Walter Pach (1883–1958)

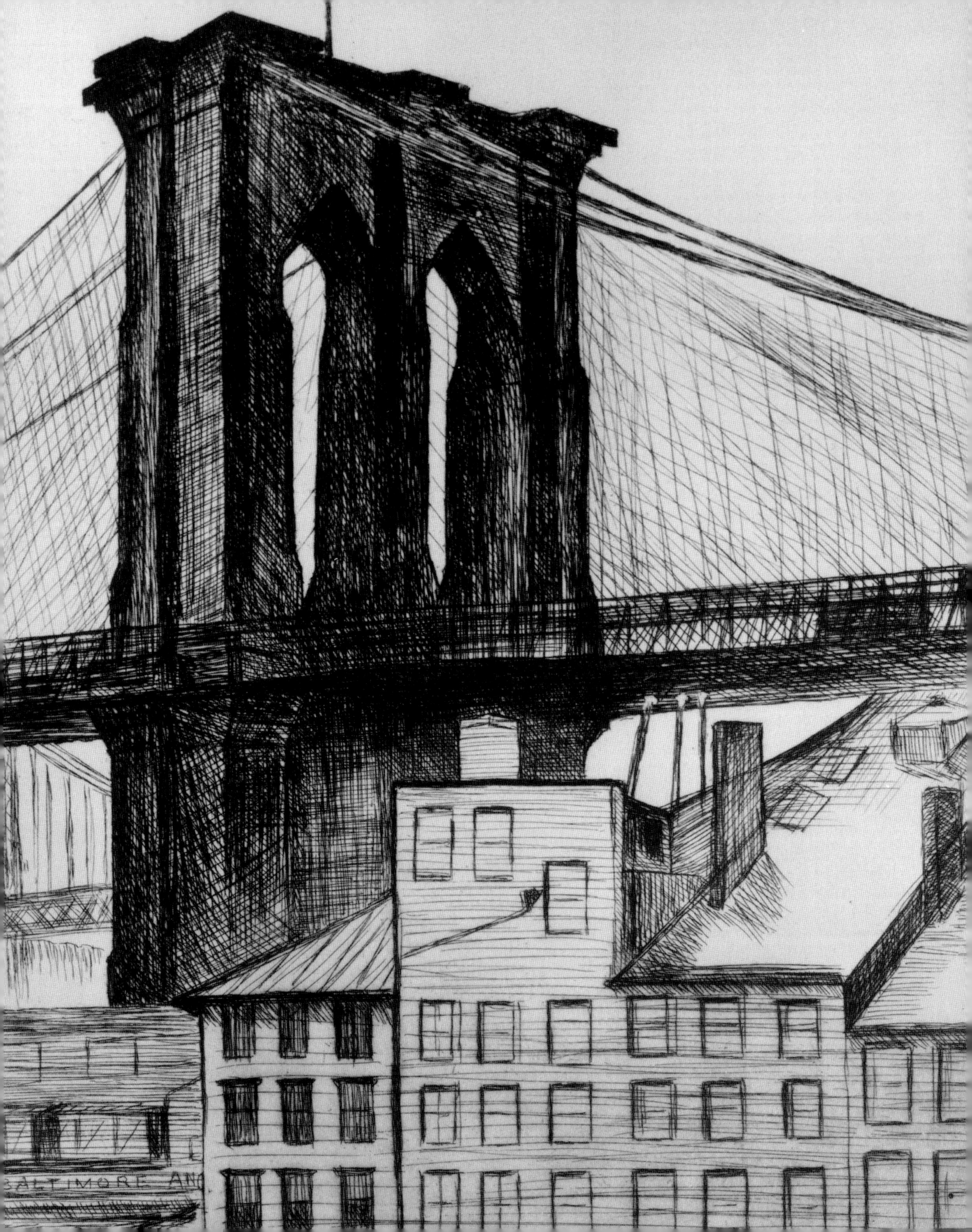
BALTIMORE AND

Walter Pach (1883–1958)

The Armory Show and the Untold Story of Modern Art in America

Laurette E. McCarthy

The Pennsylvania State University Press

University Park, Pennsylvania

Publication of this book has been aided by a grant from Furthermore: a program of the J. M. Kaplan Fund.

Frontispiece: Walter Pach, *Brooklyn Bridge,* 1919 (detail, fig. 29).

Library of Congress Cataloging-in-Publication Data

McCarthy, Laurette E.
Walter Pach (1883–1958) : the Armory Show and the untold story of modern art in America / Laurette E. McCarthy.

p.   cm.

Includes bibliographical references and index.

Summary: "Explores the career of Walter Pach (1883–1958), an influential figure in twentieth-century art and culture. As critic, agent, liaison, and lecturer, Pach helped win the acceptance of modern European, American, and Mexican art throughout the North American continent"—Provided by publisher.

ISBN 978-0-271-03740-0 (cloth : alk. paper)
ISBN 978-0-271-03741-7 (pbk : alk. paper)

1. Pach, Walter, 1883–1958.
2. Art critics—United States—Biography.
3. Art, Modern— 20th century.
4. Art and society—United States—History—20th century.
I. Pach, Walter, 1883–1958.
II. Title.
III. Title: Armory Show and the untold story of modern art in America.

N7483.P25M38 2011

709.2—dc22

2010041991

Design by Jason Harvey
Printed in China by Asia Pacific Offset
Published by The Pennsylvania State University Press,
University Park, PA 16802–1003

The Pennsylvania State University Press is a member of the Association of American University Presses.

It is the policy of The Pennsylvania State University Press to use acid-free paper. Publications on uncoated stock satisfy the minimum requirements of American National Standard for Information Sciences—Permanence of Paper for Printed Library Material, ANSI Z39.48–1992.

Contents

Illustrations

Preface

Walter Pach (1883–1958) was one of the most intriguing and influential figures in the history of twentieth-century art and culture, yet very little has been written about him and some of it is incorrect. He had the uncanny ability, and good fortune, to be at the right place at crucial moments in the history of art and he seized the opportunities presented to him to have a profound effect on modern art in the United States, Europe, and Mexico.

Born and raised in Manhattan, Pach was first exposed to art through his father, Gotthelf, an owner of Pach Brothers Studio, one of the most prestigious photography firms in the United States. The studio captured the images of the prominent social, theatrical, and political figures of the day and was the semiofficial photographer for the Metropolitan Museum of Art. While his father photographed the collections in the museum, Pach marveled at the art on view. This youthful experience, as well as other encounters with art at antique shops on the city's Lower East Side, profoundly influenced Pach's decision to become an artist and critic.

Between 1903 and 1913, Pach was a young man of two worlds: New York City and Europe. Although he lived with his parents in Manhattan most of these years, he spent many of the summer months between 1903 and 1910 in Europe, as a student and as an agent for William Merritt Chase's and Robert Henri's summer sessions abroad. In addition, he lived in Paris from the fall of 1907 until July 1908, from September 1910 through June 1912, and from August 1912 until January 1913. While living in Paris, Pach became a true insider in the contemporary art scene and developed close friendships with the most vanguard artists, writers, and thinkers of his time, including Henri Matisse, Pablo Picasso, Jacques Villon, Raymond Duchamp-Villon, Marcel Duchamp, Albert Gleizes, Jean Metzinger, Constantin Brancusi, Alexandre Mercereau, Jo Davidson, Patrick Henry Bruce, and others. These relationships were vital for the development of Pach's art and aesthetics. He also came to know many of the prominent collectors in Paris, including the Stein families, and he was on a first-name basis with the leading contemporary art dealers, among them Ambroise Vollard, Daniel-Henry Kahnweiler, Joseph Brummer, Eugène Druet, Stéphan Bourgeois, and Felix Fénéon of Galeries Bernheim Jeune. These connections helped shape Pach's multiple careers as an organizer of exhibitions, a liaison between European artists and dealers and American galleries and collectors, and a critic.

These contacts proved invaluable when Arthur B. Davies and Walt Kuhn came to Paris in the fall of 1912 to select works for the International Exhibition of Modern Art, better known as the Armory Show. Pach served as the European agent for the show and was instrumental in securing the loan of paintings, sculptures, and prints from European—particularly Parisian—artists, collectors, and dealers. Without him the exhibition would have been a completely different event. It was Pach, after all, who selected Duchamp's *Nude Descending a Staircase, No. 2* for inclusion in the Armory Show, a decision that helped change the course of modern art in the United States. He was the only individual present at the exhibition every day and at each of its three venues; in this way he had a profound impact on visitors to the show. He became, in effect, the voice and the face of modern art for many Americans. As a publicist, chief salesperson, and lecturer during the exhibition's run, Pach helped promote and disseminate to a large audience the ideas behind the modern art on view.

From the 1910s through the 1940s, Pach continued
in his role as champion of modern art—European,
American, and Mexican. In October 1914, after war
broke out on the Continent, Pach risked life and limb
to travel to Paris to secure loans from European artists
for exhibitions back in New York. He was the European
representative for the Montross, Carroll, and Bourgeois
galleries in Manhattan throughout World War I, serving
as intermediary between them and such artists as
Matisse, André Derain, Odilon Redon, Raoul Dufy,
and the Duchamp brothers. Pach helped organize
numerous groundbreaking exhibitions in the United
States, including the first large-scale shows of works by
Paul Cézanne and Matisse. He was, in fact, Matisse's
first agent in the United States, until 1924, when
Matisse's son Pierre arrived in Manhattan and was met
at the dock by Pach. Besides supporting foreign art,
Pach encouraged the New York galleries to promote the
work of contemporary Americans such as Maurice
Prendergast, Morton L. Schamberg, and Joseph Stella.
He was an advisor to the prominent art collectors John
Quinn and Walter Arensberg, helping them amass two
of the earliest and most significant collections of
modern art in the United States and introducing them
to French artists—Duchamp, Gleizes, Francis Picabia,
and Jean Crotti—who resided in Manhattan during
World War I. In 1917, Pach helped found the Society of
Independent Artists in New York and in 1923 organized
the first exhibition of contemporary Mexican art in the
United States, showing works by Diego Rivera, José
Clemente Orozco, and David Siqueiros, among others.

In addition to his roles as an agent and liaison, Pach
devoted a substantial amount of his career to his work
as a critic, and his importance in this arena lies in the
credibility with which his opinions were met and the
diversity of forums in which he presented them. His
vast knowledge of art history, his understanding of the
theories of art upon which works by the fauves, cubists,
and futurists, among others, were based, and his
personal relationships with the most advanced artists

and thinkers of his day made him the perfect candidate
to promote transnational modernism in the United
States. Pach appealed to a broad sector of the public
through presenting his ideas in popular magazines,
newspapers, and specialized journals in the United
States, France, and Mexico; he published in *Scribner's
Magazine*, the *Century*, the *New York Times*, the *Dial*,
the *Freeman*, the *Nation*, the *New Republic*, *Gazette des
Beaux-Arts*, *L'Art et les Artistes*, *L' Amour de l'Art*, *México
Moderno*, *Cuadernos Americanos*, and *Letras de Mexico*.
His books include *Georges Seurat* (1923); *The Masters
of Modern Art* (1924); *Raymond Duchamp-Villon,
Sculpteur, 1876–1918* (1924); *Ananias, or the False
Artist* (1928); *Vincent van Gogh, 1853–1890: A Study
of the Artist and His Work in Relation to His Times*
(1936); *Queer Thing, Painting: Forty Years in the World
of Art* (1938); *Ingres* (1940); *The Art Museum in America*
(1948); and *The Classical Tradition in Modern Art*,
published posthumously in 1959. Pach was the first
to translate Eugène Delacroix's *Journal* into English,
and he translated noted French art historian Élie
Faure's five-volume work, *History of Art* (1921–1930).
Through his literary work, Pach became friends with
many of the leading lights in the literary and intellectual
worlds of New York and Paris, including Wallace
Stevens, Van Wyck Brooks, Lewis Mumford, and
Alexandre Mercereau.

The history of modern art and art criticism would
have been quite different without the work of Walter
Pach. He not only championed the art of his own time,
but also had a comprehensive knowledge of art history.
In his books and articles he discussed a wide range of
subjects, from ancient Mexican and Native American
art to early twentieth-century modernism. His views
were not radical; however, they were perceived to be
authoritative and reached a wide audience at home and
abroad. His writings on modern, especially French, art
were instrumental in winning its acceptance in the
United States. In recognition of his enduring, and at
times heroic, efforts on behalf of French art and artists,

he was awarded the medal of the Chevalier of the Légion d'honneur in 1950.

Between 1907 and the 1940s, Pach lectured extensively on art in the United States and abroad. In 1918, he taught the first course on modern art at the University of California, Berkeley. During the summer of 1922, he lectured at the Universidad Nacional in Mexico City, where he met Rivera and Orozco. He later returned to Mexico City, again teaching at the university as well as at San Carlos Academy from July 1942 through July 1943. He conducted a course on modern French art for New York University students at the Louvre in the summer of 1926. In addition, he taught numerous art history classes at Bowdoin College in Maine and, in New York, at the Art Students League, Columbia University, New York University, and City College of New York (his alma mater). He was the first instructor of painting at Columbia Teachers College, Columbia University, in 1936–37. At the height of his influence—from the mid-1920s to the early 1940s—Pach crisscrossed the country, lecturing at most of the major U.S. museums, libraries, art galleries, and art institutions. During this crucial period in the history of modern art, Walter Pach was more of a household name across the United States than was Alfred Stieglitz.

Pach's support of contemporary painters and sculptors did not change dramatically during his later decades. He continued to admire the paintings and sculptures of American colleagues such as Maurice and Charles Prendergast, William Glackens, John Sloan, John Flannagan, and Arthur B. Davies, and in various articles, and through the annual Society of Independent Artists' exhibitions, he promoted their art. He also wrote essays on his favorite European and Mexican artists, including Picasso, Brancusi, the Duchamp brothers, Georges Rouault, Jacques Lipchitz, Rivera, and Frida Kahlo. He highly valued the contributions to contemporary art made by these artists; however, he could not accept the vanguard works of the abstract expressionists, viewing their paintings as "the hollowest of humbugs." In his failure to grasp the importance of the newest American works, Pach fell woefully out of touch with the contemporary art scene, which has undoubtedly contributed to the neglect of his legacy.

Throughout the 1930s and 1940s, Pach was active as an art consultant not only for private collectors, but also for museums. For example, it was Pach who arranged for the acquisition by the Louvre of Thomas Eakins's painting *Clara* (now in the collection of the Musée d'Orsay). He orchestrated the purchase of Jacques-Louis David's *The Death of Socrates* by the Metropolitan Museum of Art and was the chief advisor to the Shilling Fund, an organization, founded in 1937, designed to support the work of contemporary American artists. In this capacity, Pach was responsible for acquiring paintings and sculptures by his colleagues and then placing them in museum collections across the United States.

Despite all these activities, Walter Pach considered himself to be primarily an artist, and his art developed in accordance with the major movements of his day. His early works reveal a painter steeped in the tradition of the Old Masters and trained to portray objects in a representational manner. Confronted with European modernism, Pach changed his way of painting and attempted to incorporate the new theories into his own style. After he explored cubist and futurist elements in his pictures, Pach reverted to realism around 1919. The development of his art echoed the main tenet of his aesthetic credo—evolution. He consciously strove to learn from the past and to incorporate the lessons of the masters into contemporary works that gave voice to the spirit of his time. Although the style and content of Pach's paintings, watercolors, and etchings were not very original, his art was significant in that it addressed the vital issues of the day.

Walter Pach moved effortlessly among the leading art, intellectual, and literary circles of New York, Paris, and Mexico City in the first half of the twentieth century. Working behind the scenes, he strove to promote an understanding of and appreciation for the art of many different nations and eras, but had the most profound impact on the acceptance of modern art in the United States. He believed in the power of art to shape and affect people's lives and through his persistent crusade to make art a vital part of life, Walter Pach won the hearts and souls of artists, collectors, dealers, and art enthusiasts the world over and earned a pivotal place as one of the most seminal figures in the history of modern art and culture.

Acknowledgments

An undertaking of this magnitude required the assistance of numerous people around the world and I am most grateful to all for their help with this project. Foremost, I wish to express my sincere appreciation to Raymond Pach, Walter Pach's son by his first marriage, to Magdalene Frohberg, who passed away October 2, 2008. Since 1993, when I began my research on Walter Pach, Raymond Pach graciously opened his heart and home to my work and was enthusiastic and unfailing in his support. I would also like to thank Mrs. Nikifora N. Iliopoulos, Pach's second wife, who has been most supportive. I wish to express my deepest thanks to William Innes Homer and also to Wayne Craven, Damie Stillman, and William C. Agee for encouraging me to write this book.

During the course of my research I contacted and visited dozens of libraries, archives, museums, colleges, universities, and other institutions in the United States, France, Italy, Mexico, and Canada in my quest for materials related to Walter Pach. The most essential records are the Walter Pach papers, which are housed at the Archives of American Art, Smithsonian Institution, in Washington, D.C. I wish to thank Wendy Hurlock Baker, Marisa Bourgoin, Liza Kirwin, and Judy Throm of the Archives of American Art for their generosity and assistance with this project. Darcy Tell, editor of the *Archives of American Art Journal*, and Lawana L. Bryant, Esq., of the Smithsonian Institution also assisted me. I would also like to extend a special thanks to Claude Duthuit, Wanda de Guébriant, and Georges Matisse of Les Héritiers Matisse, who granted me access to the letters from Walter Pach to Henri Matisse in the possession of the Matisse Archives. These materials proved most insightful and were a wonderful source of information. Also, Jean-Paul Morel, one

of Élie Faure's biographers, graciously gave me photocopies of the transcribed and typed letters from Faure to Pach that are housed in the Bibliothèque Nationale, Bordeaux. These letters contained much valuable information.

Among the many others who have lent encouragement and support to this project over the years, I would like to thank especially Shirley Pach, Raymond Pach's widow, and Ginger Pach, Raymond Pach's former daughter-in-law. I am also grateful to the following for their assistance: Susan K. Anderson, Martha Hamilton Morris Archivist, and Holly Frisbee, Rights and Reproductions, Philadelphia Museum of Art; Alan Baglia and Cristin O'Keefe Aptowicz of Artists Rights Society in New York; Brianna Bedigian, Rights and Reproductions manager and Melissa McCready, Rights and Reproductions assistant, the Baltimore Museum of Art; Marc Bernstein, archivist for the New York Society for Ethical Culture; John Charlot, relative of the artist Jean Charlot; William K. Clark, volunteer archivist at the Cincinnati Art Museum; Mrs. Betty J. Davis at the Detroit Institute of Arts; Lisa L. Daugherty, trustee, the Friends of James Daugherty Foundation; Ruth Edelstein of the Fine Arts Department, the Carnegie Museum of Art; Ilaria Della Monica, the Berenson Archives, the Harvard University Center for Italian Renaissance Studies, Villa I Tatti, Florence, Italy; Rachel Di Eleuterio, librarian, Helen Farr Sloan Library and Archives, Delaware Art Museum; James Grebl, library manager, San Diego Museum of Art; Kiowa Hammons, Rights and Reproductions, Whitney Museum of American Art; Peter B. Hanchak, grandson of Wallace Stevens; Sue Hodson, curator of literary manuscripts, and David S. Zeidberg, director, the Huntington Library, San Marino, California;

Jean Jacobson, collections supervisor and Gina Garden, marketing coordinator, Museum of Nebraska Art; Norman Köhler, archivist, Staatliche Kunstsammlungen, Dresden; Peter Lockwood, relative of the artist Manierre Dawson; Mhairi Martino, Agence Photographique de la Réunion des Musées Nationaux, Paris; Eileen Morales, the Museum of the City of New York; Jacqueline Matisse Monnier, Association Marcel Duchamp; Jim Moske, managing archivist, Matthew Westerly, the Image Library, and Thayer Tolles, associate curator of American Paintings and Sculpture, the Metropolitan Museum of Art; Howell W. Perkins, manager, Photographic Resources, Rights and Reproductions, Virginia Museum of Fine Arts; Bennard B. Perlman, art historian; Marie Pessiot, chief curator of the Musée des Beaux-Arts, Rouen; Suzanne Quigley, Art and Artifact Services; Claire Rifelg of the Armand Hammer Museum; William M. Roberts, university archivist, University of California, Berkeley; Ken Rose, associate director, Research and Education, Rockefeller Archive Center; Laura Ruttum, Manuscripts and Archives Division, New York Public Library; Patricia Schuil of Research and Documentation at the Van Gogh Museum; Gregory Selch, grandson of Dr. Ruth Bakwin; John N. Serio, editor, *Wallace Stevens Journal*; Ivory Serra, photographer; Nancy M. Shawcross, curator of manuscripts, Rare Book and Manuscript Library, University of Pennsylvania; Megan Sniffin-Marinoff, archivist for Harvard University; Vincent Tovell; Orozco Clemente Valladares, relative of the artist José Clemente Orozco; Sydney C. Van Nort, assistant professor and chief archivist, City College of New York, Archives and Special Collections Division, City College Libraries; Galen J. White, former archival assistant at New York University; Cari Winterich and Tricia Smith, Art Resource, Inc.; Robert Wojtowicz, Lewis Mumford scholar; Anne-Marie Zucchielli, archivist of the Documentation du MNAM-CCI, Centre Georges Pompidou in Paris; and all others who have assisted me over the years.

The most enthusiastic and consistent support for this project has come from colleagues and friends in the field, particularly Francis M. Naumann, Allan Antliff, and John Cauman. I also wish to thank William C. Agee, Myra Bairstow, David Butler, Laura Coyle, Stacey Epstein, Jack Flam, Alice Goldfarb, Mary-Anne Martin, Percy North, Christine I. Oaklander, Jay Oles, Randy Ploog, Naomi Sawelson-Gorse, Joy Sperling, Gail Stavitsky, Michael Parke-Taylor, Virginia Zabriskie, and Judith Zilczer, who have shared many ideas and resources and have given much encouragement over the years.

Thanks also to Susan Berger, who provided some assistance with French translations; Alba Fernández-Keys for her translation of the Spanish letters; Venka V. Macintyre for her editorial comments; and India Cooper for her professional editing.

A special appreciation to Eleanor H. Goodman, executive editor for arts and humanities, and Danny Bellet, editorial assistant, of the Pennsylvania State University Press. Their patience and professionalism guided this manuscript to publication.

I am eternally grateful to my parents, John and Mary McCarthy, for their generosity, inspiration, and steadfast support. Without them this book would not have been possible. In addition, I want to express my appreciation to the rest of my family and friends who have given much assistance just by listening. Finally, I would like to thank Harold Edward Baker III, my husband, whose loving patience and encouragement were vital to this undertaking.

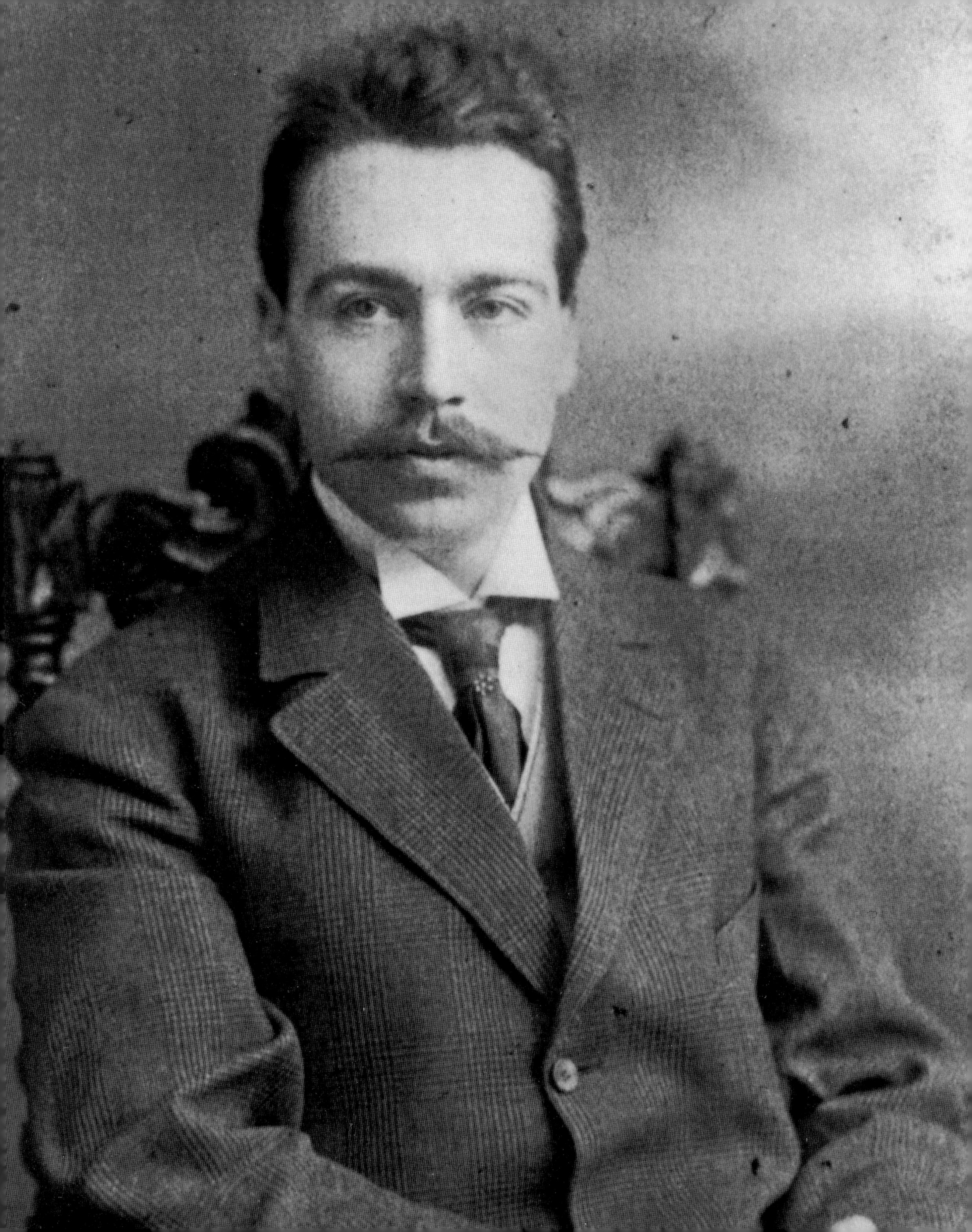

1
Family Background and Influence

Before he could walk, Walter Pach was allowed to crawl on the floor of the Metropolitan Museum of Art, surrounded by the masterpieces on view; as an adult, he would recall "no memories farther back than those of being at the Museum."[1] Pach Brothers Studio, the semiofficial photographers for the Metropolitan, was owned and operated by Walter's father, Gotthelf, and his uncles, Gustavus and Morris Pach. Living only a few blocks from the museum, Gotthelf frequently brought the child along on business trips there, letting him wander freely through its mighty halls.[2] Pach firmly believed that these excursions to the museum and the family business, not to mention the family itself, helped shape his life as an artist and critic: "As to my family background: it is sometimes considered as effecting one's fitness for a place, and it had its effect on my doings."[3]

Pach's genealogy is the story of many Americans during the nineteenth century; his father was an immigrant and his mother an American. Gotthelf Pach (fig. 2) was born in Berlin, on October 9, 1851, and was brought to the United States in 1852, not much more than an infant. His family settled in Philadelphia, but little else is known about them.[4] Walter's mother, Frances Wise (fig. 3), was born in Milwaukee on January 29, 1857. The 1860 county of Milwaukee census lists six individuals in the household, including a younger sister and a servant, but the exact relationship of the others is unclear. According to New York's 1900 census for Manhattan, Frances Wise's father was Austrian and her mother German, but other information about the family is unavailable.[5]

On September 13, 1882, Frances married Gotthelf Pach in Manhattan, in a private home, at 302 East Eighty-first Street. Professor Felix Adler (whom Pach Brothers Studio had photographed), founder of the Ethical Culture Society in America, and Judge Charles J. Nehrbas presided over the ceremonies.[6] Founded by Adler in 1876 and incorporated in 1877, the Ethical Culture Society was a religious movement that believed in the advancement of social justice for all people. The organization encouraged members to lead morally and ethically responsible lives and to engage in humane actions toward their fellow human beings.[7] Gotthelf joined the society in 1881 and must have been quite active in it for Adler to be such an important part of his marriage ceremony. Many early members of the society were from Jewish backgrounds, including Gotthelf Pach and Frances Wise. Gotthelf's father and Frances's parents were Jewish, though Gotthelf and Frances Pach themselves did not practice the faith and would not raise their children in it. The couple had two sons: Walter, born July 11, 1883, and Alfred, his junior by two years (fig. 4).

By the time of Walter's birth, Pach Brothers Studio was one of the most prestigious photographic firms in

Gotthelf Pach, photograph of Walter Pach. Private collection.

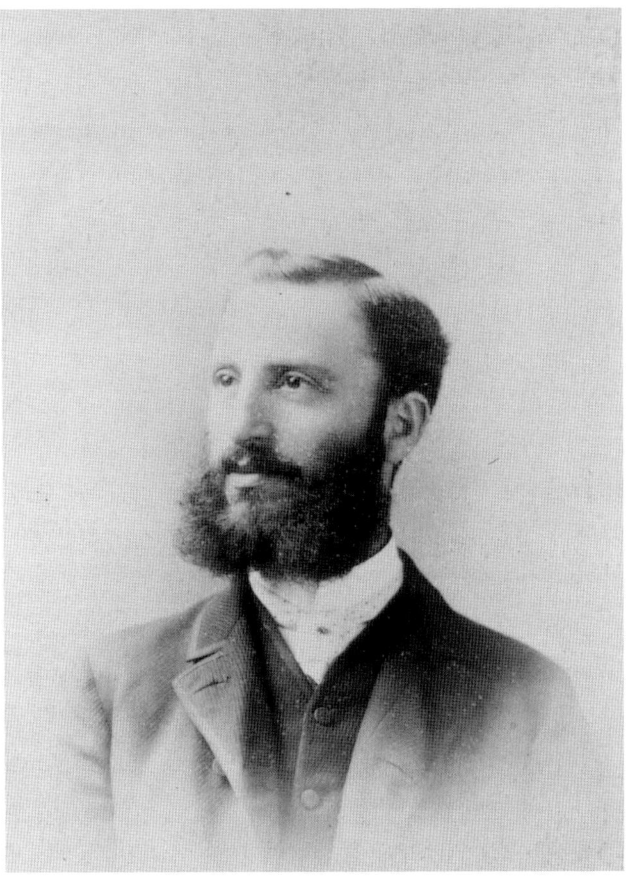

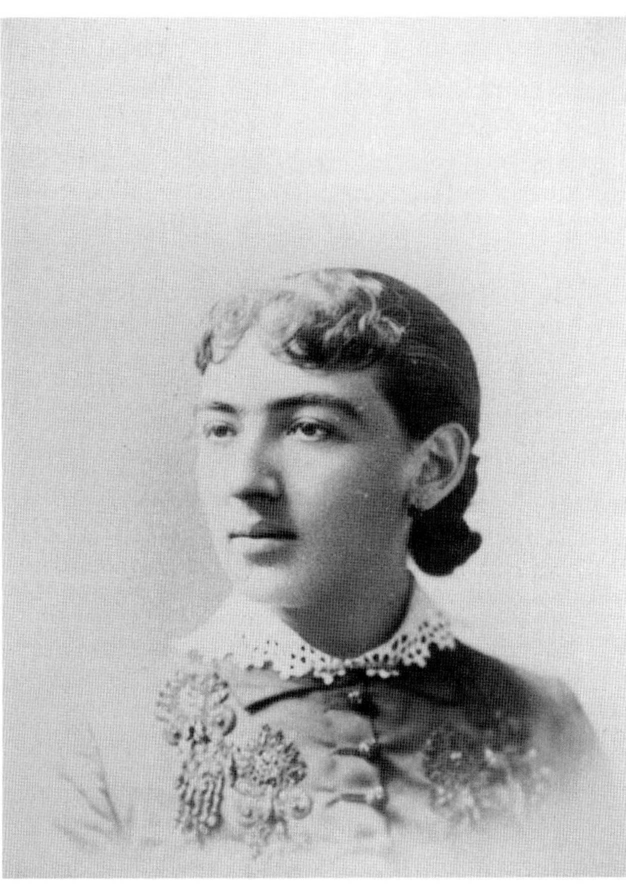

New York, rising from very humble beginnings. Although no two accounts about the founding of the firm coincide in every detail, it seems clear that Gustavus and Morris started the company in the mid-1860s and that Gotthelf moved from Philadelphia to New York sometime after that to join the firm. In the beginning, business was slow and Gustavus and Gotthelf often walked door to door throughout their Manhattan neighborhood offering to take family portraits, but they received only a few commissions. In the mid-1860s, Gustavus was diagnosed with lung problems and was advised to move to the countryside. He relocated briefly to Toms River, New Jersey, and then settled more permanently in Long Branch, a fashionable resort town on the Jersey shore. Gotthelf followed his brother, and soon the two persuaded a local cigar store owner to accept orders for portrait photographs. By 1866, the Pachs were taking outdoor views of the city from a portable horse-drawn studio and traveling from home to home soliciting work.

On one of these rounds, the brothers stopped at the oceanfront home of millionaire George Childs, who happened to be entertaining General Ulysses S. Grant and financier Anthony Drexel. Recognizing a unique opportunity, the Pachs persuaded the trio to pose for a photograph, and afterward the conversation turned to

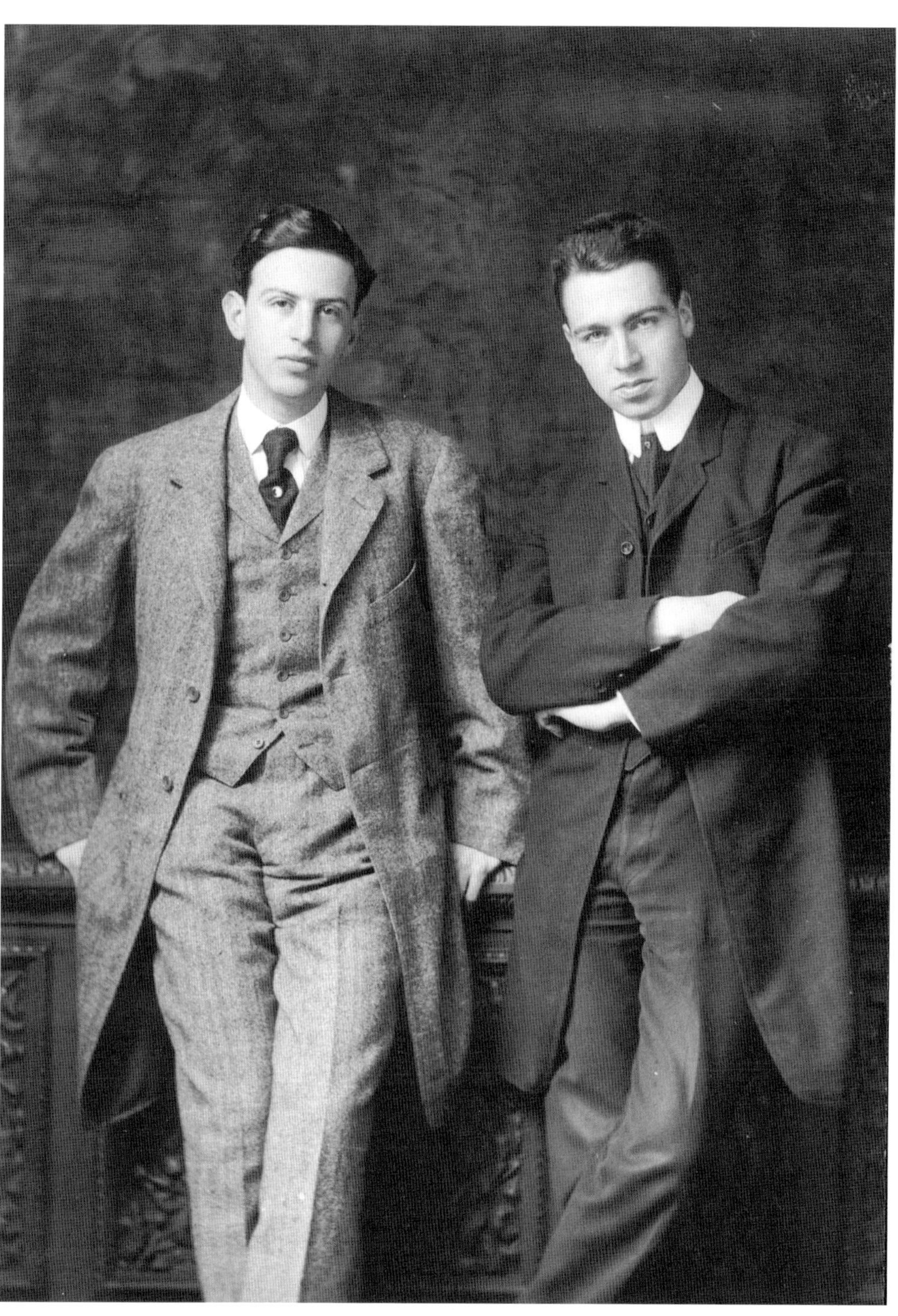

Fig. 4
Gotthelf Pach, photograph of
Alfred and Walter Pach, ca.
1905, photographic print, sepia,
15 × 10 cm. Courtesy of the
Walter Pach Papers, 1883–1980,
Archives of American Art,
Smithsonian Institution.

the future of photography, including that of the Pachs'
business. Subsequently, Drexel and Childs each gave
the Pach brothers five hundred dollars, and at last they
had the financial backing they needed to open their first
permanent studio in Manhattan.

More important, this group of distinguished
gentlemen enabled the Pachs to step into the world of
America's elite. When Grant became president, he
summoned the boys to Washington to take his portrait,
the first of many such commissions for Pach Brothers
Studio over its long existence: it photographed every
American president from Grant through Lyndon
Johnson. Also, through their contact with Grant, the
Pachs were appointed the official photographers for the
United States Military Academy at West Point. This
engagement led to the establishment of branch studios
at such prestigious colleges as Princeton, Harvard,
Columbia, Yale, Williams, Amherst, Wellesley, Dart-
mouth, and Wesleyan in Connecticut. They also
maintained studios at Long Branch and other popular
New Jersey resorts frequented by wealthy New Yorkers.

As the Pach brothers' reputation grew, many of the
most powerful, influential, and popular figures in
American politics, finance, science, letters, and theater
commissioned portraits: Theodore Roosevelt and his
family, J. Pierpont Morgan, Andrew Carnegie, Thomas
Alva Edison, Mark Twain, the vaudeville sensation the
Dolly sisters, and Tallulah Bankhead, to name but a few.
Many came to the New York studio to sit for Gotthelf
Pach in particular, now a highly sought-after portraitist.
At its height of prominence and production, Pach
Brothers Studio numbered seventeen branches, mostly
along the eastern seaboard of the United States, and
it was considered the premier photographic firm in
the country.

The studio was known for technical advancements
in photography, notably early flash photography and
the development of a type of dry plate. In the early days
of photography, photographic plates were covered with
a variety of wet substances on which the image was
fixed via exposure to a light source. This was a difficult
process: the plate had to be used within minutes of its
preparation, exposure time was long, and the materials
needed were cumbersome to transport. The dry plate
was a revolutionary new medium that made the process
much easier and greatly increased the speed with which
images could be captured. It was also much more
durable. First invented in England in 1871, the dry plate
method underwent several advancements, with the
Pach Brothers Studio making its own contribution to
the field but, unfortunately, never obtaining a patent for
its invention.[8]

Among the firm's many important clients, it was the
Metropolitan Museum of Art that made the greatest
impression on Walter Pach. Mesmerized by the art that
lined the magnificent halls of the museum, he began to
copy the paintings that graced the walls when he was a
teenager. Walter was also exposed to fine art at Pach
Brothers' tastefully appointed studios, particularly
its Windsor Arcade studio located on Fifth Avenue
between Forty-sixth and Forty-seventh Streets.
Resembling a drawing room, its reception area was
decorated with "photographic portraiture" and "pastels
and paintings" of prominent Americans such as
President Roosevelt and Jay Gould.

Located just a block from the Pachs' Broadway
studio was a "palace of magic" to the young Walter: a
curio and antique store owned by Ernest F. Eble, a
childhood friend of his father.[9] On his frequent trips
there, the boy plied Eble with questions about the
items on display, which included Old Master paintings
similar to those he had seen at the Metropolitan. While
he was curious about these pictures, he professed not to
give such dull works a second thought and instead
preferred military scenes. Soon, however, his ideas
about these boring old paintings were challenged
and changed.

The year was 1895, and twelve-year-old Walter, who
enjoyed adventure in his literature as well as in his art,
was reading *The Count of Monte Cristo* and frequenting

Eble's shop. He was enraptured by the Count and hoped to emulate the "courage, wisdom and charm" of this "superior being" in his own life. One Saturday afternoon, during a "stroll through the rooms of antiquarian stuff" at the Metropolitan in an area where Old Masters were displayed, he was shaken to his very core, his blue eyes focused on the dark, dreary paintings hanging in this section; they were precisely the pictures that his beloved Count admired.[10] Obviously, he was going to have to rethink his attitude toward this art. After two months of concentrated study, he concluded that they were, in fact, great paintings. This experience taught him a lesson he valued throughout his life: that the lack of understanding of a particular type of art was not proof that a given work was bad.

While we do not know exactly what art was in his family's home, undoubtedly there were some paintings, pastels, and photographs on the walls of the Pachs' Park Avenue apartment. The location of the apartment block, between Ninety-first and Ninety-second Streets, was not in a very fashionable part of late nineteenth-century Manhattan, yet Walter's family did enjoy some comforts and employed a live-in Irish servant, Tresa Egan.[11] Pach remembered this place as a "railroad flat"—one of his friends disparagingly referred to it as an "Irish flat."[12] By 1901, however, the Pachs owned the Windsor Arcade building, which housed the business, and other property in Manhattan. Clearly, the family was comfortable financially, and Mrs. Pach probably decorated her home appropriately for entertaining guests, which she did from time to time, though Pach recollected that the family was not very formal in its manners.

Pach was very close to his mother and confided his hopes and dreams to her rather than to his father. She was, by his account, a kind, gentle, and intelligent woman. He felt that her lively appreciation for music and the theater was inherited from her grandmother Augusta Sartorius. Her passion for the arts, and the stage in particular, was passed on to and shared with her son. Among Pach's voluminous papers is a scrapbook filled with advertisements for plays, comic operas, operettas, musical events, and magic shows. He most likely attended these events—between the ages of twelve and fifteen, several of them a month—with his parents, since Gotthelf Pach probably received complimentary tickets to numerous productions from the many stars he photographed. In addition to exposing their son to the theater, Pach's parents, especially his mother, encouraged him to learn the violin, an instrument he played for decades. Pach carried his love of the theater and music with him throughout his life, the stage and its performers becoming the subjects of many of his paintings.

Besides supporting Walter's interests in the arts, Mrs. Pach was responsible for seeing to his and his brother's education. From the scant information about Pach's early schooling, it seems that in 1894 he (and probably his brother) was enrolled at the Workingman's School, located at 109 West Fifty-fourth Street in Manhattan and operated by the Ethical Culture Society. Established in 1878 as a tuition-free kindergarten, the school was expanded in the 1880s to include an eight-grade, tuition-free elementary school open to all social classes. According to Percival Chubb, a founder of the London Ethical Society, a teacher at the Manhattan organization, and a friend of the Pachs, the teaching at the school was "based upon the Froebelian pedagogy, which was the first school to introduce manual training and systematic ethical instruction into the curriculum."[13] The program differed from that of most public institutions in its liberal approach, an emphasis on learning by doing, and the incorporation of ethics into all aspects of the children's schooling. As Felix Adler explained, the institution aimed "to give [the students] that which will secure them bread thereafter, and many of the higher treasures of human existence, we hope besides: we propose to give them a broad and generous education . . . which will prepare them for their future station in life, but also make them capable of living in a truly human way."[14] The instructors hoped to train students for their chosen profession and also to be successful and morally responsible citizens as well.

Pach's courses at the school ranged from German and natural sciences to mechanical drawing, drawing, design and modeling, and music. Although his teachers found him extremely intelligent, with strong reasoning powers, Pach was not a very good student. He did well in German and the natural sciences, but he detested mechanical drawing and had difficulty with his music class. Several teachers reported that he suffered from an "excess of vitality," became excited when disciplined, lacked restraint, was easily distracted, and often misbehaved in class.[15] This hyperactivity, while perceived as a detriment to his learning in school, would prove most useful later in life when the same energy was channeled toward his multiple careers in the field of art.

Unlike other educational curricula, the one at the Workingman's School included lessons in music, drama, and arts and crafts. Consultants in the area of art included noted painters Walter Shirlaw and George de Forest Brush. We do not know if Pach received instruction from Shirlaw or Brush, but he seems to have had some lessons in art from Percival Chubb. In an 1894 letter to his son, Gotthelf Pach wrote, "Your painting of the fire place came to me today. I was real glad to see you are learning to paint, it will be useful to your future. I trust you will ask your good Mama to give Mr. Chubb some of the pictures I have made, in return for your lessons."[16] Clearly, Pach had begun to paint, probably at the elbow of Mr. Chubb, and certainly with some encouragement from his parents.

Pach perhaps created his first painting during one of the family's regular summer exoduses from the city. Throughout his youth Walter, his mother, and his brother would escape the heat of Manhattan and travel north to Essex County in upstate New York. Gotthelf would join them on weekends, if he could escape the rigors of the business. Nestled amid the lush wilderness of the Adirondack Mountains, this area proved the perfect retreat for the boys. Here they could hike, fish, swim, and hunt. Also, the countryside offered Walter the opportunity to raise rabbits, a youthful enterprise that gave rise to one of his earliest nicknames, "Rabbits." Other terms of endearment included "Mopsy" and "Piney," the latter because his hair was quite thick and he had a cowlick that would sometimes stand up straight.

The area of the Adirondacks where the Pachs vacationed was very popular among the leading philosophical minds of the late nineteenth century, including those affiliated with the Ethical Culture Society.[17] Keene Valley, near where the Pachs stayed, was the summer home to intellectuals such as John Dewey, Thomas Davidson, and William James. It was here that Felix Adler first met Percival Chubb and invited him to join the staff of the Ethical Schools. Adler himself had a summerhouse at St. Huberts, just above Keene Valley. During the summer of 1894, the Pachs stayed at the Willey House in Essex, New York, near Keene Center. Since Mrs. Pach was closely involved with the society, she may have chosen this area to be close to some of her fellow members.

Despite his parents' association with the Ethical Culture Society, Walter did not continue at its school. Sometime after January 1895, and for reasons unknown, he was transferred to another elementary school, Public School No. 6 at Madison Avenue and Eighty-fifth Street in Manhattan. Arithmetic was certainly one of the courses there, but it is fair to speculate that the standard classes, including social and natural sciences and English, were also required. Although he had previously had difficulty in his music classes, his musical skills flourished at PS 6. He joined the school's orchestra as a first violin and played with the group throughout the regular term. Along with several others, he performed for the class's graduation. His verbal and speaking abilities became finely tuned as well, and he was chosen to represent the boys in a joint debate on graduation day. Pach also sharpened his organizational skills through his role as one of the business managers for the school paper, *The Star of No. 6.* His earlier difficulties with deportment in the classroom and performance in his studies improved greatly, and when he graduated on June 24, 1898, he looked forward to taking the scientific course at CCNY—the College of the City of New York, or City College—and then possibly going to West Point.

Pach did attend CCNY but did not go on to West Point. Founded in 1847 as the New York Free Academy, City College was a public institution. It was originally located on East Twenty-third Street and Lexington Avenue in the Gramercy Park neighborhood, close to the Pach Brothers Broadway studio. When Pach began at the school in 1898, it was a very conservative liberal arts institution. All students took classes in Greek and Latin, history, English, philosophy, natural history, drawing and aesthetics, pure sciences and mathematics, pedagogics, composition and oratory, and physical training. Since there were few secondary schools in Manhattan at this time, the program at City College entailed five years of instruction, with the first, subfreshman year, consisting of college preparatory work.[18]

During the late nineteenth century, a tremendous reformation in higher education was taking place, with the system of electives begun by Charles Eliot Norton at Harvard University gradually spreading to other colleges. In 1901, when Pach was in his third year at CCNY, its curriculum was thoroughly reformed for the first time in thirty years, in line with the elective principle. Students could choose from five distinct courses of study: classical, Latin-French, modern language, scientific, and mechanical. In their junior and senior years, students could select special subjects in their particular course of study. For the first time in the school's history, it allowed a broad range of subjects.

Although Pach intended to follow the scientific course at college, he changed his concentration sometime after enrolling and graduated with a Bachelor of

Arts degree. There are no transcripts for his years at CCNY, although in view of his German and Austrian ancestry, he probably followed the modern language course, in which German language courses were prescribed in four of the five years. It was during his college years that Pach began to develop his critical writing abilities, skills that would prove useful throughout his life. Some of his assignments for his literature class included a review of Washington Irving's "Westminster Abbey," from his *Sketch Book of Geoffrey Crayon, Gent.;* a critique of Henry Wadsworth Longfellow's poem *Evangeline;* and a piece on Claudius from Shakespeare's *Hamlet.* The title of his junior oration subject was "The Poetry of Rudyard Kipling," and that of his senior topic was "Aesthetic Tendencies in the Nineteenth Century."

This latter essay shows the first concrete evidence of Pach's interest in aesthetics. "As moderns," he wrote, "it is the tendencies of plastic art, music, and literature in our own era that we prefer to consider. That there is a close parallelism in the courses of these three great branches, we come soon to notice." The belief in the relatedness of art, music, and literature was a cornerstone of late nineteenth- and early twentieth-century aesthetic theory. This idea was undoubtedly discussed in the moral and intellectual philosophy course that Pach attended at CCNY. It could also have been debated in the drawing and aesthetics classes that he took under Leigh Harrison Hunt.

This essay hints, too, at what was to become a major precept of Pach's aesthetic theory: "The work of our moderns, has its dignity and value, as surely as that of the titans of the past. It is an integral part of the age: the great expression of a great century." Pach's belief in the integrity and importance of contemporary artistic expression, whether in art, music, or literature, remained consistent throughout his career, although his definition of the term *modern* changed over time. In this early composition, he perceived Jean-Baptiste-Camille Corot, Frédéric Chopin, and Percy Bysshe Shelley as progressive, yet they would seem dated to him a few years later.

Pach's writing also revealed an impressive understanding of the relationship between the developments in contemporary culture, society, and art. Advanced communications, he observed, were bringing together hitherto disparate civilizations, creating what he termed a "growing cosmopolitanism" among nations. This "broadening effected by modern methods of communication" was bringing the "music of the north, and the art of the Far East" to American audiences and revolutionizing the aesthetic thought of the era.[19] At a young age, Pach had already grasped the significance of the impact of new technologies on society. He understood that modern media had the power to influence and change contemporary life and to make the world a much smaller place.

During his summer breaks from college, Pach visited the Adirondacks, studied art, and worked with his father at the studio. Gotthelf taught him the tools of the trade and hoped, in vain, that his son would eventually take over the family business. Pach toiled in the darkroom and was sent out on fieldwork. One assignment was to help photograph the Manhattan skyline from the top of the old Madison Square Garden at Twenty-third Street and Fifth Avenue. The building, which was still a mass of steel girders, was to be one of the tallest skyscrapers in New York. The wind howled and gusted so fiercely at the top of the structure that Pach and his associate were almost blown off. When they finally reached the solid safety of the city sidewalk, Pach vowed to one day trade in his camera for an easel.

While Pach was never keen on the photography business, his experiences in his father's firm did affect the development of his aesthetic credo. He came to regard photography as a reproductive, not a creative, art. "This was of importance to me," he wrote, "when I saw the rise of painters who set themselves to purge their art of the merely reproductive elements in it."[20] The acceptance of photography as a fine art was a hotly contested topic in the late nineteenth and early twentieth centuries. Pach's attitude was certainly at odds with those of the leading proponents of the movement, such as Alfred Stieglitz, who promoted the medium of photography as a means of artistic expression.

This young man of artistic and philosophical sensibilities could not have hoped for a more appropriate beginning in life: exposed to paintings, prints, and photography from infancy; introduced to some of the most powerful and influential members of New York society; surrounded by a stable and comfortable family that could enjoy some of life's luxuries; encouraged to pursue his creative endeavors and introduced to the magical worlds of theater and music; exposed to a liberal and open-minded attitude toward life and the world; and through the Ethical Culture Society and his education at CCNY, taught the value of art and literature. Above all, he recognized early on the connection between art and spirituality and incorporated this philosophy into his own life. From these beginnings, Walter Pach ventured forth into the fascinating and fickle world of art.

2
Art Student Days

Pach's early exposure to art led him toward a career as an artist, though his parents, especially his father, did not wholeheartedly approve. He recalled that his "first advice about art work came from George H. Story, the curator of paintings of the Metropolitan. He set me to copying the drawings of the Old Masters saying, 'That's the way they began, themselves.'"[1] Around the age of thirteen, Pach began to work in this manner two afternoons a week and continued for two years before he advanced to making copies in watercolor and oil. It was not until the summer of 1902, however, that Pach began his formal art training. In an unpublished autobiography he wrote, "Between my junior and senior years at the College of the City of New York, I spent the summer at William M. Chase's summer school at Shinnecock, Long Island."[2] Founded in 1891, Chase's Shinnecock Summer School of Art near Southampton, Long Island, was in its last season when Pach attended an eight-week course.[3] Chase was one of America's most highly regarded painters and teachers at the turn of the twentieth century, and he had a profound influence on Pach, who vividly recalled the words that Chase spoke at the beginning of the course: "Students . . . you are entering the most ancient profession that gives us the history of our race, and you are entering the most honorable of all professions."[4]

During the summer of 1902 and until his graduation in 1903, Pach concentrated on his painting with the intention of coming to "some definite conclusion" about his future. Although his mother deeply admired and appreciated fine art, she "thought it a precarious future" and suggested that he study law instead.[5] His father was also concerned about Walter's future and, "having seen the painter as a man who made no money and had to resort to crayon-portraits etc., (less good likenesses than the straight photograph), opposed my entering on painting as a life work."[6] Pach remained undeterred by his parents' concerns and protests and decided to pursue a career as an artist when he completed college.

After graduation from CCNY, Pach began his initial intense study of art and art history by participating in Chase's summer class in Europe, based in Haarlem, the Netherlands. Throughout this journey he kept a detailed logbook in which he recorded his daily activities and his impressions of the people, places, and paintings he encountered.[7] This journal provides a fascinating glimpse of the daily routine on board a grand ocean liner and reveals in detail the life of an art student in the early years of the twentieth century. The tone of the writing reveals a neophyte embarking on a new and wondrous escapade.

Pach's earliest overseas adventure began on June 24 and lasted about three months. His mother and brother accompanied him "to Holland-America docks, via 14th St. ferry" to see him off, and along with approximately forty other students—including Morton L. Schamberg, who would be his roommate—he boarded the *Potsdam* for his first European voyage. His accommodations were anything but grand, with his cabin at the "far aft" of the ship "right over the screw," arguably one of the worst berths on the boat. Like many other travelers, however, Pach spent as little time in his cabin as possible, enjoying instead shipboard diversions such as concerts in the salon and on deck, shuffleboard, athletic games, singing, cards, parlor games, and dancing the Virginia reel. He also "lolled in steamer chair," "took photos" (which, unfortunately, have not been located), and taught himself some Dutch, a skill that would prove most useful.

Although Pach spent most of his time with the Chase students, many of whom he had met the previous summer at Shinnecock, he also mingled with the other passengers, a number of whom were foreigners. On his second day at sea he had a lengthy conversation with Nakamura Long, covering topics such as "trusts, politics, Japan, Aesthetics [and] Hokusai." Pach later explained that he "had come to be deeply interested in Japanese art in my college days and had even . . . secured from Japan a couple of books on the language and writing of the country, my object being to teach myself enough, at least, to be able to read the inscriptions on the prints and paintings, as an aid to understanding the art of them and perhaps becoming an expert on it."[8] He also collected works by Hokusai and Hiroshige. Japonisme was much in vogue among artists in the second part of the nineteenth century, and Pach's interest in such work shows that he was in tune with the latest developments in art. His appreciation of Asian art was also reinforced through his admiration for the art and aesthetics of James Abbott McNeill Whistler.

Whistler's influence on American art was profound at the turn of the past century, and Pach was one of many artists to fall under his spell. He was particularly interested in Whistler's aesthetic theories, which he undoubtedly studied at CCNY, and which most likely inspired him to write a book on aesthetics en route to the Netherlands. Several logbook entries refer to this writing: on June 28 he "showed Mrs. Doolittle and Miss Hegman my Aesthetics Book," and on June 30 he wrote that he "never knew myself to be so lazy. 'Aesthetics' is always put away untouched." Often he was seduced away from his work by his fellow students and complained that he "tried to write 'A.' but Barbier and Potter came and looked at it and gave me such a mellow brandy as I had never tasted." Finally, on July 2, he "wrote 'Finis' on p. 242 of 'A'!!!!" This text and its subject were clearly very important to Pach, and his writing of it portends his future career as a critic; unfortunately, this manuscript does not appear to have survived.[9]

After a relatively uneventful ten-day crossing, the *Potsdam* stopped briefly in Boulogne, France, before it docked in the Netherlands, its final destination. A tender brought the passengers ashore, and after they cleared customs on the dock, the pupils boarded a train bound for Haarlem. Pach was enthralled by the countryside they passed en route to Schiedam, Delft, and The Hague: "Beautiful landscape. Green fields. 'Willgen.' Canals. Windmills. Lovely quiet sunset. Black and white cattle. Wonderful houses." He and Schamberg roomed at Pension Minerva, one of the two boardinghouses booked for the group, and after they found their rooms they drove to Café Brinkmann, where they celebrated the Fourth of July at a dinner arranged by Chase and Charles Townsley, the agent for the summer session. At the café there were American flags, decorations, speeches, firecrackers, music, and wine. Pach had a "glorious time" and eventually found his way home around 3:00 A.M.

For the next two months Pach engrossed himself in the study of art and in the Dutch language and culture. The format of the summer school entailed painting in the studio, sketching outdoors, instructions and criticisms from Chase, visits to museums and private collections in Haarlem and elsewhere, and sightseeing excursions to other cities. Chase also delivered more formal lectures on Mondays and in the evenings. One topic of discussion—a lecture Pach found to be "a corncracker [and] a potwalloper"—was the state of art training at home, specifically the differences between the more progressive Art Students League and the traditional Pennsylvania Academy of the Fine Arts. Chase's more innovative approach of allowing students to paint somewhat spontaneously was often at odds with the academic tradition in which years of study and drawing after the antique were followed by hours in the life class before a student could put paint to canvas. In addition, Chase gave numerous painting demonstrations. They were sometimes attended by visitors as well as students, and the canvases that Chase dashed off during these sessions were raffled among the audience members, much to their delight.

Pach painted and sketched daily, often by the canal or on the River Spaarne, where he observed, "Everything seems so fine in this rare sunlight that it seems like painting the lily. Red roofs so fine. The handsome boats . . . wonderful, tonal reflections. Red and gray, still canals." Light, color, and atmospheric effects captured his imagination, and he attempted to translate these visions into his paintings. Pach also "worked in the studio from the model," especially during the many dreary rainy days. Locals regularly posed for the sketch classes, as did the pupils themselves, including Pach. Among the earliest located drawings by Pach is one of a young Dutch boy (fig. 5) dated 1903 that was undoubtedly done during one of these sketch classes. This charcoal shows Pach's ability as an academic draftsman.

The sketches, drawings, and paintings the students created formed the basis of Chase's biweekly criticisms, or "crits," designed to help the pupils improve their technique. Of the first crit, Pach wrote, "Fine talk by Mr. Chase . . . Rem.—Hals [Rembrandt—Hals], quality, as to [William-Adolphe] Bouguereau & [Jean-Léon] Gérôme, enthusiasm. Fine crits. Mr.

Wadsworth. Mine!" As Pach noted in this passage, Chase often lectured on the masters of the past when he discussed the work of his students, so that the latter would know what to strive for in their own paintings. In addition, Chase gave individual attention to each of the pupils, and while Pach complained on one occasion that he "knew the two landscapes were bum, but thought he might perhaps have said something better of the still life," a few days later, he was encouraged when Chase "said one of my things was the best I had ever done." This was the kind of instruction Pach needed to advance his artistic career, and, taking his teacher's words to heart, he strove daily to improve his painting technique.

A large part of the art students' education, Chase believed, should take place in the museums, where they could study Old Master paintings as well as more contemporary works by nineteenth-century artists. Pach heeded his mentor's advice and frequented the Rijksmuseum, the Teyler Museum, the Mauritshuis, and the Stedelijk Museum. He never tired of visiting these grand collections and felt that "in seeing pictures aright—just looking at the ones you want to see—the effect is not tiredness, even after this long day—but exhilaration." He was rejuvenated by the paintings of Rembrandt, Frans Hals, Anthony Van Dyck, Adriaen van de Velde, Jacob van Ruisdael, and Peter Paul Rubens, with Rembrandt's *The Company of Captain Frans Banning Cocq and Lieutenant Willem van Ruytenburgh,* better known as the *Night Watch,* having the biggest impact on him. He was awed by it, recording in his journal, "Dazzling, grandest light and luminosity, Quality, unity with divine portrait details, color, richness, tone, mystery." Pach also came to appreciate further works by what he called the "modern" painters. At this point, his definition of *modern* included nineteenth-century realist painters like Gustave Courbet; members of the Barbizon school, including Théodore Rousseau and Constant Troyon; and a few contemporaries, such as Hendrik Willem Mesdag, Jozef Israëls,

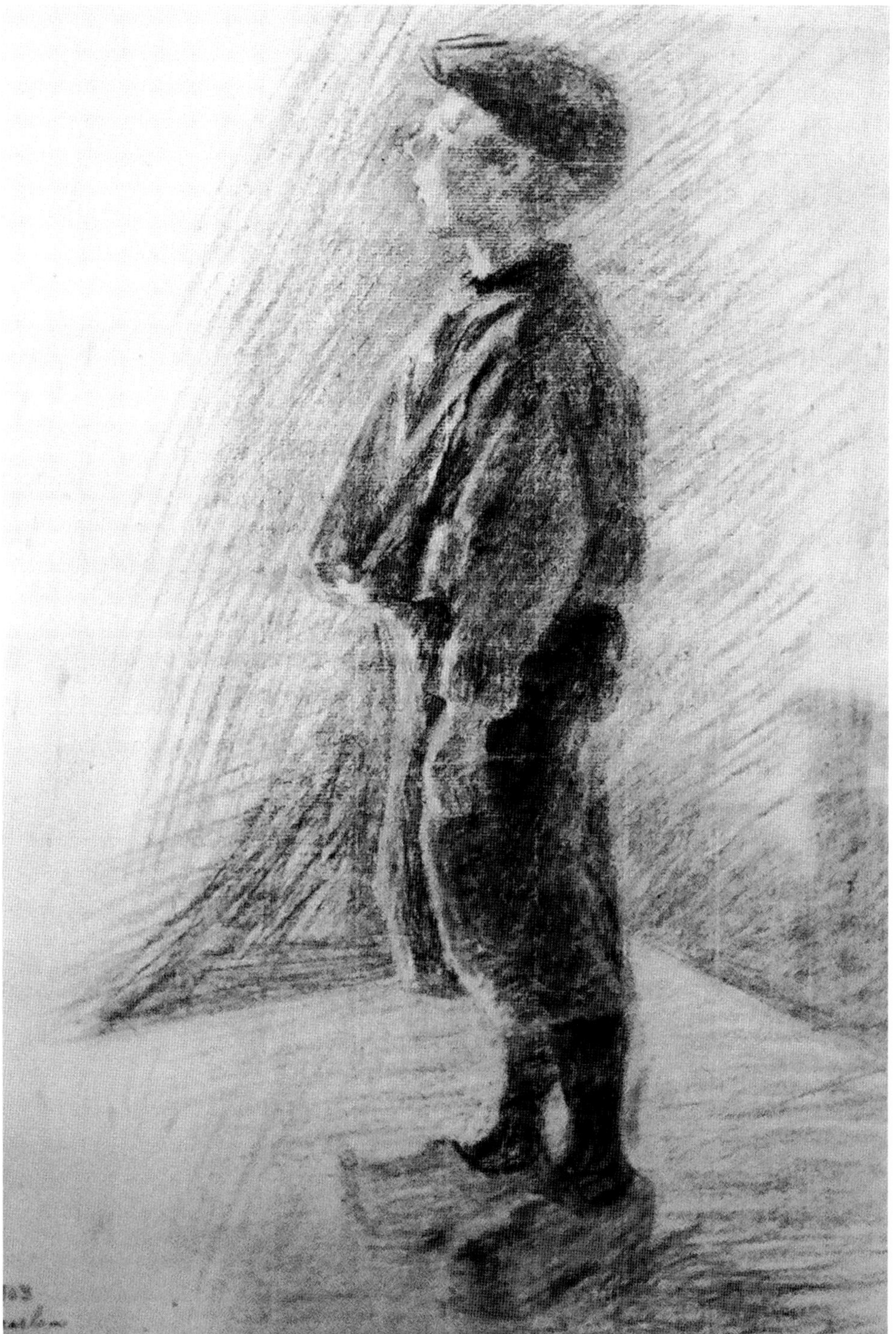

Walter Pach (1883–1958)

and most notably, Whistler. He admired their sense of light and color and tried to incorporate the lessons learned from them into his own paintings.

Another aspect of the Chase summer school that was quite a treat for the students was the frequent visits to private collections, some of which were not accessible to the average tourist. In The Hague, they went to Mesdag's collection and studio twice. They also called on Israëls. Trips such as these afforded Pach and others the opportunity to meet with professional artists and to see their work, studios, and collections. In addition, in Amsterdam, the students visited the Six Collection, formulated by Jan Six, who had become mayor of Amsterdam in 1691. Among its prized possessions are portraits of Six by Rembrandt, as well as works by Frans Hals and Albert Cuyp and furniture and porcelain. The museum remains as restricted today as it was in Pach's day. All of these outings were designed to broaden the students' education and provide further inspiration for their own art and careers.

Pach appears to have acted as the class photographer on this trip. He noted in his diary on August 6, "Everyone pleased with my photos of the class at the Mauritshuis, took orders." On August 18 he recorded, "2 o'clock photograph in the gallery of the class." On the same day, Chase wrote to his wife, "Photographed with the class in the [Frans] Hals Museum at 2 p.m."[10] Pach recorded that the "proofs" arrived two days later "amid fine excitement" and nearly everyone was pleased with the results.

Although the main purpose of the school was to train the aspiring artists in their chosen profession, Chase encouraged his pupils to absorb the culture and beauty of Haarlem, and Pach certainly took advantage of his free moments to explore the city and its environs. He frequented Amsterdam, The Hague, and Zandvoort, often in the company of fellow student Frank Wadsworth and his wife and a Miss Rheinlander. Although he complained of his lack of attention to his study of Dutch on board ship, Pach was a gifted linguist and after just one day in Haarlem was "not afraid to ask

directions in Dutch." He used these skills on the many excursions they took outside Haarlem and, for example, on their first trip to Bloemendaal acted as the interpreter for the group. He struck up a lifelong friendship with Piet van der Laan, a native of Bloemendaal and a student of classical literature. They had a mutual admiration for the works of John Flaxman, Ovid, Homer, and Friedrich Nietzsche and a love of music. Pach shared his own unpublished manuscript, "Aesthetics," with his new friend and showed him his copies of what he termed "Whistler, etc.," probably the painter's writings on aesthetics. Van der Laan posed for sketch classes and took Pach to swimming races and polo matches in Amsterdam and elsewhere. Pach also went rowing on the canal and on the Spaarne and Amstel rivers with his classmates and occasionally partook of a good "flask of whiskey" with Wadsworth and others. Evenings at the pension were often filled with games and music, and during this trip Pach managed to secure a violin in order to participate in informal recitals. He also attended concerts at the Hotel du Passage, the Grote Kerk, and the Circus Carré.

The friendships Pach made on this trip, and the profound impression that traveling and living in a foreign country made on him, were just as vital and life enhancing as the lessons in art. The close relationships that he formed with Louis Betts and his wife, the Wadsworths, Schamberg, and other students lasted for decades. The camaraderie among the students and the festivities and frivolity in which they engaged made the trip enjoyable and unforgettable. These first overseas adventures certainly whetted Pach's appetite for more voyages, and thereafter he spent every summer traveling, either in the United States or abroad.

After two months in Haarlem, Pach headed back to the United States, via London. He stopped briefly in Antwerp, where he had just enough time to visit the museum before he boarded the boat for Harwich, England. During his whirlwind tour of London, Pach spent most of his waking hours attempting to absorb as much art as possible in the hallowed halls of the National Gallery of Art, Hertford House (now called the Wallace Collection), the British Museum, and the Tate Gallery. He was impressed by the beauty of the Old Master paintings and works by John Constable and Joseph Mallord William Turner; however, he was more smitten with the "modern room" at Hertford House: paintings by Narcisse Virgile Díaz de la Peña, Troyon, Jean-Louis-Ernest Meissonier, Alexandre Decamps, Corot, and others. Pach was beginning to develop a broader taste in art, slowly moving away from the Old Masters toward more contemporary work. At the Tate, he found the British school well represented with works by George Frederic Watts, Sir Frederick Leighton, and Sir John Everett Millais, but he did not care for what he called their "art for literature's sake" style of painting. By immersing himself in a crash course, as it were, in the treasures of the British capital, Pach was further refining his eye and defining his likes and dislikes. While he had seen many paintings at the Metropolitan Museum of Art, the depth and variety of art that he encountered in the Netherlands and London were such as he had not experienced before. This first experience abroad convinced Pach of his desire to pursue a career as a painter.

In whatever spare time he managed to find during his layover in London, Pach visited most of the major tourist sights: Westminster Abbey, Big Ben, St. Paul's Cathedral, Piccadilly Circus, and the Duke of York Column. Like any good tourist, he also did some shopping before leaving for the United States and bought several Hiroshige prints, a few books to read during the crossing, and presents for his family. On September 5, he boarded a train bound for Folkestone Harbor, then took a ship to Boulogne, where he boarded the *Ryndam* with his "Wolffe, Smith & Weston" pistol in his pocket for his final ten-day voyage to New York.[11]

Upon his return, he continued his studies at Chase's New York School of Art in Manhattan and enrolled in night classes under Robert Henri, who had joined the staff.[12] Henri gave instruction in life class, portraiture, and composition, though he abandoned the traditional drawing taught at most academies. In addition, he started anatomy courses and hired Thomas Anshutz to present a series of lectures on the subject. Henri approached his own art with a sense of adventure and painted with a freedom of expression; he encouraged his students to confront their canvases in the same manner. He told them, "Know what the old masters did. Know how they composed their pictures, but do not fall into the conventions they established. These conventions were right for them, and they are wonderful. They made their language. You make yours. They can help you. All the past can help you."[13] This approach to the study of art appealed to Pach, who observed, "Robert Henri personified that form of tradition which in later days was to be called modern."[14]

Henri also believed in educating the entire individual, not merely the artist, and this was a manner of teaching with which Pach was familiar. In addition to discussing art, Henri often quoted from the writings of Émile Zola, Guy de Maupassant, Walt Whitman, or Jean-Jacques Rousseau. He also advised his pupils to attend concerts, the theater, and dance performances to develop an understanding of the world and of the interrelationship of the arts. Pach had experienced this interdisciplinary approach to instruction in his youth, and Henri reiterated what Pach had already been taught—that learning through life experience was as valuable as acquiring knowledge by rote or manual training in the classroom. Henri's belief in the possibility of the creation of a new, more harmonious society in which people could live as free human beings was also similar to tenets Pach had learned at the Ethical Culture Society. In addition, Henri's statement that "Life and art cannot be disassociated" and his understanding of the artist's role as a catalyst for change in society were precepts with which Pach wholeheartedly agreed.[15]

Through Henri's classes, Pach established lasting relationships with American artists such as Arnold

Friedman, A. S. Baylinson, and Guy Pène du Bois and with Moriye Ogihara, a Japanese artist, with whom he became particularly close. "It was an adventure for me," Pach wrote later in life, "to make friends with a Japanese possessing brilliant intelligence, the poetic sense of his people, and . . . something very near to genius for the sculpture which finally replaced painting as his work. We made friends and we remained friends."[16] Ogihara helped Pach with his reading and writing of Japanese, a language he never fully perfected. These painters and others, among them Schamberg, Charles Sheeler, John Sloan, Maurice and Charles Prendergast, and William Glackens, were to play significant roles in Pach's life, and he championed the work of several of them throughout their careers. The friendships that Pach formed during his student days were vitally important not only for his own future but also for the growth and development of art in the United States.

Little else is known about Pach's life in New York from the fall of 1903 until the summer of 1904, when he joined Chase's class in Europe as an agent for the program in London.[17] Again he kept a detailed daily logbook of this trip abroad; however, the tone of this journal is different from that of the 1903 record and reveals a more experienced and self-assured young man.[18] There is still a touch of romanticism in the writing, but the style is a bit more matter-of-fact. On June 14, Pach crossed Fourteenth Street and "drove to Holland-America dock. Got stuff aboard, and took up (8:20 am) position at 1st cabin gangway with green 'C. C. in E.' [Chase Class in Europe] on my hat." Although he admitted that he had "few opportunities to be of use" that first morning on board ship, as agent for the program he had already been invaluable in securing the cabins for the forty students and had also booked their rooms in England.

The ten-day crossing allowed Pach to acquaint himself with his fellow students and travelers and to enjoy the leisurely pace of ocean liner travel. Like most of the passengers, he spent much of his time eating,

smoking, lounging, painting, reading, and visiting with others. Among the shipboard pastimes he enjoyed were chess, dancing, shuffleboard, gymnastics on deck, and concerts. These activities helped pass the time between meals, which was quite short. Pach complained about the "ubiquity of food" on board, a characteristic of ship travel that does not seem to have changed.

After a relatively smooth crossing, the ship reached Europe. It docked first at Boulogne and then at Hoek van Holland, where Pach "saw Mr. Townsley and helped get crowd together." The group spent the day at The Hague and then caught a train back to Hoek van Holland and boarded a ship for their final destination, London, where they would spend two months. After they arrived in Harwich early the next morning, they took a train through the "English landscape"—full of "gardens, flowers, pretty houses, level roads, lots of green" with "trees black against fine sky" filled with "lots of clouds"—and reached London just before nine in the morning on June 25. Pach quickly "got people stowed in four houses on Islenloch and Glenmore Roads & Staverstock Hill" near St. John's Wood and Hampstead Heath in north-central London. Schamberg selected the house in which he and Pach would room. Another student on this trip, and one with whom Pach would become quite close, was Charles Sheeler.

The plan of the two-month course in England was similar to the one established in the Netherlands. Students drew and painted in a rented studio; sketched outdoors; received weekly instruction, criticisms, and lectures from Chase; and visited museums, private collections, and artists' studios. Pach and Townsley were in charge of obtaining art supplies, including easels and paint, for the students. Chase's discussions focused mainly on the Old Masters, but he also spoke of contemporary artists. These talks were designed to familiarize the pupils not only with the artists whom Chase considered worthy of emulation but also with those whose works he felt should be avoided. He warned his pupils, however, against slavish imitation of any other painter and encouraged them to create their own style. Pach drew in charcoal or sketched in oil in the studio almost every day and commented on his success or failure in his logbook virtually every evening. He also took his "thumb-box" with him to sketch outdoors, sometimes with Schamberg, and he painted in his room. Pach found some of Chase's criticisms to be "good crits" while others were "tough." Reviews of his work fell mostly in the "good" category, much to his pleasure and relief. The regular demonstrations were aimed at teaching the class the techniques of good painting, and the works Chase created were once more distributed to the class through a raffle.

Pach immersed himself in the museums of London, frequenting the National Gallery, the Royal Academy, the New Gallery, the Wallace Collection, the Tate Gallery, the National Portrait Gallery, and the Victoria and Albert Museum as often as possible. He still admired his beloved Old Masters—Rembrandt, Ruisdael, Hals, Titian, and Raphael, to name a few— and some British school painters such as Joshua Reynolds, Thomas Gainsborough, William Hogarth, Constable, and Turner. Pach also remained a devotee of Whistler, and when he visited Obach's Gallery in Bond Street to see the recently purchased Peacock Room he was overwhelmed by the "lovely blue, greens with lacquery golds on them in great designs."[19] However, he was finding himself increasingly drawn to nineteenth-century French artists, among them Courbet, Jean-Auguste-Dominique Ingres, and Edgar Degas and those of the Barbizon school. Pach was not yet a Francophile, but he was heading in that direction.

Among the contemporary artists the students met were Sir Lawrence Alma-Tadema, Sir Frank Brangwyn, Edwin Austin Abbey, Sir John Lavery, John Singer Sargent, and Sir James Jebusa Shannon. Pach was most impressed by his visits to Brangywn's and Sargent's studios. At the former he was enthralled by the artist's collection of "Japaneseries" and was struck by the beauty of the pottery, wood, lacquer, gold screens, and prints on display. While he was impressed with Sargent's watercolors and his Venetian scenes, he was powerfully struck by the artist's infamous portrait *Madame X.* This painting had caused quite a scandal when shown at the Paris Salon; critics had attacked both the artist and the sitter for presenting such a bold and sexually provocative image. Pach found the sheer technical skill of the artist to be profound.

Some other diversions that Pach enjoyed were outings to tourist sights, concerts, and dinners. He toured Westminster Abbey and Petticoat Lane and took train rides through the English countryside. He also indulged in his love of music by attending concerts and playing the "nice hearty English type" of violin that he borrowed. In the evenings he joined fellow students for games and sing-alongs. An avid reader and book collector, Pach regularly haunted area bookshops and Liberty's for prints by Hokusai and other Asian artists. He also taught himself "Kata-kanai" (katakana), a form of Japanese script.

Perhaps the most important aspects of this overseas excursion for Pach were the lengthy discussions on art, philosophy, and life with fellow students, particularly with his roommate, Schamberg. The two took long and frequent walks through town and on Hampstead Heath, went to museums together, and even sketched side by side on several occasions. The long "chin-chins" they had on art and life were, as Pach wrote, as "reminiscent and intimate" as the ones of the previous year. A "grand discussion" that Pach noted especially was one with Schamberg, Sheeler, and other students that centered on "photography as a means of expression." While Schamberg and Sheeler believed that photography could be used and viewed as a fine art, Pach staunchly disagreed with this opinion. Having worked in his father's studio, he found photography to be merely a reproductive, not an imitative, art form. This perspective put him squarely at odds with the more avant-garde approach to photography. During another evening on Hampstead Heath, Pach and Schamberg "talked pictures and possibilities. Collectors. Artists. America and Europe as places of residence." These young men were grappling with the intricacies of the complex world of art and trying to find their place within it. They were not, however, unaware of the larger societal issues that faced the United States in the early years of the twentieth century. Pach, for example, wrote of a conversation that turned to the topics of "the South, the negro, Henry Ossawa Tanner." While Pach may have been relatively conservative in his approach to art at this time, he was quite liberal when it came to his belief in the equal treatment of African Americans. He may well have learned this sense of tolerance through the teachings of the Ethical Culture Society or from his parents, who were socially and politically liberal. Through such discussions Pach continued to explore and develop his philosophy of art and life.

After just over one month in London, Pach left for an extended trip to the Netherlands, Germany, and France, a journey that would change his life forever.[20] On July 28 he boarded the *Dresden* at Harwich, landed at Hoek van Holland, and after a "charming ride up the Maas" met his parents aboard the *Potsdam* in Rotterdam. After a three-day visit to the museums and sights of Haarlem and The Hague, the trio departed for Germany. They arrived in Berlin on August 3 and stayed for several days before parting company for two weeks. Pach toured Berlin, Dresden, and Munich while his parents went to the spa town of Bad Nauheim, where his father took the waters for his health.[21]

Once Pach collected their belongings at the steamer office and got his parents settled, he set off to explore the art treasures of Berlin. On his first visit to what he called the "National Gallerie," now the Gemäldegalerie, he saw, "lots of Düsseldorfers and more modern rubbish but also: Liebermann, Leible, Trubner, Menzel, Lenbach & Bochlin. Big stuff not our kind—often black and often inaesthetic but big. . . . Upstairs, —stupidities, royalties, then a big room Sorolla, Jügel, Landenbesger

. . . Francisco Goya (weeeee!!!)." He took two more excursions to the museum and discovered the "grand Manet, Pissaro [*sic*], Monet, Sisley, Degas, Daubigny, Constable, Courbet." This was Pach's first exposure to many of these artists. While in Berlin he also visited the Altes Museum; however, he discovered that many works had been transferred to the new Kaiser-Friedrich-Museum (now the Bode Museum), to which he obtained entry through family friends. There he saw more of his favorite painters, including Hals, Jan van der Meer (Vermeer), Rubens, Bartolomé Esteban Murillo, and Rembrandt.

From Berlin, Pach took a "nice ride through handsome German country to Dresden," where he arrived on August 6 and remained for four days. During the brief visit he soaked up all the art the city had to offer at museums and exhibitions and enjoyed several concerts in the parks. He visited the Gemäldegalerie Alte Meister in the Zwinger Palace on several occasions and attentively studied Raphael's *Sistine Madonna* and works by other Italian painters, among them Guido Reni, Sandro Botticelli, Guarino Veronese, Tintoretto, and Titian. He spent his days there exploring the vast collections, which included "modern pictures, good Germans but not the greatest things . . . Venetians and other Italians." One day, he "began at Claude Lorraine and traversed the immense corridor, Van der Meer . . . Ruisdael, grand Hals, small Teniers, Dou and Metsu," continuing to study intently the Old Masters he had admired for several years now.

It was the works that Pach saw in the Grosse Kunstausstellung, or Great International Art Exhibition, held in Dresden, however, that profoundly affected him. On August 8, after watching a parade and troop inspection in the square, he lunched on the Elbe, then, as he noted in his diary, he

walked home and then took [the] notion to go to the exhibition again. Got into better section. Courbet, Delacroix, *Leibl*, Lenbach, *Stevens*. Lots of

Düsseldorfers; statuettes by Barye then my pets
Degas (5), Buzenne [probably Eugène Antoine
Durenne], Pis[s]arro, *Renoir,* Boudin, Carrière,
Vollon, Manet, Sisley, Daumier; English pictures,
magnificent Raeburn, Goya, Menzel; then another
swell room *Courbet* (2), Corot (2), *Monticelli,*
Inscions, Dupré, Diaz, Rousseau, Troyon; Mr.
Chase (Piloty boys) . . . Great splendid Rodin room.

He visited the show again where he "enjoyed great
Frenchmen very much." This encounter with many of
the French impressionist artists profoundly influenced
Pach. While he continued to study Old Master paintings throughout his life, after this experience he focused
his attention away from the art of the distant past and
toward the advanced French art of the late nineteenth
and early twentieth centuries.[22]

From Dresden, Pach took an omnibus and train to
Munich, where he spent two days immersed in the art
collections of yet another city. He was at the museums
virtually all day and once more studied the Old Masters
on display. After this whirlwind tour, he boarded a train
for Frankfurt and then traveled on to Bad Nauheim,
where he stayed with his parents for a few days.

On August 17, after two weeks in Germany, Pach
waved good-bye to his parents at the Bad Nauheim
train station and set off, alone, for his first trip to Paris.
He secured his ticket, then "got out Paris Baedeker
[Karl Baedeker's *Paris and Environs*] and started
investigations." He taught himself some French en
route, and by the time he arrived he had learned the
numerals and "written quite a bit." After a drink to
celebrate his arrival, he found his way, via omnibus, to
the Hôtel de Calais, on rue des Capucines near the
place de l'Opéra. He stayed in this establishment for
several days before moving to the Hôtel Angleterre on
rue Jacob, in the Latin Quarter on the Left Bank, for the
remainder of his time in Paris.

For just about a month Pach explored the city and,
naturally, gravitated toward its famed museums,

especially the Louvre and the Luxembourg. He also
visited the Musée Guimet, which housed an outstanding collection of Asian art. When he "walked down
Avenue de l'Opéra to Louvre" his first day in Paris he
was overwhelmed by the splendid stores that lined the
grand boulevard; by the shopkeepers who spoke
English; and by the wares they carried, which included
guns, pictures, and modern statues in bronze. After his
first visit to the Louvre, he wrote in his logbook, "The
museum enormous. . . . Oriented a little by walking
around—miles over very slippery uneven floor.
Velasquezs. Great Rubens in room. Venetians. . . . Went
upstairs and saw collection Thomy-Thierry. Great
Barbizons. Famous Corot of the lakes, others. Grand
Troyon of 'Le Matin.' Rousseau, Dupré, Daubigny,
Millet, Romantics, Barye and Courbet—splendid
show." His appreciation of the Barbizon school had
grown considerably over the preceding few years. After
lunch, he returned to the museum and saw "Ingres, 'La
Source,' 'L'Odalisque' etc. Big fine Troyons, Millet
'Spring.' Delacroix—Great things 'Dante' etc." With his
mind and eyes saturated with art, Pach left the Louvre
and wandered the streets of Paris to drink in the sights
of the city. That evening he dined alone, then went to
the American Girls' Club with students from the Chase
program. His first night in Paris would have been
incomplete without a nightcap at a Parisian café.

Pach knew that the best way to improve his own
painting was to study the masters of the past, and so,
like thousands of artists before him, he spent hours in
the Louvre investigating, and probably copying, works
by Leonardo, Rembrandt, Titian, Tintoretto, Diego
Rodriguez de Silva Velázquez, Veronese, Hals, and
Rubens. He did not limit himself to the Old Masters,
however, but also explored the ancient sculpture and
the decorative arts sections in the Louvre and frequented the Luxembourg and its contemporary collection of
art. Among the works that most profoundly affected
him there were the statues by Auguste Rodin and works
by Édouard Manet, Claude Monet, Alfred Sisley, and

Jean François Rafaellis, but he "did not care for the Renoirs." He was struck in particular by Manet's *Olympia,* which he found to be "grand," but "did not get into blackish 'Angelina.'" Pach had been keenly interested in Manet's art for several years and had studied the two paintings by him that were hung in the Metropolitan Museum, but this was his first exposure to some of the artist's most famed works, and he was quite swayed by their power. After careful examination of these pictures Pach "wondered how high he [Manet] might not rank among soul-men." Pach's taste in art had clearly advanced toward a deepening appreciation of late impressionists.

During his stay in Paris, Pach spent a great deal of time with fellow American artists. Among those with whom he was quite close were Patrick Henry Bruce, whom he had probably met in Robert Henri's class, and Alice Vincent Corson, with whom he seems to have been quite smitten. Bruce may have helped him find a studio in which to work: on August 25 Pach recorded in his diary, "Went to studio. Painted portrait. Two starts. Liked it," and on September 10 he wrote, "Walked to studio. Portraits going well. Nocturne—really beautiful. Talked. Philosophy." He was obviously creating paintings, which, unfortunately, have yet to be located. Others he met during this trip included the painters Frederick Reynolds, Thornton Oakley, and Victor Hugo Zoll and the sculptors Frederick Ruckstuhl and Albert Laessle. After they spent hours studying and copying paintings in the Louvre, the artists would often work in their studios or linger over dinner and a drink discussing art, life, and their careers. The talks on art usually began at the museums and ended over "drink and more talk" at Bruce's club or elsewhere. Other conversations focused on "the place of truth in the picture" and the "chance of making a hit, art in small town, love, mistresses and Paris morals." This was typical talk among young male art students of the day, and Pach was well informed of the latest issues and debates. The late-night discussions not only fueled

Pach's passion for art but also allowed him to avoid, for as long as possible, the flea-infested bed at his hotel.

While in Paris, Pach visited the usual tourist destinations—Notre Dame, Versailles, the Eiffel Tower, the Panthéon, the Hôtel de Ville, the Bois de Boulogne, Les Invalides, and the Sorbonne—went shopping, and dramatically improved his ability to speak French, becoming virtually fluent. Pach searched high and low for Japanese prints, as he had in other cities, but in a new collecting phase for him, he also shopped for impressionist prints in the stores recommended in his copy of Baedeker's. Unfortunately, it was August, the off-season in Paris. Many of the stores were closed and most of his attempts to locate prints were "highly unsuccessful in all but covering distance and seeing streets." Eventually, he did stumble on "a mine of Japanese prints" when he was not looking and also managed to locate some splendid impressionist pieces. Pach was developing an understanding of how to collect art, knowledge that would prove useful in his future career as an agent. Pach also found time to attend the theater and the opera, and, of course, no visit to the city would be complete without indulging in the favorite Parisian pastime of people-watching while sipping coffee or a drink at one of the numerous cafés that dotted the street corners of the city.

Also during this short stay, Pach had a brief meeting with Rodin at the artist's studio. When he arrived at the house on rue de Varenne he "sat on marbles till the master had taken some American ladies through. Then went in with him and showed photos." Rodin was "interested in all but most in sculpture gallery & Geo. Gray Bernard. Remembered dining with Mr. Chase and Harrison." Evidently, Pach had brought photographs of works by some American sculptors to show to Rodin, though it is unclear precisely why he had these images with him. He requested reproductions of Rodin's art but, regrettably, came away empty-handed.

Much to his dismay, Pach's first journey to Paris was very brief. On August 27, ten days after he had arrived in the city, he received notice that there was a letter from his father. Dejectedly, he "started out in obedience" to the Dépôt des Marbres, where he read the message he feared: he was told to return to Germany. Using his considerable powers of persuasion, however, he managed to convince his parents to join him in Paris. They arrived on September 10, and two days later the three traveled to London for some sightseeing and shopping before they departed for the United States from Rotterdam on September 15. During the Atlantic crossing Pach mingled with fellow passengers and read his copy of Zola's *L'oeuvre.* This might have been one of the many writings by Zola that Henri quoted in his classes; Pach's increased study of Manet's paintings during this trip might also have prompted this purchase, since Zola was one of the earliest supporters of Manet's efforts. Unlike on previous ocean journeys, Pach did not record much in his journal. Perhaps he was too travel weary from his three-month European adventure to write.

While we know that Pach returned to New York City toward the end of September 1904, there is little information about his life during that fall or the following spring. He continued his studies under both Chase and Henri at the New York School of Art through the spring of 1905 and attended a costume party at the school around this time (fig. 6). Undoubtedly, he lived with his parents. Advertisements in his scrapbooks indicate that he probably attended concerts, the theater, and the opera. Other papers show that he saw a performance by his former violin instructor Carl Hauser. Unfortunately, there is no other evidence of his activities during this period.

In the summer of 1905, Pach was again hired as the agent for the Chase Class in Europe, which this year was held in Madrid. Unlike during the previous two sessions, he does not seem to have kept a journal of his travels. Pach had received a "fine foundation in Spanish" at CCNY but probably taught himself more of the language before departing on this trip.[23] He accompa-

nied the students on the cross-Atlantic voyage that took them around the southern part of Spain and passed Gibraltar, Ronda, and Córdoba before they disembarked and boarded a train to Madrid. His responsibilities once again included securing accommodations for the students and obtaining art supplies.

The program established in the Netherlands and England was followed again in Spain.[24] Students devoted time to museum studies, studio work, and sketching outdoors, and Chase gave weekly instruction, lectures, and criticisms. The group also went on excursions to other cities and enjoyed the cultural life of the country. The main attraction in Madrid was, of course, the Prado, to which Chase took his students the day they arrived. He was most enthusiastic about the glorious paintings by El Greco but also encouraged his pupils to study and copy works by the other Old Masters in the collection, including Francisco Goya and Velázquez. The class journeyed to Toledo to view more paintings by El Greco and visited the studios of contemporary Spanish painters such as Joaquin Sorolla y Bastida. Also that summer, Chase took several students, along with Pach, to a bullfight at the Plaza de Toros de Madrid, which celebrated the festival of Corpus Christi.

After the summer session ended, Pach briefly visited France, Austria, and, perhaps, Germany before he returned to New York. In Paris, he saw the 1905 Salon d'Automne; it was at this exhibition that he first encountered the paintings of the Fauves. In *Queer Thing, Painting* he recalled, "I have a distant mental image of Rouault's pictures at the first Autumn Salon I saw, that of 1905, but I cannot recall an impression of Matisse—probably because he made none on me."[25] Pach was probably not quite ready to embrace such new and controversial art. The length of this journey is not known, but Pach was back in the United States by the end of September. He resumed living with his parents in their Park Avenue apartment, continued his training under Chase and Henri, and frequented the

Metropolitan Museum of Art to copy works in its collection. He also participated in his first museum exhibition with the acceptance of *The Toledo Bridge,* an oil painting undoubtedly inspired by the previous summer's excursion, into the Sixth Annual Exhibition of the Fellowship of the Pennsylvania Academy of the Fine Arts, which opened on November 16, 1905.[26]

The year 1906 was filled with new adventures and changes for Pach in his professional and personal life. In March 1906, he met John Sloan, a fellow artist who became a lifelong friend. Sloan was substituting for Henri in the men's life class at night at the New York School of Art. He wrote of Pach in the diary he kept at the time, "After the evening class, had a talk with some of the members. Hatch, Van Sloon, Boss, Pach, Levy. They are all of interest. . . . In Pach, I think it is all ideals, he don't work up to them—and yet, it is difficult to say. He might turn out the best but I miss my guess if he does."[27] Sloan recognized that Pach's intellectual and

philosophical proclivities sometimes hindered his abilities to translate his artistic thoughts into concrete form in paintings, a hindrance that would plague Pach throughout his artistic life.

In the summer of 1906, Pach accompanied Henri's class to Madrid; he had been hired as the agent for the program. The course was similar to the Chase programs in Haarlem, London, and Madrid. Students worked in a studio and sketched outdoors, visited museums, and enjoyed leisure-time activities. Among the pastimes Pach enjoyed were another bullfight at the Plaza de Toros and musical performances. During this trip he met the English poet Ezra Pound, though the two did not form any lasting friendship.[28] This was yet another eventful summer for Pach artistically and culturally.

After the official summer session ended, several pupils, under the guidance of Pach and Louis G. Monté, the other agent for the class, traveled to Paris and other cities before they departed for the United

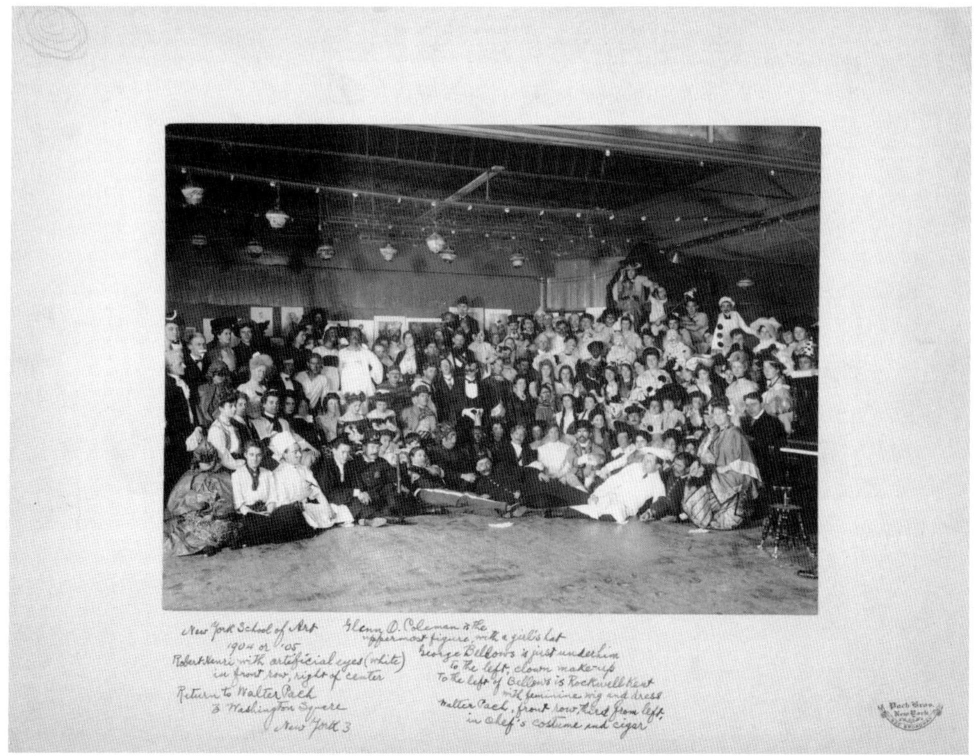

Fig. 6
Gotthelf Pach, photograph of New York School of Art costume ball, 1904 or 1905, photographic print, black and white, 25 × 20 cm. Courtesy of Walter Pach Papers, 1883–1980, Archives of American Art, Smithsonian Institution.

States. They spent one week in Paris sightseeing and visiting museums. Pach complained to Henri that his "great disappointment in Paris was missing the Durand-Ruel private collection," but he reported that he saw "some beautiful things. Manet's 'Absinthe Drinker' etc. Some Courbet, Puvis [de Chavannes] and Monet at the store."[29] At this early date, Pach was visiting one of the most important vanguard art galleries in Paris, Durand-Ruel, and was beginning to establish an understanding of the art market there. After Paris, a few of the pupils accompanied Pach to Brussels and Bruges, where they met British artist Frank Brangwyn and other friends. In Antwerp, they visited the cathedral and the museum, and in Leiden they saw a Rembrandt exhibition. After a brief stay in Haarlem, the group departed for London for their voyage home. As an agent for the program, Pach was responsible for seeing to the students' return passage to the United States on board the *Erturia,* and he promised Henri that "every detail—the various boxes of class paintings and copies as well—was in order."[30] He also helped arrange for Henri's return voyage to the United States.

Pach remained abroad for several weeks after the students' departure, having "a good look at the National Gallery" and "a visit to the A. B. [Arthur Burdett] Frost family" before he returned to Haarlem, where he worked in a studio over Café Brinkmann for two weeks.[31] Pach painted a portrait of one of Mr. Brinkmann's sons, several oil sketches, and copies after paintings in the museums.[32] It was during this time that Pach first encountered the work of Vincent van Gogh. In *Queer Thing, Painting* he recalled, "Painting in Holland for a time, I found myself going out of my way, on returning from my studio every evening, in order to take a street where I could see certain drawings in the window of a bookshop. Finally I went in and inquired the name of the artist and was told that it was van Gogh, which left me not much wiser than I had been, since no mention of his genius or even his existence had yet reached me."[33] Pach was among the earliest

Americans to form a sincere appreciation of van Gogh's art, and later in life became one of the first critics to write about him.

When Pach returned to New York in the fall of 1906, he established his own studio in his father's building at 935 Broadway, declaring himself no longer a student.[34] Although he continued to live with his parents in their Park Avenue apartment, he now had a place of his own. As a herald of his new life as an artist, he submitted a painting inspired by his recent trip to Spain, *Open-Air Restaurant, Bombilla,* to the jury of the National Academy of Design. Much to his delight, the work was accepted to the Winter Exhibition of the Academy, a sure sign of his status as a professional artist.[35]

3
The Formative Years

The years between 1907 and 1910 were a time of transition in Pach's life, "the turning point in my career," as he wrote.[1] He had declared himself a professional artist in 1906 and opened his own studio, yet his parents, and his father in particular, were not very enthusiastic about his choice. Gotthelf admired the works he saw at the Metropolitan Museum of Art and believed that mastery of painting would be a useful skill for his son to possess, but he opposed Walter's decision of "entering on painting as a life work."[2] Instead he advised him to try translations, journalism, and criticism. Realizing he could not yet support himself as a painter, Pach begrudgingly acted on his father's suggestions and began to write, lecture, and translate on a regular basis. He had mixed feelings about this work. He complained bitterly that "time spent on such matters has cut into my painting time very seriously," yet he also strongly believed that his work in this vein provided a valuable service to the public.[3] He would struggle throughout his life to balance his multiple roles of artist, critic, lecturer, dealer, and historian.

In early spring of 1907, Chase laid plans for a new summer class abroad in Florence, and Pach was once again asked to serve as an agent for the program.[4] As before, he secured the students' accommodations, both on sea and land, and found a suitable studio space for the class. Another of Pach's responsibilities was to enlist students for the course and answer any inquiries regarding the program. He wrote to Alice Klauber, a prospective pupil,

> Mr. Chase, as our most eminent painter and teacher needs no further introduction. Mr. Monté has been some seven times to Europe—by himself and as director of parties, covering Italy thoroughly three times. He is a specialist on art-theory, history and pedagogics, and during his tenure of office at Teacher's College, Columbia University and other institutions, he has lectured before many important classes. He is recognized as one of the leading authorities on his subject.
>
> This will be, for me, the sixth season with classes of this order. Should you care for references as to my work with them in painting and art-knowledge, languages and European management, I think even a random selection from the couple of hundred students with whom I have been associated, would satisfy you.
>
> We have arranged the trip to afford the maximum of profit and enjoyment to the party, while bearing in mind the character of its personelle [*sic*] where possible, and economizing its means wherever such a course in no wise interferes with the comfort to which Americans in Europe are accustomed.

Pach was quite persuasive in his publicity campaign, and Klauber did indeed join the program. To ensure the "maximum of profit and enjoyment to the party," he departed for Italy before the group to make final arrangements and to obtain the students' art supplies, such as paints and easels.[5] Pach had obviously taught himself enough Italian to perform these services, a skill that would also enable him to act as an interpreter for the class.

The group departed from Boston aboard the White Star Line's *Romanic* on June 8, 1907, for an art-filled two-month excursion to Italy, and Chase met the students in Florence. The program for this year's class differed slightly from those of previous years in that it placed more emphasis on the history and appreciation of art. The students avidly studied the riches of the Uffizi Gallery, the Pitti Palace, and the numerous churches in Florence. Models were hired to pose daily in the studio, and the students were encouraged to work outdoors as well, sketching figures and landscapes. Chase devoted "two consecutive days weekly to instruction of the class," and Pach and Louis G. Monté presented the lectures on the "History of Art, Architecture, Sculpture, and Painting."[6] This trip marked the beginning of Pach's formal career as a teacher, a role through which he inspired future generations toward a love of art.

Although Pach formed close friendships with several of the students on the program—including Klauber, Clifton Wheeler, Edith Bell, and Joe Harvey—the most lasting and significant relationship he developed at this time was with Magdalene Frohberg (fig. 7), a native of Dresden, who would become his wife. The Frohbergs were originally from France but had immigrated to Germany. The family was highly educated, and Frohberg's father was the royal surveyor for the king of Saxony. Magda, as Pach called her, had hoped to pursue a medical career, but she was not accepted into school. A strong and independent woman, she was determined to earn her own livelihood and sent out more than one hundred applications for work, eventually finding employment in a bookstore in Florence

that was run by a German woman. When Pach visited the shop, he became quite taken by Frohberg, and the opportunity to spend more time with this charming young woman may have been one of his motives for lingering in Italy through the autumn of 1907.[7]

Pach's main reasons for remaining abroad were to continue his art studies and to develop more fully his painting technique. He roomed at the Pensione Innocenti while in Florence, and most of his days were spent studying the art in museums and churches and making copies of various paintings. Yet he also had the unique opportunity to meet with the collector Charles Loeser, heir to Loeser's Department Store in Brooklyn, who had settled in Florence after graduating from Harvard in 1886. Loeser was among the first American collectors of Paul Cézanne's work. He began acquiring paintings by Cézanne as early as 1896, so that by the time Pach was in Florence in 1907, Loeser had accumulated quite a collection.[8] Exactly when and how Pach met Loeser is unclear, but the two shared both a love of art and a passion for fine music, and they remained friends for decades. Many an evening was spent at Loeser's home, La Gattaia, on the Viale Michelangelo, examining his fabulous collection, particularly the Cézannes. These visits afforded Pach the opportunity to come to a better understanding of the artist's connection with older masters and to recognize more fully his highly original achievement. Pach also met Loeser and other colleagues at the city's various cafés, including the Café Reininghaus on the Piazza Vittorio Emanuele II.

During this summer, Pach was also a guest of the Stein families at their villas in Fiesole, just outside Florence.[9] Gertrude and Leo Stein had settled in Paris in 1903 and by 1907 had amassed quite a collection of avant-garde Parisian art. They hosted a famed informal salon for artists, writers, and musicians at their apartment at 27 rue de Fleurus. Their brother, Michael, and his wife, Sarah (Sally), were also collectors and had also moved to Paris around 1903. It is unclear precisely

Fig. 7
Gotthelf Pach, photograph of
Magdalene Frohberg Pach.
Private collection.

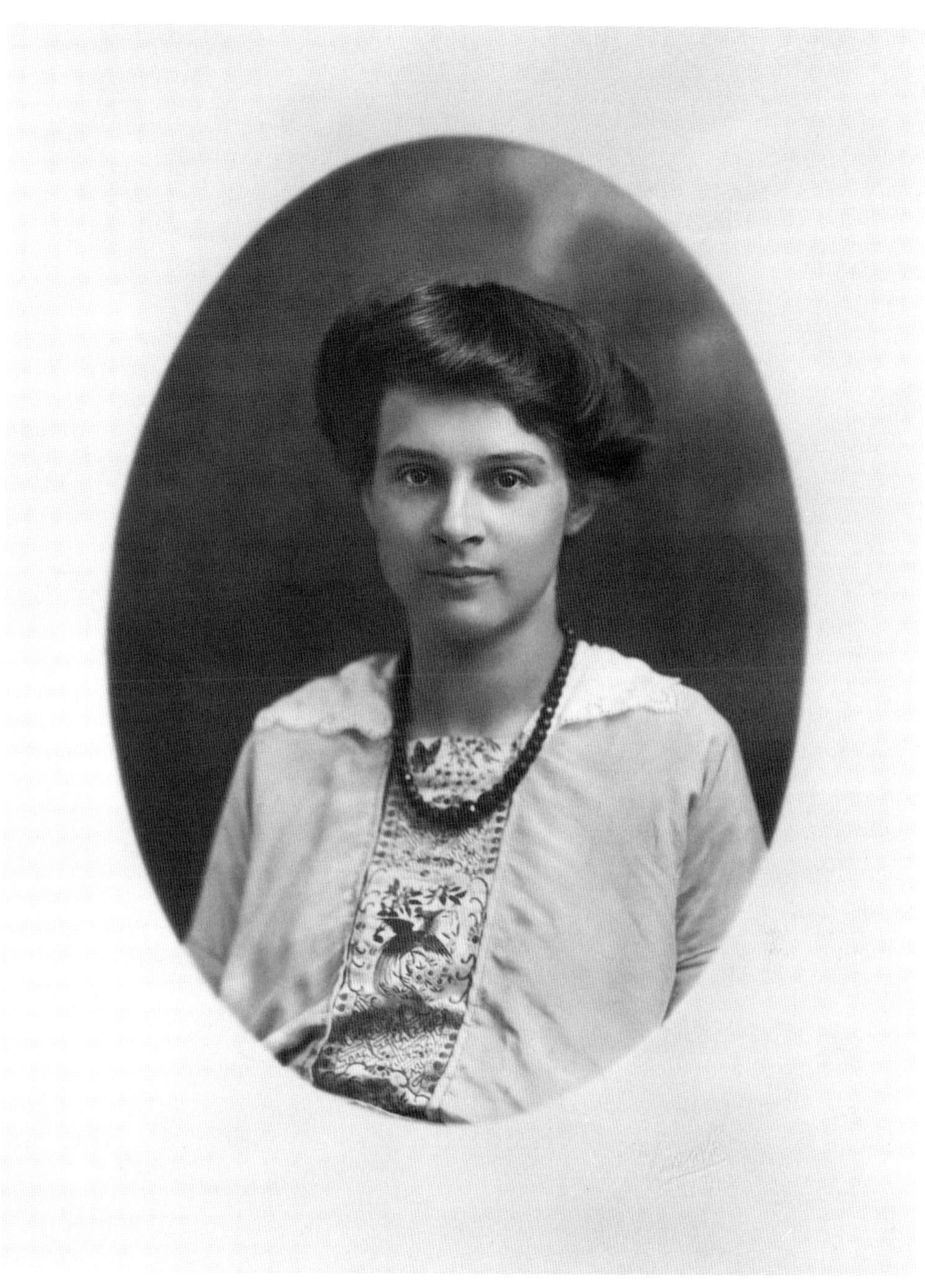

where, when, and how Pach initially met the Steins. In a 1956 interview with Aline Saarinen for her book *The Proud Possessors,* Pach recalled that at his first meeting with Gertrude Stein she showed him Pablo Picasso's *Portrait of Gertrude Stein.*[10] The earliest this could have taken place was late in the previous summer, 1906, since the painting was not completed until then.[11] Pach was in Paris in August 1906; however, he never mentioned meeting the Steins to Robert Henri, with whom he was corresponding, or to anyone else, which would have been a natural thing for him to do. Unfortunately, there is no written record of Pach's response to this work, nor is there any further indication of where and when he first met Gertrude Stein.

The Steins were very gracious hosts and introduced Pach to several of their friends and colleagues. It was at Michael and Sarah Stein's Villa Bardi in Fiesole that Pach first met Henri Matisse, and while he did not know much of the artist's work at the time, he found the man most amicable, and the two would share a lifelong friendship.[12] That same summer, Leo Stein invited Pach to visit the noted Italian Renaissance scholar Bernard Berenson, but unfortunately, Berenson was not at home, and it would be some years before the two would meet.

In the fall of 1907, Pach settled down for his "first winter in Paris," a momentous development in the young man's life.[13] Soon after his arrival, he reported to his new confidante Alice Klauber, "My studio is very satisfactory—perfectly furnished, comfortable and adequate to my needs in painting still-life and compositions—portraits too if I get a chance, but for models I still go to a school."[14] Between October 1907 and July 1908, Pach lived in an apartment at 9 rue Campagne première, a small street located a few blocks south of the intersection of boulevards Montparnasse and Raspail. The area was a thriving art community in the early years of the twentieth century. Sculptor Elie Nadelman had quarters nearby, as did American artists Jo Davidson, Maurice Sterne, and Pach's friend Patrick

Henry Bruce. Another artist friend with whom Pach became reacquainted at this time was the Japanese painter Moriye Ogihara.[15] Pach and Ogihara spent many hours together discussing art, and Pach acted as an interpreter for the Japanese artist when the two visited the studios of the sculptors Rodin and Emile Bourdelle.

In Paris, as in Florence, the Steins were among those who helped introduce Pach to modern European art and artists. Leo and Gertrude Stein, on rue de Fleurus, and Michael and Sarah Stein at 58 rue Madame, all lived very near Pach's apartment. By November 1907, Pach had become a regular guest at the famous Saturday night salons held at each of the families' dwellings.[16] At the Steins' apartments he studied intently works by Matisse, Picasso, Paul Gauguin, Cézanne, Henri de Toulouse-Lautrec, Maurice Denis, and Pierre Bonnard, among others, and had the chance to meet some of these artists. The first time he spoke with Picasso, probably in French (or perhaps in Spanish, since he spoke both languages), was at Leo and Gertrude's apartment. Pach recalled, "We were looking at a big Matisse on the wall. 'Does that interest you?' asked Picasso. 'In a way, yes' (this was one of the first occasions when I saw such work), 'it interests me like a blow between the eyes. I don't understand what he is thinking.'"[17] The Matisse painting was, according to noted Matisse scholar Jack Flam, probably *Bonheur de vivre* (not *Blue Nude,* as some have conjectured).[18] This and other works by Matisse that Pach saw at the Stein apartments clearly confounded him, and it would take him months to come to terms with the new approach to painting they embodied.

Pach was so taken by his "stirring days" at the Steins' that he wrote about them to Guy Pène du Bois, a friend and former schoolmate from Robert Henri's class and the art critic for the *New York American,* who responded with "an urgent request for an article on Matisse." Pach set out for the quai Saint-Michel and Matisse's studio to "renew the acquaintance formed during the preceding summer in Italy."[19] He spent hours with the artist, who explained the evolution of his art from the paintings done in a naturalistic style through those made under the inspiration of van Gogh. Where Matisse lost him, Pach confessed, was in his most recent works. "It was one thing for me to feel the passion of Giotto (or some of it) before the frescoes in Florence," Pach said in *Queer Thing, Painting;* "it was an entirely different thing to recognize the emotion in this unfamiliar conception of the picture."[20]

As Matisse scholar John Cauman observed, "Despite his esteem for the painter, Pach found it difficult to write about work that he only partially understood."[21] Nevertheless, he wrote the essay and sent it to Pène du Bois with high hopes for publication. Pach wrote Klauber in January 1908, "Did you see my Matisse article in the Hearst paper? It should be out now, or soon."[22] He must have also written Ogihara, who replied, "How about the article on Matisse?"[23] In February 1908, Pach complained to Klauber, "Do you know, I've not seen hide nor hair of that Matisse article yet—nor the check for it which is even more annoying. Every mail is a likely one for it now. As you can imagine, the Steins' eagerness for it is only second to my own."[24] Unfortunately, when Pach sent the article to Pène du Bois, he also sent photographs of Matisse's works, which were deemed too sensational by the editor of the *American*'s Sunday supplement. In March 1908, he told Klauber, "I hear, in a round about way that my Matisse article was not used (though my orders were positive and explicit)."[25] Although this article was never published, it was a milestone for Pach, marking the beginning of his career as a writer on modern art.

Pach's initial response to Matisse's art reveals a certain naïveté about avant-garde French art, but even though he failed to grasp immediately the ideas behind these vanguard paintings, he sensed that Matisse's works were vitally important, and he was determined to unlock their secrets. "Month after month of my first entire year there, I kept up a bitter struggle with the

problem,"[26] Pach wrote later in *Queer Thing, Painting,* and he reported to Klauber in November 1907, "I've been to Mr. Leo Stein's and the Matisses haven't gained any. I've about given it up."[27] He persevered, though his progress was slow. Later in life he admitted, "It was only when I settled in Paris for my first long stay that I had the opportunity for repeated seeing of the things and for a relating of them to arts that could explain them, where before I was holding to the masters of chiaroscuro—a technical element of no use to Matisse in his investigation of pure color. It was a help, though I was obstinately slow about accepting help, when Sarah Stein made a comparison between the color in Matisse's work and that in the enamels of the Byzantines."[28]

Not confident in his response to Matisse's art, Pach discussed his work with Monet, a painter he admired, during "a splendid two hours" he had with him in Giverny in November 1907.[29] Pach asked Monet if he saw the qualities in Matisse that others had perceived. "There was not an instant's hesitation in his reply of 'Nullement,'" Pach told Klauber.[30] Monet's reaction helped alleviate Pach's sense of inadequacy in understanding Matisse's pictures, and he wrote Klauber that after his meeting with the famous painter he "felt easier—even about the big still-life in rue Madame."[31] Pach was probably referring to one of the many Matisses that lined the walls of Sarah and Michael Stein's apartment, perhaps *Blue Still Life.*

Determined to understand Matisse's art, he visited the artist at his studio on Monday afternoons to study his technique and listen to his philosophy of art; however, Pach was never a pupil at his more formal school, organized by Sarah Stein and others in 1908. Pach did not approve of these students' adoration of Matisse, or their blatant imitation of his style. He told Klauber, "Since Matisse has been teaching, the bunch is worse than ever, they now all claim that they don't know anything."[32] Later in life, Pach had some second thoughts about not joining the school and wondered "what it would have meant to my work had I had the sense to profit by his atelier, during that short time that he accepted pupils." Yet the other students, Pach observed, "were the cause, very largely, that I did not go to his school. . . . They were (with exceptions) a bad lot, the wild-eyed type—largely non-Frenchmen—who apparently looked on Matisse as crazy, and who wanted to be the same way."[33]

After three months of studying Matisse's paintings and struggling to comprehend their lessons fully, Pach reported, "I should never have to reproach myself with having given the Matisse pictures an insufficient trial. I've gone to see them, thought over them and the arguments intended to uphold them, studied the masters they're supposed to descend from. . . . But my progress has been small. The drawings remain fine—I see a certain color and a certain possibility in some of the still-lifes (principally) that I didn't at first but otherwise I've not changed much."[34] Finally, in the spring of 1908, he could state with some confidence, "I do feel lots more at rest about Matisse—admitting some points, denying others, thinking him a man of great possibilities (did I tell you I saw an early landscape of his that was splendid in color?) and not by any means incapable of big mistakes."[35] These days with Matisse and the Stein families helped Pach forge lasting and deep friendships that were vital for his crucial role in bringing modern European art to American audiences in the near future.

Pach's response to Picasso's early work was much more favorable than his reaction to Matisse's paintings. Much to William Merritt Chase's chagrin, Pach admired a Blue Period drawing by Picasso that the two saw together in the window of Clovis Sagot's shop on rue Laffitte; Pach also admired the paintings by Picasso from his Blue and Rose periods that he saw on the walls of the Steins' apartments. In these works, Pach saw a continuation of the great tradition of painting as practiced by El Greco, Goya, Degas, Puvis de Chavannes, and Toulouse-Lautrec. In *Queer Thing, Painting*, Pach wrote that he understood Picasso's paintings as

representing "earlier conceptions of picture-making," and he connected Picasso's art with works by past masters.[36] Pach believed that all great art was grounded in the traditions of the Old Masters and that art was an evolutionary process in which each succeeding generation built on the truths of the past to create its own vision. This evolutionary theory of art was quite common at the time and formed the basis of Pach's own aesthetic credo.

Picasso's most recent paintings, however, posed greater challenges for Pach, who simply could not see how these newest works fit into this evolutionary concept of art. The paintings that Picasso made "under the influence of Negro sculpture," as Pach would observe in *Queer Thing, Painting* in 1938, were "complications of the Spaniard's later evolution."[37] Pach struggled with these paintings as he had with Matisse's art and wrote Klauber early in February 1908, "Picasso's latest are still incomprehensible, but I expect to make the connection between them and his earlier wonderful things."[38] Perhaps he was remembering the lesson he learned as a teenager, when confronted with the Count of Monte Cristo's love of Old Master paintings that he himself had dismissed. Pach was determined to understand this new aesthetic and was confident that, eventually, he would do so.

During this nine-month stay, Pach became a true insider in the Parisian art world. While he spent many days at the Louvre or the Luxembourg, he also frequented art galleries such as Galerie Kahnweiler, Galerie Druet, Galerie Bernheim Jeune et Cie, Vollard, and Durand-Ruel et Cie. These dealers had been known for carrying works by Corot, Eugène Delacroix, Gauguin, and Cézanne, yet in the early 1900s, they also began to display paintings and sculptures by some of the Fauves—Maurice de Vlaminck, Charles Camoin, Pierre Girieud, Kees van Dongen, and André Derain— and other contemporary artists, including Fernand Léger, Picasso, and Georges Braque. Pach frequented these galleries and studied intently the works on view.

He also visited the major Cézanne retrospective at the Salon d'Automne in October 1907. In addition, in 1908, he saw the "two big exhibitions of van Gogh": a display of one hundred of the artist's paintings held at Bernheim Jeune and one of thirty-five works, lent mainly from private collections in Paris, at Druet's.[39] Pach had been an admirer of van Gogh's work since that day in Haarlem in the fall of 1906 when he spied several pieces in a store window. Pach developed close friendships with many of the dealers whose galleries he visited, and he familiarized himself thoroughly with the art they exhibited, thus becoming conversant with the latest developments in modern European art.

While in Paris, Pach became especially close to the dealer Joseph Brummer. When he looked back on his first long stay in Paris, Pach recalled, "Perhaps the most important effect of that season was my friendship with Joseph Brummer, the greatest connoisseur of ancient art in the world today and a profound appreciator of modern art. I owe him a great deal of debt for the understanding of the classics gained in visits with him to the Louvre . . . and his own outstanding collections."[40] Brummer was Pach's guide in Paris and his mentor, and the two would remain lifelong friends. Through him Pach learned a deeper appreciation for ancient art. More important for his future careers as critic and agent, he gained a greater understanding of the inner workings and intricacies of the Parisian art market.

Pach's main priorities while overseas were to study art and improve his painting technique. Of course, while there were "miles of pictures to see in Paris, the Louvre always challenging you to answer its riddles and enticing you with its delights, the current shows that you hate to miss," there were also "visitors, old friends—and possible customers and Diversion presenting herself in every possible form. (Of course I don't mean amusement, but turning aside from work)."[41] Among the visitors to his studio was Chase, who stopped briefly in Paris en route to and from

Florence and on the latter occasion invited his favorite student to join him for a drink at the famous Café du Paix.

Pach knew that his dream of remaining abroad was contingent on his earning a living. Soon after his arrival in Paris, he set about trying to find literary work. He reported to Klauber, "My staying here will depend on circumstances. My brother writes that I can most likely have a position in my old college [CCNY] if I want it—in February. But it would be lots better for my work to stay here and if I can put some articles through and nothing turns up at home, I may do so."[42] In February 1908, he submitted a manuscript based on his November visit with Monet to *Scribner's Magazine* "(on a venture) and asked at the same time for the commission to write a Cézanne article."[43] His short essay on Monet was published in the June 1908 issue of the journal, and his request to write an article on Cézanne was granted.

Pach's essay on Cézanne, which appeared in December 1908, was the first substantial piece on the artist to be published in the United States, and as such it laid the groundwork for America's understanding and acceptance of Cézanne's art. By 1908, Pach was quite familiar with Cézanne's art and the criticism concerning it written by artists, art historians, and critics, including Emile Bernard, Julius Meier-Graefe, and Roger Fry. He found Meier-Graefe's concept of the evolution of art particularly fascinating and incorporated some of his ideas into the essay. Pach judged Cézanne's "passion for form as a pure abstract quality" and his concern with "what is within—the structural, the significant" as the defining marks of his art.[44] He believed that Cézanne's preoccupation with form and structure was not unique, but was more pronounced in his works than in earlier paintings by other artists, thus separating him from his predecessors. While he believed that Cézanne's work differed from what had gone before, he also thought that the artist had followed the traditions of the "classic" school of art and felt that the greatness of

Cézanne's contribution to art lay in his ability to bridge past and future generations. Pach's assessment of Cézanne's contribution to the history of art and his admiration of the artist's greatness were not revolutionary, but this was the first time the artist and his art had received such attention in the American media.[45] More important, the essay established Pach's reputation as a critic of modern art.

Sandra Phillips wrote the first scholarly article devoted to Walter Pach, and more particularly his art criticism, in 1983, five years before his papers were available to the public. In her essay, Phillips aptly recognizes that Pach played "a major role in American cultural history in the early twentieth century," and she also credits him "more than any other single person . . . with recognizing the importance of modern French art and bringing it to the attention of his countrymen."[46] As for Pach's criticism, Phillips argues that his views were very much a reflection of those of his contemporaries such as Roger Fry, Bernard Berenson, Élie Faure, and Meier-Graefe. From these critics, and others, Phillips observes, Pach adopted the concept of the evolutionary aspect of art and made it the main focus of his criticisms.

Pach's first long stay abroad may have been profitable artistically and personally, but he faced financial obstacles and had to admit, "I imagine that I shall have to go back and look up work in the fall: my jobs have been too much of the 'odd' and unreliable variety the last few months."[47] Among other efforts to fund his European sojourn, in February 1908 he sublet his "little studio" in Paris and traveled to Belgium and the Netherlands to find work. In Brussels, he made copies of paintings for colleagues, including Klauber, and tried to find portrait commissions. He also seems to have had one of those "odd" jobs there, but the details of this employment are unknown. Before he returned to France, he stopped in the Netherlands to see if he could "pick up any more jobs at portrait painting," but was unsuccessful.[48] His parents also felt another season abroad might not be feasible. When they visited Paris

in July 1908, Gotthelf offered to take his son into the family business, and Pach apparently could not refuse. He confided to Klauber, "Here is the big burden of my news: I am going home."[49] Pach did not return to the United States immediately, however, but spent part of August and September 1908 in Italy. He returned to the Pensione Innocenti in Florence, where he was warmly welcomed, visited the Stein family at their Villa Bardi, and renewed his acquaintance with Magdalene Frohberg.

After having experienced the exciting atmosphere of the contemporary Parisian art world, Pach found it extremely difficult to adjust to life back in New York City. He told Klauber, "I should have to . . . say something of my feelings on being back in New York. I fear they are not very good feelings. I don't believe I like much here except a few people. The family is fine, and the old friends, the painter bunch—is the same—only too much so, for the year abroad has made me different and while personally they are as fine as ever . . . we look at things so differently now."[50] Pach's view of art and his acceptance of the advanced work of painters such as Matisse and Picasso were at odds with the ideals espoused by his former classmates and mentors. He had grown and changed dramatically in his year abroad both artistically and emotionally and was having a hard time relating to those whose art and ideas on art had remained the same.

Pach lived with his parents and worked for Pach Brothers Studio, but he knew that his days at his father's business were numbered. He wrote to Klauber, "I have not got the business-thoughts and the art-thoughts to hold their places—so to speak, to keep out of one another's way and confusion is sometimes the result."[51] Throughout the fall of 1908 and the early months of 1909, Pach worked hard at developing his careers as a critic, translator, and lecturer. He was working on an article on American artists for the *Gazette des Beaux-Arts* and he was commissioned to write an essay on Cézanne with the cooperation of his friend the American collector Charles Loeser, but it was never published. In addition to these assignments, Pach had "a pretty good dose of translating scientific German" and French articles for various companies and did some translations (mainly French and perhaps German) for friends, including Arthur B. Davies, whom he probably met through John Sloan.[52] He also reignited his public-speaking work with a lecture on art in Springfield, Massachusetts, sometime in January or February 1909.

Arguably the most significant career move for Pach during this period was the launch of his work as an intermediary, or agent. His first endeavor in this arena was on behalf of Bryson Burroughs, curator at the Metropolitan Museum of Art. He had probably been introduced to Burroughs through Pach Brothers Studio, still the main photographers for the museum. As the story is recounted in a 1941 article and in John Rewald's book *Cézanne and America: Dealers, Collectors, Artists, and Critics,* the Metropolitan had been offered the magnificent Cézanne *Self-Portrait* now in the Phillips Collection in Washington, D.C. Burroughs told Pach that the trustees would never approve such a purchase because the work was too modern, but if Pach could "persuade someone to buy it and present it to the museum, the picture would be accepted." Remarkably, at such an early date Pach had the connections and influence to make such a transaction possible. He "made tracks down to the office of Benjamin Altman, art collector and department store owner," and convinced him to advance the sum to buy the work.[53] Much to Pach's dismay, however, Burroughs did not welcome the news after all: he feared that the furor the acquisition would cause among the trustees and in the press would make Altman so angry that he would ultimately refuse to give his collection to the museum. This was an eye-opening experience for Pach, awakening him to the intricacies and politics of the art and museum world of New York.

Not all of Pach's time was spent on work and art, and he found many entertainments away from the job and the easel. He indulged in one of his favorite pastimes by attending performances of *Othello* and *Don Pasquale* at the Metropolitan Opera House. Also, after a three-year hiatus, he took up the violin again; much to his surprise and delight, he was still able to carry a tune. On his commute to and from work he read nineteenth-century romantic novels, the perfect escape from the noisy crowds on the streetcars. He also continued his studies in the art and literature of Japan and China and read several texts that were specifically related to painting. One of them was Ogden Rood's *Modern Chromatics,* which he found to be "a very important book" and which undoubtedly was useful in his own painting endeavors.

In the summer of 1909, Pach was offered a full-time, permanent position with Pach Brothers Studio, but when he was informed that he was expected to work six days a week for fifty weeks of the year, he opted to take his chances as an artist, critic, and agent and left his father's business. He wrote Klauber, "It simply transpired that I could not possibly keep on with the photography if I had any notion of being a painter."[54] Soon thereafter, Pach became increasingly more engaged in working as an agent and dealer, both for himself and for other artists. He arranged with Klauber, who lived in San Diego and had, it seemed, opened an art gallery or shop, to send works to her for shows in California and wrote to her in November 1909,

> I think besides the sketches I can find some Goya etchings and some photos or something. Also if you want more sketches I know lots of men (or several anyhow) who would doubtless be willing to send. You must also use your discretion somewhat as to prices: for the two things I have picked out and also for the two I got from my good friend Joe Garvey the minimum is $15. each. I always put $35. for this size on the card when I have them in the exhibitions here and it is a fair price though not an exorbitant one. If you can sell them for enough to give us more

than the $15—so much the better. I think I will include my Tintoretto copy of an "Unknown Man"—price $75. I asked $125 when it was exhibited at Smith College Museum, which bought one of my things. Perhaps by sending time I shall have something else and shall put an inventory and price-list in the box.

I am enthusiastic over the shop. It will give you employment that I should think would prove fascinating, and such places—not just commercial and (what is more dangerous and even more to be avoided) not "arty"—are exactly what this country needs. . . . When you get things going I feel pretty sure I could get a number of the big men to send you things. Meanwhile please write me without hesitating about anything you want, even if you're not sure I can get it. How about the frame-lady in Venice? I have just made arrangements to sell her things through a dealer here.[55]

These ventures in selling art and in organizing exhibitions took up more and more of Pach's time and energy and would prove increasingly to be among his most important and lasting contributions to the history of modern European and American art.

During this period, Pach also continued in his literary endeavors, some of which he had begun during his stay in Paris the previous year. He had been engaged by Roger Marx, editor of *Gazette des Beaux-Arts,* for an essay on American painters and corresponded with Winslow Homer, J. Alden Weir, William Merritt Chase, and other living American artists to request reproductions of their works for the article. The resultant piece, "Quelques notes sur les peintres américains," was a brief survey of American painting from John Singleton Copley to Robert Henri.[56] It was among the earliest articles published in France on American art, particularly contemporary artists, and it served to introduce many of these painters to French audiences. This was the first such occasion in which Pach served as an ambassador for American artists in France, but it would not be the last. In conjunction with his article, Pach stopped by Sloan's studio in 1909 and requested from his friend "some photos and three etchings." In March 1909, Pach again called on Sloan, who "delivered the copper plate 'Fifth Avenue Critics' to be forwarded to the Gazette des Beaux-Arts in Paris."[57] Unfortunately, the plate was held for duty at the Customs House in New York when it was returned from Paris and, according to Sloan, Pach "made affidavits" for its release.[58] Under the current customs laws, objects such as etching plates were considered utilitarian objects, not art, and could therefore be subject to tariffs. Pach would be called upon on numerous occasions to testify on behalf of artists and their art in this ongoing battle over taxes on contemporary art.

Late in the summer of 1909, Pach received commissions for other articles, one of which, "Manet and Modern American Art," appeared in the *Craftsman* in 1910. In this piece, Pach traced the origin of the pronouncement that "art to be really significant must be born of its own time, an expression of its immediate environment" to Manet.[59] He used this view to uphold his support of the work of his American contemporaries—including Glackens, Sloan, Henri, George Luks, Maurice Prendergast, and Davies—who, like Manet, painted the contemporary life and peoples of their own country. Pach agreed with Manet's argument that since each society was different, it produced an art unique unto itself. This belief in the existence of national schools and the idea of race as a determining factor in cultural expression were not Pach's innovation but were part of the mainstream artistic and social criticism of the time. These concepts had been popularized by writers such as Hippolyte Taine, whose work Pach knew. Other ideas professed by Pach in this essay that were part of the aesthetics of his day included the belief that a genius was born, not made, and the concept that art, music, literature, science, and politics were interrelated. Pach perceived life, and thus art, as a continuum and saw a parallel between Manet's era and his own. While his views were not very original or unusual, Pach's writings appeared in popular periodicals, thus bringing contemporary aesthetic theories to a wide audience throughout America.

In January 1910, Pach, Jerome Myers, Everett Shinn, Henri, and Luks met at Sloan's studio to have a "'pow-wow' over an exhibition or society or something" that would offer American artists venues other than the National Academy of Design for showing their work.[60] Thus was born the idea of an Independent Exhibition. Henri, Sloan, and Walt Kuhn became the prime movers behind the show and were responsible for raising funds and securing the exhibition space. Others who backed the cause were Rockwell Kent, Guy Pène du Bois, Glackens, and Davies. Pach suggested that William Merritt Chase, J. Alden Weir, and Childe Hassam be invited to participate in the exhibition, but Sloan "opposed this violently," as he felt they represented the type of art against which the independents were organizing.[61] In March 1910, Pach stopped by Sloan's studio and informed him that "Stieglitz of Photo Secession is hot under the collar about our show"; clearly, by then Pach had made the acquaintance of Alfred Stieglitz and had probably visited his gallery, 291.[62] On April 1, 1910, the first (and only) Exhibition of Independent Artists opened, with three paintings and three drawings by Pach in the show. It became a huge media and cultural event, and though sales were not great, the artists deemed the exhibition quite a success.

Although Pach was no longer a pupil of Chase's, he remained in contact with his former mentor, and when Chase resumed his summer course in 1910, he asked Pach to serve once more as agent for the trip.[63] Pach arranged for the students to visit several Italian cities, including Naples, Capri, Rome, and Siena, before they settled down in Florence for two months of instruction from Chase, with lectures on art history again provided by Pach and Louis G. Monté. Besides the usual course of copying paintings, working in the studio, and

sketching outdoors, the class was invited to Chase's home, Villa Silli. Located near Fiesole, the house was surrounded by greenery and provided a refreshing escape from the hot, busy city. This was the last season that Pach worked with Chase. Mentor and pupil would soon drift far apart as Pach became more and more absorbed with and involved in the contemporary art scene in Paris, a world that Chase simply could not understand and was unwilling to accept.

Pach could not resist the lure of Paris, and his previous stays had only whetted his appetite for a lengthier visit. After the Chase summer class in Italy ended, he departed Florence for the city of his dreams. From September 1910 until June 1912, Pach lived in an apartment at 3 rue des Beaux-Arts, near the École des Beaux-Arts. He described his home away from home to his friend Sloan: "I am in a first-rate studio— near the river, Louvre and Notre Dame: just what I wanted."[64] Although the space may have seemed ideal or even romantic to Pach, his "airy attic" studio could be reached only by climbing a daunting five flights of stairs.[65]

One of Pach's main reasons for this lengthy sojourn abroad, as in 1907–8, was to improve his painting skills. Although he no longer considered himself a student, he attended the Académie Ranson in Paris and took classes with Paul Sérusier and Maurice Denis. He explained that Sérusier had been "particularly recommended to me by Henri Matisse."[66] This school was founded in December 1908 by Paul Ranson, a member of the circle of artists known as the Nabis. When Ranson died in February 1909, Sérusier, Denis, and other members of the Nabis began teaching at the academy. Sérusier taught the theory of colors, and Denis instructed the students in composition and painting. Although Pach undoubtedly learned new techniques of painting through these teachers, it was their theoretical and spiritual inclinations that more deeply attracted and affected him, particularly their belief in the connection between art, life, and spirituality. While Pach found some of their teachings to be completely compatible with his beliefs, Denis' proclamation, "It is well to remember that a picture—before being a battle horse, a nude woman, or some anecdote—is essentially a plane surface covered with colors assembled in a certain order," was a concept that Pach had been struggling to accept since his first encounter with Matisse's art in 1907.[67] The concept that painting was an art not merely of imitation but also of creation was one that Pach gradually came to accept during his years in Paris at the beginning of the twentieth century.

When Pach settled in Paris in the fall of 1910, he decided that he needed to improve his French—both speaking and writing—and enrolled in a course at the Lycée Charlemagne, a public institution affiliated with the Association Philotechnique. The school was part of the free public education system in Paris and was associated with the socialist movement in France. At this tuition-free night school, located in "an abandoned convent in a very poor part of the city," Pach took classes in literature, composition, and oration. His fellow pupils were middle-class working men and women who "wanted to round out the more or less defective schooling of their earlier years."[68] By attending these classes, Pach not only became more fluent in French but also met many like-minded individuals and expanded his knowledge and understanding of French literature and current politics.

Soon after his arrival in Paris, Pach renewed his friendships with the Stein families and once again became a regular guest at the Saturday evening gatherings. Gertrude Stein wrote one of her famous "portraits" of Pach in these years, and Pach became quite friendly with her partner, Alice B. Toklas.[69] Pach and Toklas shared a love of music and attended several recitals and concerts together. Toklas also edited some of Pach's essays.[70]

Pach also remained in close contact with fellow American artists at home and abroad, acting as a liaison and guide for them, as well as for American tourist friends, when they visited Paris. He brought several American artists to the Stein apartment on rue de Fleurus during this time. In February 1911, for example, he wrote Toklas, "My friend [Joseph] Stella has been unexpectedly delayed in Italy over a stupid question of a passport which he needs to go abroad. So he will not be here in time for next Saturday night."[71] When Stella did finally arrive in Paris, he spent much of his time with Pach. Pach also corresponded regularly with his friends back home, among them Charles Sheeler and Morton Schamberg, and apprised them of his activities. Ever the gracious host, he also took visiting American friends to dances at the Moulin de la Galette, dinners at the Restaurant du Concon, and concerts and plays.

Pach could not ignore the famed Parisian nightlife and took advantage of the multitude of attractions the city offered. His taste in the performing arts was—like his interests in the visual arts—quite eclectic. He attended performances of French plays such as *La vie de bohème* and saw a matinee appearance of the celebrated French actress Sarah Bernhardt in Alexandre Dumas' *La dame aux camélias*. He also enjoyed concerts by the most famous musical virtuosos of his day, such as world-renowned violinists Fritz Kreisler and Eugene Ysaye, and Harold Bauer, regarded as one of the greatest living pianists. In addition, he had the great good fortune to see the famed modern dancer Isadora Duncan perform. Pach remained interested in traditional music, theater, and dance but was also fascinated by contemporary artistic expression in various media.

Like many other young men, Pach frequented the smoky cafés and cabarets of Paris such as Au Lapin Agile. In *Queer Thing, Painting,* he gave a vivid description of this place—and could not resist throwing in a comment about the escalating prices of modern art:

There was a cabaret, in those pre-war days, that kept up the old tradition of such places. For the cabaret as a species of theater with hired entertainers is a comparatively recent development [Pach was writing this in 1938]. Formerly it was a place where poets and musicians forgathered to exchange ideas and get an audience—picking up what material advantage they could, often just food and drinks—with always the hope of reaching patronage which would pay. That was the character of old Frédéric's place, and it was astonishing that it kept up amid the commercialism of twentieth-century Paris. The walls were crowded with paintings and drawings by the artists who came there; among them was a fine Picasso of his early Bohemian days, and when Frédéric finally sold it to a German picture-dealer, the price he got was a thousand times what it had cost him in hospitality to the painter, some ten years before.[72]

Pach was leading what he perceived to be the life of the typical Parisian painter, and he became a denizen of the usual haunts of the artists of his day.

It was during these years in Paris that Pach developed close friendships with most of the leading lights of the Parisian art world, relationships that would prove vital for the history of modern art in the United States. Among those he came to know quite well were Picasso, Matisse, Braque, Gino Severini, Constantin Brancusi, Derain, Odilon Redon, Roger de la Fresnaye, and Raoul Dufy. He also became friendly with Italian artist Umberto Brunelleschi and met the Portuguese modernist Amadeo de Souza-Cardoso at Brunelleschi's home.[73] Among the closest bonds Pach formed were those with the Duchamp brothers—Jacques Villon, Raymond Duchamp-Villon, and Marcel Duchamp. Through the Duchamp brothers, Pach became a member of the Puteaux Group and appears to have been the only American artist and critic to be directly associated with them.[74]

Beginning in 1910, this circle of cubist painters and sculptors gathered on Sundays at Jacques Villon and Raymond Duchamp-Villon's studio in the Parisian suburb of Puteaux and met on Mondays at Albert Gleizes's home in nearby Courbevoie. These artists were joined by poets and writers such as Alexandre Mercereau, Guillaume Apollinaire, Roger Allard, and André Salmon. Through these gatherings Pach developed close relationships with Francis Picabia, Jean Metzinger, Léger, Apollinaire, Robert Delaunay, Marie Laurencin, André Mare, and Mercereau, and the camaraderie among them proved vital for his understanding of contemporary artistic and literary theories.

Most of the artists associated with the Puteaux Group worked in a style of cubism related to that practiced by Picasso and Braque; however, they were more theoretical and didactic in their approach to their art than either of these pioneering painters. As art historian R. Stanley Johnson has noted, "There were several different concepts of Cubism which co-existed during the Cubist epoch."[75] The discussions at the homes of Gleizes and the Duchamp brothers revolved around discovering analogies between art, mathematics, literature, music, and science. From the analytical explorations of this group came Metzinger and Gleizes's 1912 tract *Du "Cubisme,"* which, art historian Robert Rosenblum noted, "articulated fully for the first time a philosophical basis for Cubism. . . . Their rationalizations about the nature of Cubism as an art that reflects such modern concepts as relativity, simultaneity, and four-dimensionality soon became, in fact, commonplaces in many pseudo-scientific explanations of Cubism."[76] Art historian Allan Antliff has observed, "Indeed, in their exposition of the cubist aesthetic published in *Du Cubisme* (1912), Gleizes and Metzinger argued that the dynamic temporal transitions of cubist *passage* combined with accumulated imagery from the artist's memory to evoke a unanimist intuition of the artist's thoughts in the mind of the viewer."[77] "Unanimism," Antliff noted, was French poet Jules Romain's term for a "theory of collective consciousness."[78] Among the main proponents of this movement were Pach's close friends: the Duchamp brothers, Gleizes, Metzinger, Picabia, and Mercereau. *Du "Cubisme"* was published at virtually the same time as the Section d'Or exhibition. This show, which many have regarded as a culmination of the cubist movement, and which Pach visited on more than one occasion, was held at the Galerie de la Boétie in October 1912. Nearly two hundred works by more than thirty artists, including most of the Puteaux Group, but not Picasso and Braque, were on display. The title was given to the show by Jacques Villon and, as noted scholar John Golding observed, "seems to indicate some dissatisfaction with the term Cubism as applied to their work, and was probably intended to imply that the paintings shown had a more profound and rational basis."[79]

Stimulated by the intellectual atmosphere of these gatherings, Pach incorporated some of these ideas into his own aesthetic credo. The belief in the connection between art and music had been a part of his philosophy for years, but through these artists he came to embrace the concept of a relationship between painting, sculpture, science, and the modern world. His perception of the works produced by these painters and sculptors was substantially influenced by the ideology they espoused. For example, in 1938 he explained, "When Duchamp painted for us his drama of the forces of stability and instability (which is my interpretation of the canvas entitled *The King and Queen Surrounded by Swift Nudes*), he was dealing with ideas that only our age with its new conceptions of space and reality could imagine."[80] Pach was among the first to recognize and promote Duchamp's genius. He staunchly believed that Duchamp was one of the greatest artistic minds of all time, an opinion that proved to be quite prescient.

Soon after arriving in Paris in 1910, Pach met Élie Faure, a noted physician, philosopher, and art historian, whom he first came to know through Faure's 1910 essay on Cézanne.[81] Pach was so moved by the Frenchman's observations on the painter that he "exclaimed aloud at something on a printed page when no one else was present."[82] A few months later, Pach heard Faure lecture on "architecture, the social art," at the University of the People, and shortly thereafter he went to see him. When Pach arrived at the address given him, he was surprised to find himself "among a group of patients awaiting treatment" at a doctor's office.[83] The physician, it turned out, was Faure. The two men took an instant liking to each other and remained friends until Faure's death in 1937.

Another acquaintance Pach made in Paris was Egisto Fabbri Jr., an expatriate American artist and collector.[84] Born and raised in New York, Fabbri was the nephew of one of the early partners of J. Pierpont Morgan and had studied art under J. Alden Weir. Several years after his father died, he moved to Florence with his mother, brothers, and sisters. Thereafter, he relocated to Paris and settled in a studio in Montmartre. Pach had heard of the gentleman and his collection, particularly his numerous Cézanne paintings, and he wrote to ask permission to see them. As he recalled in 1938, "A courteous reply led me to an old studio building in Montmartre, where, after a climb of six flights . . . I found myself under a skylight, and before an easel on which a good picture was in progress. Though I remonstrated, Mr. Fabbri took it away, saying I had come to see Cézanne's work and not his, upon which he brought out one magnificent thing after another by the old painter of Aix, rounding off the feast by a few other things, including some drawings by Ingres."[85] Once more, Pach was acquainting himself with some of the major collectors of modern art in Paris, connections that would facilitate the introduction and promotion of modern art to the United States in the years to come.

While in Paris during these years—between 1910 and 1913—Pach visited artists in their studios regularly and tried his best to see the endless number of exhibitions at the museums and galleries. He was particularly struck by the pictures by Bonnard and by Matisse's *La musique* and *La danse,* mural-sized paintings that were on view at the Salon d'Automne of 1910. He frequented Vollard's, Druet's, Durand-Ruel's and, most often, the Galerie Bernheim Jeune et Cie. Among the most exciting and stimulating shows he saw were major exhibitions of paintings by Renoir, Bonnard, and Henri Rousseau and the celebrated cubist exhibition, the Salon de la Section d'Or, held at the Galerie de la Boétie. This show was organized by André Mare in collaboration with several artists, including Pach's friends Duchamp-Villon, Laurencin, Villon, and de la Fresnaye. Pach also saw, for the first time, Duchamp's painting *The Chess Players (The Chess Game),* a work that he would later acquire. Although he was most interested in the latest developments in painting, he continued to study older masters such as Ingres. By visiting such diverse exhibitions, Pach was training his eye and studying intently the lessons these artists had to teach. He was trying to equip himself with a thorough knowledge of the history of nineteenth- and early twentieth-century French art, information that would prove especially useful in the months to come.

Pach, who had a keen intellectual curiosity, was deeply interested in philosophical inquires, and in Paris he explored new aesthetic ideologies while also trying to refine his own artistic credo. In the fall of 1911, he enrolled in Un cours de bonheur (reconnu d'utilité publique) (A Course in Happiness [state-approved]) at the Lycée Charlemagne in Paris.[86] The aim of the course was, according to Pach, to discover the true nature of happiness and to make "disappear the social misunderstanding" that he believed would "dissipate when those who do not know will have penetrated to the truth of art." The curriculum focused on poetry, philosophy, art, aesthetics, literature, music, and ethics. Students and teacher met weekly, except for a Christmas break, from October 1911 through March 1912; Pach kept a journal that contains a summary of the topics discussed in those sessions.

Under the guidance of their instructor, Henry Marx, students in the class were taught to seek and discover an acceptable philosophy of life. Pach wrote, "It's a matter of defining the object, the philosophy of our course. What is its relationship with ethics? We will see at first that there is not only one ethic, but also at least three. From the first attempts to explain the universe, man has followed one of three principal routes: that of the priests, that of the scientists, that of the artists." The pupils investigated the psychology and philosophy of religion, science, and art. In the process of these discussions, Pach concluded that the real interpreter of truth was art and that the moral code of the artist was the ideal ethic to follow. Students also debated the definitions of science, beauty, nature, and art. In his journal Pach concluded that art "is an arrangement of the ideas and the sensations that produces in us all the phenomenon of the exterior and interior world." He finally accepted the idea that art is not merely the imitation of external nature but is an exteriorization of the internal sensation that one experiences in response to outside stimuli.

The theory of the evolution of art was another topic of exploration and debate—a theory with which Pach had become familiar through his reading of Meier-Graefe's *Die Entwicklungsgeschichte der modernen Kunst,* Faure's essay on Cézanne, and other writings on aesthetics, and one he embraced as a major tenet of his own theory of art. The students also addressed the connection between art, life, and spirituality, which Pach had encountered first in his early schooling at the Ethical Culture School in New York and more recently in his classes with Sérusier and Denis at the Académie Ranson. Through his studies with Matisse, Sérusier, and Denis, and during his visits with the Duchamp brothers, Picabia, and Gleizes, among others, at Puteaux, Pach came to understand the necessity of the artist's role as a revealer of universal truths.

The students also discussed the theories of the symbol and of individuality. Pach found that the true symbol was reached when, for example, "in a painting of bathers or a still life Cézanne reveals to us the integrity and the harmony of the world such as they were visible to him before his subject." He also expressed his belief that the "personality—not that which colors the work and distinguishes it from others—but that which confesses itself, which incorporates itself absolutely in the work is the great necessity for the highest art." Furthermore, he came to believe that "it is only in remaining true to ourselves that we discover that the line that joins us all is straight: the differences between us are only of the surface—in going deeper into our individualities, we see that what is a symbol for one is a symbol for all." Pach perceived universality among all peoples and firmly believed that art could, and should, be used as a societal force to bring humankind together in unity and harmony.

Through these classes Pach was able to define more clearly and articulate his understanding of art and the place of the artist in society. He explained that this course "put in light the master of the most pure race [the artist], the one whose activity addresses itself only to that which is most essential in the interpretation of the world, in the creation of the future. It is the artist. . . . He is the master-revealer of the divine in humanity." Pach came to see the artist as the most intuitively evolved of beings, who could, and should, expose the divinity in us all. He also came to believe that, through the creation of art, the artist partakes of the divine. This belief remained at the core of his aesthetic theory throughout his life.

During these years Pach was actively engaged in literary work for American and European journals. Some of the articles he wrote were on American artists and his friend and concert companion Alice Toklas helped edit these essays. Pach's writing on Winslow Homer was the most substantial of his articles published in France at this time, and in it he endorsed the theory of a native school of art. Pach felt that Homer's greatness lay in his respect for the power of nature, his admiration for tumultuous movements and great spaces, and his straightforward definition of forms.

These characteristics, Pach believed, reflected the force, integrity, and poetry of a race of the frontier, the American people. In his estimate, Homer ranked with the masters of French art such as Ingres and Corot, because his paintings combined "the feeling of nature that one spoke of in the past, and the aesthetic of which one speaks today."[87] Pach's promotion of American art and artists in France was relatively unusual for his time, and he helped establish the canon of masters of American art. His belief in identifiable characteristics of "Americanness" in American art remains part of the discourse on American art to this day.

The subject of the other major essay that Pach wrote at this time was Renoir, and he had been waiting to write this article for almost three years. Pach had had a brief interview with the artist in June 1908, but, as he observed, it was "not enough to make an article of—too much interrupted."[88] In March 1911, Pach visited Renoir at his studio on two occasions to interview him, and after much discussion and correspondence with the artist regarding the context of the article, Pach submitted his manuscript to the publisher. In this article, Pach again espoused his belief in the theory of the evolution of art when he observed that Renoir "placed himself in line with the great colorists of the past." Pach furthermore proclaimed that, like the great masters of the past, Renoir also recognized that "color has a nature and function apart from the questions of representation."[89] The idea that color could exist as an aesthetic value separate from its role in the creation of a recognizable object in painting was a tenet of avant-garde art theories and a practice endorsed by Pach's contemporaries, such as Matisse and Denis. Pach's use of this ideology as a tool with which to evaluate Renoir's work reveals his position within the mainstream of contemporary art criticism.

While in Paris, Pach continued in his work as an agent, mainly for friends and collectors back in the United States, particularly Arthur B. Davies. He would recall, "When I went abroad again in 1910, he [Davies] had me send him photographs from Florence of works he could not come by otherwise, and our correspondence kept up when I bought for him (or, finally for Miss Bliss) a landscape by Cézanne."[90] The Cézanne referred to in this letter is *La route.* Pach arranged its sale with the assistance of his good friend Loeser, who was still in Florence at the time. In April 1911, Loeser wrote Pach in Paris:

> Vollard dropped in on me about 10 days ago. He had brought with him a big & most beautiful Cézanne that I had much admired in his rooms in Paris, but which I had no thought of ever possessing at his price 30,000 frcs. Still I had suggested that we might effect an exchange. This we finally agreed upon here. I giving him no less than four Cézannes in exchange for the one. . . . One of these exchanged pictures is "Costa's," so that now if you are to see this & the others with a view to your German friend acquiring it, or another, you should go to Vollard's without delay. . . . I see no reason why you should not prearrange with Vollard to receive your fitting commission of 10% on her purchase. Why should you give the benefit of your brains, your time, your experience to others—gratis?[91]

Pach was clearly working as an agent on behalf of clients both in the United States and Europe and was probably paid the standard 10 percent commission on the sales he made—a finder's fee that still exists in many parts of today's art world. The "German friend" referred to in this letter may have been an acquaintance of Pach's friend Magdalene Frohberg (although the painting mentioned was not purchased by this "friend" but was eventually sold to American collector Lillie Bliss with the assistance of Davies). Through these and other dealings with collectors such as Loeser, and gallery owners such as Ambroise Vollard, Eugène Druet, Paul Durand-Ruel, and Félix Fénéon of Bernheim Jeune et Cie, Pach became an important player in

the intricate world of the Parisian art market. He helped broker the sale of art to American collectors and positioned himself to be a vital source for the importation of modern art to the United States in the years to come.

Pach spent the summer of 1912 in Italy. Before he left Paris, he had given up the lease on his old apartment, and when he returned in the fall he found a new home at 83 boulevard Montparnasse. He continued to paint, visit with friends and fellow artists, and spend long hours at the museums and galleries. The most significant project with which Pach became involved in the fall of 1912, however, was the monumental task of helping organize the International Exhibition of Modern Art, better known as the Armory Show.

4
The Armory Show

Pach's involvement with the International Exhibition of Modern Art—better known as the Armory Show, so called for the location where it was held in New York City—was vital for the scope and success of the undertaking; the extent of his participation, however, has only recently been fully investigated, and he is just beginning to receive the credit he is due.[1] His first contact with either the Association of American Painters and Sculptors (AAPS) or the show itself was through a circular he received in 1912 that invited him to participate in the exhibition. His affiliation with the event as more than a potential exhibitor, however, began in the summer of 1912 while he was living in Paris. Pach recalled that he "had read, in New York papers sent me by my mother, about the modern art group of which [Arthur B. Davies] had become president, and I wrote him that—knowing, as I did, many of the most important artists, collectors and dealers—I should be glad to offer him any assistance I could."[2]

Davies admired Pach for his knowledge of modern art and knew that, given Pach's connections, his support and participation would be essential for the success of the exhibition. Davies quickly took Pach up on his offer and in June 1912 laid plans for a trip to Paris to choose art for the exhibition, but "domestic troubles" prevented him from going abroad in October as planned. Instead, he sent Pach a letter in which he explained,

> The reason for writing now is with reference to Walt Kuhn and the coming exhibition at the 69th Inf [antry Regiment] Armory in Lexington Ave. Kuhn sailed for Hamburg to see the Sonderbund at Cologne & to enlist for our show such artists as may promise of the newest tendencies—good work of an International character anywhere—The hanging space will be very large and lots of new men we hope to bring to the front. . . . To those of us and men like yourself the possibilities loom tremendous yet so many can only see another opportunity of showing their work—we look for the higher organic

life in the intuitive future. I believe that you can do much for Kuhn in every way. . . . So I am asking a favor of you again for which I hope I may reciprocate happily some time.[3]

Davies requested that Pach introduce Kuhn to Pach's colleagues in Paris. To Kuhn himself, Davies suggested, "You might go back to The Hague stopping in Brussels where there is a big movement and lots of interesting things. Pach can inform you of much of the work done there."[4] In another letter he told Kuhn, "Walter Pach has an article about the coming exhibition . . . in 'L'Art et [les] Artistes.' He may not mention it unless you do."[5] This article was probably "Le mouvement artistique a l'étranger: Etats-Unis," published in *L'Art et les Artistes* in September 1912, which briefly mentions the exhibition and the rumor of Davies's voyage to France. Once Kuhn reached Paris, however, Pach's participation became much more substantial. Although he was never an official member of the AAPS, Pach became the primary liaison between the artists, collectors, and dealers in Europe and Kuhn, Davies, and the association in New York.[6]

When Kuhn arrived in Paris at the end of October 1912, he immediately contacted Pach, who took him to several galleries and studios. Kuhn wrote Vera, his wife, "Tomorrow Pach and I go calling on some artists." He later reported, "Have spent the last 2 days looking over the local proposition—will begin selection tomorrow. . . . Pach is very agreeable and extremely useful—the other fellows however like those at home, they take all they can get and don't want to move a finger."[7] Overwhelmed by the task at hand, Kuhn wired Davies and asked him to come over; Davies arrived in November. In just over one week's time, Pach escorted Kuhn and Davies to the galleries of Vollard, Druet, Kahnweiler, and Bernheim. He also took the two men to meet several artist friends and collectors, including Constantin Brancusi, André Dunoyer de Segonzac, Odilon Redon, the Duchamp brothers, and the Stein families. In *Queer Thing, Painting,* Pach noted that when they visited Brancusi's studio Davies remarked, "'That's the kind of man I'm giving the show for.' And on the spot he bought for his own collection the exquisite little *Torso of a Woman*."[8] At the Puteaux studio of Jacques Villon and Raymond Duchamp-Villon, Kuhn and Davies saw works by all three Duchamp brothers, though the youngest, Marcel, was not present when they visited. Pach recalled in *Queer Thing, Painting,* "I remember how, in 1912, when I had left the Steins' [Sarah and Michael] apartment in the Rue Madame with Arthur B. Davies, that extraordinary appreciator made a respectful bow to them—on the other side of the door."[9]

Davies and Kuhn may have had the opportunity to meet some of these dealers, artists, and collectors through other Americans in Paris, such as Alfred Maurer and Jo Davidson, whom they also met while abroad; however, Pach was their main contact. He knew the Parisian art world intimately and shared with them a level of knowledge of and familiarity with its workings the others simply could not provide. Also, he fully understood the intricate workings of the art market, having been acting as an agent/dealer for a number of years. He was, however, also biased; therefore, the tour of the avant-garde Parisian art scene that Davies and Kuhn received was selective and reflected Pach's own personal tastes, interests, and friendships. The paintings, sculptures, and works on paper from which Davies and Kuhn could choose had, in essence, been preselected by Pach. In a sense it was merely up to Davies and Kuhn to narrow the choice from among numerous works to which he had directed them.

After a frantic ten days in Paris, Davies and Kuhn left for the United States and, basically, left Pach in charge of virtually all aspects of the European section of the exhibition. Davies and Kuhn stopped briefly in London on their way back to the United States to see the Grafton Gallery exhibition of postimpressionist art. From Queenstown, England, en route home, Kuhn sent Pach a note asking him to contact the gallery and obtain permission to borrow works for the show in the United States. Pach corresponded with Robert Dell and Roger Fry of the Grafton Gallery, Henri Matisse and his wife, Leo and Michael Stein, Alice B. Toklas, Bernheim, and Druet regarding the loans of pictures from London. It was Pach who secured the loan of Matisse's *Blue Nude,* a painting that became one of the most notorious works in the exhibition. He also arranged with the Steins and Toklas to borrow two Picassos they had lent to the Grafton Gallery show. It is doubtful that these works would have been lent without Pach's contacts and his powers of persuasion; because of his close friendship with the Steins and Matisse, Pach was easily able to secure them. In addition to obtaining these loans he arranged for the pieces to be insured, collected, packed, and shipped to and from New York.

Although Davies and Kuhn gave Pach detailed instructions on the particular pieces they wanted for the show, the availability of works was uncertain, and they left it to his discretion to choose what would be sent to the United States. Kuhn assured him, "We have absolute confidence in your decision in all matters which may arise."[10] Pach did, in fact, select not only almost all the avant-garde Parisian art but also most of the nineteenth-century French art that was sent to the exhibition. He revisited the galleries, collectors, and artists personally to make his selections. The dealers with whom he negotiated included Stéphan Bourgeois, Vollard, Druet, Daniel-Henry Kahnweiler, Durand-Ruel, and Félix Fénéon of Bernheim. The task was not always easy, as some dealers were more difficult than others. For example, Kuhn wrote, "Sorry you are having trouble with Kahnweiler," then urged Pach to "try to make a deal with Kahnweiler but do not sacrifice too much."[11] Pach summoned up all his skills of diplomacy and settled matters quite well. From Bourgeois he secured a painting by Cézanne and two by van Gogh. The largest loan came from Druet, where Pach selected works by van Gogh, Gauguin, Toulouse-Lautrec, Cézanne, Maurice Denis, Henri-Edmond Cross, Charles Camoin, Albert Marquet, and Georges Seurat, among others. From other commercial enterprises he chose paintings by Bonnard, Paul Signac, Vlaminck, André Derain, Picasso, Monet, Camille Pissarro, Sisley, and Henri Rousseau. Vollard and Druet in Paris also lent lithographs and colored reproductions in addition to paintings. Pach also convinced his good friend Egisto Fabbri to lend two drawings by Ingres.

Pach was also responsible for gathering together the pieces from The Hague and Germany that Kuhn had selected before he arrived in Paris. Artz and deBois of The Hague lent twenty-two "oeuvres d'art," including works by Redon and van Gogh, as well as lithographs and colored reproductions after paintings by these artists and by Renoir, Gauguin, Cézanne, and Édouard Vuillard. Pach corresponded with this gallery regularly before the show. The dealers Hans Goltz of Berlin and Heinrich Thannhauser of Munich lent dozens of paintings and lithographs. Once Kuhn and Davies left

for the United States, Pach handled virtually all the correspondence with these establishments.

In addition to returning to the commercial galleries and private collections, Pach revisited the artists' studios. He saw, among others, Sousa-Cardoza, Rousseau, Braque, Emile-Antoine Bourdelle, Derain, Picasso, Patrick Henry Bruce, Morgan Russell, Robert Delaunay, Gleizes, de la Fresnaye, Léger, Dufy, Alexander Archipenko, Picabia, and the Duchamp brothers. Kuhn had specifically asked him to borrow plaster casts by Brancusi, Archipenko, and Manuel Manolo. In 1963, Archipenko recalled, "In the year 1912, one morning, the delegate, Mr. Walter Pach, came into my studio, and selected for exhibition three of the more conservative of my statues, and some drawings."[12] At Picabia's studio, Pach persuaded the painter to lend two canvases, including *Dances at the Spring,* which became one of the sensations of the show. He also convinced Picabia and his wife to come to the United States to see the exhibition for themselves, which they did.[13] Pach went to Matisse's studio, though the French painter was not there, and corresponded with the painter regarding loans for the show.

It was Pach who was responsible for securing the most notorious work of the show, Marcel Duchamp's *Nude Descending a Staircase, No. 2* (fig. 8), which was largely responsible for making the Armory Show a huge success and a popular cultural event. In a 1967 interview, Duchamp explained how he came to be invited to the Armory Show: "By Walter Pach. He had come to France in 1910, and he had made friends with my brothers, through whom we met. Then in 1912, when he was entrusted with the task of gathering paintings for that show, he saved a lot of room for the three of us. We had shown him what we had, and he left. He took four of my things: the 'Nude Descending a Staircase,' the 'Young Man,' the 'Portrait of Chess Players,' and 'The King and Queen Surrounded by Swift Nudes.'"[14]

Since Pach was the only American artist to be affiliated with the Duchamp brothers and their Puteaux

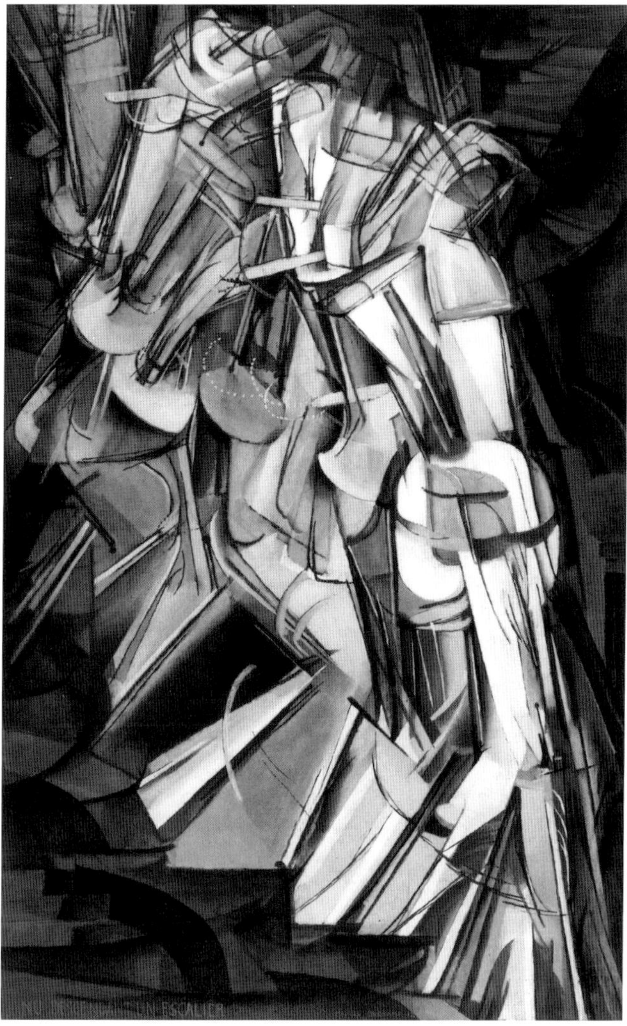

Fig. 8
Marcel Duchamp, *Nude Descending a Staircase, No. 2,* 1912. Oil on canvas, 57 ⅞ × 35 ⅛ in. Philadelphia Museum of Art, The Louise and Walter Arensberg Collection, 1950 (1950-134-59). Photography by Graydon Wood, 1994. © 2011 Artists Rights Society (ARS), New York/ADAGP, Paris/Succession Marcel Duchamp.

circle, he alone was responsible for securing loans from these painters. He chose paintings by Jacques Villon and sculptures by Raymond Duchamp-Villon and also borrowed works from Metzinger, Gleizes, and others. If it were not for Pach, it is unlikely that the artists of this group would have lent their works to the exhibition. In fact, this was the case in general. Most of the Parisian artists did not know Davies or Kuhn and had never heard of the AAPS, but virtually all the artists in Paris who sent works to the Armory Show knew Walter Pach personally, and they entrusted their art to him, more than to the organization that he represented. Pach corresponded with many of them before the show opened, as well as during and after the exhibition. For example, the German sculptor Wilhelm Lehmbruck sent a letter explaining that he had sent two sculptures and six etchings for the exhibition. The French sculptor Bourdelle wrote him a note that included a drawing describing how one of his pieces should be mounted. Nadelman jotted a short card informing Pach of the addition of another plaster to the exhibition. Dunoyer de Segonzac's father wrote Pach to arrange for his son's paintings to be collected for the show (his son had already left Paris). Other correspondents included Robert and Sonia Delaunay, the Duchamp brothers, Odilon and Camille Redon, Brancusi, and Sousa-Cardoza.

As the European representative for the AAPS, Pach had, according to Kuhn, "full authority to act for the Society."[15] In this capacity, he was responsible not only for securing the loan of paintings and sculptures in Europe but also for determining the value for which the art was to be insured and for obtaining the insurance. Kuhn reported to Vera, "Pach has friends in the insurance business here, and will help me with that." Later, however, he complained, "Pach was o. k. to take me around to dealers and introduce me, but when it came to business he was nix—I settled all insurance matters in good shape."[16] This statement was not entirely true, for Pach handled most of the insurance matters for the exhibition. He also contacted the packers, shippers, brokers, and customs agents and oversaw the collection and transportation of the European works to and from the United States. For his part, Kuhn did give him the names and addresses of the various European agents and packers with whom he needed to correspond, and Pach certainly could not have done this without his assistance. Pach's familiarity with the European art market and his fluency in French and German, however, were invaluable and expedited these processes enormously. All this work took place in a remarkably short time. Just over one month from the time Davies arrived in Paris, Pottier, the shipper Pach had hired, was in the process of finishing the construction of the crates for transport of the artworks to the United States.

Davies and Kuhn intended to present a variety of contemporary European art, but when the final selection was made there were some notable lacunae, including many of the German and Russian avant-garde. Most accounts of the Armory Show state that the reasons for these absences were that Davies and Kuhn felt the Germans had not made any significant contribution and that there simply was not enough time to acquire a more thorough representation of vanguard European work, including Russian works. A much more plausible explanation for the lack of non-Parisian advanced art is that Pach was a dedicated Francophile, and much of the selection was up to him.

Another group that was missing from the show was the Italian futurists, and almost every account of the Armory Show states that they were excluded because they insisted on being shown together.[17] In the 1988 edition of his book on the exhibition, by contrast, Milton Brown suggested that the futurists "may have been committed to European exhibitions during that time."[18] Bennard Perlman also noted in his biography *The Lives, Loves, and Art of Arthur B. Davies* that the futurists had a conflicting commitment in Italy and would not participate in the New York show.[19] Primary and other secondary sources—most of which have been available to scholars since 1972—prove this was indeed the case.[20] At the Chicago venue of the show, the AAPS published a pamphlet titled *For and Against: Views on the International Exhibition Held in New York and Chicago*. Printed in this brochure was a one-page piece called "As to Futurists." Most likely written by Pach, it included the following short statement:

The Futurist artists were personally seen last Fall by Mr. Davies, Mr. Kuhn and Mr. Pach in Paris, and had the most cordial invitation which could possibly be extended to any individual or group of men. Indeed, an entire room at the Exhibition was offered them, so that their artistic individuality might be preserved intact, if they so desired. While absolutely disposed to exhibit with us, the circumstances of their engagements with European Exhibitions prevented their being able to send the pictures to America.[21]

Pach reiterated this statement, almost verbatim, in a letter written on December 21, 1920, to Katherine S. Dreier, an American artist and collector: "There was no representation whatever of The Futurist group at the International Exhibition of 1913. The Futurists were invited to exhibit and were told they could have a room to themselves if they wanted it, so as to keep their artistic individuality intact. After some time they told me it would be impossible to send their pictures to America because of other engagements."[22] Clearly all had done their part to include this group in the Armory Show, and accounts that state otherwise are inaccurate.

Pach both volunteered and was recruited for public relations activities in Europe and the United States. Kuhn asked him to secure "a 'thumb nail' biography of *all* the important men" who were to participate, and he specifically requested a "snap shot of the Duchamp Villon brothers in their garden."[23] Kuhn felt such information would greatly help with the publicity for the exhibition. A photograph of Raymond Duchamp-Villon, Jacques Villon, and Marcel Duchamp in the garden of the older brothers' Puteaux studio did appear in the *New York Times* in April 1913, and Pach undoubtedly furnished the original image of the siblings. He also enlisted his father's company to make reproductions of this photograph, which were circulated to the newspapers. In addition, Pach Brothers Studio photographed many of the paintings and sculptures displayed at the

Armory Show. These "fine photographic reproductions," as well as color prints and postcards, were available for sale at the show's venues. Finally, Pach was advised to speak with the dealers in Europe concerning their desire to advertise in the catalog produced for the show.

Pach had not initially planned on leaving Paris to come to the United States for the show, but his curiosity about this huge exhibition must have been aroused, and he probably felt that he had a vested interest in a positive outcome for his friends in Paris. As he was saying good-bye to Davies and Kuhn at the railway station in Paris, he said to them, "I guess I'll have to go over to New York to see that show." Davies purportedly "slapped Kuhn on the back and said, 'Didn't I tell you we'd get him'?" According to Pach, Davies and Kuhn had wanted "some one who knew the artists as well as their work to be the spokesman for the public"; they felt that Pach could continue to be of service to their cause.[24]

On February 17, 1913—with Walter Pach present— the International Exhibition of Modern Art at the Armory of the Sixty-ninth Regiment in New York City opened to a curious crowd. Unfortunately, few photographs of the interior of the New York Armory Show exist. Certainly one of the most often reproduced images of the show is the view of the main European gallery (fig. 9). Pach, it seems, took this now famous photograph. This was but one of the many services he provided for the Armory Show.

Pach worked at the exhibition throughout its entire run in New York, Chicago, and Boston and was the only person to be at each of the venues every day from the time the doors opened until the exhibition closed. His main responsibility was chief sales agent, and he kept notebooks in which he recorded purchases. Soon after the show opened he enthusiastically reported to Duchamp-Villon that they had sold several of his pieces and had an order for a bronze cast of one of them. In addition, he wrote Vollard on March 8, "Exhibition unprecedented success. One hundred seventy works

sold."[25] Pach was responsible for most of these sales and tried to negotiate other acquisitions as well. He also sold photographs of the works that were available at the various venues.

Through his work as sales manager Pach met some of the foremost collectors in the United States and became an advisor to several of them. In Manhattan, he was introduced to John Quinn, a lawyer and art enthusiast, who was legal counsel for the AAPS.[26] Quinn made his first purchase at the New York venue of the Armory Show on February 22, 1913. Eventually, he bought paintings, sculptures, and works on paper by Duchamp-Villon, Villon, Jules Pascin, Odilon Redon, André Dunoyer de Segonzac, Paul Signac, Puvis de Chavannes, André Derain, Manolo, Alexandre Blanchet, and Girieud from the exhibition. Many of these works were acquired on Pach's recommendation. He recorded in his notebooks that Quinn had made more than five thousand dollars' worth of purchases for himself and bought works for friends. Also in New York, Pach met Arthur Jerome Eddy, a Chicago lawyer, who acquired several works from this venue and eventually amassed quite a collection of modern art. Walter Conrad Arensberg, an art collector and poet, and his wife, Louise, who lived in Boston, visited the exhibition in Manhattan and bought "a colored lithograph . . . through Mr. Pach."[27] Pach also sold a watercolor to the collector Agnes Ernst Meyer, wife of Eugene Meyer, who owned the *Washington Post*. In addition, Pach most likely arranged for Arthur B. Spingarn, another New York lawyer with whom he would become quite close, to buy two lithographs, one by Redon and another by Gauguin. He reported the success of the show to Michael Stein: "Total number of sales in N. Y.—237 (this includes about 50 lithographs Cézanne, Renoir, Denis, Gauguin, Vuillard, Bonnard). Our *great* sale was a glorious Cézanne landscape to the Metropolitan Museum. That just about made me wild with joy. . . . Among the important sellers were Redon, Derain, Duchamp-Villon and his brothers."[28] It was

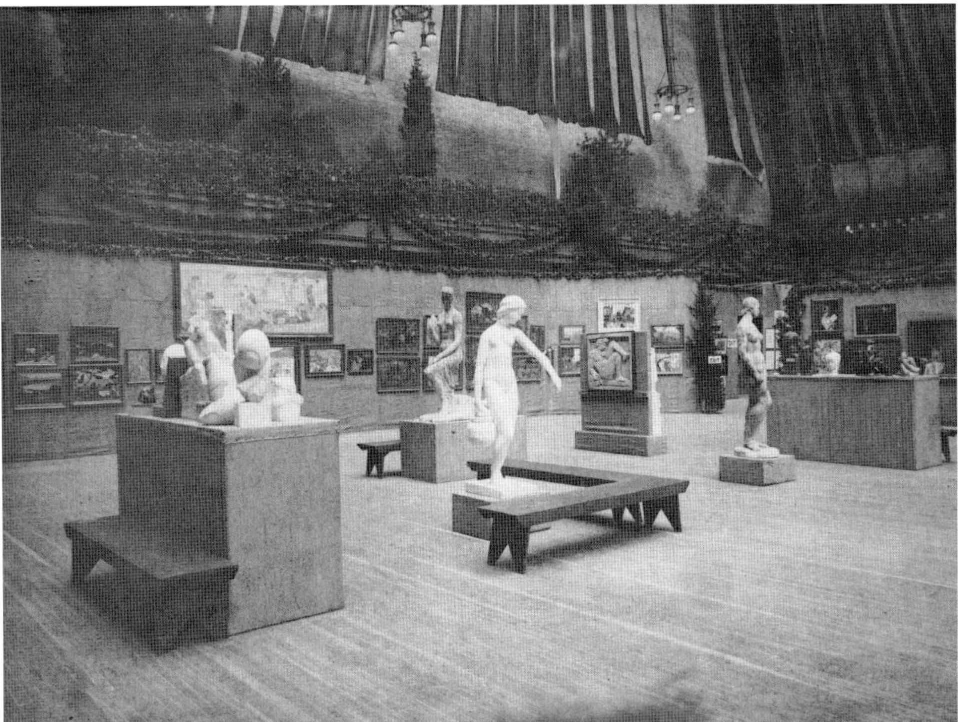

mainly through Pach's efforts that these sales took place, among them the purchase of Cézanne's *View of the Domaine Saint-Joseph,* also known as *La colline des Pauvres* (fig. 10), by the Metropolitan Museum of Art with the aid of his good friend Bryson Burroughs.

Pach also met numerous artists, critics, and writers who came to the show, both those who supported the art and those who did not. Among the detractors were Kenyon Cox and Royal Cortissoz, critics whom Pach knew well. Picabia, in the United States at Pach's invitation, came to the exhibition often and saw his friend frequently. Another artist who frequented the show was Carl Zigrosser, who met Pach around this time:

> I also met Walter Pach outside Keppel's, and he opened up other vistas for me, glimpses of foreign shores. Although American-born, Pach had a slightly foreign aura about him. He and his walrus mustache appeared somewhat Spanish, and indeed he taught Spanish at night school. He smoked French cigarettes, the *paquet blue* of Maryland tobacco, or strong Italian cigars, *toscani.* He had exotic tastes in food; he introduced me to Chinese restaurants. They were cheap and neither of us had much money. We also talked about art and literature. From Pach would come intimations of exciting experiences in Paris, or casual references to Matisse, Redon, Jacques Villon, or Elie Faure.[29]

Zigrosser had been working as a researcher at Keppel and Company, a well-known print shop and art gallery, since 1912. He and Pach shared an interest in contemporary prints. Zigrosser captured Pach's persona perfectly. With his large mustache and the lingering smell of French cigarettes, Pach had a somewhat mysterious and glamorous air, making him seem exotic and exciting to many young American artists, who saw him as a link to

Walter Pach (1883–1958)

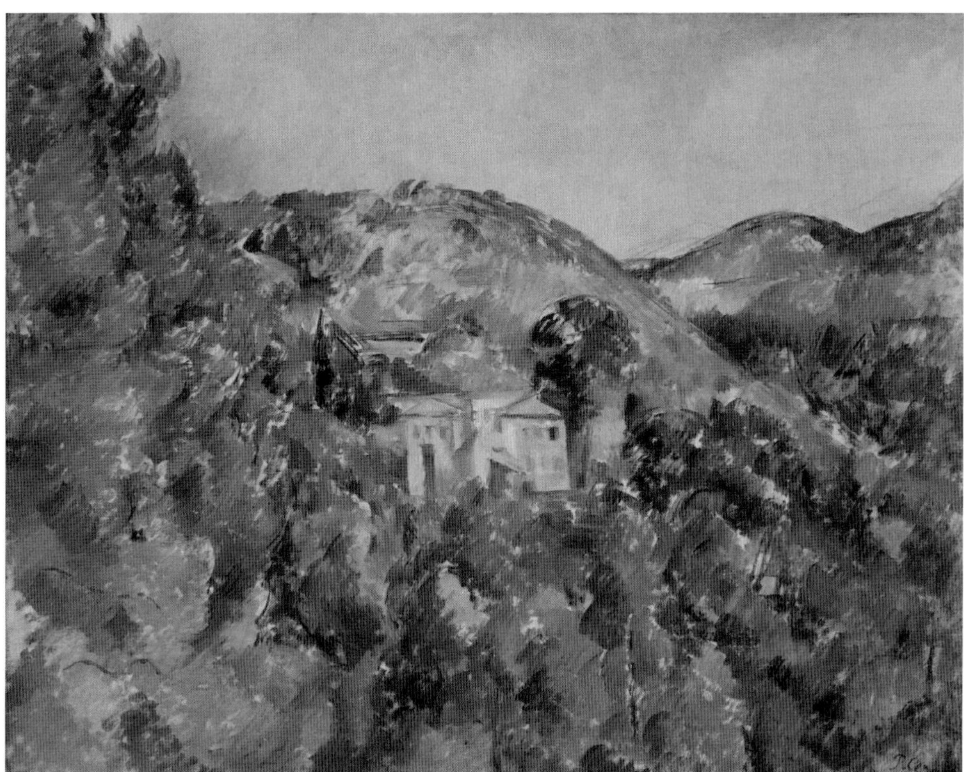

Paul Cézanne, *View of the Domaine Saint-Joseph,* late 1880s, oil on canvas, 25 ⅝ × 32 in. (65.1 × 81.3 cm). The Metropolitan Museum of Art, Catharine Lorillard Wolfe Collection, Wolfe Fund, 1913 (13.66). Image © The Metropolitan Museum of Art (photo: Malcolm Varon).

the modern, Parisian art world. "During the period of the Armory Show," Zigrosser wrote, "I naturally turned to Walter Pach for enlightenment. But the artist seemed unable to explain or justify all the startling innovations, since he, in spite of more experience and an artist's training, took for granted many things which puzzled the neophyte." Zigrosser would have liked Pach to explain a little further how he had come to understand and accept the avant-garde art on view at the show, but Pach was unable to do so, and probably had little free time. "A long time afterwards," Zigrosser wrote, "he confided to me that his own acceptance of the extreme forms of distortion in postimpressionist art had not been accomplished without considerable doubt and effort on his part." Zigrosser was one of many who felt that Pach was a highly learned person who had a great depth of knowledge on art, but one who "could not transmit its spirit or essence to another, because, as it turned out, he had not actually made it part of him-

self."[30] He found Pach to be too ponderous in his pronouncements on art, with little passion for it. Pach also met the poet Wallace Stevens around this time, probably at the exhibition, and perhaps through Walter Arensberg; wherever they met, the two became fast friends and remained so for life.[31]

The Armory Show closed in New York on March 15 and was dismantled and, in part, transported to the Art Institute of Chicago. Pach and Kuhn boarded the Twentieth Century Limited on March 20 and headed west to oversee the operation. Frederick James Gregg, an Irish-born critic hired by the AAPS for publicity work, had already departed for Chicago. Kuhn reported to his wife, "Pach and Gregg took off their coats and worked like beavers."[32] The three of them, aided by the staff of the Art Institute of Chicago, installed the show in one day. This greatly reduced version of the exhibition contained mainly the European works and a few American pieces.

Pach's main responsibility at the second venue of the show was, again, to serve as sales manager. Although sales were not as numerous as at the New York venue, several works did sell in Chicago, and Pach attempted to negotiate other acquisitions. Kuhn reported to Davies, "Pach sold 3 Sousa Cardozas to Eddy Yesterday. Also several lithographs. It looks as though he'll make many sales."[33] Eddy also bought a painting by Vuillard. He requested that Pach translate into English the titles of the pieces he bought at the New York venue, which were on display at the Art Institute of Chicago, for inclusion in the catalog produced for the Chicago show. Another buyer in Chicago was Manierre Dawson, a painter, civil engineer, and architectural draftsman whom Davies had told Pach to look up if he had the time. Dawson recorded his first meeting with Pach in his journal: "The man with the moustache and tremulous hands who seemed in constant attendance saw me as the most lingering of spectators. Engaging me in conversation, I found him most interesting and informative. His name is Walter Pach."[34] After visiting Dawson's home, Pach selected one of Dawson's paintings, titled it *Wharf Under Mountain,* and surreptitiously hung it in the American section of the exhibition. This unrecorded work was the only abstract painting by an American and the only work by a Chicago artist in the exhibition. From Pach, Dawson bought a painting by the Portuguese modernist Amadeo de Souza Cardosa and Marcel Duchamp's *Nu, esquisse (Sad Young Man on a Train).*

Most accounts of the Armory Show state that Chicago had the highest attendance record of all the venues and attracted the most publicity, which is true, but many reports have it, not entirely accurately, that students from the Art Institute of Chicago burned or hanged in effigy Matisse; or Matisse and Brancusi; or Matisse, Brancusi, and Pach. According to Pach, "Further publicity followed when the students at the Art Institute held a meeting of protest and a majority of them voted for condemnation. This was put into effect by the burning in effigy of one of Matisse's big nudes, also a figure representing myself and . . . an image of cheap little *September Morn*—which, of course, was not in our exhibition."[35] A reproduction of *September Morn,* a French academic painting by Paul Chabas, had recently been displayed in a downtown dealer's window, until the "defenders of morals" in Chicago had it removed from view. One newspaper article showed students protesting outside the art institute, one holding a sign that read, in part, "Morn," probably referring to the work about which Pach wrote. The press reported the demonstration on April 17, the day after the Armory Show closed, one newspaper announcing, "The Men's Life Class association of the Art Institute will present the 'Trial of September Morn' this afternoon and evening at Fullerton hall in the Institute building." "It had been the intention of some students," said the reporter, "to burn a figure of Matisse in effigy, but authorities stopped this projected sacrilege."[36] Instead, the students held a mock trial of Henry Hair Mattress, found him guilty of crimes against art, and burned copies of three of Matisse's paintings, *Blue Nude, Luxury,* and *The Gold Fish.* Clearly, the exact nature of events in Chicago is uncertain.

In addition to working as chief sales agent, Pach was the main spokesperson for the vanguard art at all three venues of the show, a role for which he was well qualified. Milton Brown and other art historians who have written about the Armory Show record that Eddy and Charles Francis Browne, president of the Society of Western Artists, lectured to packed houses in Fullerton Hall at the Art Institute of Chicago. Few accounts mention that Pach, too, lectured in Fullerton Hall the evening the exhibition opened. Walt Kuhn told Elmer MacRae, "They did root up Pach about 10 P. M. to have him give a lecture."[37] On April 5, Pach received a letter from New York that read, "I am anxiously awaiting your 'lecture,' [which] ought to make fine reading in the New York papers."[38] The speech referred to in this note may have been the one delivered by him on March 24, or perhaps he gave a second talk in Chicago. In any event, it is clear that Pach was called upon to present formal lectures that explained the modern art exhibited in the Armory Show. He was also pressed daily in the galleries to speak informally about the modern art on view with the crowds that came to see the show.

According to many accounts of the show, only a handful of artists, critics, and collectors appreciated the new art; those outside this exclusive circle, namely, the general public, so the story goes, ridiculed the art and did not understand it at all. Pach had a different view on the audiences' understanding of the new art. He wrote Michael Stein, "You would be *astounded* at the amount of intelligence I find in my rounds of the galleries (I am chief salesman as you know)—even as a small fraction of the comment, it more than makes up for the idiots."[39] Among the thousands of visitors who attended the exhibition, Pach found several who shared his enthusiasm for the advanced art of the Continent. He wrote Robert Koehler of the Minneapolis Art Institute, "I am full of confidence that the impression on all classes of the big public of Chicago has been a profound one and that it will continue to grow for many many years."[40] It was largely through Pach's efforts that some came to accept, and even appreciate, the art on view; he became, in effect, the face and voice of modern art in the United States.

Less than one week after the show opened in Chicago, Pach wrote Stein again, this time reporting the show's unqualified success:

> I never saw the like of it. Of course it's because only a couple of us are working Davies, Kuhn, Gregg, MacRae and me to be more exact and the proposition, with its thousand ramifications, Chicago, Boston, etc., etc., etc. is gigantic. But we are going to put a mark on American thought that will simply be indelible. We have done it already. Total attendance in N. Y. about 100,000—most all paid. Yesterday

and today in Chi [cago] about 20,000 people! each. . . . Matisse, I really believe, awakens more interest than any one else in the show and I do not have to work hard to keep up my hopes of a sale or two from the splendid long wall he has to himself here, the first thing you see as you enter. Davies made the plan for the hanging here, and designed it that Matisse should first meet the eye and set a pace— annunciate the character of the exhibition. . . . Not one article showing real critical insight of importance has appeared.[41]

Although only a small group of individuals attempted to understand and appreciate the contemporary works, and few critics discussed them with any clarity, Pach saw hope for the acceptance and advancement of modern art in the United States. When the show closed in Chicago, Pach and MacRae were left in charge of the tricky task of separating the works into two categories: those destined for the next venue and those that were to be returned to New York for dispersal to their owners.

The final destination for the show was Copley Hall in Boston, where a further reduced version, which contained only European works, was put on display for three weeks, from April 28 to May 19. Pach was again present at the show each day, and once more he was the chief sales agent and main spokesperson for the vanguard art. Several authors have written that the Boston venue was a disappointment, and some even called it a failure. Others, including Pach, saw Boston in a different light. Attendance was not as large as in Chicago or New York, but in just over three weeks more than twelve thousand people visited the show, and the Copley Society "made a small profit."[42] Pach made a few sales in Boston, mainly to Walter Arensberg, whom he came to know quite well. He later recalled,

> Of all our visitors to the Armory Show, it was a rare one indeed who made such a record for assiduity

and interest as Walter Arensberg. . . . When we were able to prolong the exhibition and let it go to Boston, he not only came to study the pictures at old Copley Hall, where they were shown, but had me come repeatedly to his house in Cambridge for long evenings of talk about them. . . . His approach to modern art was not merely literary, but was based on his interest in philosophy, one which developed across the years, through his studies in psycho-analysis.[43]

Pach, who found Arensberg to be a willing convert to modernism, enthusiastically supported the latter's purchases, which included Villon's *Sketch for "Puteaux Smoke and Trees in Bloom No. 2"* and two lithographs.

While in Boston, Pach lectured at the Copley Society and at Wellesley College. He reported to Kuhn that he "delivered one of the most eloquent and stirring addresses on art that ever came down the pike" at the women's college.[44] From Pach's point of view, Boston was clearly not a complete failure. When the show ended, he and MacRae were responsible for overseeing the packing, customs inspection, and shipping of the paintings back to their owners. Pach carried on much of the correspondence with the artists, dealers, insurance companies, and customs agents until all accounts were settled—a process that would take more than three years.

In addition to carrying out his numerous other responsibilities, Pach wrote several essays for the show, two published separately, *The Art of Odilon Redon* and *A Sculptor's Architecture,* and three published in the pamphlet *For and Against,* "Hindsight and Foresight," "The Cubist Room," and "As to Futurists." These writings were designed to guide the public toward an understanding of modern art, and in them Pach seized the opportunity to espouse his theory of art. For example, in *The Art of Odilon Redon,* he wrote, "The work of Redon has the quality of reaching out to the future while preserving its just relation with the

past—and is therefore classic."[45] In this definition of the term *classic,* he promoted his belief in the evolution of art and his conception of the artist as intermediary between his ancestors and his progeny. Pach, who viewed painting, sculpture, music, literature, and architecture as an "exposition of life," felt that contemporary work should reflect modern life, and he argued this point in his pamphlet *A Sculptor's Architecture.*[46] "Hindsight and Foresight" was a defense both of modern art and of the chronological arrangement of the works presented in the Armory Show; in it Pach reinforced the philosophy of the exhibition that hoped, in part, to show the unbroken chain of development from the art of Ingres to the paintings of Duchamp. In "The Cubist Room," Pach explained that while Cubism was "a radical departure from preceding forms," it was not a subversion of the basic principles on which the great art of the past was founded. The nineteenth century, he declared, had brought realism to its furthest potential; therefore, a new art was needed that "should be not an imitation, but what it has eternally been— expression."[47] Cubism was, according to Pach, the logical and natural result of artists' search for a new means of communication. He praised the cubists and asked his readers to judge them not as disrupters and rejecters of tradition but as preservers of the past and architects of the future. Pach was not alone in expounding a belief in the evolutionary aspect of art; other contemporary American critics who wrote of the development of art as an evolutionary process included Christian Brinton and J. Nilsen Laurvik. However, because Pach knew intimately the artists whose works were on view, and because he was at the Armory Show daily, his words rang with more resonance for American readers and many of his ideas still ring true today.

Pach undertook other literary jobs aimed at educating the public about the modern art on view at the show and publicizing the event. He translated two lengthy pieces on Cézanne and Gauguin written by Faure. These materials were on sale at the show. In addition, he published notices and reviews of the exhibition in *L'Art et les Artistes, La Chronique des Arts et de la Curiosité: Supplement à la Gazette des Beaux-Arts,* and *La Vie.* All these endeavors were aimed toward educating the public and raising awareness of the event.

Last, but not least in his own mind, Pach participated in the Armory Show as an artist. He submitted five oil paintings and five etchings, all very representational works that did not reveal any influence of the avant-garde European art with which Pach was familiar and that he selected for the show. The oils were *Flowers; Wall of the City; Girls Bathing; Casentino Mountains;* and *Portrait of Gigi Cavigli, of Arezzo.* The five etchings, all executed in Europe, were *Mary, Renoir's "Liseuse"; Gothic Virgin; St. Germain des Prés—Night;* and *St. Germain des Prés—Day.* The wealthy collector Henry Clay Frick bought *Flowers* (unlocated) and another New Yorker, Richard Sheldrick, bought an edition of *Renoir's "Liseuse."* According to MacRae's accounts, Pach may also have sold other etchings in New York.

Pach's incentives for becoming so deeply involved with this historic event were undoubtedly complex and diverse, but his main reason was that he was a staunch supporter of modern art. He truly admired the European, particularly French, artists and their works and wanted to see them promoted and sold in the United States. Monetary gain was not a motivating factor. There is no documentation to indicate that Pach received any commissions from dealers in Europe. The only payments we know he received were from the AAPS. He was reimbursed for his expenses at the various American venues and in May 1913, after the show closed, was paid twelve hundred dollars for "services rendered," which included his work as the European representative, his role as chief sales agent at the three exhibition sites, his writings, and his lectures in conjunction with the show.[48]

Pach's contributions to this historic exhibition were enormous and cut to the very core of the show. Beyond the very important practical work he executed so

effectively, Pach was really the only one of the group capable of shaping the modern French section as an accurate representation of current avant-garde work in Paris. The quality and quantity of the French works flowed naturally from Pach's intimate knowledge of the vanguard painters and sculptors, the dealers and collectors, in Paris. Among the loans he garnered were works—Matisse's *Blue Nude,* Brancusi's *Sleeping Muse* and *Mlle. Pogany,* Picabia's *Dances at the Spring,* and Duchamp's *Nude Descending a Staircase, No. 2*—that gave the show its notoriety and made it the success that it was. As chief sales agent Pach was responsible not only for the sale of more than two hundred works but also for cultivating an appreciation for modern art among American collectors. His assiduous efforts to place works with them had far-reaching consequences for American taste.

5
Pach the Artist, 1903–1919

Despite his many other activities, Walter Pach considered himself primarily an artist. The surviving drawings, paintings, and prints that he made between 1903 and 1919 can be divided into four styles. Constituting the first group are realistic, somewhat academic works—for example, *Dutch Boy,* 1903 (fig. 5)—that reveal the influence of his American teachers William Merritt Chase and Robert Henri. The second group comprises paintings and prints that reflect Pach's awareness of the impressionist and postimpressionist paintings of French artists such as Renoir, Monet, Cézanne, Matisse, and the Fauves. The third group is cubist in style and reveals Pach's response to the paintings of his friends Duchamp and Villon and others of the Puteaux Group. In the final group are paintings that combine cubist and representational elements and signal a shift away from any abstraction in his work.

Between 1905 and 1913, Pach exhibited frequently. His paintings were accepted into several prestigious exhibitions, passing a jury of his peers for inclusion in shows at the Pennsylvania Academy of the Fine Arts in Philadelphia; the National Academy of Design in New York; the Corcoran Gallery of Art in Washington, D.C.; and the Salon des Indépendants in Paris. He participated in his first group invitational at the New York School of Art in the spring of 1907 and the first Exhibition of Independent Artists in 1910. Many of the works that Pach exhibited at these venues, among them *The Toledo Bridge; Open-Air Restaurant, Bombilla; Hay-Built, Haarlem;* and *Dutch Lowlands,* were clearly inspired by his trips to Europe with the Chase and Henri summer schools between 1903 and 1910.[1] Pach also participated in the 1913 Armory Show and other group exhibitions in New York and other cities across America throughout the teens and became viewed as a core member of the modernist vanguard.

During two extended trips to Paris between the fall of 1907 and the beginning of 1913, Pach's style changed from a dark and somber palette, reminiscent of his teachers Chase and Henri and of Goya and Velázquez, to a method influenced by his investigation of the impressionists, postimpressionists such as Cézanne, and Matisse and other Fauves. Among the extant paintings that clearly reveal the stamp of Pach's mentors is *Portrait of Mr. Ogihara* (fig. 11). Painted in Paris in the fall of 1907, this work presents the sitter wearing a painter's smock, indicating Ogihara's profession. Pach's portrayal of Ogihara was realistic, and his method recalls Henri. In Pach's work the pigments were slashed onto the canvas in broad sweeps of the brush, and the details of the clothing and figure were not distinctly defined. The bottom portion of the canvas was left unfinished. The blank background and the compressed space focus the viewer's attention on the figure and the handling of the paint.

Etchings such as *St. Germain des Prés—Day* (fig. 12) and *St. Germain des Prés—Night* (fig. 13) reveal Pach's fascination with French architecture and his interest in capturing the scene under differing light conditions—an approach he would have learned from the impressionists, especially Monet. The images are not very original in their style but are quite beautiful. According to one source, his depictions of the church of Saint-Germain were drawn "on the copper as it looked from his window at 3 bis, rue des Beaux Arts."[2] It is probable that Pach had access to a printing press while in Paris and pulled his own prints as he had done in New York.

In several paintings from this period, Pach employed softer colors in pastel hues and brighter lighter tones, indicating the influence of the impressionists. He did not, however, adopt their technique of introducing pure pigment onto the canvas in short, unblended strokes; rather, he applied his oils in broad, flat bands. Instead of shading his colors to build three-dimensional forms, as he had done in earlier works, he used layers of translucent hues to create the effect of depth. This technique may have been inspired by Cézanne's late

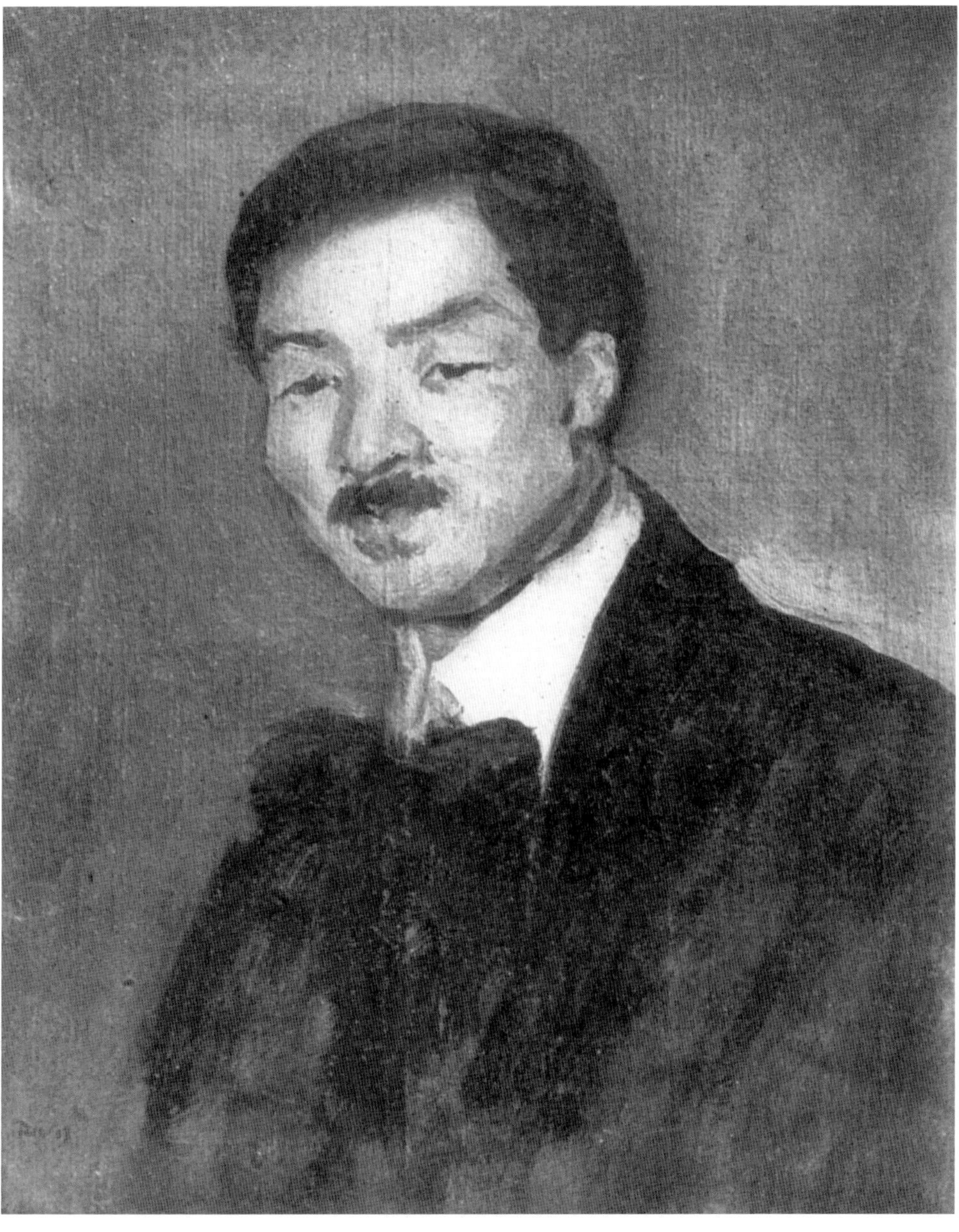

Fig. 11
Walter Pach, *Portrait of Mr. Ogihara,* 1907, oil on canvas, 20 × 16 in. Collection of Mrs. Nikifora N. Iliopoulos.

Fig. 12
Walter Pach, *St. Germain des Prés—Day,* 1911, etching, image 4 15/16 × 3 13/16 in. (12.6 × 9.7 cm), sheet 14 15/16 × 9 15/16 in. (38 × 25.2 cm). The Metropolitan Museum of Art, Rogers Fund, 1922 (22.26.3). Image © The Metropolitan Museum of Art.

Fig. 13
Walter Pach, *St. Germain des Prés—Night,* 1912, etching, image 5 9/16 × 3 13/16 in. (14.2 × 9.7 cm), sheet 11 15/16 × 8 15/16 in. (30.4 × 22.4 cm). The Metropolitan Museum of Art, Rogers Fund, 1922 (22.26.4). Image © The Metropolitan Museum of Art.

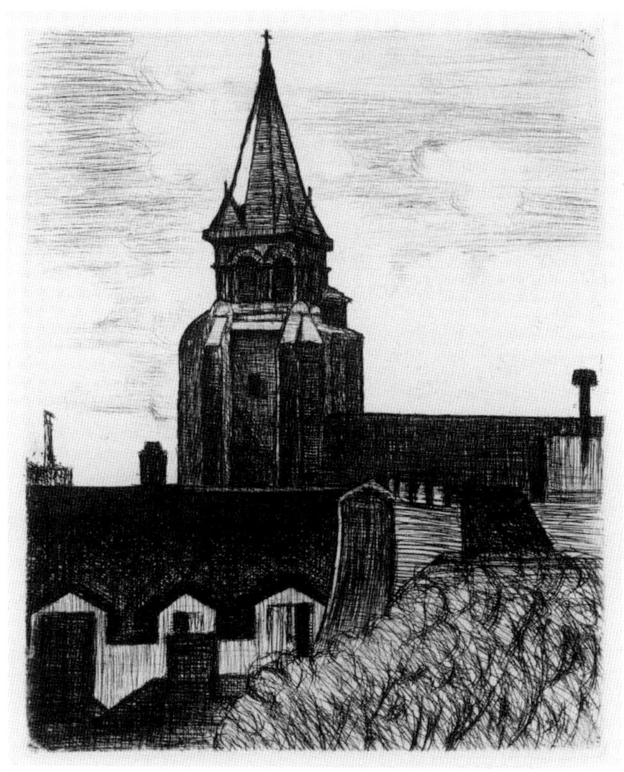

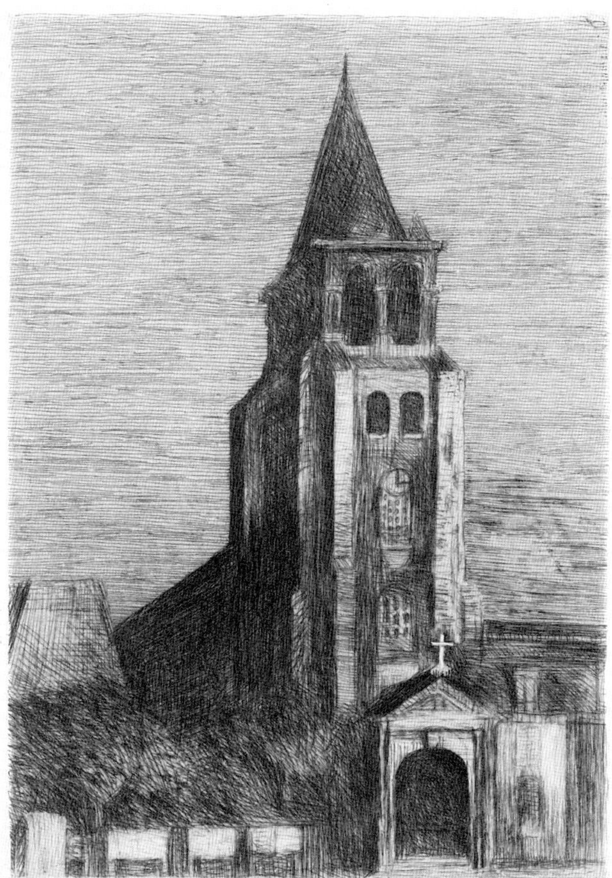

paintings and watercolors, which Pach had seen in two exhibitions in Paris. In a few paintings from this time, Pach experimented even further and his use of bright, bold, almost prismatic colors and a simplification of forms in these works reflect the influence of Matisse and other Fauve painters.

Clearly confident that he had produced paintings of some merit, Pach accordingly sent six works to the jury of the Salon des Indépendants in the spring of 1908. Much to his delight, all the paintings were accepted, quite a coup for a young American artist. All except one were for sale. Regrettably, none has been located.[3]

In June 1912, after almost two years in Paris, Pach departed for a lengthy trip to Italy. He again visited Florence but also spent several weeks in Arezzo and Perugia. This was a working vacation; Pach painted, and he also studied Piero della Francesca's frescoes in Arezzo. Leo Stein, in his pronouncements on modern art, with which Pach was familiar, hailed della Francesco as a precursor to cubism and urged many artists to make the pilgrimage to Italy to study paintings by this master. Several of the paintings Pach made during this sojourn are extant, one being *Portrait of Gigi Cavigli of Arezzo,* depicting a young neighbor of Pach's (fig. 14). This portrait of Cavigli was clearly influenced by the della Francesca frescoes in the church of Saint Francis in Arezzo. The monumentality of the figure and the simplicity of the composition recall the murals by the Italian master, and the three-quarter-length pose and the sparse background in the portrait are reminiscent of compositional devices della Francesca used in his work. The solidity of the forms and the realistic style seen in this painting reveal Pach's continued fascination with and admiration for past masters and reflect his belief in the relevance of older art to the modern art of his day.

The five oil paintings and five etchings that Pach exhibited at the Armory Show were most likely done in Europe between 1910 and 1912. The oils included *Portrait of Gigi Cavigli of Arezzo* and *Casentino Mountains* (plate 1). *Casentino Mountains* appeared in a newspaper article

alongside a reproduction of Matisse's *The Red Madras.* Both were compared to works by residents of Dunning, the local hospital for people with psychiatric disabilities. Pach did not seem to mind being placed in the company of Matisse, an artist he greatly admired. No two artists could be further apart, however, in their respective styles. Pach's sentimental scene of young girls in a landscape setting rendered rather awkwardly in pretty pastel colors was quite different from Matisse's *The Red Madras,* with its bold colors and forthright statement. Pach's painting reveals an artist who has not quite mastered the depiction of the figure in the landscape, and though representational, it is not naturalistic. The five etchings he sent to the exhibition were *Mary, Renoir's "Liseuse"; Gothic Virgin; St. Germain des Prés—Day* (fig. 12); and *St. Germain des Prés—Night* (fig. 13). Regarding the style of these works, Pach explained, "All my pictures at the Armory were of my pre-Cubist days; they ended that same year of 1913." By this remark, Pach meant that the works he exhibited at the Armory Show were realistic and representational in style and were unaffected by the cubist art of Marcel Duchamp and others of the Puteaux Group that would greatly influence his art for the next several years.

Pach stated that between late 1913 and 1919 he "worked under the influence of the great new school of France."[4] The school to which he referred was undoubtedly that of the Puteaux Group, more particularly, the Duchamp brothers, Gleizes, and Metzinger. Inspired by Duchamp's *Nude Descending a Staircase, No. 2* (fig. 8), Pach, as well as numerous other American painters, began experimenting more with cubism after the Armory Show. Among the first works that he produced in this new style were *Progression No. 1 (Flowers)* (plate 2) and *Progression No. 3 (Aquarium)* (plate 3). He wrote Manierre Dawson in November 1913, "I kept up writing as long as I could and was on the point of bursting into a thousand pieces. Then I opened the safety valve (i.e. began to paint) and have enjoyed myself royally. The long vacation from it may even have done me good.

I am working ever so differently from what I did before; much better too, there are cubistic things in it."[5]

Both these paintings are cubist in style and reveal the change in Pach's style after the Armory Show. They were included in a 1913–14 traveling exhibition of modern American art that Pach helped organize. This show opened at the Carnegie Institute in December 1913 and traveled to the Montross Gallery in New York, the Detroit Museum of Art (now the Detroit Institute of Arts), the Cincinnati Art Museum, and the Peabody Institute in Baltimore in 1914. These two paintings generated quite a few lines of press, most of which were short and not very favorable. The *Detroit Times* reported that among the modern works were those by "Walter

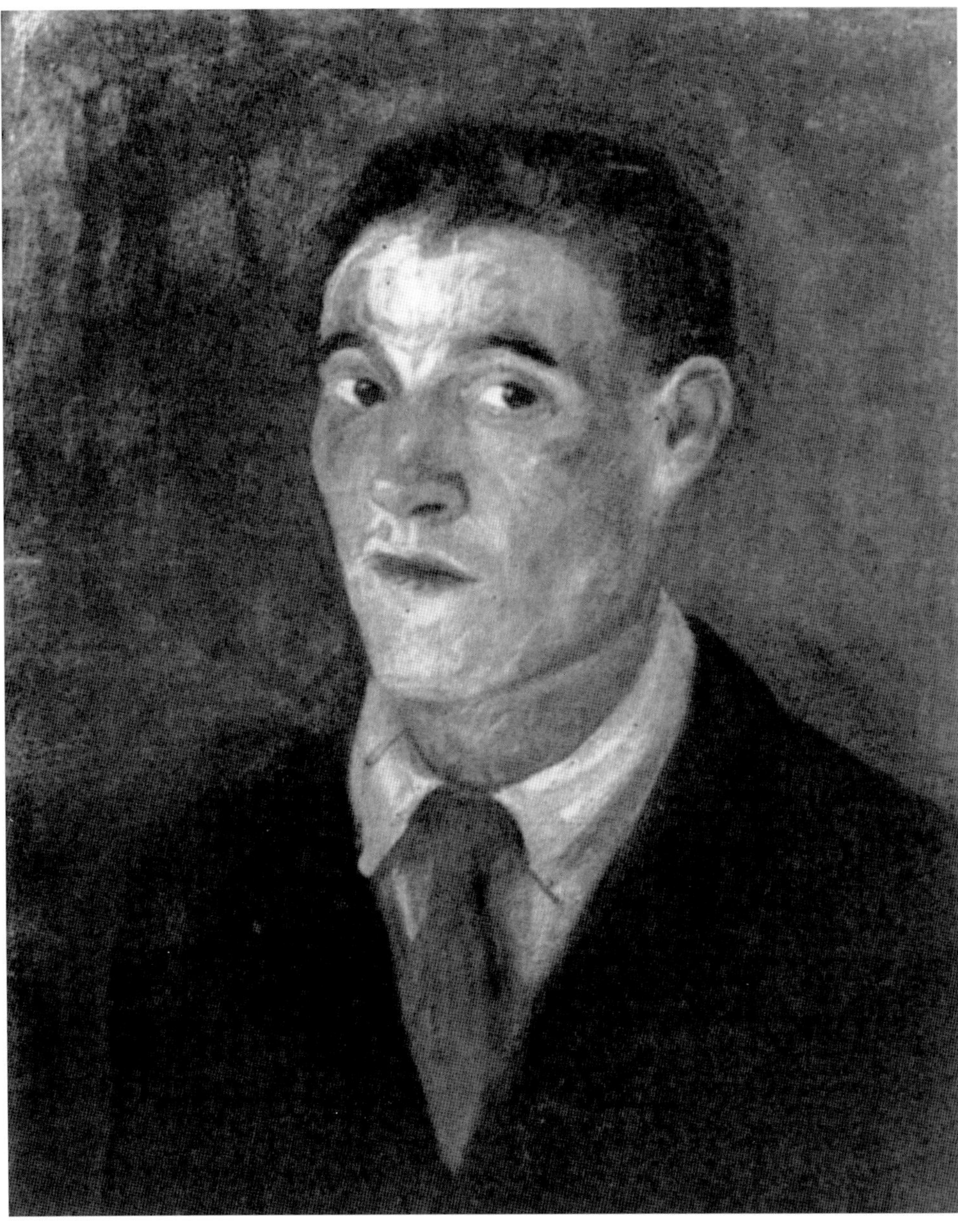

Fig. 14
Walter Pach, *Portrait of Gigi Cavigli of Arezzo,* 1912, oil on canvas, 24 ¼ × 18 ¼ in. Collection of Mrs. Nikifora N. Iliopoulos.

Pach, whose cubist 'Progressions' are bad paintings of fish, flowers and fruit."[6] A critic for the *Detroit Journal* explained, "A group by Walter Pach shows increasing peculiarities of light, shade and movement, treated in characteristic modernist style."[7] Mary L. Alexander of the *Cincinnati Times Star* complained, "Walter Pach's 'Still Life' [*Progression No. 1*] and 'Gold Fish' [*Progression No. 3*] are among the unintelligible canvases."[8] A *Cincinnati Commercial Tribune* reviewer criticized one of his entries as "something that looks like the latest fashion in millinery, a green hat trimmed in vegetables, with the title, 'Progression No. 2.'"[9]

The longest critique of Pach's work was, in fact, the most favorable. About *Progression No. 1,* the *Baltimore Evening Sun*'s art critic wrote,

> Perhaps one of the most striking things about all of the work of the cubists is its solidity, the sense of mass, which it conveys to the observer. It is not a question of color, which is often too strident, but of length, breadth and thickness, which in many instances seems remarkably well expressed. This is especially noticeable in Walter Pach's "Progression" of "the flowers in the flashlight." Study this picture thoughtfully from a position just within the classic statuary room, and you cannot fail, I am sure, to get a remarkable impression of the concrete roundness and body of these flowers, in spite of the fact that they are painted in squares and have so many corners.[10]

Pach's paint application in broad, flat areas and his use of intersecting planes of color in this painting achieve a certain impression of depth and solidity, but the forms remained relatively flat and decorative. He again uses lines and angles to refract space while maintaining the integrity of the forms in his watercolor *Progression No. 3 (Aquarium)*. The fish and tank remain recognizable, but they appear to float in the fractured space within the picture.

Another admirer of Pach's work was Walter Arensberg, who traveled from Boston to New York to see the exhibition at the Montross Gallery. In March 1914, Arensberg wrote Pach, "I must thank you again for so much of the pleasure of my brief visit to New York. The exhibition was tremendously fresh and fine. . . . Many of the pictures—and your own among the most vivid—are intact in my memory. . . . you bring to the study of appearance something incalculably more penetrating and faithful then mere observation. You certainly give the impression of telling the truth, the whole truth, and nothing but the truth."[11] Arensberg quite rightly observed what Pach was attempting to do in his canvases, namely, to give the impression of appearances but not to portray them realistically. Probably encouraged by the response to his paintings in this exhibition, Pach experimented further with cubist and futurist elements in several watercolors dated 1914, two of which are *Landscape* (fig. 15), which Arensberg probably purchased at this time, and *Untitled (Cubist Still Life)* (plate 4). In both these works Pach employed the cubists' vocabulary of lines, angles, and planes to refract the surfaces of his works into multiple facets. Forms remain recognizable and retain a sense of three-dimensionality, but the space around them is flattened into a repetitive pattern of colors.

Soon after Duchamp arrived in the United States in June 1915, Pach painted his portrait (fig. 16) and sent Matisse photographs of this and another work, remarking, "These are two oils that I like better than what I have done. . . . I believe that the difference of design between the painting of Magda and the other more recent of Duchamp is due in great part to my "regimen" of research in the manner more or less cubist such as you had seen in that watercolor that I made in Paris. I continue therefore these studies, where I am freer from the hindrance of appearance, and believe draw there a freer vision and a knowledge more firm of aesthetic values."[12]

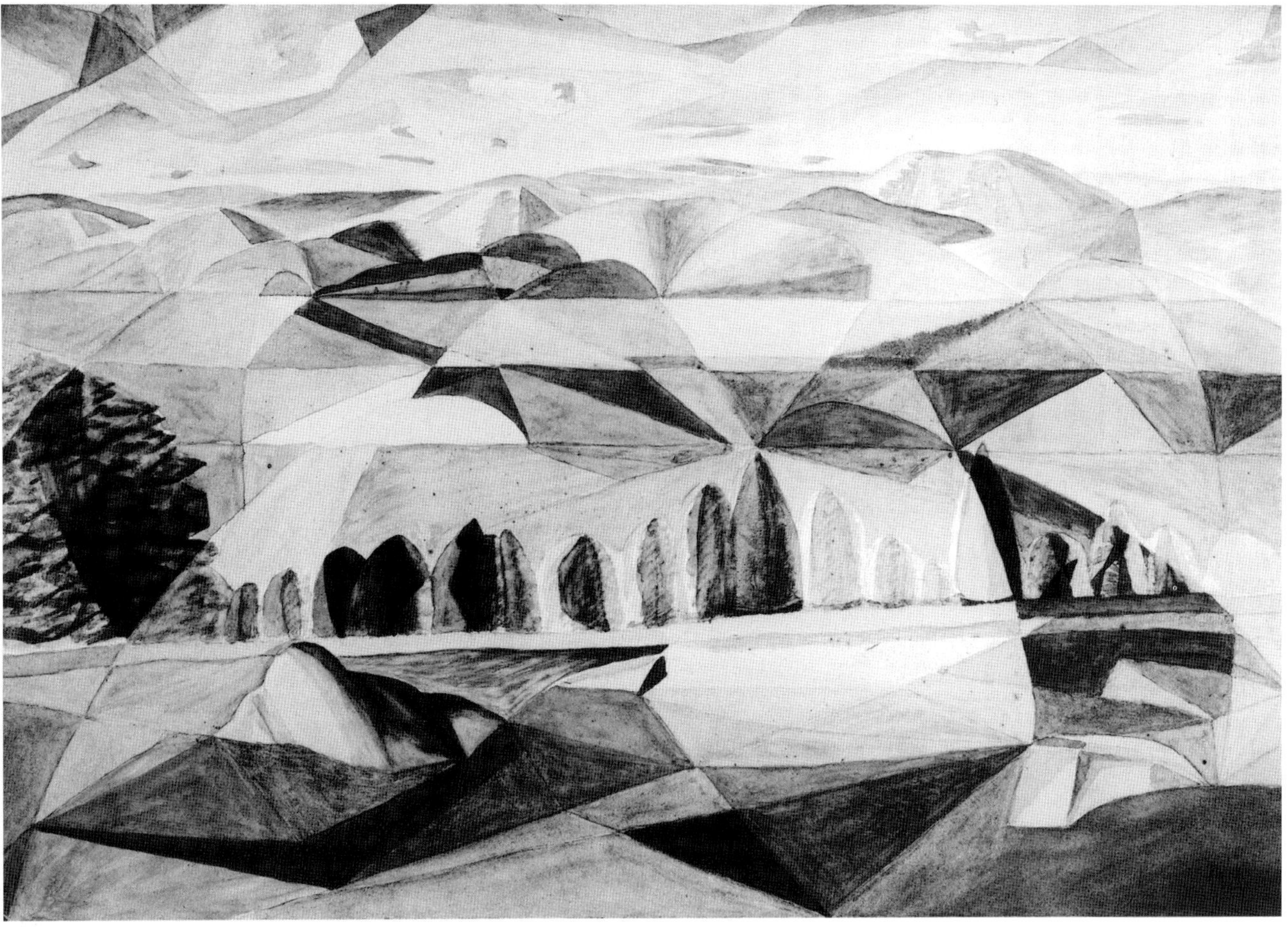

Fig. 15

Walter Pach, *Landscape,* 1914, watercolor over graphite. Philadelphia Museum of Art, The Louise and Walter Arensberg Collection, 1950 (1950-134-516).

Matisse responded, "Now I must tell you that I viewed with pleasure the two photographs of portraits that you have sent me, and that I have noticed great progress in the second work, the portrait of a man—from the point of view of 'style'—but I must also say I find it a bit cold. I think that the progress you'll soon make will consist of warming up your formula a bit, which is pretty but severe. When your new skills are definitely secured, you will be able to relax and show the sensitivity which is present in the portrait of your wife."[13] The portrait of Duchamp is mainly representational in its approach, though the forms are a bit elongated and exaggerated. The solid, pale background helps focus attention on the sharp and well-defined features of the figure. Pach was extremely proud of this work and exhibited it regularly throughout his lifetime.

During 1916, Pach created some of the most intriguing paintings of his career. In May, he wrote to Matisse, "At present I have had in hand a view of New York with many cars in movement. I am going to treat it in a schematic fashion."[14] Later in the year he reported that the "painting of the view of New York that I am making is perhaps the last where I will employ the geometric forms—which have served me well, besides aiding me to obtain a structure more firm."[15] Although the precise paintings to which he referred in these letters remains unknown, two of his most well known works, *The Cathedral* (fig. 17) and *Sunday Night (St. Patrick's at Night)* (plate 5), were both executed in 1916, and either could fit the description.

In *The Cathedral,* Pach used geometric forms to create the impression of solidity and structure. Simultaneously, by reducing the buildings and figures to their basic shapes and rendering them in a schematic fashion, he evoked the sensation of movement. The strong vertical thrust of the church—Saint Patrick's Cathedral on Fifth Avenue between Fiftieth and Fifty-first Streets—contrasts with the horizontal line of the avenue, and the pronounced vanishing point reinforces the feeling of motion in the work. Pach's

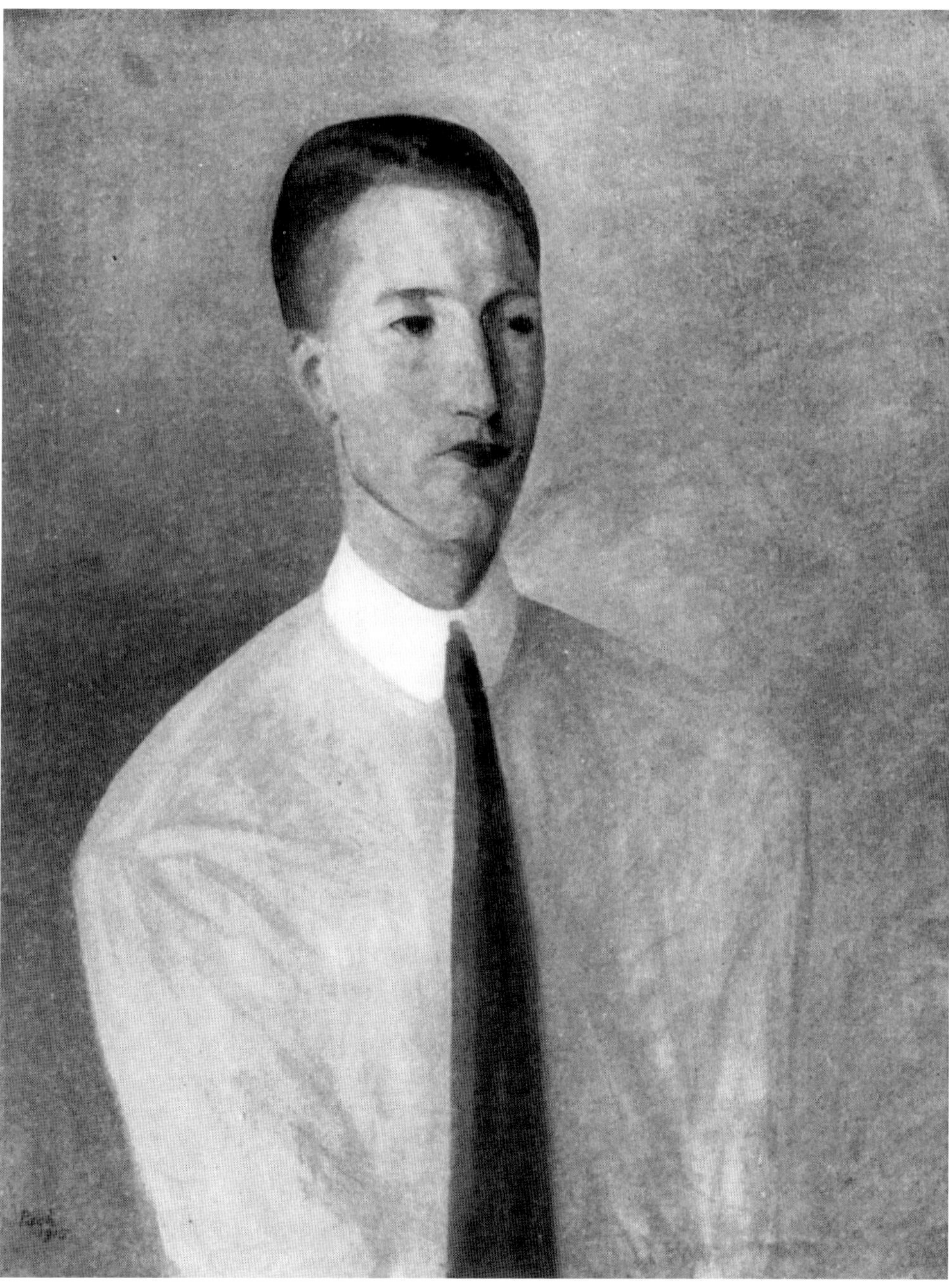

Fig. 16
Walter Pach, *Marcel Duchamp,* 1915, oil on canvas, 28 ½ × 21 in. Collection of Mrs. Nikifora N. Iliopoulos.

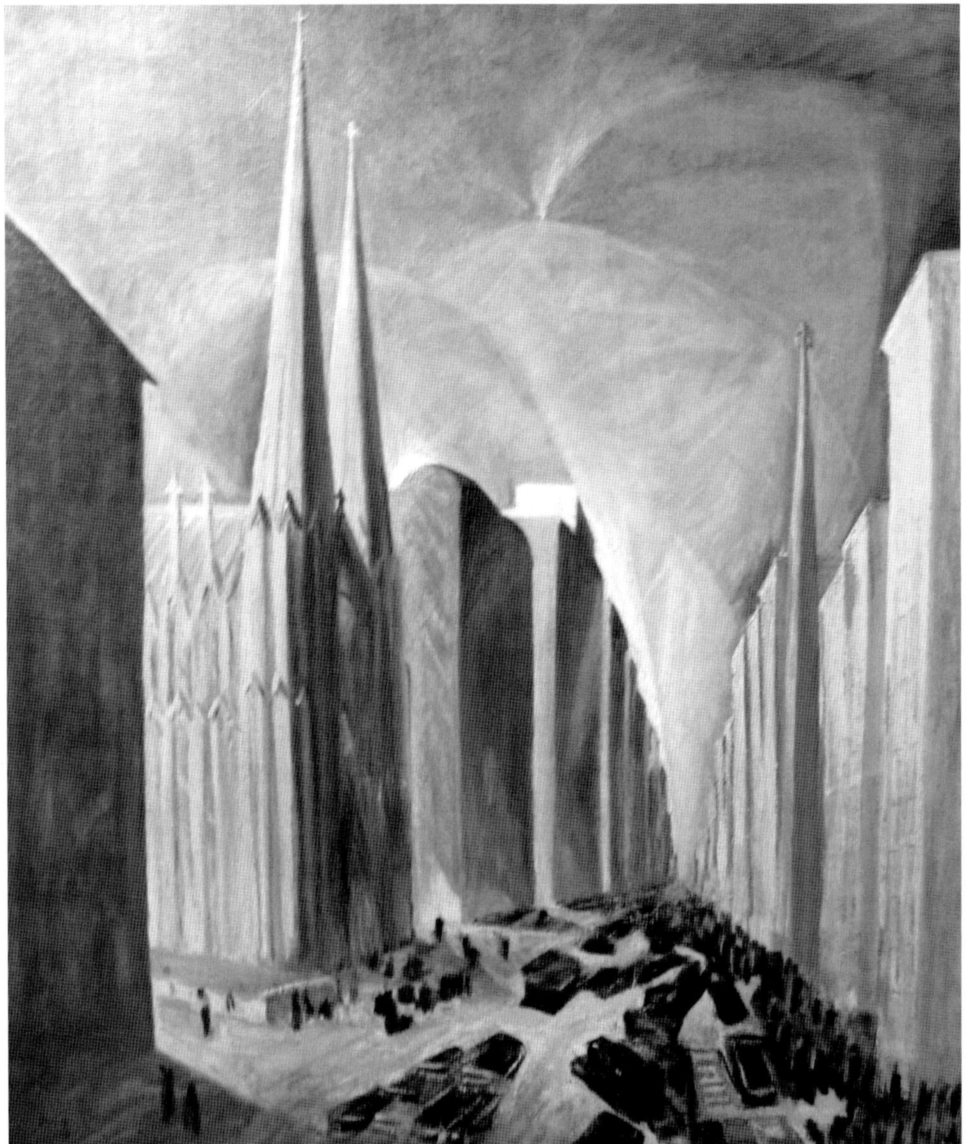

attempt at re-creating the impression of dynamic movement was probably influenced by works created by Duchamp, Gleizes, and other Puteaux Group members, some of whom were in New York at the time. Allan Antliff has argued that "the example of Gleizes's paintings, combined with the marked antiwar sentiments he shared with Pach, may have inspired his American friend to focus on a similar continuum: one connecting the collectivizing force of Christian pacifism with the contemporary unanimism of America's

great metropolis."[16] This interpretation is quite plausible, as Pach shared these artists' interests in ideas of space, time, and technology and believed that modern art should find subjects and forms to reflect and reveal contemporary life.

Antliff further observed that the French literary movement of unanimism could also have inspired the subject and style of this painting, which he sees as containing "surprisingly political overtone."[17] Unanimism, Antliff noted, was French poet Jules Romain's

Walter Pach (1883–1958)

term for a "theory of collective consciousness."[18] Among the main proponents of this movement were Pach's close friends the Duchamp brothers, Gleizes, Metzinger, Picabia, and Alexandre Mercereau. Undoubtedly, Pach was aware of the concept of unanimism that was discussed among this group, and he may have, as Antliff argued, "combined unanimist aesthetics with a pointed reference to the institutional preeminence of Christianity in a bid to encourage his ideals" in paintings such as *The Cathedral*.[19] Yet it is difficult to say with exactitude that *The Cathedral* and other works treating Saint Patrick's Cathedral were directly influenced by unanimism. Perhaps Pach was merely contrasting the old church architecture with the modern dynamism of contemporary New York.

The closest that Pach came to abandoning any reference to reality in his art during this period was in *Sunday Night (St. Patrick's at Night)*. This work clearly shows the influence of the Puteaux Group and the futurists. It also has certain similarities with the paintings of Pach's American futurist friend Joseph Stella. In this depiction of the cathedral Pach created a picture in which the objects were dissolved into simple geometric shapes—rectangles, triangles, circles, and squares. The strong horizontal, vertical, and diagonal lines in the painting imply movement: the forms are in flux, one overlapping and blending into the next, thus stimulating the sensation of dynamism.

Pach exhibited this work at the first annual exhibition of the Society of Independent Artists under the title *Sunday Night*. Later, the title was changed to *St. Patrick's at Night*. Without benefit of the later title, viewers had difficulty discerning the subject of the painting. For example, the *Nation* critic Frank Jewett Mather Jr. found "Walter Pach's bit of cubist symbolism called Sunday Night very soothing and fascinating, without having the least idea of what it's all about. It looks like a smoothly working machine under iridescent illumination, is rather hypnotizing."[20] This comment aligns Pach's work with the ideals of his Puteaux

Group friends—Duchamp, Gleizes, and Metzinger, in particular—who in their paintings and writings celebrated the machine age and its aesthetic.

In the summer of 1916, the Pach family vacationed for three weeks in Ashokan, New York. During this time, Pach gave a great deal of thought to his painting and told Matisse that he had made some notes on the landscape and that "certainly there are some signs that the study of form and pure color that I have made in my studio react on these simple notations of the effect of sun, of mist, etc. My goal . . . is to arrive at the point where each touch will be at once inspired by a sensation and controlled by a schematic idea."[21] He was still pondering the paintings he had recently done and was responding to other artists' reactions to them.

In the fall of 1916, Pach created *Petrouchka* (fig. 18), one of the most complex paintings of his career.[22] This work was inspired by the ballet of the same name with music by Igor Stravinsky, composed in 1910. Pach placed a program from an October 19, 1916, performance at the Manhattan Opera House in his scrapbook, suggesting that he viewed the ballet that evening in New York. The vision that stimulated Stravinsky's creation was, according to the composer, "A puppet suddenly gone mad who exasperates the patience of the orchestra by his diabolical cascades of arpeggios. The orchestra retaliates in turn, with menacing trumpet blasts. The outcome is a terrific noise, which, after reaching its climax, ends in the sorrowful collapse of the poor plaintiff puppet."[23] Pach probably chose *Petrouchka* as a subject for his work based on his fascination with music and the ballet in general and because he had recently seen it performed. However, he could have selected the ballet as the theme for a painting for other reasons. By giving artistic form to a dance composition, for example, he may have meant to suggest the connection between the arts, a connection in which he firmly believed. In addition, he was aware of the ballet's historic importance. According to Alexandre Tansman, Stravinsky's biographer,

"*Petrouchka* had shaken the musical art of the period."[24]
By selecting this ballet as a theme for a painting, Pach
may have been aligning himself with what was perceived to be among the earliest compositions of the
modern era. Furthermore, Stravinsky's ballet was a
parable for the battle between evil and good in humanity. Since Pach painted his work in the midst of the
horrors of World War I, with news of his friends being
wounded and perishing at the front in Europe, his
picture could be interpreted as a comment on the
carnage of war.

Although basically representational in style, *Petrouch-*
ka contained elements similar to those found in Pach's
more modern works and marked a transitional stage in
his career. The figures, particularly the magician, are
objectively depicted, but their shapes and scale are
distorted. The forms are not three-dimensional solids
existing in space but appear pasted on the surface of the
canvas and are refracted into prismatic schemes. Pach
attempted to find artistic equivalents for the music and
the dance, but he did not try to represent accurately the
scene enacted before him. He presented the dancers,

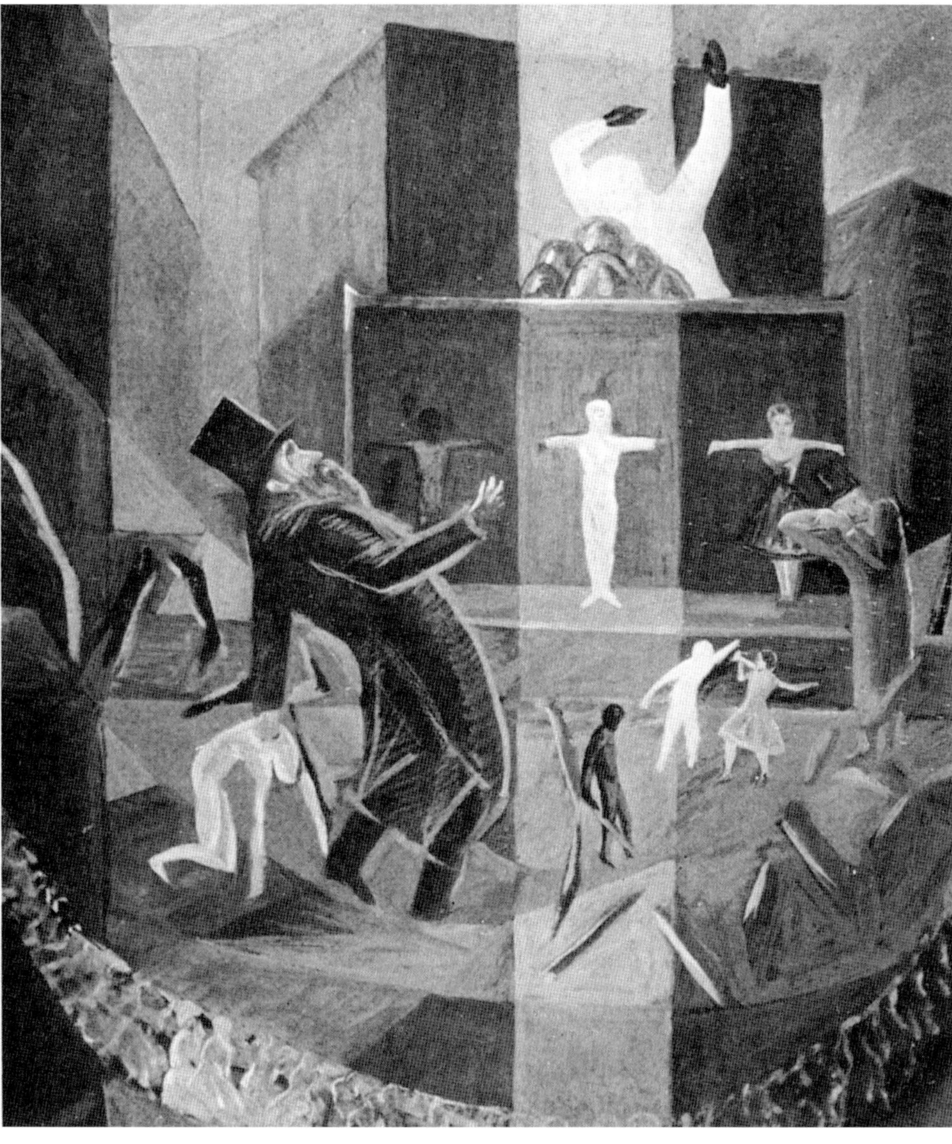

Fig. 18
Walter Pach, *Petrouchka*, 1916,
oil on canvas, location
unknown.

Walter Pach (1883–1958)

puppet, and magician in stiff, stylized poses that makes them resemble props, and he used stark, simple forms to mirror the harsh content of the narrative. In addition, by using strident contrasts of scale, sharp lines, and severe angles, he strove to create a visual counterpart to the cacophonous music of the piece.[25]

During the early months of 1917, Pach submitted two pictures, including *Petrouchka,* to an exhibition of modern art at the People's Art Guild. Organized by John Weichsel, the guild had socialist leanings and was "an association of artists and lay art lovers of diverse creeds bent on placing the art problem of our day on a sound public foundation."[26] Other participants in the show included Pach's friends Picabia, Metzinger, Sheeler, Stella, Picasso, George F. Of, Derain, and A. S. Baylinson. Once more Pach's art was placed in company with works by some of the vanguard painters of the day.

Also in 1917, Pach painted *The Lily of the Valley* (plate 6), a work that might have been inspired by the tragic death of his mother in May. Painted in a cubist/futurist style, the work shows a coffin or deathbed in the foreground with an anonymous mourner collapsed atop it and others hovering nearby. Other figures, more ethereal in appearance, seem to float in the background. The colors are muted, and the sense of scale between figures and objects is severely distorted. This painting may represent the artist's response to his mother's death or a reaction to the destruction and carnage of the war; both events were deeply disturbing to Pach.

The later months of 1917 brought about changes in the range of Pach's artistic production. He designed a set for Wallace Stevens's *Bowl, Cat, and Broomstick,* a series of four one-act plays satirizing "new" poetry. The production, by the Wisconsin Players, opened at the Neighborhood Playhouse in Greenwich Village on October 23. This project was quite an experiment for Pach, though he does not discuss it in detail in any of his writings. During this time Pach seems to have also branched out into porcelains. He wrote Robert Harshe of the Carnegie Institute, "Mr. Montross spoke to me of

an exhibition of applied arts you are arranging and suggested that you might care to show some of the porcelains I have been engaged on lately." Pach only had "small pieces" that were unsuitable for this particular show, and thus had to decline the subsequent invitation.[27]

Toward the end of 1917, Pach participated in at least three group exhibitions. He sent *The Lily of the Valley* to the October opening exhibition of Montross's new season, and in December he was represented by two works in the Exhibition of Watercolors by American Artists held at the same gallery. In addition, he submitted two pictures to the Exhibition of Paintings by the "Moderns," held at Vassar College, also in December. Among other artists who participated in the Vassar show were Derain, Edward Hopper, Metzinger, Diego Rivera, Schamberg, Sheeler, and Max Weber. Pach's continued inclusion in important shows of modern art reveals that his art was held in high esteem among his peers and that he was still considered a relevant figure in the avant-garde art movement of the day.

Beginning in 1918, Pach's painting style underwent a gradual shift from his cubist phase to a more pronounced combination of cubist and representational elements. His subject matter also began to vacillate between depictions of the contemporary world and images from the past, or a combination of the two. Among the paintings from this period is *"La Maja de Goya"* (plate 7), based on a Spanish operetta of the same name that was performed in New York in 1918. The beautifully costumed performers are not realistically rendered. One stands in the foreground of the picture, while the others form a curved line behind her. In the background are the familiar elements of refracted light and space. The bright colors and brilliant light could have been part of the staging of the operetta.

Another work displaying both cubist and naturalistic elements is *The Automobile (Fifth Avenue)* (fig. 19). In this watercolor, Pach's primary approach was representational—the vehicles, figures, and buildings

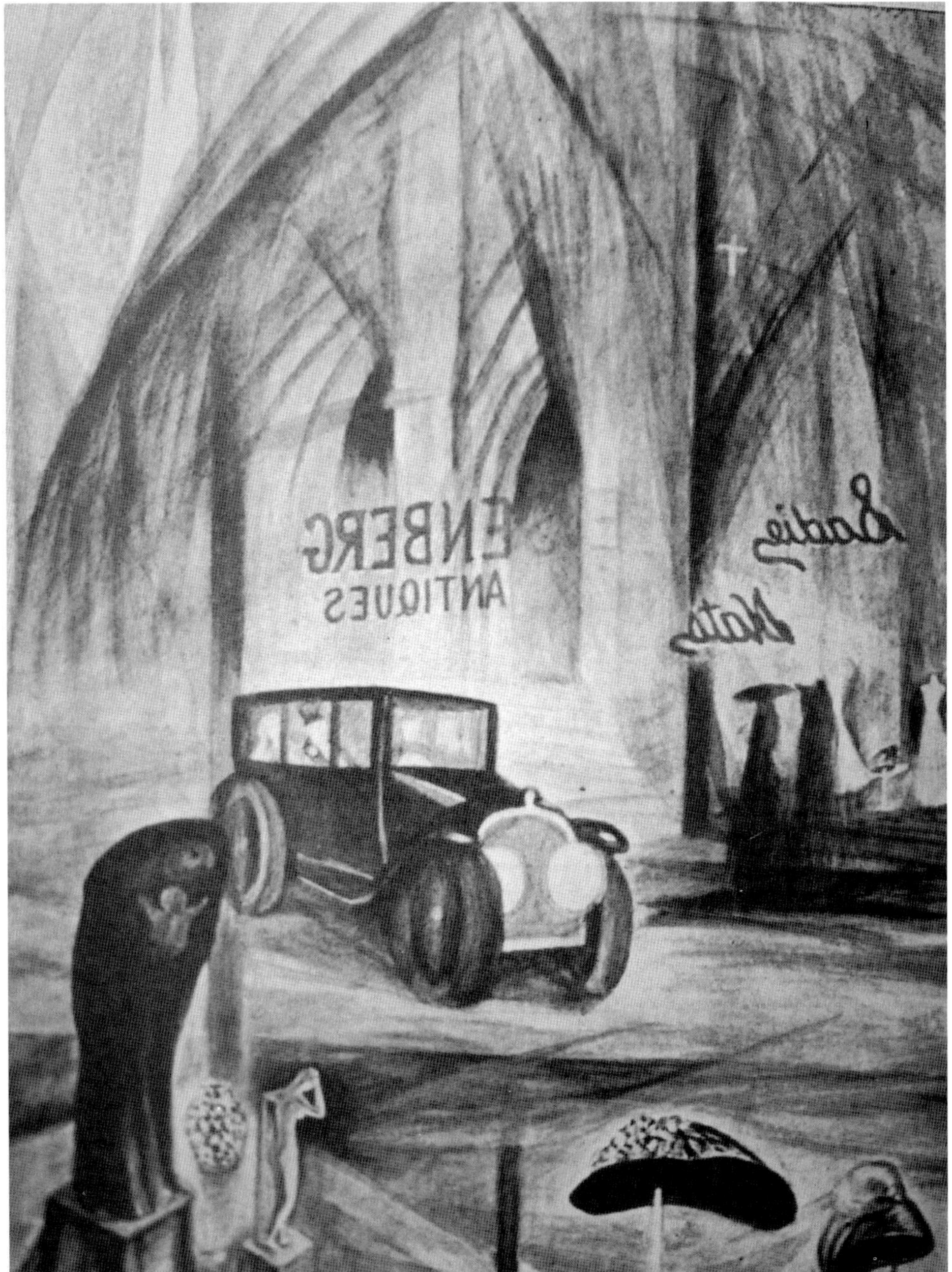

Fig. 19
Walter Pach, *The Automobile (Fifth Avenue),* 1919, watercolor, location unknown.

are clearly recognizable objects—yet the schematic manner of depicting forms that he used in earlier paintings such as *The Cathedral* (fig. 17), *Sunday Night (St. Patrick's at Night)* (plate 5), *Petrouchka* (fig. 18), and *The Lily of the Valley* (plate 6) remains present in this image. The church in the background—probably Saint Patrick's—is sketchy compared with the clearly defined sculpture of the Virgin and Child in the foreground shopwindow. In this image, Pach seems to be consciously contrasting the fashionably dressed individuals in the shining new car and the latest styles of Sadie's Hats with the church architecture and antique statuary. He presented the old and new existing side by side in the dynamic, modern city of New York. This concept of juxtaposing the past and present may have been inspired by the beliefs of Duchamp-Villon, whose vision of the modern world paid tribute to the traditions of the past and simultaneously embraced the latest technological advances, such as contemporary automobiles. It also may have been influenced, as Antliff argues, by the unanimist beliefs of Mercereau and other members of the Puteaux Group.

Pach's transitional phase, this period when he combined cubist and realist elements in his art, was quite short-lived, and by the end of World War I he was returning to full-fledged naturalism. As his style became more decidedly naturalistic, much of his subject matter became more specifically American. These changes were not unique to Pach; rather, they were consistent with the general developments in the art of both his European and American colleagues. By continuing to alter his approach to art, Pach remained relevant, and while his works were not revolutionary in form or content, they were significant in that they continued to address the vital issues of the day.

Modern Art Exhibition Organizer

The Armory Show ignited widespread interest in avant-garde painting and sculpture throughout the United States, and before the exhibition even closed in Boston, officials from museums, galleries, and art organizations across the nation wrote to the AAPS and requested loans from the show for their institutions. Kuhn wrote Pach,

The office is now being overrun by various groups and individuals who are anxious to get up traveling sections of our show, or in any case secure the names of purchasers. I had a long consultation with Mr. Davies on the subject, and we came to the following agreement which we think absolutely necessary: That as far as the association is concerned, there are to be no other fractional exhibits out of our show, and under no condition will we give the name of purchasers. There is no doubt that a lot of these small piece shows would discount the effect of our exhibition. Davies tells me that you were practically of the same opinion, which I was glad to hear.[1]

Although Pach may have been "of the same opinion" as Kuhn and Davies, he had his own ideas, and by the summer of 1913 the coalition was starting to show some signs of dissolution. Kuhn wrote, "Davies phoned me this AM. He sure was glad to see me and it gradually leaked out that he has grown tired of too much *Pach.* D[avies] says Pach is merely a man with an acquired encyclopedia and *no personal judgment.* I was right when I thought that it would only be a matter of time and he would get wise to Mr. W.P. Pach has evidently been rubbing it in and hung too heavily on D's neck."[2] Pach was strong-willed and could be a bit overbearing in his demeanor, and while he had an encyclopedic knowledge of the history of art, he was often too ponderous in his pronouncements. For his part, Kuhn

was fiercely protective of his relationship with Davies (and others) and was clearly pleased with Davies's change of attitude toward Pach, whom Kuhn seems to have viewed as a rival. Kuhn had already taken a slight dislike to Pach when the two worked in Paris in the fall of 1912, and his aversion to him grew in the following years.[3] Davies, Kuhn, and Pach were all very forceful personalities in their own ways, and it is easy to imagine that without the major task of the Armory Show to keep them focused, they would inevitably have splintered into disagreement; however, they managed to put their differences aside to help mount exhibitions of advanced art following the Armory Show.

Soon after the Armory Show closed, an exhibition of cubist and futurist paintings was held in Milwaukee, Cleveland, Pittsburgh, New York, and Philadelphia from May through the summer of 1913.[4] The display was sponsored by the Gimbel Brothers department store of Milwaukee. It included works by Pierre Dumont, Gleizes, Arpad Kesmarky, Léger, Metzinger, Gustave Miklos, and Villon. Since Pach knew virtually all these artists, it is highly likely that he was somehow involved with the arrangements for the exhibition. He received a letter from Duchamp-Villon dated April 18, 1913, stating that a commission agency had requested a group of cubist paintings for the United States, probably a reference to this exhibition.[5]

The first show of contemporary art in the United States with which Pach can be linked definitively was an exhibition of works by American artists that opened at the Carnegie Institute in Pittsburgh on December 1, 1913, and traveled to the Montross Gallery in New York, the Detroit Museum of Art (now called the Detroit Institute of Arts), the Cincinnati Art Museum, and the Peabody Institute (now the Peabody Gallery of Art) at Johns Hopkins University in Baltimore.[6] The show was originally organized by Davies and Kuhn under the auspices of the Art Society of Pittsburgh, and they seem to have been largely responsible for the Pittsburgh and Manhattan venues. Pach, however, arranged the appearance of this groundbreaking exhibition in Detroit, Cincinnati, and Baltimore from March through May 1914 and was also responsible for recruiting at least one artist, Manierre Dawson, to the cause.

Soon after the show opened in Pittsburgh, Pach began writing museum personnel across the country to secure additional venues for the exhibition. In December 1913, he wrote to the director of the Cincinnati Art Museum:

> The Art Society of Pittsburgh having requested a group of paintings from the artists most in sympathy with the modern developments in France, the following men are now holding an exhibition at the Carnegie Institute in Pittsburgh: Arthur B. Davies, Maurice Prendergast, Walt Kuhn, William Glackens, George F. Of, Joseph Stella, C. R. Sheeler Jr., M. L. Schamberg, Allen Tucker, E. L. MacRae and myself. Since the paintings have gone so far, and since other cities on hearing of the exhibition have applied for it, we thought we might as well let it go on for the rest of the season and I accordingly write to ask whether you would want it for your gallery. The enclosed notices will tell you something of it, the article in our conservative "Evening Post" being interesting as showing how opinion has been turning in favor of modern work since the International Exhibition when papers like the "Post" were generally our determined opponents.[7]

He wrote an almost identical letter to Clyde Burroughs of the Detroit Museum of Art and sent him "a catalogue" of the show and "advance notices from New York papers." Being the adept salesperson that he was, Pach put his best pitch forward and stated, "So many applications have been received from the galleries of various cities that we have decided to continue it for the rest of the season, which is now completely scheduled off save for the month of January. . . . I am writing to two other galleries so that the letters may arrive at about the same time and would beg you to let me know promptly if you want the exhibition for the Detroit Museum as the time is short and we must make arrangements as soon as possible."[8]

How could they refuse?

Through his keen negotiating skills, Pach secured both the Cincinnati and Detroit venues and managed to book the Peabody Institute as well. The Exhibition of Modern Art was seen at the Detroit Museum of Art from March 1 to 14, 1914. At the Cincinnati Art Museum, the Special Exhibition: Modern Departures in Painting; "Cubism," "Futurism," Etc. ran from March 19 to April 5, and the show, under the same title, was hung at the Peabody Institute from April 15 to May 15. Pach handled almost all the administrative details for these venues before, during, and after the exhibition and corresponded with museum officials regularly. He arranged for insuring and shipping the art and forwarded catalogs, photographs, and press notices concerning the exhibition's success to the institutions involved. He was also responsible for obtaining payment from the museums that covered shipping and insurance fees as well as from the artists, who each paid a portion of expenses.

The art displayed in this exhibition varied at each institution depending on the sale and withdrawal of pieces. In Pittsburgh, forty paintings by Davies, Glackens, Kuhn, MacRae, Of, Pach, Maurice Prendergast, Schamberg, Sheeler, Stella, and Tucker were shown.[9] The Montross Gallery catalog lists forty-one pictures by title and includes works by Dawson, Henry Fitch Taylor, and Howard Coluzzi that were not exhibited at the Carnegie Institute. Also mentioned in the New York brochure were drawings in watercolor, colored pencil, pastel, and chalk. Several works were not for sale, and those that were ranged in price from ten dollars for a charcoal drawing by Dawson to three thousand dollars for *The Great Mother* by Davies.[10] In Detroit, Cincinnati, and Baltimore about seventy-six works—oils, pencil drawings, watercolors, and pastels—were exhibited, but not all appeared in the accompanying catalogs.

The success of the undertaking in igniting interest in the new art can be judged by the number of newspaper articles devoted to it, the attendance records, and the sale of at least nineteen pieces. The show received mixed reviews in the press, but as one critic wrote, it was "probably the most important event in art circles this week."[11] The museum officials were also pleased with the results. John H. Gest, director of the Cincinnati Art Museum, reported, "The collection was extremely well received here and interested a large number of people, who studied it rather carefully and succeeded rather surprisingly in appreciating the trend of your work."[12] Shortly after the opening at the Peabody Institute, director Louis H. Dielman informed Pach, "The exhibit is drawing large crowds."[13] Among the sales was one of Pach's "cubistic" watercolors, either *Progression No. 2* or *Progression No. 3.*[14] Some of the works that were sold from the New York venue of the show were bought by Quinn, who had begun to amass quite a collection of modern art, some of it under Pach's guidance. Without Pach's efforts it is highly unlikely that this exhibition would have traveled to Detroit and Cincinnati. He was responsible for bringing advanced American art to midwestern audiences at a very early date and, perhaps, helping influence artists and collectors there toward an appreciation of modernism.

Sometime amid the flurry of activities in February 1914, Pach and Magdalene Frohberg married.[15] Initially,

the couple had planned to wed in Dresden, but there is no evidence that they traveled abroad at this time, and they probably were married in New York. They may have had a religious ceremony, since Frohberg was Lutheran, but the exact circumstances of their wedding remain unknown. They lived with Pach's parents for a short time at 1135 Park Avenue, but by mid-March they had a place of their own at 33 Beekman Place.[16] As Pach explained to Dawson in April 1914, "Getting married, moving to the above address, fixing the place up (that was the tremendous work) and keeping up with other necessary jobs has made my time fuller than at most other periods I have known. We are just beginning to feel settled now and soon shall be sending out cards."[17] This was the young couple's first home, but it certainly would not be their last.

Following the Montross Gallery's lead, several other commercial enterprises in New York began to show contemporary paintings and sculptures in the years following the Armory Show. Most of these establishments had not dealt in modern art before, but none wanted to miss the opportunity for sales generated by the newfound interest in contemporary works. Further, new galleries opened that focused specifically on modernism. Pach became the European representative for three Manhattan galleries: Montross, Carroll, and Bourgeois. He served as the intermediary between these dealers and artists such as Matisse, Derain, Redon, Dufy, and the Duchamp brothers. In addition to supporting foreign works, he encouraged the New York galleries to promote the art of Americans such as his good friends Maurice Prendergast, Schamberg, and Stella.

Throughout the 1910s, Pach helped arrange many exhibitions of modern art in the United States and negotiated sales of works by contemporary European and American artists in New York City and elsewhere. Later in life he explained, "By means of the Armory Show and other exhibitions I made, and my writing, a tremendous amount was done for the whole of America, and precious help (through purchasing here) went back to France."[18] Pach was instrumental in spreading modern art across the United States, beyond the confines of the elite art world of the East Coast. He usually worked behind the scenes, preferring to remain out of the limelight, and he also worked for scant pay. His motivations were unselfish—a love of art and admiration for his fellow artists—although others would not see him in such an altruistic light. Regarding these early exhibitions, Pach explained in *Queer Thing, Painting*, "We decided to follow up the International with more exhibitions. Only a few people would get the benefit of them at first, but in the long run a taste for real things in art would be strengthened. Duchamp-Villon agreed to assemble in Paris a large group of works that would carry on the idea of the Armory through the season of 1914–1915."[19]

One of the individuals who wished to see more exhibitions of modern art was John Quinn. In her analysis of Quinn as a collector, Judith Zilczer noted that despite the increasing number of venues selling contemporary art, he wanted "more direct control of the new market in modern art" and looked about for a place to make this happen.[20] From the outset, Quinn envisioned Pach as a vital force in the undertaking, and in November 1913, he sent a letter to Mrs. Charles C. Rumsey, in which he wrote, "The idea of a gallery for the exhibition and sale of contemporary art, both European and American, about which Mr. Pach tells me he has spoken to you, has appealed to me as the best means of furthering the appreciation in America of vital living art. . . . Our artists and public need a gallery conducted by such a man as Mr. Pach as a guide to the best art of today."[21]

In 1914, Quinn approached Harriet C. Bryant, proprietor of the Carroll Galleries, and suggested that she expand her decorating business to include the exhibition and sale of vanguard European and American art. It is unclear whether Quinn provided financial backing for the gallery; however, his subsequent purchases certainly helped sustain the business. Pach

became one of the prime movers in this enterprise; among his main responsibilities were securing loans of art from the Continent and organizing exhibitions of contemporary European and American art.

Throughout the spring and summer of 1914, Pach worked tirelessly to arrange for shows of modern work in New York for the coming season. In April, he wrote enthusiastically to Matisse about the show of American modernists that had been held at Montross a few months earlier, commenting that they (most likely meaning Davies, Kuhn, and Pach) had convinced the dealer that a show of works by Matisse should be the "pièce de resistance" of the 1914–15 season.[22] In July, Pach wrote to Souza Cardoso that Bryant had asked him and his associates to invite European artists to exhibit the following season. He had also been corresponding with Duchamp-Villon about the show at the Carroll Galleries. These were but a few exhibitions that were being planned; however, history would soon intervene and jeopardize all their plans. Pach later recalled, "But then came the war, my friend [Raymond Duchamp-Villon] was mobilized, as were all the other men of military age, and there was no one to carry out the plans and to ship the works to America. At first the beautiful shows we had planned seemed lost, but when the battle of the Marne had been fought and we felt sure . . . the Germans would not take Paris, it was decided that I should go abroad and collect the promised exhibits."[23]

In October 1914, Pach undertook the dangerous wartime journey to France. He arrived in Paris on October 15 determined to acquire as many works as possible from Matisse and other colleagues for display in the United States. Immediately after his arrival, and with much urgency, he sent a note to Matisse's studio and asserted that he had "other similar commissions to occupy himself" but that Matisse's exhibition was "the only one for M. Montross and our Association."[24] In his later years, Pach recollected, "I had gone to Paris as the representative of Montross and of the Carroll Galleries (officially—in reality it was out of interest in having the work of the Armory Show continue)." He did not receive any salary or commission for this work: "I got my expenses—not a cent over my expenses."[25] Pach was not in the business for the money. His journey to Paris during the war was a true labor of love, as was so much of his work on behalf of all artists.

With boundless energy and determination, Pach visited scores of his painter and sculptor friends, as well as dealers and collectors, during his whirlwind month-long trip. Time was of the essence, and Pach spent day and night calling on Picasso, Dufy, Rouault, Redon, Brancusi, Derain's wife, and others. He rallied the artists and encouraged them to send works to the United States. In his autobiography, he recalled, "Redon, Dufy, Rouault, and others had responded again to our call, and New York answered their confidence and proved that the enormous success of the Armory was no accident: Americans were ready to support a better art than what they had been offered before in current production."[26] Pach was one of those "ready to support a better art," and while in Paris he purchased Derain's *Portrait of Madame Derain* from the painter's wife. He considered this work to be one of Derain's finest paintings, and it remained a treasured possession throughout his life. He later remarked, "I was deeply impressed with it when I first saw it on the wall of his studio in October 1914, when he was at the front and had been wounded. The money I paid for it meant an almost unreasonable sacrifice for me, but it enabled Mme. Derain to travel to see him in the hospital."[27] Pach was a true romantic at heart.

Since Matisse was not in Paris, Pach wrote Michael Stein, who told him where to find the painter and encouraged him to convince the artist of the necessity of sending his works to the United States. When Matisse returned to Paris, Pach visited with him several times and also introduced him to Duchamp-Villon at the sculptor's Puteaux studio. Before Pach left France, Matisse made a quick portrait etching of him as a token of his affection and friendship (fig. 20). Pach, while he was in Paris, also managed to create at least one watercolor of his own, which he probably gave as a gift to Matisse. By the time he left France on November 18, Pach had secured the loan of dozens of paintings, sculptures, and works on paper from artists, collectors, and dealers for the Montross and Carroll galleries for the upcoming season in New York—a tremendous effort in the best of circumstances, but a monumental feat in the midst of war.

When Pach left for Paris, he left a very pregnant wife behind; Mrs. Pach was due in December. While her husband was away, Magda spent a good deal of time with her in-laws. Pach's mother wrote him in Paris that she saw Magda "once or twice a week and am always glad to be with her" and reported that she looked well.[28] On December 26, 1914, Raymond Pach was born (he would be their only child).[29] Raymond was named after Pach's good friend Raymond Duchamp-Villon. He was raised "in the German Lutheran faith" and "baptized into the Episcopal Church."[30] Pach was not a very religious person, so he left this aspect of his son's upbringing to his wife.

Perhaps because of the stress of travel, work, and marriage, Pach's health began to shown signs of weakness. Sometime in 1914, he began to suffer from what he called attacks of colic, described as bouts of acute abdominal pain. He also suffered from kidney problems, as did his father and his uncle, Oscar. He did not, however, go to a doctor at this time to have his illness diagnosed. He simply waited for the problem to pass and hoped it would not recur again for a while.

Pach's hard work in Paris paid off in the form of numerous exhibitions in New York City in late 1914 and throughout 1915. Soon after he had returned from overseas, Pach met with Davies, Kuhn, and Quinn to plan the 1914–15 season at the Carroll Galleries. The First Exhibition of Works by Contemporary French Artists opened in December 1914 and closed on January 2, 1915; Pach's friends Derain, the Duchamp brothers,

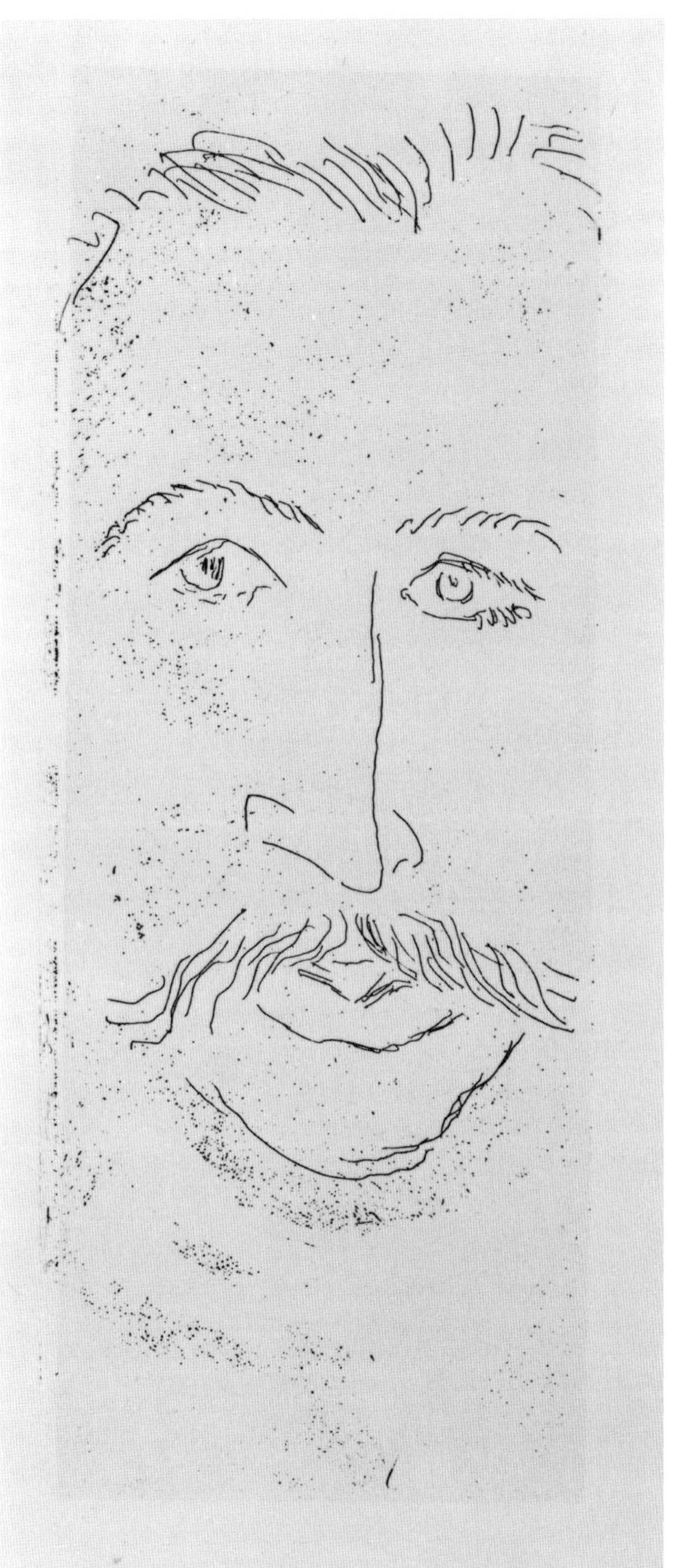

Henri Matisse, *Portrait of Walter Pach,* 1914, etching, plate 6 ⁵⁄₁₆ × 2 ⅜ in. (16.1 × 6.1 cm), sheet 10 ⅝ × 7 ½ in. (27 × 19 cm). Stephen C. Clark Fund (43.1951), The Museum of Modern Art, New York, NY. Image © The Museum of Modern Art/Licensed by SCALA/Art Resource, NY. © 2011 Succession H. Matisse/ Artists Rights Society (ARS), New York.

Gleizes, Dufy, and André and Paul Véra were among the exhibitors. The Second Exhibition of Works by Contemporary French Artists opened shortly after the first show closed and ran until February 13. It consisted of oil paintings, sculptures, and ceramics. Among the artists represented were Redon, Rouault, Duchamp-Villon, Paul Véra, Jean-Paul Lafitte, Louis Valtat, Gustave Moreau, Auguste Chabaud, Maurice de Vlaminck, André Dunoyer de Segonzac, Dufy, and Renoir. There was virtually no downtime between exhibitions at the Carroll Galleries; the Third Exhibition of Contemporary French Art opened on March 8 and ran until April 3, 1915. Among the forty-six works shown were paintings and sculptures by Picasso, van Gogh, Gauguin, Derain, Duchamp, Duchamp-Villon, Roger de la Fresnaye, Gleizes, Metzinger, Georges Ribemont-Dessaignes, and Villon. This show was much more cubist in its orientation than the previous one and included some of the most experimental art of the day, such as Picasso's *The Guitarist* and Duchamp's *The Chocolate Grinder I* and *Chocolate Grinder II*. Since Pach knew all the living artists involved, he was responsible for securing the loans from these painters, and he corresponded with them regarding sales. He also wrote the very brief introductions to the small brochures printed for the exhibitions. In addition, Pach borrowed a painting by Gauguin, *A Tahitian,* from Matisse, who wished to sell the work.[31] Theodore Druet, a well-known Parisian art dealer and a colleague of Pach's, lent the *Still Life* by van Gogh.[32] Although Bryant was theoretically the director of the gallery, Pach took charge of the exhibition, probably at Quinn's request. In fact, Pach had a hand in virtually every show mounted at the Carroll Galleries in these years.

Through his trip abroad, Pach also helped organize the first major show of works by Matisse in the United States, held at Montross Gallery from January 20 to February 27, 1915. Pach was an indispensable contact for Matisse and, as Matisse scholar John Cauman has noted, was "Matisse's principal promoter

stateside" until the artist's son Pierre arrived in 1924.[33] Pach handled virtually all the administrative details for the show: securing works and photographs from the artist, borrowing pieces from dealers such as Bernheim, and arranging for the shipment and insurance of the art. Matisse's works arrived in mid-January 1915, and Pach supervised their unpacking and hanging. While the exhibition was on display, Pach corresponded with Matisse regularly and kept him apprised of public and critical reaction and sales.[34] Early in March 1915, he sent Matisse a list of the works that had sold at the show, which included fifty-four lithographs, seventy etchings, and six sculptures. Montross took a rather large, 50 percent commission. Pach also reported on Henry McBride's favorable review of the show. McBride, he noted, was "the only one among the critics who is worth reading."[35] With the success of the undertaking, Montross asked Pach to acquire more works, prints in particular, from Matisse for sale through his gallery, and the artist obliged. The monotypes Montross ordered arrived at the beginning of March and sold immediately. "Mr. Davies," Pach informed the artist, "bought them all for himself."[36] A month later Montross asked for more lithographs. As a gesture of thanks, Matisse gave his good friend Pach a monotype, adding to Pach's growing collection of contemporary art.

Besides organizing the one-person show at Montross Gallery, Pach arranged for the sale of Matisse's prints through the Carroll Galleries. In March 1915, he wrote the artist, "Miss Bryant, director of the Carroll Galleries asks me to order from you a copy of each plate of your series of etchings, those which were at Montross and the others. I have not fixed a price for her, but I suppose that she would want the same conditions as Montross."[37]

In addition to organizing exhibitions of European art, Pach was interested in promoting contemporary American art and helped Quinn arrange a show of works by his friend Maurice Prendergast at the Carroll Galleries. The exhibition opened in February

1915 and consisted of twenty-nine paintings and thirty-one watercolors. When he wrote about the exhibition later in life, Pach observed, "One show we arranged of a work by a native painter at the same gallery as housed the Redons, Picassos, etc., gave the most inspiring evidence that Americans could no more than import modern art—they could produce it. The exhibition I speak of was that of Maurice Prendergast."[38] Pach had known the artist and his brother, Charles, for many years and was a staunch supporter of Maurice's work. From this show Quinn purchased seven oils and nine watercolors, mainly on Pach's recommendation.

In addition to these undertakings, Pach began to assist the French dealer Stéphan Bourgeois, who had opened a gallery in New York in 1911, with exhibitions and other dealings. In October 1915, the two started planning a show of contemporary European art that would open the following spring. Pach wrote Matisse immediately:

> Yesterday I was able to arrange an exhibition more or less exactly as I wished—and in a gallery that has some advantages that the Montross gallery has not. First Bourgeois Gallery has only sold works from the best schools: Rembrandt, Greco, Goya, the Primitives very important, Chinese and Gothic sculptures, Cézanne, Van Gogh, Toulouse-Lautrec, Manet, etc., etc. . . . Bourgeois Gallery is only three rooms but with the best daylight possible, magnificently equipped, in the quarter the most chic of all New York, and his clientele is the most serious and even distinguished—to the point of view of the collectors who have bought there. We have the ambition of offering especially one of the great paintings of Seurat. . . . We will invite Signac, and then you, Derain, Rouault, Dufy, Picasso and Braque (this last has never been sufficiently represented here). Then Duchamp and Gleizes who are here would contribute something, and Of, Stella

and me. . . . The exhibition will probably be in the month of March. All the expenses: packing, insurance, transport and return of the works not sold will be paid by us.[39]

To this invitation Matisse responded, "I thank you for arranging to show my monotypes as part of your exhibition at Bourgeois, and since you still wish to add one or two paintings (one or two?) of small dimensions, plus a few drawings, I am overwhelmed."[40] For this show, Pach also requested loans from Bernheim, and Pach suggested to Matisse that the latter send his paintings through this dealer. Pach also contacted Signac regarding the loan of Signac's work and of a Seurat painting, but Signac declined. The planning for this exhibition continued throughout the fall of 1915 and into 1916.

Pach longed to return to France, but he remained stateside throughout the war, promoting contemporary European and American art through exhibitions for the Montross, Carroll, and Bourgeois galleries. His remarkably energetic constitution was pressed to its limits. Early in 1916, Pach helped arrange an exhibition for Montross of seven oil paintings and thirty watercolors by Cézanne, borrowed from Fénéon of Bernheim Jeune.[41] This was one of the largest showings of Cézanne's work in the United States to date, giving American audiences a broader perspective on the artist's oeuvre. Pach also had a hand in another show at Montross, the Exhibition of Pictures by Jean Crotti, Marcel Duchamp, Albert Gleizes, Jean Metzinger (also referred to as "The Four Musketeers Show"). Duchamp, Gleizes, and Crotti were living in New York at the time, and all were friends with Pach. This show introduced some of the most avant-garde French art of the day to the New York art scene, causing quite a stir and once more forcing many American artists to rethink their ideas about art.

One of the biggest shows with which Pach was involved in the spring of 1916 was The Exhibition of

Modern Art Arranged by a Group of European and American Artists in New York, held at Bourgeois Gallery. Initially, the strong Continental character of the show offended some American exhibitors, but, as Pach informed Matisse, "the petty nationalism that one had tried to throw inside has failed to advance, and I am certain of that (see my preface in the catalogue, I respond there without note)."[42] In the show were oil paintings, pastels, drawings, and monotypes by French painters and sculptors such as Cézanne, Matisse, Metzinger, Duchamp (*The King and the Queen Surrounded by Swift Nudes*), Picasso, Georges Seurat (*Study for "A Sunday on La Grande Jatte"*—now in the Metropolitan Museum of Art), Signac, van Gogh, Hunt Diderich, and Duchamp-Villon, as well as works by Pach and some of his American colleagues; among these were Arnold Friedman, Maurice Prendergast, Schamberg, and Stella. Pach served as agent for the European artists and dealers who lent their works, and he also wrote the preface to the catalog. After the show closed, Pach reported to Matisse, "The exhibition at Bourgeois was a success and I am doubly happy of it, because the effect amongst the public is very important and then the fact of having obtained and justified the support of M. Bourgeois is a solid base for the developments to come. . . . All the works sold have been acquired by some Americans; the foreign artists, or their representatives have deals unique with me, who is American, and have received the amounts resulting from their sale from me, who is in some manner the secretary of the group."[43] In 1917 and 1918, Pach helped organize two more such shows, which included the artists previously mentioned and others such as Americans John R. Covert, Glackens, John Marin, Man Ray, Sheeler, George F. Of, Oscar Bluemner, and Abraham Walkowitz and French artists Robert Delaunay, Henri Rousseau, and Gaston Lachaise.

Since the Parisian art market was at a standstill during the war, many European artists turned to Pach for assistance in selling their work in the United States, and Pach gladly obliged. In May 1916, Gino Severini, the Italian futurist, wrote to Pach and asked whether an exhibition of Severini's work would be possible in New York.[44] Pach replied with several letters and contacted Alfred Stieglitz and Marius de Zayas on the artist's behalf. After a year of corresponding through Pach and de Zayas, Stieglitz in 1917 finally gave Severini his first one-person show in the United States, at 291. Pach also corresponded with Souza Cardoso and attempted to arrange an exhibition of his work at de Zayas's Modern Gallery. Unfortunately, the show did not materialize.

In the fall of 1916, Pach once more became heavily involved with planning exhibitions for the following year. The battle for the acceptance of modernism in the United States was being hard fought, as Pach explained to Matisse: "It is not always a rapid process, but we make some progress, new amateurs present themselves from time to time, the public becomes always a little more favorable, finally it is in driving in the direction that we have taken that we will form a solid group of appreciators of sincere efforts." Pach and Bourgeois met again to organize a show that would help advance "the art in which we believe." Pach told Matisse, "M. Bourgeois has had the idea of asking you to gather a small group of painters who have been more or less around you, who have exhibited in the same sections of the Salons, who would be sympathetic to you in a word. I have thought that these would be Rouault, Derain, Dufy perhaps. But you would be entirely free (within the limits of the space of his gallery) to form the ensemble that would please you."[45]

Unfortunately, the conflict in Europe made it extremely difficult to insure and ship works of art from France, and the show that they envisioned was postponed. Pach informed Matisse, "We are doing all that is possible to advance the appreciation of modern art here. Despite a strong opposition we gain ground."[46] Late in 1916, he dispatched another letter to Matisse reporting that a show consisting principally of modern European paintings already in the United States was planned. Furthermore, he explained, "an exhibition of you only, or of you and the painters that you would choose as neighbors, would come better next year where we hope the conditions are more favorable."[47]

Ever on the lookout for new art galleries or bookstores with art and art books, Pach discovered one of Erhard Weyhe's book and print enterprises around this time. When he walked by the shop, he saw "a modest row of books in a plumber's show-window"; upon further investigation he noticed, much to his delight, that they were all art books. He also found that inside the store were lithographs and other prints by artists such as Toulouse-Lautrec. As he later recalled, "I entered [and] my fate as a regular customer was sealed."[48] Pach became a frequent visitor to the bookseller, especially after his friend Carl Zigrosser was brought on board to oversee the print shop. Pach, among others, recommended Zigrosser to Weyhe and vice versa.

Besides the war, another major obstacle to the acceptance of modernism was the conservative sector of the New York art world. Painters and critics such as Kenyon Cox and Royal Cortissoz denounced the new art and created an atmosphere unfavorable for its reception. Although a few collectors such as Quinn and Arensberg purchased contemporary works, large-scale private and public support was not forthcoming. Financial markets in the United States were unstable because of the war, and the scanty disposable income available to people was not spent on art. Yet artists and dealers persevered, with Pach quietly working in the background, providing encouragement and expertise.

In May 1917, tragedy struck Pach's family; his mother, Frances Wise Pach, died. She had undergone "long months of suffering" before she passed, an experience that deeply affected her son.[49] Pach had always been especially close with his mother and was devastated by her death. While Pach's family suffered this crisis, he steadfastly continued his work on behalf of his foreign colleagues. He remained convinced of the need

for the European artists to have their works shown in the United States, and he kept up his correspondence with them and assisted in the sale and exhibition of their works. Severini wrote several times in reference to his exhibition at Stieglitz's 291 gallery, thanking Pach for his assistance and praising him for his efforts. He also congratulated him on the success of the first Independents and authorized him to use any works not sold from the 291 show for other exhibitions in the United States. Pach also corresponded with Madame Redon regarding the works by her husband that remained in the United States and wrote to Brancusi regularly. These artists had faith in Pach's ability to sell their works and maintained utmost trust in his integrity.

Most of Pach's work in organizing exhibitions during these years involved modern European art, but he was interested in American art as well. For example, en route home from a summer of teaching at the University of California, Berkeley, in 1918, Pach, with his family, stopped in Santa Fe, visiting the Palace of the Governors, where he met Dr. Edgar Hewett of the museum. Pach was drawn to the art of the region and enthralled by the Native American art he saw on display. He purchased several tiles for himself and for his friends Morton Schamberg and Charles Sheeler.[50] This was the beginning of a lifelong love affair for Pach; he rapidly became engrossed in studying Native American art and culture and promoting it within the New York art world. He, along with John Sloan, was one of the first to do so. When Pach arrived back in New York, he quickly approached the Metropolitan Museum of Art and made a proposal for an exhibition of "Indian Art." He reported to Hewett, "Immediately after my return to New York I went to see Bryson Burroughs, the Curator of Paintings at the Metropolitan Museum and laid the idea before him. He liked it quite as much as I had hoped he would and said he would speak for it if he had the chance: Dr. Robinson, the Director, being the one who must past on it [sic]. I wrote Dr. Robinson, who replied that the idea was a very interesting one but that lack of space combined with an agreement made with the Museum of Natural History to leave Indian matters to the latter institution forbade his taking up the plan."

Undeterred, Pach approached several commercial galleries in New York; however, as he informed Hewett, "the interest in art matters seems so utterly banished for the time being that I am in some doubt whether our efforts would not be nearly fruitless—I mean as compared with results we might obtain at a time when it would be easier to get the attention of the public and important men."[51] Although the plan did not come to fruition at this time, neither Pach nor Hewett abandoned hope.

Devastating news arrived in the fall of 1918: one of Pach's closest friends, Raymond Duchamp-Villon, had died. Duchamp-Villon had contracted typhoid fever while working in a hospital at the front in 1916 and suffered for two years before he succumbed to uremia, a disease of the blood cause by kidney problems. Pach was crushed. He wrote Quinn, "I can not say what his loss means to me—I had counted on being with him again after the war."[52] The war and its carnage haunted and infuriated Pach, and he struggled in his heart and mind with his inability to serve. Pach was not a pacifist; he was exempt from the draft because of flat feet.[53] He debated whether to offer his services as an interpreter but felt that he was "more use in my studio than at the front."[54] Pach, like the rest of the world, was greatly relieved when the armistice was announced and the war ended in November 1918.

Throughout the late 1910s and the 1920s, Pach continued his support for modern art in the United States by helping to organize other exhibitions in the country. In the spring of 1920 he was asked to create a show of the latest modern works for the Worcester Museum of Art in Massachusetts. Because of his reputation as an insider in the contemporary American art scene, he was left to make the final selection of pieces that would be sent. He personally invited

Charles Prendergast, Gaston Lachaise, Reynolds Beal, and Haley Lever to participate. Among the other artists whose works were shown at the Exhibition of Modern Art by Contemporary Artists were George Bellows, Jerome Blum, Catherine C. Critcher, Stuart Davis, William Glackens, Robert Henri, Leon Kroll, Jonas Lie, Maurice Prendergast, Mary C. Rogers, Morton L. Schamberg, Henrietta M. Shore, John Sloan, Maurice Sterne, Florine Stettheimer, and Max Weber. Pach was responsible for securing most of the works by these artists, all of whom he knew personally, and through this show he helped promote modern American art at yet another venue outside New York art circles.

Toward the end of 1920, Pach was approached by the exhibition committee of the Art Gallery of Toronto to assist with their Exhibition of Paintings by Contemporary American Artists, which ran from January 8 through February 6, 1921. The preface in the catalog noted, "In order to have the modernists adequately represented we were fortunate in securing the co-operation of Mr. Walter Pach, Treasurer of the Society of Independent Artists. About twenty pictures of the ultra-modern movements in painting selected by him and shown together in one of the rooms, may be taken as thoroughly representing the American adherents of Cezanne, Van Gough [sic] and Gaugin [sic]."[55] Among those whom Pach selected were his friends and colleagues, including Hugh Breckenridge, Arthur B. Davies, Marsden Hartley, Alfred Maurer, George F. Of, Maurice Prendergast, Morton Schamberg, Charles Sheeler, and John Sloan. This show helped bring modern American art to yet another audience beyond Manhattan, this time an international one.

Also in the early 1920s, Pach was involved with two shows of works by Vincent van Gogh. He was one of the earliest and most avid admirers of the artist's paintings, which he had discovered in a bookshop window while working in Haarlem in the fall of 1906. In the summer of 1917, while on vacation at the beach at Edgemere, near Rockaway Park, Long Island, Pach met

Johanna van Gogh-Bonger, Theo's widow and Vincent's sister-in-law, and her family.[56] Their friendship had grown in the intervening years, so when the Montross Gallery began organizing an exhibition toward the end of 1920, Pach was contacted for assistance. This was one of the earliest and largest displays of van Gogh's art in the United States and consisted of thirty-two oil paintings and thirty-five watercolors, drawings, and lithographs. Two works in the exhibition, *Portrait of Adeline Ravoux* and *The Sower,* were acquired by Theodore Pitcairn. The Pitcairn family fortune was amassed through the Pittsburgh Plate Glass Company (now PPG Industries), founded by Theodore's father. The middle of three sons, Theodore was a minister as well as an avid art collector, purchasing works by Monet, El Greco, and three by Van Gogh. In 1923, Pach seems to have been involved with the exhibition of van Gogh paintings in the Exhibition of Dutch and Flemish Pictures XV to XX Century, from the Goudstikker collection, held at the Anderson Gallery that spring. He corresponded with Johanna van Gogh-Bonger (who was back home in the Netherlands) regularly and ensured the pictures' safe return. In gratitude, she sent him an exquisite drawing by Vincent van Gogh to add to his growing art collection.

Among other exhibitions with which Pach was affiliated during these years was the Exhibition of Modern German Paintings from the Detroit Institute of Arts, held at the Des Moines Art Association April 7–21, 1924.[57] It is probable that Pach was assisted in the Des Moines endeavor by Wilhelm Valentiner, who became director of the Detroit Institute of Arts in 1924 and had organized an exhibition of German expressionism at the Anderson Galleries in New York in 1923. Among the artists represented in Des Moines were Otto Mueller, Karl Schmidt-Rottluff, Max Pechstein, Oskar Kokoschka, and Erich Hekel. This was a groundbreaking exhibition of avant-garde European art that had never before been seen in places such as Des Moines, Iowa.

In 1926, Pach organized an exhibition of part of John Quinn's enormous collection of modern art at the Art Center in Manhattan.[58] Located on East Sixty-fifth Street at the time, this organization was funded by the Rockefeller family and was home to several art-related groups. Knowing the collection intimately, he wrote the introduction to the catalog and an article for the *Art Center Bulletin.* "It would be difficult to overestimate the importance of the exhibition of works from Mr. John Quinn's collection at the Art Center," Pach declared. He believed that Quinn's collection served as "a guide for both artists and art-buyers alike."[59]

In 1928, Fiske Kimball, director of the Philadelphia Museum of Art and a personal friend of Pach's, contacted him regarding a show of modern French art for the museum. Kimball wrote Pach that he was in search of good examples of work by Gauguin or van Gogh and thought Pach might be able to help track some down. Pach suggested that Kimball contact the dealers César Mange de Hauke (who ran a subsidiary of Jacques Seligmann and Company in New York City) and Stéphan Bourgeois, both of whom carried works by these painters. He also suggested that Kimball call on the collector Mrs. Lewis Larned Coburn of Chicago, who, he was told by de Hauke, had a "magnificent Gauguin of Tahiti" that she would be willing to lend. In addition, Pach provided Kimball with an introduction to Theodore Pitcairn and recommended that he borrow the *Portrait of Adeline Ravoux* and "a small picture 'The Sower'"—one of several versions of this painting—from the collector (now in the Armand Hammer Museum in Los Angeles).[60] Kimball did not know about the Pitcairn collection, which was located only eighteen miles outside Philadelphia. He informed Pach that when he telephoned for an appointment he found that Pach's name was "an open sesame," providing him access to a private collection to which Pach alone seemed privy.[61]

The gallery that Pach worked most closely with in the 1920s was Joseph Brummer's establishment. Pach and Brummer had known each other for years and had similar interests in historical as well as contemporary art. In 1921, Pach introduced the Prendergast brothers, Charles and Maurice, to Brummer, who subsequently gave them a show that spring. In 1924, Brummer mounted an exhibition of works by Georges Seurat with which Pach was involved and for which he wrote a foreword. Also in 1924, while vacationing in Saint-Tropez during the summer, Pach met Roger Fry and, after several discussions, arranged for a solo exhibition of his work at Brummer's gallery that ran from January 19 to February 7, 1925. As Fry recounted the story to British painter Vanessa Bell, "There was an American artist and writer on art here, Walter Pach—rather a terror in some ways but very much up on modern art and knows all the artists rather well. He's arranged an exhibition for me with a friend of his who keeps a very select gallery."[62] Fry's observation points again to one of the character flaws that others found in Pach: he took art, and himself, too seriously. Pach was not oblivious to his faults, as he readily admitted to his friend Carl Zigrosser: "People have to be tolerant with my one-sided point of view. I am quite conscious that I *am* one-sided but of course add insult to injury my [*sic*] thinking it is the right side."[63]

Between 1928 and 1930, Pach also assisted Brummer in putting together shows devoted to two of the Duchamp brothers: Jacques Villon and Raymond Duchamp-Villon. Pach remained a staunch supporter of both artists' work and wrote the foreword to the exhibition catalogs. The two Villon shows that were mounted, one in 1928 and the other in 1930, consisted of paintings, engravings, and drawings, most for sale. It was probably through or at this exhibition that Pach made the acquaintance of Ida and J. Caesar Guggenheimer. He was a respected lawyer, and Ida was a budding art dealer and civil rights activist. The Pachs and Guggenheimers (especially Walter and Ida) developed a very close relationship and remained good friends for years. Toward the end of 1928, Brummer and

Pach began work on the Memorial Exhibition of the Works of Raymond Duchamp-Villon. Opening in January 1929, it was one of the most comprehensive exhibitions of the artist's work in the United States and consisted of drawings as well as plaster, terra-cotta, marble, stone, bronze, cement, wood, wax, and clay sculptures. The show was quite successful, and several pieces sold both during its run and after it closed, some to Pach's friends, including Beatrice Stein and Ida Guggenheimer.

During the 1920s, some in the New York art world questioned Pach's vehement promotion of modern European art, ignoring his staunch support of American artists. Pach not only helped organize and promote exhibitions of modern European art but also wrote reviews of the shows and made acquisition recommendations to his acquaintances. Many artists, critics, and museum personnel felt that this type of multilevel involvement with both dealers and collectors was completely unethical, and Pach was highly and routinely criticized for his roles in these dealings. These sentiments were openly expressed at a debate on the attitude of museums and collectors toward contemporary American art at the Waldorf-Astoria, sponsored by the Society of Independent Artists in the spring of 1926. With Pach and Rockwell Kent as the main speakers, the floor was open to remarks from the audience. Kent used the platform to launch an attack against Pach and his Francophile leanings. He assailed the museums and collectors who bought European works and admonished dealers and their allies, especially Pach, who encouraged museums to uphold the system of patronage that supported the purchase of non-American art. Pach argued against nationality as a rationale for the support of a particular artist or group of artists. Quality, not nationality, mattered, he contended, and museums should buy and display the best works they could afford regardless of who made them. When audience members Alfred Stieglitz and Gaston Lachaise joined in the assault against Pach's art and critical writings, John

Sloan, president of the Society of Independent Artists, intervened and redirected the discussion back to American art and museums. This was a very divisive issue within the New York art world. Through his gallery, Stieglitz was supporting a small coterie of American modernists, artists whom Pach did not particularly promote. Further, throughout the 1920s, there was a shift in American taste in the arts away from European, modernist, and abstract art toward art that was representational in style and more American in subject matter—works that would be defined as American scene and regionalist painting in the 1930s. Although Pach strongly supported many contemporary American painters and sculptors—Maurice Prendergast, John Sloan, Morris Kantor, Homer Boss, and A. S. Baylinson, to mention but a few—many saw him as only a Francophile and viewed his ideologies as Eurocentric and therefore unacceptable and un-American. This may be one of the reasons that Pach has been ignored in many American art histories.

In the 1930s and 1940s, Pach's role in organizing exhibitions became much more limited, and he was now called upon only occasionally. In 1934, he helped organize the Maurice Prendergast Memorial Exhibition for the Whitney Museum of American Art. Pach had been a promoter of Prendergast's work for more than two decades. He lent two works from his own collection for the show and wrote the foreword to the catalog. In 1940, he assisted with the planning of the Origins of Modern Art show held at the Arts Club of Chicago. Pach organized the seventy-two works on view into thematic sections rather than chronologically: Form, Color, Realism, Vision, Composition, Abstract—Crescendo, Exotic, Science, and so on. As Pach described it in his foreword, this methodology had been used at two other exhibitions the previous year in Boston and New York. Pach's use of it indicates his awareness of new approaches to the study of art history. In his groupings of art, Pach compared Old Masters with more contemporary artists: della Francesco with Courbet and

Renoir, Rubens with van Gogh and Maurice Prendergast, and Nicolas Poussin with Matisse and Picasso, for example. For the Fine Arts Society of San Diego in 1941, Pach curated Watercolors of an Earlier Day, with works by Claude Lorrain, Pissarro, Cézanne, Thomas Gainsborough, John Trumbull, Winslow Homer, and John Marin, among others, borrowed from private and public collections throughout the United States. In late 1943 or early 1944, Pach became affiliated with the Mortimer Brandt Gallery in New York. During this time he and Robert Lebel, a noted French art scholar, dealer, and collector in exile in the United States during the war, selected a group of modern French paintings for an exhibition at the gallery. In 1945, Pach, one of the earliest admirers and promoters of works by African American artists, served as the juror for The Fourth Annual Exhibition of Paintings, Sculptures, and Prints by Negro Artists, held in April at Atlanta University. According to the show's brochure, the exhibition included fifty-one oils, twenty-three watercolors, ten prints, and five sculptures. Among the artists represented were Jacob Lawrence, Romare Bearden, and Horace Pippin.

By the late 1940s, Pach's role within the contemporary art scene began to diminish significantly and his influence to wane rapidly. Increasingly, he was viewed by many artists and critics as a part of the historical past, not as an active and relevant participant in the latest developments in the American art scene.

7
Society of Independent Artists

Although exhibitions of contemporary art in the United States began to increase after the Armory Show, Pach believed that there was a need "for an exhibition occurring regularly, year in and year out, which should bring together the public and the artists who felt the vital movement of the time. That was the statement of the case made in 1916 by Morton L. Schamberg."[1] Many agreed with Schamberg's sentiments, and during the summer and fall of 1916, a group of artists, writers, musicians, and many of the New York intelligentsia, among them Pach, Duchamp, Crotti, Picabia, Gleizes, Stella, Sheeler, Schamberg, John R. Covert, Erik Satie, and Wallace Stevens, gathered at the Sixty-seventh Street apartment of Walter and Louise Arensberg—who had probably been introduced to Stella, Sheeler, and Schamberg by Pach—to discuss this issue. From these meetings the American version of the Society of Independent Artists (SIA) was established.[2]

The SIA adopted the "No jury, no prizes" motto of the Société des artistes indépendants in Paris and dedicated itself to providing all artists the opportunity to show their works freely. These aims were set forth in the Certificate of Incorporation signed on December 5, 1916, by Ray Greenleaf, John R. Covert, Homer Boss, Pach, and Arnold Friedman.[3] The main goals of the society were to hold annual exhibitions independent of any jury, to promote "solidarity among American artists" and cooperation with foreign artists, and to organize lectures and readings and distribute brochures and pamphlets that promoted the mission of the organization. The SIA sought to provide an intellectual atmosphere and an exhibition arena free from the constraints of the established jury and prize system of the old-guard New York art world. The group also hoped to promote the cause of modern art through lectures and writings, and it encouraged an open dialogue between American and European artists.

As the driving force behind the SIA, Pach was involved with virtually every aspect of the corporation.

In the fall of 1916, he engaged the services of Quinn as the legal advisor for the society.[4] With Pach's assistance, Quinn prepared bylaws containing twelve articles that reiterated the main goals of the society; explained membership options; outlined operating and management procedures; detailed the duties of the officers; and created finance, hanging, and membership and propaganda committees. Membership in the SIA was divided into regular and honorary categories and was unlimited in number. Any artist, American or foreign, who filed an application and paid initiation fees and annual dues could become a member and exhibit his or her work.

A board of directors managed the business and administrative affairs of the SIA. This governing body elected a president, one or more vice presidents, a treasurer, a secretary, and other officers annually. The original directors of the SIA were Bellows, Boss, Covert, Katherine S. Dreier, Marcel Duchamp, William Glackens, Ray Greenleaf, Rockwell Kent, John Marin, Pach, Charles Prendergast, Maurice Prendergast, Man

Ray, Schamberg, Sloan, Stella, and Maurice Sterne. The officers for 1916–17 were Glackens, president; Charles Prendergast, vice president; Pach, treasurer; Covert, secretary; and Walter Arensberg, managing director. Pach would serve as treasurer for twenty-one years. The responsibilities of this post included signing the checks, drafts, and orders for the payment of money by the society; endorsing all instruments of funds received by the group; and keeping the accounts.

Since the primary function of the SIA was to present yearly exhibitions, the directors began planning the first show in the fall of 1916, and Pach was involved with each stage of the operation. The first task was to locate an arena for the event. In October, he reported to Quinn, "I hope to hear, by the end of the week anyhow, whether we can get the building I saw for the Independents. It would be a great step if we could as there are few places in New York that would do."[5] The board of the SIA envisioned a large exhibition that would require a substantial space, and, accordingly, the Grand Central Palace on Lexington Avenue between Forty-sixth and Forty-seventh Streets was chosen as the site for the first show. Planning for the exhibition continued throughout the fall and into the new year.

Of course, funds had to be raised. Twelve guarantors, including the Arensbergs, eventually supported this initial exhibition. Pach served as the chairman of the finance committee and was responsible for the budgetary arrangements. He told Quinn in January 1917, "I do not think we have to fear that the guaranty-fund list will be incomplete. We have part of it now."[6] Pach also obtained loans of foreign works and agreed to act as sales agent for the organization.

Early in 1917, Pach drafted the circular sent by the SIA to painters, sculptors, and the press. In this publication he announced a spring show "in which all artists may participate independently of the decisions of juries."[7] The pamphlet explained that the organization was based on the "No jury, no prizes" principle and presented the requirements for admission to the SIA.

The flyer also stated the directors' decision—suggested by Duchamp—to hang works in alphabetical order. Pach believed this method of installation would relieve "the hanging committee of the difficulties raised by their personal judgments as to the merits of the exhibits."[8]

The response to the brochure was overwhelming, and soon after its release Pach enthusiastically reported to McBride, "Applications are simply pouring in and the success of the show is certain. Also I believe we shall do what we most want: reach the kind of people who have no chance to show otherwise. In time I think we shall really get good stuff that does not exist today."[9] He also wrote to Quinn, "In two weeks over six hundred applications have come in. We are going to have a good many of the known men and, I believe, some worth-while stuff from the unknown men. That is what I am interested in. . . . The more I am in the thing, the bigger it looks to me for the future of art here."[10] The open-door policy of the SIA encouraged artists at all levels of training and competency to participate in the undertaking. The directors of the organization understood that the quality of art submitted for display would be uneven; however, Pach was convinced that the equal opportunity provided by the SIA was important for the growth of art in America. He was also certain that the exhibition would reveal workers of great talent, hitherto undiscovered.

The "no jury" tenet on which the society was founded was tested before the first show opened by the submission of a urinal titled *Fountain* and signed "R. Mutt" by Marcel Duchamp. There are several accounts of the circumstances surrounding this incident, which proved divisive for the SIA.[11] Zigrosser thought that Duchamp's prank was "designed especially to get Walter's goat," since Pach "was very earnest and ponderous about 'art' and also very proper about morals."[12] In Pach's version of events, the object was rejected from the exhibition and was not present at all. Pach explained that the executive committee voted to exclude the work to avoid fine or imprisonment for outraging public decency. He furthermore stated that the directors' function was "distinct from that of a jury, which is a body that passes on aesthetic merits." According to Pach, Duchamp's *Fountain* was not dismissed because its artistic value was questionable; rather, the artist was not "permitted to place in the exhibition an object which by its nature would have aroused such disgust and resentment among the members and visitors of the Society as to endanger the continuance of the work which had been undertaken."[13] With the future of the society at stake, Pach and others ruled against the inclusion of Duchamp's piece in the show. The immediate result of this decision was that Duchamp resigned from the SIA. He informed Dreier, "I have resigned from the board of directors on account of a serious disagreement with the ruling spirit of the Society."[14] Pach and Duchamp had a "celebrated falling down or out" over this issue, as William Ivins recalled, and it took more than a year for the schism to heal fully.[15] Despite this setback, the SIA opened its first show on April 10, 1917.

Perhaps the most controversial aspect of the initial exhibition was the installation of the works. In his foreword to the catalog, Pach wrote, "The arrangement of all the exhibits in alphabetical order, regardless of manner or medium, is followed with a view to freeing the individual exhibit from the control of merely personal judgments which are inevitably the basis of any system of grouping."[16] In another, later explanation of this manner of hanging the art, he wrote, "Suggested by Marcel Duchamp as a result of his observation of the Independents in Paris, this new move consisted in hanging the show alphabetically, according to the place among the twenty-six letters which chance assigns to each name."[17] By this method, so the argument went, the public was made to judge the art solely on its own merits and was not presented with the subjective opinions and aesthetic sensibilities of a hanging committee.

Another problematic feature of the initial exhibition was its size—more than twenty-five hundred paintings, sculptures, prints, and other objects were in the show. Pach wrote John Marin and explained that to help visitors understand the art displayed, the officers "decided to have a Director take charge every afternoon, and for him to ask five of his artist friends to assist him to meet whoever came to the Exhibition and would like to know more about the pictures."[18] Through this effort, the management of the society hoped to educate the public about the principles underlying the works on view. As a director, Pach was called upon to perform this duty and was an ardent spokesperson for the contemporary art on display.

The initial season for the SIA was beset with fiscal and administrative problems. Although the first exhibition attracted publicity and visitors, it was a financial failure. In May 1917, Pach reported to Dreier,

Referring to the guaranty joined in by you and others totalling $10,000, we had expected to borrow upon this guaranty, prior to the opening of the exhibition. But the funds contributed by the membership and the credit obtained through the guaranty permitted us to get along without calling on this fund until now. . . . We are confronted with a deficit. This compels us to call upon the guarantors to pay the amount they have guaranteed. We should be glad if you would send us your check to the order of "The Society of Independent Artists, Inc." in the sum of $500. A copy of this letter is being sent to each of the guarantors.[19]

Some collectors, including Quinn and Dreier, purchased some art, but only forty-five works sold. As treasurer, Pach was responsible for detailing the expenses of the society to the sponsors. He explained that monies obtained from gate receipts and membership dues were insufficient to cover the costs of the undertaking. Because of the fiscal problems encountered by

Walter Pach (1883–1958)

the SIA, several directors resigned their posts, among them Katherine Dreier. By late 1917, fifteen new members managed the board of the SIA, and all the officers, except Pach, were replaced.

Although the show was not a monetary success, Pach was convinced that it met some of the goals set forth by the directors. He firmly believed that the society had "accomplished a very great work in promoting an understanding of contemporary art and sympathy with it." The alphabetical system of hanging had won converts, and artists and critics, in general, approved of the exhibition. He felt that the show confirmed "that no other agency now existing can do so much for the bringing together and advancement of American art."[20] Although beset with infighting and criticism, the organization persevered and weathered its first stormy season, mainly through Pach's tenacity.

Soon after the first show closed, the trustees of the SIA began to plan the Second Annual Exhibition. The tasks of organizing, advertising, mounting, and running the large-scale exhibition were enormous, and most of the burden fell to Pach. One of the biggest ordeals of the second season was to find a suitable place for the show, as the government had commandeered the Grand Central Palace for use as a base hospital. Initially, the SIA decided to erect a tent in the Moorish Garden on the south side of 110th Street between Broadway and Riverside Drive, but this scheme was abandoned. Pach explained to Quinn, "We have been obliged to give up the tent idea for the Independent show. I think you will be glad of that and—considering the splendid location we have found—I am too. . . . We are in a big store— 42nd St. between Broadway and Sixth Avenue."[21] Pach helped secure this site at 110–114 West Forty-second Street. He also contributed two works to the show and wrote the foreword to the catalog.

In the foreword, Pach stated, "The Society's ideal is one of freedom; to continue the work under present conditions is to affirm our belief in the principle and to respond to the example of self-possession which

French artists have given by pressing on in their work within hearing-distance of the battle."[22] He believed that the SIA exhibitions were a vital source of encouragement to foreign artists, a spark of hope that helped them continue their work during the devastating conflict on the Continent. Pach saw his involvement with the society as part of the war effort, as he explained to Matisse: "It is hard to have these operations on the back but I consider that, since I do nothing for the war, it is a way of fulfilling my duties as a member of the Society."[23] The support given to the SIA by artists and the public proved, according to Pach, that "a nation doing its utmost in a great war still felt art not to be a dispensable luxury, but a profound and vital need, and that it must continue its development uninterruptedly."[24] While his friends were fighting for freedom on the battlefields of Europe, Pach was waging war for the cause of modern art in the United States.

In the early months of 1919, Pach was once again knee-deep in the planning of the SIA's annual exhibition, which was held in the Roof Garden of the Waldorf-Astoria Hotel at Thirty-fourth Street and Fifth Avenue. Pach made a poster for the show; borrowed paintings from Quinn, as he had done in 1917 and 1918; and was again involved in almost every aspect of the undertaking. He wrote McBride,

> One of the reasons [for not writing] has been work on the Independents and as they are in some degree to be counted among your progeny, you are also in some degree responsible for the work we're having. The important point is that signs seem to point to our success this year, and if we do put it firmly on its legs, we'll feel repaid for everything we've done. It is certainly easier than it was even last year, to say nothing of the Inferno we went through in 1917. The idea of the Waldorf scared me a bit at first, and I've just turned in an article for the next issue of the *Dial* (March 22nd) wherein I defend the society against charges of being suddenly successful, the charges

being the ones which I thought of. I also defend the alphabetical system.[25]

In that *Dial* essay, Pach admitted that some art displayed in the exhibition was mediocre, yet he defended the "No jury, no prizes" motto of the society and extolled the virtue of an open enterprise that served as a battleground for new ideas. The large-scale show, he argued, afforded the opportunity for anyone to submit and show his or her art. Furthermore, he assured his readers that among the works exhibited were paintings and sculptures of great importance through which the younger generation expressed thoughts central to the age. He attributed the "vitality of the Independent principle" to its correspondence with the "deep current of evolution" alive in his day, a current in which all members of society were given recognition and the right to exist.[26] Pach steadfastly promoted the show as the most important avenue through which innovative thoughts in art could be explored and by which the public's understanding of contemporary works would be enhanced.

For the 1920 show, Pach enlisted the aid of yet another attorney friend (and a fellow artist), James N. Rosenberg, to write a letter "to the collector of internal revenue asking that our exhibition be relieved of collecting the war-tax on the sale of tickets."[27] Rosenberg graciously agreed to Pach's request and, before the show opened, sent him a "certificate of exemption from the collection of federal taxes on admission to your fourth annual exhibition," assuring Pach that "there was no difficulty at all entailed in securing exemption."[28] This would save the SIA quite a bit of money.

A unique feature of the SIA's 1920 show—for which Pach was partially responsible—was the inclusion of watercolors by contemporary Native Americans. Pach had been trying to organize a showing of these artists' works since returning from Santa Fe in 1918, and in 1920, he arranged for Edgar Hewett to meet with John Sloan and Robert Henri to discuss the matter. Hewett

and Mabel Dodge agreed to loan works for the exhibition, and in early February Hewett reported to Pach that "the arrangement for the Indian Art Exhibition was consummated." He added, "I think the idea is an excellent one, and am very grateful to you for your encouragement of the plan from the beginning."[29]

While Pach worked tirelessly for the cause of the SIA, not all involved saw his role in a particularly positive light, and early in 1920 Hamilton Easter Field, a director and the recording secretary, asked to be excused from the publicity and membership committees because he could not cooperate with Pach.[30] Field took his grievance to the press, and in an article published in the *Brooklyn Daily Eagle* he accused the SIA, and Pach in particular, of mismanaging publicity and favoring certain artists. Pach replied to Field's allegations, and the debate that ensued caused a fracture within the SIA. As a result, Pach was ousted as treasurer. According to Helen Sloan, John Sloan's second wife, the controversy stemmed from Field:

> He [Field] and Walter had . . . problems. . . . Field wanted to be able to put his favorites forward of the artists that were exhibiting and of course it was hit or miss, if you had money you could show. . . . He claimed that Walter was promoting his friends by giving photographs of their work to the publicity people who came from the newspapers. Well the photographs were whatever the artists brought in and they just lay around on the table. So this was a piece of manipulation on Field's part. . . . He really would have liked to have elbowed Walter aside and to have sort of taken the thing over.[31]

John Sloan, the SIA's president, threw his strong support behind Pach.

Through Pach's diligence and enthusiasm, the Fourth Annual Exhibition was the first of the SIA shows to post a monetary gain, and the deficit previously incurred was replaced by a surplus in the treasury.[32] Not only had sales increased but attendance had nearly doubled since the previous year, and membership in the organization had grown by one-fourth. As Pach reported to Rosenberg, "We sold twenty-six works [and] . . . had 7193 paid admissions this year as against 3455 last year."[33] The SIA's progress was hailed by its directors in a brochure sent to the members in which Pach wrote, "The support of the Society during the past four years by artists in every section of the country, from the most radical to the most conservative, from the young unknown workers to the men of the most eminent position, is the best augury for the continuance of the Independent idea."[34] Despite infighting and setbacks, and a serious bout of influenza, Pach persevered and helped ensure that the SIA continued its mission as a venue for contemporary art.

While the 1921 season for the SIA was relatively quiet, in the spring of 1922, the organization was once more beset by controversy within the board of directors as Field launched another public attack against Pach, accusing him of improperly handling the publicity for the exhibition and showing favoritism toward his friends.[35] Although Pach had previously been ousted as treasurer, Sloan had named him to the financial committee, much to Field's chagrin. This dispute resulted in Field's resignation from the SIA and his establishment of a rival organization, the Salon of America. Undeterred by the disturbance in the ranks, Pach worked tirelessly to get the show off the ground. He personally encouraged artists he knew to submit their work, and arranged, as he had in 1920, for a special section that featured contemporary Native American art, courtesy of Dr. Edgar Hewett.

For the 1923 SIA annual exhibition, Pach arranged a show of a group of works by many of Mexico's leading painters.[36] Among the participants were David Siqueiros, Jean Charlot, Carlos Mérida, José Clemente Orozco, Diego Rivera, and Rufino Tamayo. Pach had met most, if not all, these artists the previous summer.

This historic event was the first display of its kind by these artists in the United States.

Another "unusual and remarkable event took place during the run of the 1923 Independent exhibition," this incident, too, involving Pach. A New York City police officer took offense at a painting depicting the New Testament scene in which Jesus performs his first miracle, turning water into wine. The artist, J. Francis Kaufman, portrayed "Congressman [Andrew] Volstead, William Jennings Bryant, and William H. Anderson, all in modern dress expressing disapproval" of Christ's actions.[37] Kaufman's painting was clearly an anti-Prohibition statement—the Volstead Act reinforced the Prohibition amendment to the Constitution. Bryant was an avid speaker in favor of Prohibition, and Anderson was superintendent of the Anti-Saloon League. The officer served A. S. Baylinson, secretary of the SIA, a summons and charged that the painting was "an outrage to public decency." The SIA lost the case in the city magistrate's court and appealed to the state supreme court, and in the fall of 1924, Pach was called in to testify. As Carl Marlor noted in his history of the SIA, "Pach's testimony helped develop the concept that there were pictures of Jesus Christ painted with persons in contemporary garb hanging in the Metropolitan Museum of Art, New York City, the Dresden Museum in Germany and the Louvre, Paris and these pictures were in no way construed as an outrage to public decency."[38] Pach's words helped win the case, which strengthened artists' rights to exhibit their creative work freely in the United States; however, as John Loughery observed in his biography of John Sloan, this incident showed that the battle for the complete acceptance of freedom of expression in art was far from won.

While questions about the need for the SIA began to surface in the mid-1920s as other venues for the exhibition of contemporary art appeared and flourished, Pach and Sloan felt that the society and its open-door policy still provided the most democratic

arena in the United States in which to showcase work
by living artists—American and foreign.[39] Both artists
and critics expressed concern about the level of
competence displayed in some of the works on view,
noting the often startling juxtaposition of paintings by
accomplished artists such as Sloan and Glackens with
amateurish pictures by nonprofessionals. Nevertheless,
Pach and Sloan were steadfast in their commitment,
and throughout the 1920s and 1930s the SIA's annual
exhibition provided a showcase for new and diverse
talent, with painters and sculptors such as Adolph Gottlieb, Reginald Marsh, Mark Tobey, and Robert Laurent
participating in the shows. After a tumultuous start and
several strife-filled seasons, the structural organization
of the SIA stabilized and the annual exhibition gained a
steady footing, thanks in large part to the efforts of
Walter Pach. By the time of its twenty-fifth anniversary
in 1941, however, the SIA had run its course. With
increasing financial difficulties—a problem that had
plagued the society since the early 1920s and particularly during the Depression—and the United States'
entry into World War II, the organization was nearing
its end. In 1944 the SIA held its final annual show.

8
Liaison, Agent, Dealer, and Advisor

Pach had begun acting as an intermediary between artists and collectors, and as a dealer, as early as 1908, and while he was active in this vein until the Armory Show, his work in this capacity grew enormously during World War I and into the 1920s and 1930s. Pach was usually the first person contacted when anyone wanted to buy or sell modern, especially foreign, works in the United States. John Quinn, Walter and Louise Arensberg, and other major collectors, as well as museum leaders such as Fiske Kimball and Bryson Burroughs, turned to Pach as a trusted advisor. Friends, colleagues, and family acquaintances sought Pach's counsel when acquiring art, particularly modern art. Pach assisted individuals who wished to sell historical art and was instrumental in placing many works—some major—with museums, collectors, and private dealers in the United States and abroad. He guided budding art dealers, among them Pierre Matisse, Henri's son. Through these and other negotiations Pach quickly found himself heavily involved in the primary and secondary art markets in the United States.

During the war years and through the early 1920s, Pach worked on behalf of many modern European artists, Matisse being the one he promoted most enthusiastically. As noted earlier, Pach was instrumental in organizing Matisse's 1915 show at the Montross Gallery. Afterward he became a dealer himself, reporting to Matisse in the autumn of 1915, for example, "Meanwhile I have sold three monotypes myself and send you their price—being four hundred and fifty francs—by money order, in this letter."[1] In January 1916, Pach arranged for the Arensbergs to purchase Matisse's painting *Portrait of Mademoiselle Yvonne Landsberg* (fig. 21), now in the Philadelphia Museum of Art. He assured the artist that the picture had been acquired by "an amateur[,] the most interesting but not very rich (he is a writer of great merit, one of my best friends, M. [Walter] Arensberg)."[2] In March 1916, he wrote Matisse, "I have sent the etchings that remain to Miss Alice Klauber of

San Diego California. Last night she advised me that she has sold eleven until then."[3] Matisse responded in April, "Your letter gave me great pleasure. I wrote a note at once to Miss Alice Klauber, whom I remember seeing with you in Florence—almost 10 years ago."[4] Pach, through Klauber, introduced Matisse's art to the West Coast at a very early date, thus spreading European modernism beyond the art circles of the East Coast. Pach continued to serve as Matisse's primary agent in the United States until 1924, when Matisse's son Pierre arrived in New York. He arranged for Matisse to consign works to galleries such as Weyhe in Manhattan and brokered the sale of the artist's work to collectors as well.

From the Armory Show in 1913 until 1924, Pach's primary employer was John Quinn, and through Pach's agency Quinn amassed one of the most significant collections of modern art in the United States at the

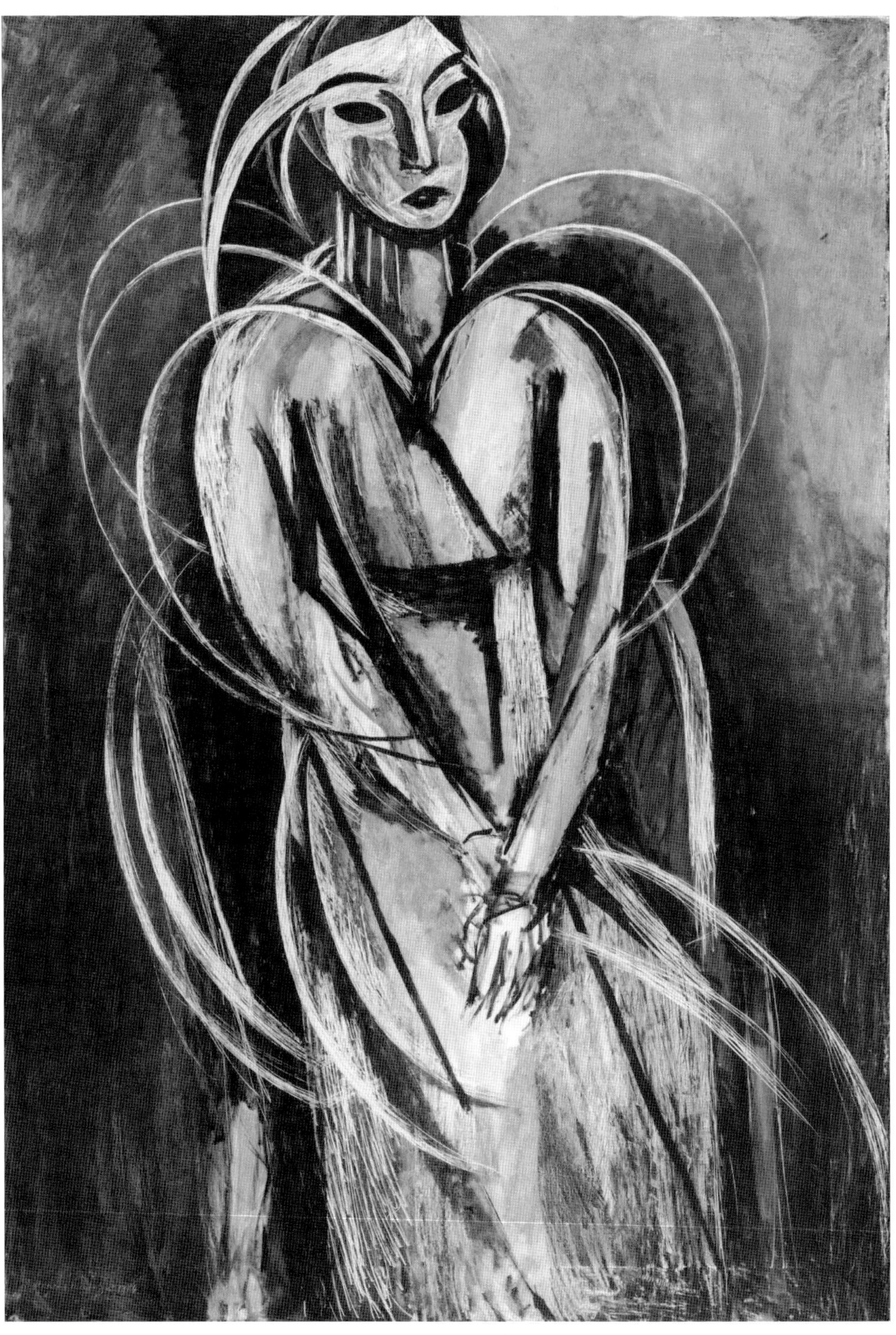

Walter Pach (1883–1958)

time.[5] Among the numerous works that Pach helped Quinn acquire between 1915 and 1917 alone were thirty-five etchings, three monotypes, two drawings, and two paintings by Matisse; three paintings by Villon; four sculptures by Duchamp-Villon; four pictures by Dufy; drawings and an oil study by Dunoyer de Segonzac; eight watercolors and oils by Derain; six works by Picasso; four paintings by Gleizes; six pastels and paintings by Redon; two paintings by Robert Delaunay; ceramics and other works by Rouault; and works by American artists Sheeler and Joseph Garvey. Many of the French pieces had been consigned to the Carroll Galleries, which Quinn backed. Also through Pach, Quinn bought Duchamp's preliminary oil sketch *Nude Descending a Staircase, No. 1* (now in the Philadelphia Museum of Art), which Arensberg had wanted.[6] Pach also corresponded with Brancusi regarding the latter's sculptures *Mademoiselle Pogany* and *Golden Bird,* which Quinn had purchased, and about the collector's desire to acquire the original version of *The Kiss,* a copy of which the sculptor had given to Pach.[7] These are merely some of the sales Pach helped broker for Quinn.

Pach's negotiations with European artists on Quinn's behalf entailed tremendous time, energy, and effort. Much of this work involved voluminous translations of letters to and from artists in France. While Pach was obliging, he sometimes felt overwhelmed, as he explained to Quinn:

I have been thinking of the matter of my remitting to the French artists in the fall. After the letters I have had to write this week (Rouault, Segonzac, Dufy, Derain, Duchamp-Villon and various others resulting from my work for the exhibitions) I hesitate about going in for another bunch. It always means adding a few lines of my own—or more than a few as they always ask questions, have news to give, or offers of some sort to make—and that takes up my time more than would seem possible at first

glance. While I don't want to shirk anything that is for a good cause if there is no one else to attend to it, I do think that Miss Bryant's interest in the matter—since you intend her to have a commission, aside from what she has done in the way of sales this past season—might bring this correspondence within her province. . . . I do not announce this as a final decision at all: if you had special reason for desiring me to attend to the affair, I should do it, as I appreciate too fully the support you are giving the art I believe in today, to decline any similar request. Only—this season my time has been so cut up that it will be necessary for me to concentrate my attention next fall on the magazine work, translations and other such matters as I may get to do and let other people keep up the art-campaign. However if you really prefer to have me take care of the remittances I will do it willingly—once I sit down to write to these fellows, it is a pleasure— also to get their letters.[8]

Knowing he needed Pach's help to acquire the art he wanted, however, Quinn insisted that Pach continue the correspondence with the European artists.

These letters primarily concerned the sales of the artists' works in the United States, but they also contained the latest news from France. Many painters and sculptors, including Derain, Duchamp-Villon, Dunoyer de Segonzac, and de la Fresnaye were at the front, and Pach kept Quinn informed of their daily activities during the war. Many artists in war-torn Europe viewed Pach as a lifeline, someone who could forestall disaster for their professional lives during the conflict on the Continent. They were immensely grateful to him for his intercessions on their behalf, and to return the favor, they often made him gifts of their art. In an unpublished manuscript, Pach quoted Gleizes, who had written to him from his post in one of the forts at Toul: "Thanks for the noble effort that you are making for us. We stand for France today, and through the action of your people in keeping up an interest in art at such a time, we learn to understand the character of America—and we are grateful to you as artists and as men."[9] As an agent for his comrades in France, Pach viewed his work as his contribution to the war effort and as vital to the morale and livelihood of the artists he supported.

Besides working as Quinn's agent, Pach personally introduced the collector to some of the French artists who fled to the United States during World War I; among them was Duchamp, whom Pach met at the dock when the latter arrived in June 1915. Quinn also probably met Jean and Yvonne Crotti, Francis Picabia and Gabrielle Buffet-Picabia, and Albert Gleizes and Juliette Roché through Pach. Before Duchamp arrived in Manhattan, Pach wrote Quinn,

> The best letter—with a piece of surprising news— was from Marcel Duchamp. . . . The surprising thing is that he wants to leave France, in fact is quite decided to. He has been dissatisfied there for some time, and I imagine his not serving in the war makes his position less pleasant. He says he would be glad to come to New York, provided he can earn his living here. . . . I shall write him of what I think are uncongenial conditions for him here, but shall look about at various institutions where there could be a place for him. . . . He is one of the finest young men I know, with one of the most brilliant minds. Do you think of any institutions that might have room for him?"[10]

After Duchamp arrived in New York, Pach did everything in his power to find employment for his friend, enlisting Quinn's help in the undertaking. He wrote the collector, "Duchamp is really quite determined to do some sort of work that will save him from the necessity of living by the sale of his pictures and I was wondering whether it would be any good to speak to Miss Belle Greene for him again. She did not know of anything in the spring."[11] Quinn responded, "I doubt very much whether Belle Greene would be able to place Marcel Duchamp. Would you like to have me speak to her? If you would I shall gladly do so."[12] Pach accepted this offer and explained,

> Duchamp has been again to the French Museum (Institute Français) 599 Fifth Avenue, where I introduced him in June. The director (if that is his title) Mr. Juen . . . now informs Duchamp that there is probably need for a person to catalogue, arrange and otherwise look after the growing library of the Museum. . . . Miss Greene—who is at present secretary, I believe—is likely to be made president. The place would be an exceptionally suitable one for Duchamp from every standpoint. . . . Also Duchamp is very serious in his wish to earn his living at something outside of his painting; and in view of the character of his work, I am in complete sympathy with his desire to keep his mind free of any consideration of money in thinking about his painting. . . . So if, as you say, you would not mind speaking to Miss Greene for him, I am convinced it would be a good thing. At my request, she tried to find a place for him before he came to America, but was unable to do so. I would speak to her again myself . . . but I had just met her once through a note of introduction from my father.[13]

Pach eventually persuaded Quinn to arrange a meeting between Greene and Duchamp. After his interview with Greene, Duchamp happily reported to Quinn, "She decided to ask the President of the French Institute for: 4 hours in the afternoon every day (from 2 o'clock to 6) and $100 a month. My hope is surpassed."[14] Once again, Pach had done a good turn for a dear friend.

Pach also introduced his French friends to collectors Walter and Louise Arensberg, who had moved to Manhattan from Boston around 1914. He had made the acquaintance of Walter Arensberg at the Armory Show's New York venue and had become quite friendly with the couple during the exhibition's appearance in Boston. The Arensbergs began buying contemporary works soon after they arrived in New York, purchasing "a Gleizes, a de la Fresnaye and a Picasso etching from the [Carroll] Gallery," undoubtedly on Pach's recommendation.[15] Arensberg also tried to buy some of Duchamp's work through Pach in the spring of 1915.[16] After Duchamp arrived in the United States, in June of that year, he stayed at the Arensbergs' apartment— through Pach's intercession—until October, after which time he lived across the street from Walter and Magda Pach on Beekman Place. In another effort, Pach assisted Arensberg with a literary review the latter was working on; Pach wrote to a young poet friend, Jean LeRoy, who was at the front in Europe, and sent requests for articles to various artists abroad.

At his home at 33 Beekman Place, Pach entertained numerous American and European artists, collectors, writers, and dealers. In November 1915, he wrote Henry McBride:

Tomorrow (Wednesday) evening Gleizes, Marcel Duchamp and Crotti are coming to my place, also the Prendergasts and perhaps George F. Of. It just occurred to me that perhaps you might care to drop in, if you are not engaged. You would make or renew acquaintance with the French artists (Gleizes either met you in Paris or has an introduction to present to you, I forget which) and it might be that they could give you news for one of your nice Parisian Paragraphs. . . . The main thing is that we shall surely have some good talk and it would be a pleasure if you could join us.[17]

Also in November, the Pachs invited Quinn and Arensberg to dine with them, though only Quinn could attend the dinner. Wallace Stevens joined them afterward. The Pachs' apartment had become a gathering place for members of the New York and Parisian art and literary worlds, and we can be fairly certain that Pach thoroughly enjoyed every minute of it.

Pach's work for Quinn took many forms; on January 18, 1916, he testified in court about the taxes on some contemporary art. Quinn told Duchamp-Villon, "Our common friend, Mr. Pach lunched with me today after considering with me the evidence which I am going to have him give tomorrow before the customs court on the point that the Seramics [sic] by M. Rouault are works of art and not objects of utility and hence that they are entitled to be admitted duty free."[18] Pach had been called upon before on this issue, and his expert opinion would be sought again. He and Quinn were at the forefront of the battle to have the duty on imported contemporary art removed, and while they had won the first round in 1913, when the tariff was repealed, the struggle continued. Pach felt his work in this vein was of great assistance to his artist friends in Europe.

The question of what to do with the Carroll Galleries and its inventory weighed heavily on Quinn in 1917, and he contacted Pach to discuss the matter of "the Carroll Galleries French paintings and drawings."[19] Harriet Bryant had informed Thomas Curtin, Quinn's assistant, that she wanted to have the French pictures still in her possession sent to the Artist Packing and Shipping Company and packed there. Fearful that the inventory might go astray, Quinn summoned Pach to his office to discuss the problem, and as a result of this meeting and other conversations, Pach assumed control over the remainder of the gallery's inventory. Unfortunately, some art entrusted to the gallery was unaccounted for, and payments that Bryant said she had rendered were left owing. Pach supervised the packing of the pieces at the gallery and followed Quinn's advice to have Bryant "certify to you all of the works that she has on hand, by name of artist or consignor, by title or subject-matter of work, and price in francs, and that you receipt to her for those works respectively."[20] Pach also took on the responsibility of informing the artists and dealers concerned that the establishment was closed and that he had possession of their works.

Bryant was not at all pleased with the way matters were being handled. She complained to Quinn, "That Mr. Pach should be disgruntled and complain that he had no money return for his activities is a surprise and something of a shock to me—Certainly his often-voiced desire to serve the cause of 'fine art' in America should have made him less exacting, particularly in view of what *you have done, Kuhn* and *Davies* as well as my humble self."[21] Ever supportive and protective of Pach, Quinn replied,

> My recollection is that you cheerfully agreed not merely to pro rate with Mr. Montross Pach's expenses abroad, but to make the remittance of $20 a week to his wife. Having at that time agreed to it as part of the inducement to Pach to go abroad, it comes with ill grace on your part, it seems to me, to make a point of it now. . . . I know nothing about Mr. Pach being "disgruntled" or complaining that he "had no money return for his activities." . . . I have always felt that he deserved a very great deal of credit and appreciation for the courage and self-sacrifice shown by him in going abroad to collect those works in the early stages of the war and without one dollar of compensation to him. But I suppose Mr. Montross is no more appreciative of Mr. Pach's efforts for him in getting the Matisse exhibition.[22]

Quinn was in no mood to play games with Bryant and was staunchly on Pach's side in the matter. Dealings with Bryant grew strained; consequently, it took nearly two more years to settle all the accounts from the 1914–15 season at the Carroll Galleries. Pach placed some of these works with other galleries in New York, including Bourgeois and Ehrich, and tried to sell some himself, an arduous feat in good economic times, but

an especially hard one during the war. The art market was very slow, and he confessed to Quinn that he "had no opportunity to sell any of those things" though he had written a number of collectors.[23] Eventually, after the war, Pach made arrangements for the return of the paintings and prints to the artists in Paris, using a large portion of the only commission he ever received from his work as an agent for Quinn to cover the costs of the shipment back to France.[24]

Pach correctly believed the art market would return to business as usual after the war; as he observed, "right after peace came, people began to buy a few pictures again."[25] Soon after the armistice was signed, Pach was back negotiating sales with dealers such as Vollard and Bourgeois, with artists, and with collectors. Just after the beginning of 1919, Pach received a letter from Frederick C. Torrey with unexpected news; Torrey wished to sell Duchamp's painting *Nude Descending a Staircase, No. 2,* which he had acquired from the Armory Show. Torrey wondered, "Considering the high price of gasoline do you think anyone would pay a thousand dollars for the Nu Descendant? Walter Arensberg wrote to me about purchasing it that year I met him in N.Y. but I was not in a selling mood. It has lately occurred to me to write now and offer it to him but it occurs to me at the moment that someone within your knowledge might be quite as much interested, and if so would be glad to know of my willingness at the moment to let it go."[26] Perhaps because of some agreement, either verbal or nonverbal, Pach first offered this work to Quinn instead of Arensberg, who would have been the logical choice. Quinn refused the painting, but Arensberg leapt at the chance. Pach made all the arrangements in expeditious fashion, and just one month after he had broached the subject, Torrey shipped the painting to Arensberg and wrote Pach, "Your speedy activity takes my breath away."[27]

In 1919, on Quinn's behalf, Pach sent a proposal to Matisse, Derain, and Picasso expressing the collector's desire to see the latest examples of their work with an eye to acquiring more pieces for his collection.[28] At Quinn's request, Pach suggested that the artists submit photographs of their most recent paintings and sculptures for the collector's perusal. He wrote Matisse, in particular, that it was important for him to be represented in Quinn's collection by "an appropriate number of works which will show the range of your art and its place in the modern movement."[29] Pach also sent each artist a personal note on Quinn's background and his interest in contemporary art. As an extra incentive he added, "In addition to Mr. Quinn's general desire to add good examples of work by living men to his collection, there is the great advantage of sales direct by artists to Mr. Quinn being exempt from the ten percent tax."[30] Quinn, Pach, and others fought long and hard to have the taxes on the importation of contemporary art exempted. As Pach explained to Matisse, Derain, and Picasso, "The fifteen per cent United States customs duty was taken off modern art. And again in the late [1918] Revenue Act taxing art sales, Mr. Quinn, on behalf of the artists, and at his own expense, made the briefs and a trip to Washington and the arguments there which resulted in sales by living artists of their own work being exempt from the ten per cent tax which was imposed upon all other art sales."[31] Although this round was won, the battle on this particular issue was far from over.

By 1920, Pach had become Quinn's private art consultant, agent, and secretary and he remained in this position until Quinn's untimely death in 1924, although Henri Roché was also advising the collector during these years. Pach's main role was as a liaison between the collector and the European art market. While he had not charged for his translation work before, matters were different now, and he wrote Quinn, "When you first asked me about translating letters for you, you spoke of paying me for the work. I did not say yes or no on that point because I felt I would rather not have any payment for it unless it ran to a good deal of time and trouble and I feel so now. . . . The amount runs to over ten thousand words, all told—French to English and English to French . . . [so] the price paid the translator averages $4.00 per thousand words."[32] Quinn accepted Pach's terms because he knew these letters were vital for his seemingly insatiable appetite for new works from France. The content of these letters often regarded overdue or neglected payments for works that Quinn agreed to purchase. Pach found this task to be "vexatious" and truly dreaded having to ask the collector repeatedly to pay his debts. Pach also helped broker sales with auction houses and dealers in Paris, advised Quinn on purchases in New York, and recommended books and magazines for Quinn to read, thus becoming indispensable.

Toward the middle of 1923, Quinn and Pach began discussing the future fate of the remarkable collection that these two had amassed over the past decade. The urgency of this decision would soon become paramount, as Quinn was losing his battle with cancer. During this period, Pach had meetings with New York lawyers and real estate developers Alexander M. and Leo S. Bing about establishing a permanent museum of modern art, with Quinn's collection as its base. Pach had probably met the Bings through their mutual friend Lewis Mumford. The Bings, Pach informed Quinn, intended to raise funds for donating two empty houses for such an undertaking and they "had in mind all the time a permanent gift to the public." Although, as Pach wrote Quinn, "they would not be willing to furnish the buildings," they "would be glad to make contributions to the fund, if one were raised, for having the long-term exhibition which should lead to a permanent museum of modern art."[33] Regrettably, Quinn was not pleased with this idea, and the destiny of his collection remained unsettled, but not for long.

While on summer vacation in Saint-Tropez in 1924, Pach received the distressing news of John Quinn's death. Quinn's health had been deteriorating throughout the year; nevertheless, Pach was shocked by the turn of events and wrote Curtin,

I was on the very point of writing an acknowledge-
ment of your letter of July enclosing the copy of Mr.
Quinn's letter to Hugo Brehme of Mexico City,
when I chanced to see from the window Mr.
Brancusi, the sculptor, who was spending the day in
the small town here where I am working. I ran out
to meet him and almost the first thing he told me
was that Mr. Quinn had died. . . . It is a deep loss
and grief to me. . . . You know what it means to the
artists—both those whose friend Mr. Quinn was in
a personal way and those who simply had the
encouragement of knowing that there was such an
art lover in the world. . . . I cannot get it through my
mind that Mr. Quinn is gone. It will be very long
before any of us realizes what this means.

For Pach, Quinn's death was a devastating blow to the
world of modern art. He offered to assist Curtin in any
way, "especially in the matter of the collection."[34] Curtin
immediately took Pach up on his offer and began to
correspond with him about the collection and its
dispersal, a task that would occupy both men for the
next two years. During a two-week stay in Paris in
September 1924, Pach approached several dealers
whom he knew and asked their opinion about the
auction of the collection. When he returned to Manhattan, he informed Curtin that his French dealer friends,
among them Félix Fénéon of Bernheim and Joseph
Hessel, felt that the sale should not be held in New York
City; he had discussed with his foreign colleagues the
possible costs of selling the works in Paris and advised
that a complete catalog of the collection would be
necessary. He had spoken, he told Curtin, in an "unof-
ficial way only," with people at the Metropolitan
Museum about acquiring the collection.[35] Regrettably,
the executors of the Quinn estate would not heed his
advice. Pach was one of many artists, collectors, and
museum officials who were extremely disappointed
that the collection was not acquired by any museum or
public institution. Instead, the works were sold at

auction at the Hôtel Drout in Paris in October 1926
and at the American Art Association in New York in
February 1927.[36] Several of Pach's friends, colleagues,
and acquaintances, including Alexander M. Bing and
Harry and Ruth Bakwin, bought paintings from these
sales, many on Pach's advice.

While Pach's job as an advisor to Quinn was quite
formal, his role as an agent/liaison/dealer with other
major collectors was less so. For example, he arranged
for several acquisitions, among them paintings by the
Duchamp brothers, for Walter and Louise Arensberg.
From time to time he sent Abby Aldrich Rockefeller,
Duncan Phillips, and Etta and Claribel Cone of
Baltimore photographs of paintings, prints, and
sculptures for their consideration, and while they did
not buy any of these works, they all acquired paintings
by Pach. Whether Pach recommended any particular
purchases to Frederick and Helen Birch Bartlett is not
known; however, he probably provided them with
introductions to European dealers.[37] It was certainly
Pach who made arrangements with Stéphan Bourgeois
and Fénéon for Adolph Lewisohn's purchase of Seurat's
Study for "A Sunday on La Grande Jatte," now in the
Metropolitan Museum of Art (fig. 22).[38]

Pach also lent friendly counsel to newcomers to the
field of collecting. Sometime before 1926, Pach met
Harold Tovell, a collector of modern art from Toronto,
who was also a member of the education department at
the Art Gallery of Toronto.[39] The two probably first met
at Brummer's Gallery in New York. In the late summer
or early fall of 1926, Tovell acquired Marcel Duchamp's
painting *The Chess Players (The Chess Game),* now in
the Philadelphia Museum of Art. Originally purchased
by Quinn from a Carroll Galleries exhibition in 1915,
the picture had been reacquired by Duchamp sometime after Quinn's death in 1924. From Monaco,
Duchamp wrote Tovell, who was in Brussels, "The
painting is packed now and I will have it shipped as
soon as I get back to Paris (Oct 1st) to your office
address."[40] It is likely that Pach introduced Tovell to

Duchamp while all three men were in Paris during the summer of 1926, and he probably also encouraged Tovell to acquire *The Chess Players (The Chess Game)*. Eventually, Pach owned this painting, which he then sold to Walter and Louise Arensberg. Pach also assisted the Tovells on their purchases of works by Duchamp's brothers Jacques Villon, who became a very close friend of the family, and Raymond Duchamp-Villon. He also shared with Mrs. Tovell his enthusiasm for Delacroix, an artist whose paintings both collected. Other friends and colleagues to whom Pach lent advice and for whom Pach acquired works were New York collectors Gerda and Beatrice Stein, Alexander and Florence Bing, Leo Bing, Wallace Stevens, and Ida and

Caesar Guggenheimer, many of whom visited the Pachs while they were in Paris between 1929 and 1932. Ever the gracious hosts, the Pachs took their guests to exhibitions and to visit Villon and other artists in their studios. Often these collectors purchased works they saw, undoubtedly on Pach's recommendation.

Other young collectors to whom Pach gave some early guidance were pediatricians Drs. Harry and Ruth Bakwin.[41] Pach first met Ruth Morris Bakwin through his friendship with her stepfather, Francis Neilson, and her mother, Helen Swift Morris Neilson. Mr. Neilson was one of the editors for the short-lived journal the *Freeman,* to which Pach was a regular contributor. Ruth and her sister, Muriel, posed for Pach when they were

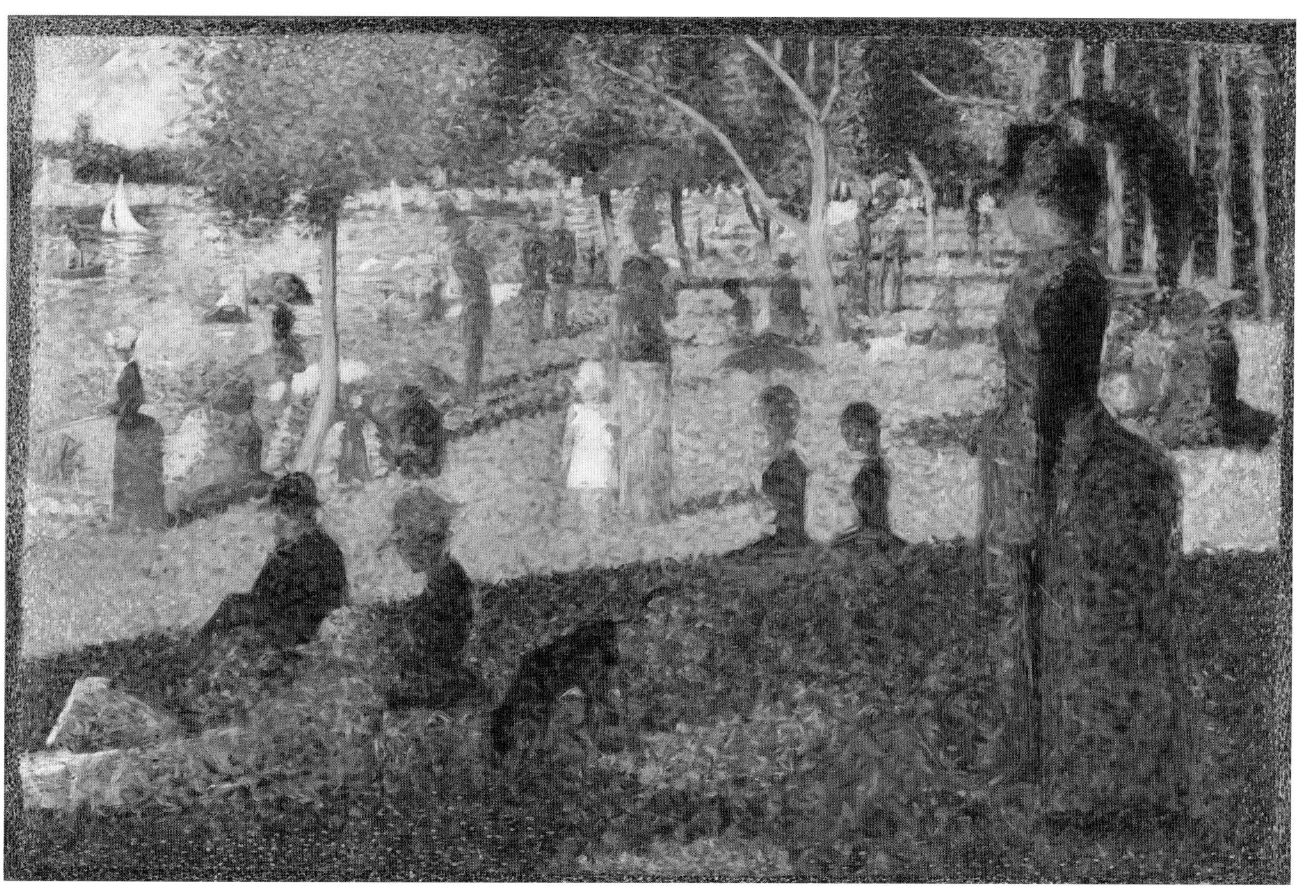

Fig. 22
Georges Seurat, *Study for "A Sunday on La Grande Jatte,"* 1884, oil on canvas, 24 ¾ × 41 in. (70.5 × 104.1 cm). The Metropolitan Museum of Art, Bequest of Sam A. Lewisohn, 1951 (51.112.6). Image © The Metropolitan Museum of Art.

young girls, she in exchange for Spanish lessons for an upcoming trip to Madrid. Pach, she recalled, "went to art museums with the family, and recommended different art exhibits and shows," and while she "did not feel that he influenced her taste at that time . . . he did make recommendations that were crucial." Pach suggested that the Bakwins buy paintings from the John Quinn estate, and as Ruth wrote, "when the Bakwins took Pach's advice and told him about the four paintings they purchased from the Quinn Estate in 1926, he was pleased with their choice; André Derain's 'Old Woman,' Henri Matisse's 'Artist and his Model,' Paul Gauguin's 'Caribbean Woman with Sunflowers,' and Georges Rouault's 'Head of a Clown.'"[42] It was through Pach that the Bakwins met the famed Parisian art dealer Ambroise Vollard, from whom they purchased a number of works, and Vincent van Gogh's nephew and namesake. Also through Pach they made the acquaintance of painter Maurice de Vlaminck, with whom they became quite close and from whom they bought several landscapes. In addition, Pach introduced the Bakwins to French art historian, dealer, and curator Robert Lebel. Among the acquisitions they made from him was Cézanne's *Portrait romantique*. The Bakwins also acquired one of their prized possessions, Cézanne's *Jeune Italienne accoudée*, from Pach in 1928. The Bakwins shared Pach's belief that "a work of art was based on more than painterly skill, that it reflected the mind and spirit of the artist, and that it needed to communicate with the viewer."[43] While Pach may have been directly responsible for only one of their acquisitions, indirectly he played a large part in helping to shape the Bakwins' substantial collection of modern art.

Pach also advised museums on their acquisitions of modern and historical art and even brokered the sale of some major paintings. When Alfred Churchill became the first director of the Smith College Museum of Art, he turned to Pach for assistance in acquiring works and through Pach's advice purchased several paintings, including Courbet's *Preparation of the Dead Girl.*

Through his work at the Armory Show, Pach helped place the first painting by Cézanne, *View of the Domaine Saint-Joseph* (fig. 10), in an American museum—the Metropolitan Museum of Art. Throughout the 1920s and early 1930s, Pach sent photographs of paintings for sale to Bryson Burroughs, curator at the Metropolitan, although the latter did not acquire any at the time. In the 1920s, Fiske Kimball approached Pach and asked him to purchase, on behalf of the Philadelphia Museum of Art, one or two etchings by Delacroix from Weyhe's gallery or other establishments in New York. Pach had recommended the acquisition of Delacroix's prints in his 1928 book *Ananias, or the False Artist* as an example of how museums could find first-rate but undervalued works at reasonable prices, instead of paying exorbitant amounts for bad, but popular, art. Soon after he received Kimball's letter, Pach popped around to Weyhe's and chose "two fine Delacroix etchings" that cost only fifteen dollars each.[44] He set aside two other prints by Delacroix at another gallery, J. B. Neumann's, that were, as he explained to Kimball, a bit more expensive at eighteen dollars apiece. Kimball was most grateful for Pach's quick response to his request. Other museums to which Pach offered acquisition recommendations included the Detroit Institute of Arts; the Phillips Collection; and the Museum of Fine Arts, Boston.

In 1931, while in Paris, Pach negotiated one of the most significant sales of his career. He wrote Burroughs at the Metropolitan in January, "I have now stumbled on one [painting] that is surely that [a museum picture] and, though I am not going in for picture hunting as a practice, I thought I should send you the photograph of this [Jacques-Louis] David. It is his *Socrates Receiving the Hemlock* of the Salon of 1787" (fig. 23). He assured Burroughs that "the condition of the picture is flawless."[45] Pach knew its owners, who were asking the princely sum of eighteen thousand dollars for the canvas. Burroughs replied that though the board of the museum was in "a most economical mood," he would make a strong effort to convince them to acquire the work. He also, of course, asked if there was any "concession in the price" and if the owners would send the painting to the museum for the trustees to see.[46] When the painting arrived for viewing, Burroughs wrote Pach, "It is grander even than I had imagined—what a noble work—We are all very much excited and most enthusiastic—Such condition! Not even rubbed! It will be one of the masterpieces here, one of the outstanding works of permanent interest."[47] After several letters, and much negotiation, Burroughs gleefully cabled Pach on March 31, "David bought Hooray."[48] This painting remains one of the most significant works in the collection of the Metropolitan Museum of Art.

Toward the beginning of 1931, Pach wrote Susan Eakins to propose placing a painting by her husband, Thomas, whose work he had admired for decades, in the Louvre. Overwhelmed by the gesture, she immediately sent Pach several photographs of portraits that would be available and told him that she preferred to "present" the work to the Louvre, rather than "sell" it to the museum.[49] Negotiations ensued between Pach; Susan Eakins; Kimball; Burroughs; and officials at the Louvre, particularly Jean Guiffrey, the chief curator. It was Burroughs's idea to "try to wrangle Clara (1) or The Bohemian (2) out of the Pennsylvania Museum [Philadelphia Museum of Art]."[50] After an exchange of several letters, the group settled on *Clara* (fig. 24). Susan Eakins was most pleased with the selection, and officials at the Louvre graciously accepted the generous gift, which they acknowledged was given through the "intermediary" Walter Pach. Bureaucracy in museums being what it is, and with the addition of overseas shipment, it took several more months before the picture actually arrived in Paris and was presented to the museum.[51] This was quite a coup for American art, and the transaction would never have been considered by the French government if Pach had not been involved. This painting was later transferred to the collection of the Musée d'Orsay, Paris.

Throughout the 1910s, 1920s, and 1930s, Pach acted as a broker for friends and colleagues—both American and European—and helped them sell modern and historical art in the United States, either through retail galleries or privately. After Morton Schamberg died in 1918, Pach helped organize his memorial exhibition at the Knoedler Gallery in New York City. When the show closed, he and Charles Sheeler took on the responsibility of trying to sell the paintings that remained in the estate. Pach wrote Quinn, "Sheeler brought from Philadelphia the rest of the Schamberg pictures that we decided to keep, and turned them over to me this week. Beside what was left from the exhibition, I have now about ten paintings that were not shown at Knoedler's. I shall be glad to show them to you any day, if you would like to see them."[52] Unfortunately, Pach was not very successful, and he eventually gave the works to the Charles Daniel Gallery in New York. During a trip Pach made to Issy, France, in the summer of 1921, Matisse asked him to try to sell some pastels by Redon that Matisse had bought for his father, as well as some Old Master paintings.[53] Eventually, Pach negotiated the sale of the Redons from Matisse's collection to Quinn. Pach also persisted in his efforts to sell modern French paintings and prints left in his care during the war years, meeting with some limited success. For example, in the spring of 1925 he sent Jean Metzinger a check for a picture Pach had recently sold. The artist thanked Pach, released him from all responsibility for his other works still in New York—many of them left from the war period—and told him to "dispose of them as you wish."[54] Pach also tried to sell works, and occasionally succeeded, for collectors such as Alexander and Florence Bing.

While in Paris between 1929 and 1932, Pach approached several artist friends in the United States with a proposition to promote American art in Paris. One of the departments at the Louvre, the Chalcographie, housed six or seven thousand engraved plates from which prints were made and sold to the public.

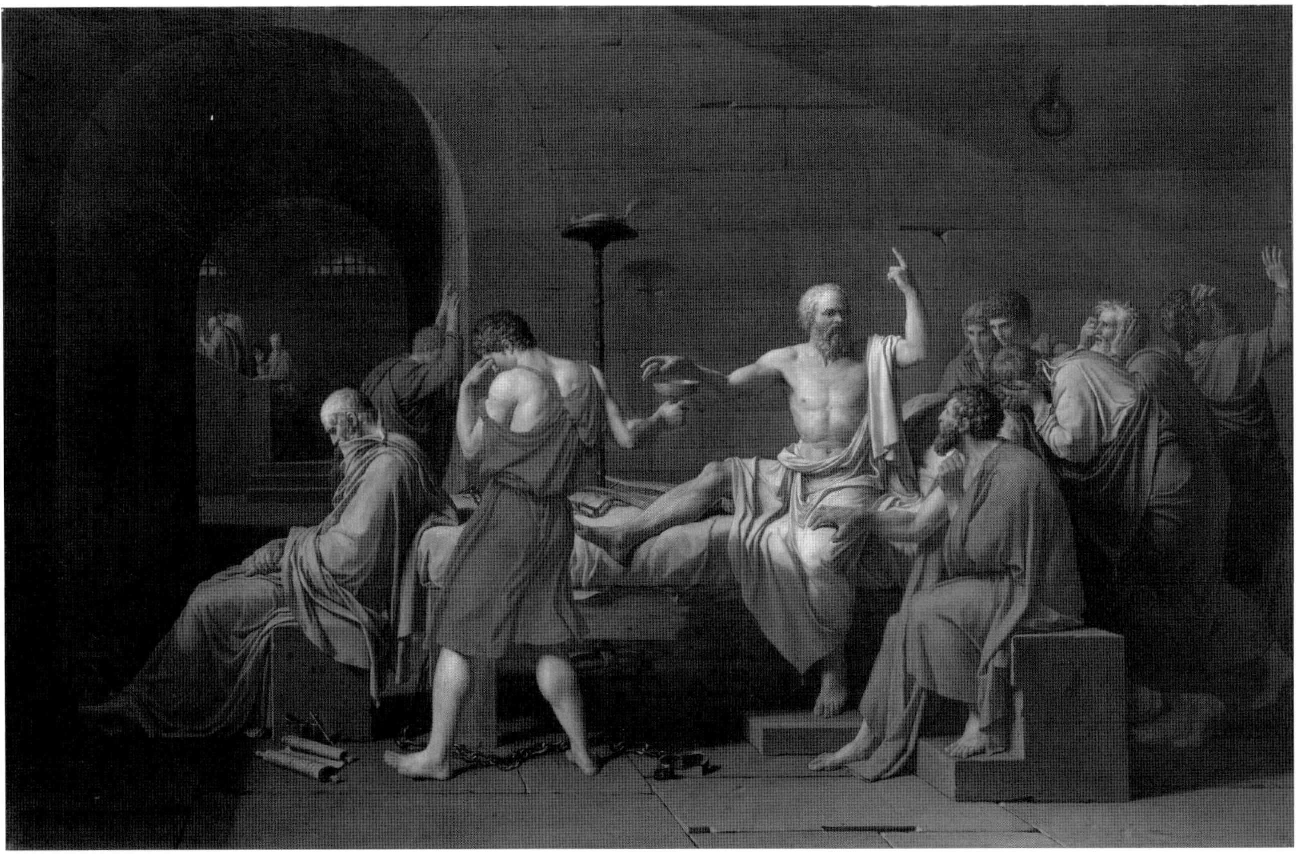

Fig. 23

Jacques-Louis David, *The Death of Socrates,* 1787, oil on canvas, 51 × 77 ¼ in. (129.5 × 196.2 cm). The Metropolitan Museum of Art, Catharine Lorillard Wolfe Collection, Wolfe Fund, 1931 (31.45). Image © The Metropolitan Museum of Art.

The director of this department approached Pach and asked him to recommend American artists for the collection. Pach's first thought was of Sloan. He told his friend that the museum would not pay the artists directly for the plates, but they would receive a royalty of 10 percent on the sales of prints. He knew that this was not a great financial reward but assured Sloan, "It *is* an honor, and can be of value to one as propaganda."[55] Pach donated one of his own works and also wrote to Childe Hassam, who sent a plate. Pach's negotiations on behalf of his friends and colleagues resulted in several sales, quite an achievement considering that the art market in New York and elsewhere remained relatively weak.

Élie Faure was the most consistent and persistent of those who asked for Pach's aid in selling works in the United States. The pictures offered came from Faure's personal collection and from clients of his in France. Most of these paintings were nineteenth-century French and older works. Pach sometimes consigned the pictures he could not sell to dealer friends in New York, such as the Ehrich Galleries. Pach usually received at least a 10 percent commission on sales of works from Faure, although his friend sometimes had to insist he take it. He was also compensated for his efforts in the form of prints and other art for his personal collection.

Pach returned to the United States in the fall of 1932 and spent much of the next decade earning a living as a

Walter Pach (1883–1958)

writer and lecturer, but he was also involved in a few undertakings to promote modern art. In the early months of 1937, he became connected with a new venture, the Shilling Fund. The late Alexander Shilling, an American painter and etcher, bequeathed his "modest estate" to two colleagues and suggested that "they use his money for the benefit of artists."[56] Lawyers Arthur Strasser and Fred Stein (a relative of Leo and Gertrude Stein), executors of the estate and friends of Pach, established the Shilling Fund on March 15, 1937, and asked Pach and others to participate.[57] The mission was to provide awards to artists of American birth or residence whose works would be selected by a committee and presented as gifts to American museums. This was a revolutionary idea. Strasser and Stein asked Pach to head this committee, whose initial membership included John Sloan, Edward M. M. Warburg (art collector and trustee of the Museum of Modern Art), George Grosz, Talbot F. Hamlin (of the architecture department of Columbia University), and dealer Joseph Brummer. After Grosz and Warburg resigned their post for reasons of work and the war, Wilhelm Valentiner of the Detroit Institute of Arts and sculptor Hugo Robus became members. It was Pach, however,

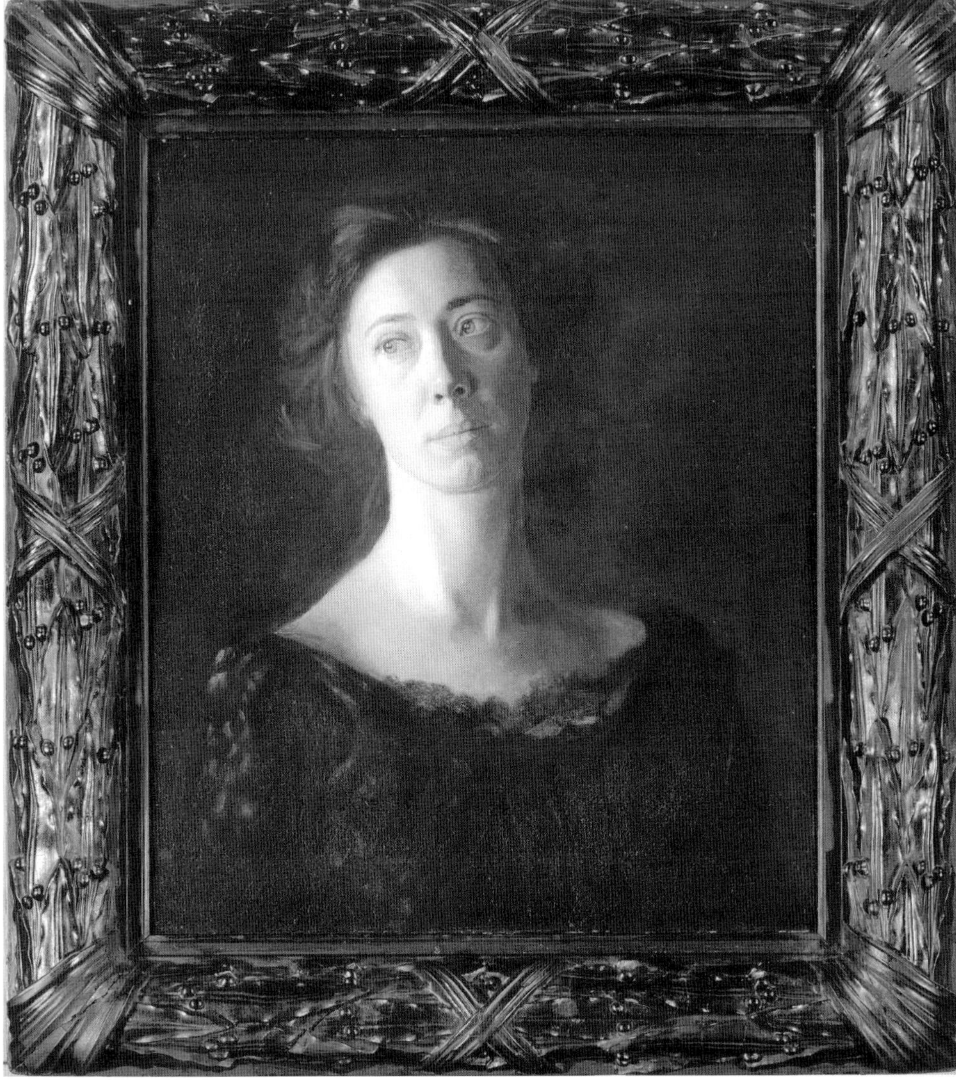

Fig. 24
Thomas Eakins, *Clara* (Clara J. Mather), ca. 1890, oil on canvas, 61 × 51 cm. Musée d'Orsay, Paris. Photo: Réunion des Musées Nationaux/Art Resource, NY (photo: Hervé Lewandowski).

who took charge of the selections. In 1946, he was approached by Strasser and Stein and offered an annual fee for his services as the fund's principal advisor. The two men had compensated Pach in the past, but this proposal was different. They wrote that they wished "to assure ourselves of the continuation of your services to the Fund in so far as that is compatible with your other activities."[58] Over the course of ten years, Pach would receive a thousand dollars a year. His wife would receive the same benefits if he died. Understandably, Pach was overwhelmed by this generous proposition, which would give him much-needed financial relief, and accepted at once. He worked in this capacity until at least 1956, dispersing many paintings and sculptures to museums across the country, in the process influencing their collections and those who came to visit these institutions. Among the works given were John Flannagan's *Figure of Dignity—Irish Mountain Goat* (fig. 25), to the Metropolitan Museum of Art in 1940; Jacob Lawrence's *Subway—Home from Work* (fig. 26), to the Virginia Museum of Fine Arts in 1944, this being the first painting by an African American artist to enter that collection; Hugo Robus's *Reunion,* to the Cleveland Museum of Art in 1946; Philip Evergood's *No Sale,* to the Baltimore Museum of Art in 1946; and George Constant's *Sea, Sun, and Sky,* to the Pennsylvania Academy of the Fine Arts in Philadelphia in 1956. The Art Institute of Chicago, the Brooklyn Museum of Art, the Toledo Museum of Art, the Museum of Fine Arts in Boston, the Philadelphia Museum of Art, the Los Angeles County Museum of Art, the Detroit Institute of Arts, and the Phillips Academy in Andover, among others, were also recipients. Little research has been done on the Shilling Fund, which was defunct by 1960, and its archives have yet to be discovered; however, with Pach's able assistance, it became a great source of support for many American artists.

In the 1940s, Pach's influence within the contemporary art world of New York began to wane, and he found it more difficult to find work of any kind. So,

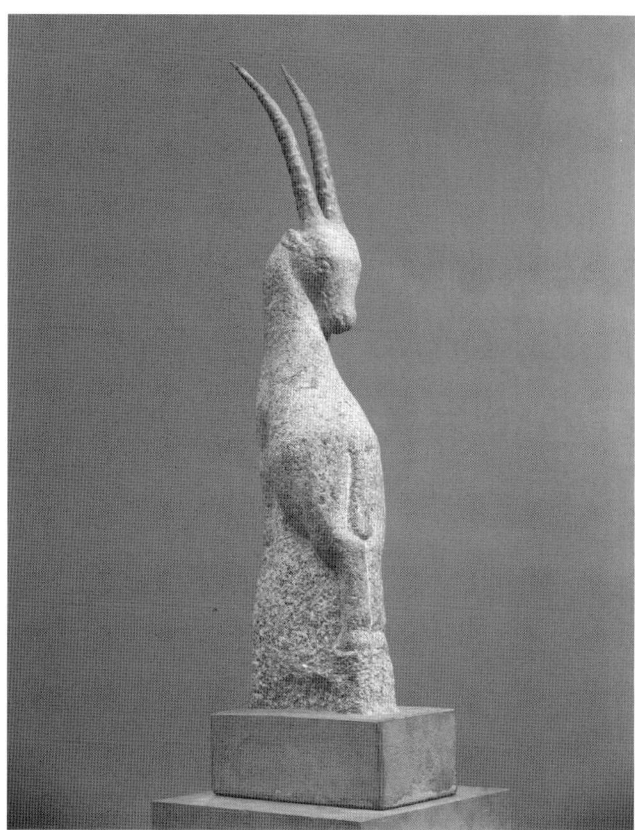

Fig. 25

John Flannagan, *Figure of Dignity—Irish Mountain Goat,* 1932, granite and cast aluminum on concrete plinth, 53 ¾ × 14 ⅛ × 8 ¾ in. (136.5 × 35.9 × 22.2 cm). The Metropolitan Museum of Art. Gift of The Alexander Shilling Fund, 1941 (41.47). Image © The Metropolitan Museum of Art.

when he was approached in the spring of 1942 by M. M. Pochapin, merchandising director of the Publishers Service Company, and asked to sit on the board of judges of a new organization, he agreed. The Art Appreciation Movement, whose other members included John Sloan and Reginald Marsh, was a loosely organized group headquartered in New York that called itself a "great Public Service Movement" and whose mission was to bring art to the American people. It was "designed to appeal to the great masses of people" and would "be promoted through the use of full-page and double-truck display advertising in the greatest newspapers of our country, preceded by huge public dinners and banquets, and supplemented by radio and direct mail advertising, plus every other dignified approach toward interesting the public in a great cultural enterprise."[59] Artists were asked to consign paintings to the "campaign" as a "Public Service." The price of these pictures would range from five to one hundred dollars. "This is a campaign," Pochapin wrote Magda Pach, "to arouse the desire to own beautiful oil paintings, not on the part of a few thousand people, but in the minds of millions of people."[60] The idea of placing oil paintings in every American household was a goal in which Pach firmly believed, and the Art Appreciation Movement's mission was one he felt compelled to support. He consigned five paintings to the cause and asked for prices well below his normal range. The salary for his

services was twenty-five dollars a week. After less than six months, the Art Appreciation Movement ran into difficulties, and Marsh and other members resigned. Pochapin tried to continue under the new title of Art Movement, Inc., holding exhibitions in department stores such as Wanamaker's in Philadelphia and Rich's in Atlanta, but the organization did not succeed.

In the mid- to late 1940s, Pach was involved as an agent or liaison for several New York galleries, although the details of his work are unknown. Pach reported on his 1948 income tax return that the Robert Lebel Gallery, New York, had paid him $1,330 for his services. He was also paid $50 by E. Ehrenzweig Gallery and $100 by Schaeffer Galleries; all three employers were located in Manhattan. In addition, he declared $740 in

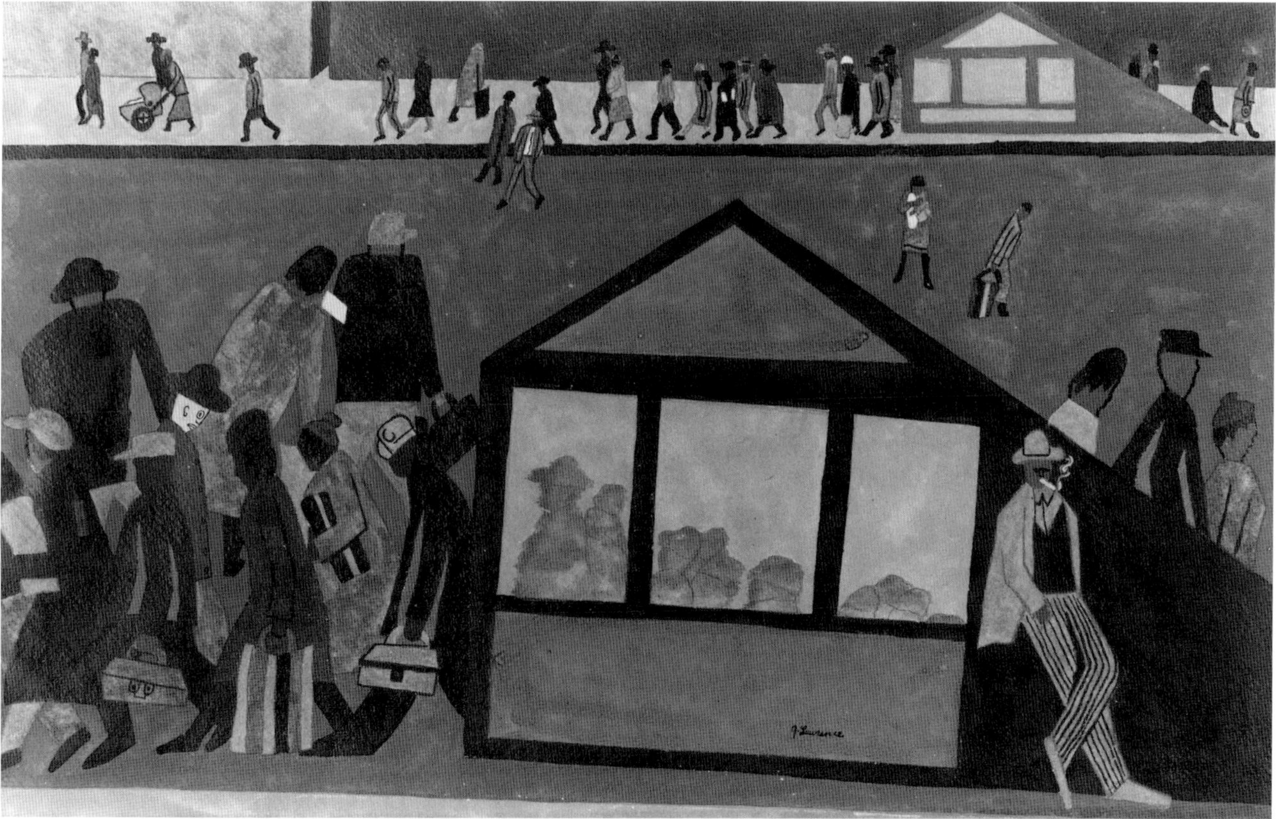

Fig. 26

Jacob Lawrence, *Subway—Home from Work,* 1943, watercolor on paper, 14 × 21 ¼ in. (35.6 × 54 cm). Virginia Museum of Fine Arts, Richmond. Gift of The Alexander Shilling Fund. © Virginia Museum of Fine Arts (photo: Ron Jennings). © 2011 The Jacob and Gwendolyn Lawrence Foundation, Seattle/Artists Rights Society (ARS), New York.

expenses for a seven-week trip to Paris in the spring of 1948.

Another way in which Pach was involved with the secondary art market in the United States was through the sale of paintings, prints, and sculptures from his own collection. In September 1936, he approached Duchamp about selling *Sad Young Man on a Train,* which Pach had acquired from Manierre Dawson in 1922. Apparently, he had been offered thirty-five hundred dollars for the painting and was tempted to accept. He had written to Duchamp that he would give him 20 percent of this sum, or seven hundred dollars, quite a handsome commission for a secondary sale. Pach did not mention the name of the buyer. A year lapsed before Duchamp responded that he was "flabbergasted" by the price of thirty-five hundred dollars and asked Pach if he would be willing to "cut out this 20%" and reduce his share "by an amount between $2,000 and $2,500"; he would be happy, he said, with a hundred dollars. In reality, however, he wanted the picture to join its "brothers and sisters in California" in the Arensberg collection. Pach eventually sold Duchamp's picture to Peggy Guggenheim in 1942.[61] Three years after that, he parted with the artist's painting *The Passage from the Virgin to the Bride,* which went to the Museum of Modern Art in New York.

Toward the end of 1948, Pach began to reorganize his resources; among the first decisions he and Magda made was that they could part with some of their collection. He contacted Sotheby Parke-Bernet to consign paintings, prints, and a few sculptures. On January 6, 1949, a significant portion of the collection was offered at Parke-Bernet's New York gallery, with results that were not good. Pach reported to Paul Sachs at the Fogg Art Museum that among the things that sold was van Gogh's drawing *Landscape at Arles* (presently in the collection of the Art Institute of Chicago) for forty-one hundred dollars and Delacroix's *Tiger Resting* for fifteen hundred dollars. After the miserable results of the auction, Pach sent letters to

Paul Sachs and other colleagues and offered the works to them, at reduced prices, of course.

Among the prized possessions he sold at this time was Duchamp's *The Chess Players (The Chess Game),* which he had acquired from Harold Tovell around 1928. On the advice of Alexander Bing, Pach first approached Walter and Louise Arensberg in May 1949, setting his price at six thousand dollars; initially, the Arensbergs declined. Pach then spoke with Fiske Kimball at the Philadelphia Museum of Art, relaying that he had offers from a private collector and dealer who were willing to pay seventy-five hundred dollars for the picture. Kimball, however, wrote Arensberg immediately after he heard from Pach and also contacted Albert Gallatin for his opinion. The negotiations for the sale of this painting persisted for months, and it was not until the early summer of 1950 that Pach finally sold *The Chess Players* to the Arensbergs. Toward the end of June, Duchamp dropped by Pach's apartment to tell him that he had received a letter from Arensberg in which he said he would buy the piece for four thousand dollars, "with an initial payment of $1,500 and the balance at intervals running through 1951." Pach accepted the deal, though it was far less than he was asking for the canvas. He told Arensberg that he would now "be free of the importunities of the dealers, several of whom have been coming to me periodically about the canvas."[62] He confessed that a barrage from Peggy Guggenheim's assistant had forced him to sell Duchamp's *Sad Young Man on a Train* to Guggenheim. Arensberg sent the first deposit at the end of June and instructed Pach to ship the painting "direct to Earl Stendahl, 7055 Hillside Avenue, since he will uncrate it and hang it for us."[63] Pach complied without delay. Funds from all these sales, Pach admitted to Arensberg, would add to "the reserves of money on which I shall live when I get out of teaching, writing, and the other means I have of earning."[64] Pach, it would turn out, was overly optimistic in his hopes of retiring.

On top of his work as an agent and liaison between artists and collectors, Pach acted as a mentor to a few novice art dealers, notably Matisse's son Pierre and Ida Guggenheimer, in New York in the 1920s and 1930s. In the autumn of 1924, Matisse wrote Pach that Pierre was leaving France on his advice to find employment at a gallery in New York, preferably a "modern one."[65] Furthermore, he told Pach, "The Steins approve of it and they share my belief that if you allow it he would benefit greatly from your advice. Could you please do whatever you can to help him?"[66] Matisse was entrusting his son to a friend's care and guidance, and the friend did not disappoint him. On a cold Monday morning, Pach stood at the dock and greeted Pierre Matisse on his arrival in the United States. He proved to be a godsend to the young man, who barely spoke English and had arrived during the week of Christmas, a time when gallery owners were not particularly anxious to meet with prospective competitors. Pach gallantly guided him through opening a bank account and finding a place to stay. He also introduced him to his numerous colleagues in the art world. One, the bookseller and print dealer Erhard Weyhe, gave Pierre his first break: an exhibition of his father's work with a preface to the catalog written by none other than Walter Pach.[67]

Soon after Pach had met Ida Guggenheimer, in the late 1920s, he began advising her on the New York art world, the art market, and her role in both. He understood the difficulties of the current art market and had a warning for his friend:

> Selling pictures is a very difficult game and that you must not be disappointed if you find customers rare. (They may even seem non-existent). All up and down the streets around 57th St., they are offered the pick of the world (also, to be sure, a lot of things that are poor pickings). For dealers are watching like hawks for anything that looks at all salable,— and they watch even more hawkishly for the possible buyer—for whom they will do anything, so long as they can get him to their galleries. If he *is*

a buyer the pictures (plus some diplomacy and compliments) will do the rest. You have very slender resources to compete with them in a busy city where people have so narrow a margin of time and interest in Art. In Paris, it's their business to see it and acquire it. In New York it's the fifth wheel to the wagon.[68]

While overseas between 1929 and 1932, Pach stayed fully abreast of all the activities regarding modern art in the United States through letters to and from colleagues back home and through a subscription to *Art News,* which, he informed Lewis Mumford, "covers everything pretty thoroughly."[69] Arguably the biggest art event of 1929 was the opening of the Museum of Modern Art in New York. Pach knew virtually everyone involved with this venture, including Abby Aldrich Rockefeller, one of the founders, and Alfred Barr Jr., the first director. He told Guggenheimer that the museum should "do very much" in the way of advancing the modernist cause and advised her, "You ought, I think, to get into contact with Mr. Barr, the director. He is a young man who should be glad to receive any friend of mine; I think he is well disposed toward me as are all, probably, of the committee." "The most important person," he informed her, "in the whole outfit is Mr. A. C. Goodyear, the chairman. He is a most important collector, his purchases include Villon, Baylinson, and Kantor. Our acquaintance began when, having read an article of mine praising the two Americans, he wrote to ask me how he could get to see their work."[70] Even at a distance of a few thousand miles, Pach stayed connected to the power structure in the art world of New York.

The new Museum of Modern Art provided much grist for the artistic gossip mill, and in January 1930 Pach wrote Guggenheimer and Mumford about the first two shows at the museum: Cézanne, Seurat, Gauguin, and Van Gogh, and Paintings by Nineteen Living Americans. Even from a distance, Pach felt compelled to be involved in the discourse on modern art that was swirling around the New York art circles. He wrote Guggenheimer, "I know you have been often to see the remarkable pictures at the Modern Museum (the French show) and can see that I was right about the importance the place would acquire. I have just seen the list of Americans in the second show and, while I cordially agree with many—or perhaps most of the choices, I disagree very much with others."[71] Pach was beginning to have serious misgivings about the management of the museum, concerns that were shared by Mumford, who wrote Pach that since Barr "*began* by making compromises," he doubted whether there was any chance that the museum would "ever get properly on its feet." Mumford disapproved of the museum's choice of Walt Kuhn, Rockwell Kent, and Lyonel Feininger for the American show and felt that the selection was an "attempt to get, not the best pictures available, but those that are owned by their patrons."[72] Pach agreed with his friend's sentiments but also confessed that he "was glad not to be in New York and so escape having to say what I thought of the running of that place." He confided, "The Metropolitan is ever so much better in its acts—even if it is less 'modern,' (the word gets more baneful to me all the time)."[73] As the tone of this last statement indicates, Pach was beginning to rethink and reassess his approach to modern art. Although he continued to admire and promote the work of contemporary artists in the United States and France, he was becoming much more interested in historical art.

9
Writings on Modern European and American Art

The battle for the acceptance of modern art in the United States was fought not only in the galleries but also in the press, and in his writings on the subject Pach was at the forefront of the fight. He was one of the few critics of the time who knew intimately the progressive Parisian and American painters and sculptors and their styles. Although he did not always fully fathom all the theories behind the new movements, Pach understood their significance and hailed their creators' efforts in his essays. Pach's ideas on modern art were not revolutionary in content; however, they were perceived as authoritative, and his importance in the field of criticism rests not only on his expertise in the area but also in the diversity of forums in which he presented his views. His monographs and books were distributed in the United States and France, and his articles appeared in popular periodicals, newspapers, and specialized journals, including *Scribner's Magazine, Harper's Weekly,* the *New York Times,* the *Dial,* the *Freeman,* the *Christian Science Monitor, Gazette des Beaux-Arts, L'Amour de l'Art,* and *L'Art et les Artistes,* bringing his views on modern art to an international audience. Although his ideas were not particularly original, they helped shape the intellectual atmosphere of early twentieth-century American art criticism.

In his essays on modern art, Pach consistently presented an aesthetic credo with several main tenets: the theory of the evolutionary aspect of art; the belief that art was creative, not mimetic, and that it did not have to represent reality accurately; the idea that art was a creation unique unto itself; an understanding of the correlation between art, life, and spirituality; the belief that art was the outward and necessary expression of an individual's emotional response to the world; and the conviction that the true artist must be the voice of his or her generation and the revealer of universal truths. The view of art as an evolutionary process was not unique to Pach; he shared this ideal with critics and colleagues such as Roger Fry, Julius Meier-Graefe, and Élie Faure, whom he admired. Pach also professed that art was a product of its time and place and partook of

national characteristics, a philosophy that echoed Hippolyte-Adolphe Taine's analysis of art as a result of "race, milieu, and moment."[1] In addition, he embraced Clive Bell's theory of significant form and accepted the Englishman's assertion that there was an inextricable connection between form and idea in a work of art. Pach professed, "According as one or the other of these phases tends to become dominant, we speak of art as classical or romantic."[2] All artists, Pach believed, could be placed into one of these two categories. Although he felt that all art, if it was true art, was worthy of recognition, he maintained that classical art contained qualities that "meet the universal in man's nature" and was therefore the type of art toward which artists should strive. Culled from various sources, and formulated over several years, Pach's mature aesthetic credo, which did not change dramatically over his career, reflected the cultural context and philosophical ideologies of the late nineteenth and early twentieth centuries.

Although he sometimes complained about his work as a critic, Pach nevertheless enjoyed most aspects of it. He wrote, "While my writing has been a source of necessary income to me, it also means more than money. I am always desirous of reaching out to people who are interested in art and to speak for the things I believe in (not that I think of myself as a propagandist—except for art as a whole)."[3] Pach was passionate, albeit sometimes ponderous, about art. He firmly believed that it was his moral duty to educate the American public about the social value of art and the essential need for it in everyday life.

Pach's career as a critic of modern European and American art officially began with his 1908 publication on Cézanne and continued to grow throughout the late 1900s and 1910s. Several of his articles during this period promoted American art and artists. In his essays on Winslow Homer and John Sloan, published in *L'Art et les Artistes* in 1912 and 1914, Pach endorsed the theory of a native school of art and celebrated the American characteristics of the artists' works.[4] For Pach, Homer's respect for the power of nature, his admiration for tumultuous movements and great spaces, and his straightforward definition of forms reflected the force, integrity, and poetry of the American people, a race of the frontier. Homer, Pach believed, ranked with Ingres, Corot, and other masters of French art because his paintings combined "the feeling of nature that one spoke of in the past, and the aesthetic of which one speaks today."[5] Pach praised Sloan for his ability to capture the essence of contemporary life in the United States, while he compared Sloan's illustrations with those of the renowned British artists George Cruickshank, William Hogarth, and John Leech and at the same time perceived a correspondence between Sloan's prints and the work of Honoré Daumier. Sloan, he felt, attained the same depth and intensity that foreign

geniuses of the past had achieved. Although Pach was not unique in his support of an indigenous style, he was among the first to declare American artists the equals of European masters.

Pach's role as a leading authority on modern art began in earnest with his writings and translations for the Armory Show and blossomed throughout the 1910s, 1920s, and 1930s. The Armory Show presented an overwhelming array of modern art to American audiences, and in the articles he wrote immediately afterward Pach attempted to explain the theories behind the works and to establish their connection with the past. In 1914, William C. Brownell, of Scribner's publishing house, asked Pach to write a series of articles on modern art and then "suggested a whole volume on the modern school."[6] Unfortunately, this project did not come to fruition at this time. However, Pach's seminal piece, "The Point of View of the 'Moderns,'" was published in the *Century* magazine in April 1914 as one of five articles in the series "The Transitional Age in Art"; the others were John White Alexander's "Is Our Art Distinctly American?," Edwin H. Blashfield's "The Painting of Today," Ernest L. Bluemenschein's "The Painting of Tomorrow," and Jay Hambridge and Gove Hambridge's "The Ancestry of Cubism." Pach was pleased with his article in general, but he complained to artist Manierre Dawson, "I worked hard on the 'Century' article but it did not look as I wanted it to in the magazine—with those bum repros stuck into my text and that letter of Duchamp-Villon's omitted which I had counted on to cover matters I skipped through limited space."[7] Obviously the editors added their own touches and photographs to his manuscript, a practice that would infuriate Pach throughout his life.

In his essay, Pach set forth the theories on art he had been developing for years. He believed that art was a living thing and that its purpose was to convey to the viewer the specific emotion the artist deemed vital in the most concise way possible. This aim was consistent throughout the history of art, Pach felt, but the method used to achieve this goal changed with each generation. Since each era had its own spirit, every period needed to find its unique form of expression, yet each epoch built on the past. The modern movement, he argued, began with Cézanne, whose work evolved from past masters. Cézanne, however, represented only one element of the modern era—classical art; Redon represented its opposite—romantic art. The impressionists, Pach stated, employed aesthetic qualities instinctively, whereas "with Cézanne we have the all-important evolution in an art where they are sought for consciously."[8] Redon, by contrast, was a figure of immense significance for the development of art as an embodiment and revelation of the inner world of reality. Pach traced the roots of cubism to Cézanne, particularly his "composition of volumes," but noted that "the Cubists take the elements of expression from the forms and colors of nature, and use them not to represent objects, but to produce an organism which will contain in terms of art what a given subject means to them in terms of sensation. . . . The Cubists have already shown the possibility of an expression in painting without representation."[9]

Pach's article was illustrated with several black-and-white images: Brancusi's marble bust *Mademoiselle Pogany,* Duchamp's *Nude Descending a Staircase, No. 2,* Stella's *Battle of Lights, Coney Island,* and Maurice Prendergast's *Sea-Shore,* thus placing American art on par with European modernists. These illustrations brought the art into the homes of those readers who could not see the works firsthand. Writings such as this, as well as by Henry McBride, Christian Brinton, and other contemporaries of Pach identified the modern "masters" and helped formulate the hierarchical canon of modern art that became the basis for the traditional history of Western art as taught to generations of college students and others.

Pach followed up this piece with another for the *Century,* "Why Matisse?," which was published in the

February 1915 issue and coincided with the artist's solo exhibition at Montross Gallery in New York. Pach championed Matisse as an artist who found the means to express the essentials of the modern era and who eliminated all that was unnecessary from painting. He likened Matisse's art to that of the ancient Greeks, Persian plate makers, and Gothic stained-glass artisans. "It is in harmony with their principles," Pach wrote, "that Matisse is important as a continuer of the great heritage of the past, as being one of the truest exponents today of 'the classic point of view.'"[10] In Matisse's art, Pach found proof for his theory of the evolution of art. He believed that, like all great artists, Matisse had one foot in the past and another in the future while remaining in, reflecting, and revealing the present. Noted Matisse scholar John Cauman sees this article by Pach as "a collaboration between the author and the artist."[11] To foster further understanding of Matisse's art, Pach presented a translation of some of the artist's own writings about his works. Pach hoped that both his and Matisse's words might guide the public toward a better appreciation of modern French art.

Also in February 1915, Pach was in negotiations with two publishers regarding either several articles or a book on modern art. As Pach told Quinn, he was again approached by Brownell of Scribner's publishing house. He was also talking with Mitchell Kennerley, publisher, art patron, and director of Anderson Galleries, a gallery and auction house in New York, who proposed a series of "essays on the various modern men" and then suggested a full-length manuscript on the topic.[12] Quinn had intervened on Pach's behalf with Kennerley, and the venture would have involved all three men planning "the general synopsis of the work."[13] In regard to this book, Pach told Lewis Mumford that he spent "the whole summer of 1915 and the whole summer of 1917 trying to write it, but only got a third of the way through—, assigning to myself as a reason that I could not afford to write a book on which I should not get any payment for a year or two, but really hedging because of the difficulties of it."[14] Quinn advised Pach to try to negotiate a magazine deal with Scribner's for a series of articles and a book deal with Kennerley. He also suggested that Pach discuss the project with Frederick Gregg, for Pach reported to Quinn, "I saw Gregg today and made sure he no longer thought of writing the book on modern artists. There was no reference to you in what we said."[15] This statement reveals Quinn's desire to be at the forefront of the modern art scene in New York, with Pach as his right-hand man. Regrettably, this plan did not materialize, and it would be eight more years before a similar undertaking would meet with success.

A few months after these events, Quinn wrote a letter to Allan Dawson of the *Globe and Commercial Advertiser,* a New York–based newspaper, in which he showed his admiration for Pach as an individual and his appreciation of him as a critic:

Mr. Pach is a gentleman of cultivation and learning and is an artist of fastidiousness and great cultivation. I know most of the art critics in this town and know or know of the work of contemporary critics abroad. The crying need of art criticism in this country is someone who not only knows the classics and the old masters of art but who is familiar with the work of the men of today, the men who may be the classics of tomorrow.

Mr. Pach is a learned man in art. He knows the literature of the subject, both of early art, the great masters of art, and the men of today. He knows the great traditions. He has the feel of the subject. He has all the learning of the subject at his finger ends and I state that of my own knowledge.

Besides being an artist he is an expert critic of paintings and knows how to judge and appraise a picture. Besides being an artist and learned in the history of art, he has a personal knowledge of many of the leading artists of today both here and abroad. He has perhaps a more intimate knowledge of

foreign living artists than any man in this country. In addition to this he is an excellent writer and has contributed articles to such magazines as the Gazette des Beaux Arts, The Century, Scribner's, Harper's, the International Encyclopedia and other important publications.

Mr. Pach is a facile writer and has had much experience with newspaper work. He is a man of agreeable personality, absolutely incapable of writing an unfair or biased criticism, and equally incapable of depreciating a good work because of any personal reason, or of over-praising a poor work. In short I think he would make an ideal critic. . . .

I believe that Mr. Pach would make the art criticism in The Globe notable; in fact I believe that before very long his contributions would come to be regarded as the best art criticism that we would have.[16]

Quinn was obviously a great admirer of Pach's knowledge about art and his keen intellect, and though Pach was not hired, Quinn remained a staunch supporter of his friend's artistic sensibilities and writing skills.

Throughout the war, Pach continued to promote modern French art in newspaper articles and periodicals in the United States. His March 5, 1916, *New York Times* article, "French Art and War," was a response to an editorial in the *Times* that declared that the war had swept away all the recent developments in art, particularly postimpressionism and cubism. Alarmed that such a rumor was being spread in his hometown, Pach took pen in hand and vehemently denied the false accusations. The modern artists—some of whom, such as Marcel Duchamp, Jean Crotti, Francis Picabia, and Albert Gleizes, were living in New York—were, Pach affirmed, "continuing the advance to new truths without a hint of going back."[17] Furthermore, Pach predicted that modern art, particularly French modern art, would triumph. In another essay, "Modern Art

Today," in the April 29, 1916, issue of *Harper's Weekly,* Pach pointed to the current exhibition of European art at Bourgeois Galleries as proof that modern art was alive and well. The illustrations carried in this article, which once more brought the art to a larger segment of the American population than could visit the galleries and see the works in person, included Georges Rouault's *Superman* and Georges Seurat's *Study for "A Sunday on La Grande Jatte."* Pach took the opportunity to congratulate Alfred Stieglitz, N. E. Montross, Marius de Zayas, and other dealers for their recent shows of modern art and used this venue to dispel, once more, any rumors that modern art had died with the war.

One of Pach's most significant publications of this time was his 1918 article "Universality of Art" for Carl Zigrosser's journal, *Modern School.* As scholar Allan Antliff has noted, Zigrosser sent Pach his 1917 pamphlet on the project and enlisted his support and participation. Antliff observed that Zigrosser had "intended to seek out contributors who had 'an individualist and libertarian perspective' to write on art and other issues," and Pach was an early choice of contributor to the periodical.[18] In this piece Pach reiterated his central ideas on art and his appreciation of modern works. He firmly believed that art had a social value; it not only could, but also absolutely should, help people toward an understanding of one another and their differences. This concept of art as a force for social good was one Pach shared with several of his American and French colleagues. Allan Antliff has argued that Pach's essay was an "exposition of unanimism" whose main theme was that "unanimist cubism could play a role in overcoming nationalist hatreds and social divisions fostered by World War I."[19] "Unanimism," Antliff writes, "was a theory of modern collective consciousness popular among French literary and artistic *avant-garde,* including many Cubists, in the years leading up to World War One."[20] He sees the theories Pach set forth in this article as being directly related to and a result of his friendship

with French intellectuals and writers of the Puteaux Group and the unanimist circle, including the Duchamp-Villon brothers, Gleizes, Metzinger, Léger, Jules Romains, and Alexandre Mercereau. While Antliff's conclusion that Pach saw cubism as "an important artistic step toward the goal of universal brotherhood" is valid, Pach had formulated similar concepts of art as a means to universality among nations and humankind much earlier than his affiliation with the Puteaux Group.[21] Through the Ethical Culture School and its teachings, Pach had embraced the concept of art as a social force. In addition, he would probably have heard such beliefs espoused by his friend Élie Faure—whom Antliff describes as "an anarchist-leaning radical"—as early as 1910 and through lectures at the University of the People in Paris at the same time.[22] His course at the Lycée Charlemagne in 1911–12 further reinforced these tenets, and since his return to the United States in early 1913 for the Armory Show, he had promoted these thoughts in his writings.

Pach's work with Zigrosser on the *Modern School* continued in 1918 and 1919. In the July 1918 and August 1919 issues, several of van Gogh's letters were published, through Pach's intercession. Pach assisted Zigrosser with the October 1918 edition of the journal, devoted to France. He contributed an article on his avant-garde poet friend Jean Le Roy and enlisted Wallace Stevens to translate the poet's work *Moment of Light.* Stevens clearly did this as a favor for his friend, for he confided in Zigrosser, "The truth is that I was not nearly so impressed by it as Walter Pach was."[23] Pach acquired a Redon lithograph to illustrate Le Roy's poem and translated a short article by Faure titled "Paris in War-Time." The April–May 1919 edition of the journal was dedicated to Walt Whitman, and Pach arranged for André Derain, Rockwell Kent, and Raoul Dufy to provide illustrations.

Toward the end of 1918, Pach began writing for the *Dial* magazine and, for a brief period, was consulted "about all art-matters" for the journal.[24] Founded in

1840 as a publication centered on transcendentalism and reinvented in 1880 to address socially humanitarian themes, the *Dial* was under the editorial control of Scofield Thayer when Pach became involved with it. Thayer, a graduate of Harvard University, was a close friend of T. S. Eliot, giving him entrée to the leading literary and artistic circles of the United States. By 1920, Thayer had transformed the *Dial* "into a journal of art and culture; the liberal political agenda had become implicit and diffuse, absorbed into a radical and clearly focused aesthetic agenda."[25] Among the artists and writers who contributed to the publication were Van Wyck Brooks, Sherwood Anderson, Bertrand Russell, Ezra Pound, Charles Demuth, and Redon. Pach already knew some of these people and soon became close with others. He wrote only a handful of articles for the *Dial,* as his colleague and friend Henry McBride assumed the position of chief art critic in 1920.

One of Pach's most important pieces for the journal was on his old school chum Morton L. Schamberg, who had died tragically in the autumn of 1918. Pach's review of Schamberg's retrospective at M. Knoedler and Company was the first substantial writing on the artist and helped establish his place as a modernist of the first rank. Pach discussed the change of Schamberg's style from colorist to cubist and attributed this development to a shift from instinct to reason as the guiding force behind the artist's work. In Schamberg's growth from student to mature artist, Pach found affirmation of his own evolutionary view of art. He saw Schamberg as a leader of his generation who gave visual expression to the spirit of his day. "His paintings in the Cubistic manner were among the very first in America and will probably long remain among the best," Pach asserted.[26] As Ben Wolf observed in his 1963 monograph on Schamberg, Pach "had the rare and perceptive intuition and foresight (as had McBride) to realize that his ex-classmate had caught the spirit of the new century and that Schamberg's work would increase in meaning with the passage of time."[27] Pach was among

the earliest critics to recognize and promote Schamberg's talent.

Two other influential essays that Pach wrote for the *Dial* were on Native American art. Published in January and March of 1920, they coincided with the showing of Native American art that Pach had arranged at the annual Society of Independent Artists exhibition.[28] Pach was but one of a number of American artists to champion the work of Native Americans as art. In these writings, he argued for the preservation of the culture and art of the Native Americans of the American Southwest. He believed that "at its best to-day it is equal to the best they ever produced" and felt that their art attained "the dignity that inheres in national and religious things, for it belongs to the whole of the people and informs every phase of their lives, from the great ceremonies of prayer and thanksgiving to the making of clothing, ornaments, and the objects of daily use."[29] Their work, according to Pach, was a living art of today that was deeply connected with the lives of the past. He expressed concern over the "government agents" who were trying to "civilize" the Native Americans and erase all trace of their ancient and noble heritage. Yet however much Pach admired the art of the Native Americans, he still referred to the people as backward, weak, and "among the great Primitives." He wrote, "They are Primitives in the true sense of the word, their form and content deriving from an immediate response to the scenes they depict, the simple means of execution being suddenly raised to their intensity of effect by the conviction and enthusiasm of the artists."[30]

Noted art historian William Jackson Rushing has observed that Pach's January 1920 article was important "not just because its author was an integral part of the early American avant-garde. In it one finds a compendium of themes central to the cultural primitivism inherent to Euro-American intellectual and spiritual life in the late nineteenth and early twentieth centuries. . . . Indeed, it is probably because Pach *was* a purveyor of modernism that one finds these ideas informing his perceptions of Native American art." Rushing argued that although Pach "encouraged a shift from thinking of Native American objects 'as relics of a savage period,' to seeing them in the startling new light of art, his vision was clouded by the duality of race/evolution."[31] For Pach, race was a determining factor in the development of art. He felt that people of certain ethnic backgrounds created works in a style peculiar to them; German art had a certain look, as did that of the Italian Renaissance. Pach's approach was not that unusual for his time; his notions about race and culture were very much influenced by Faure's and Hippolyte Taine's theories of race and ethnicity.

The end of 1919 brought a new enterprise for Pach; the *Christian Science Monitor* approached him about writing for the publication. Ever the salesperson, and always in search of new venues to disseminate his views on art, Pach sent the editor a letter with a list of the most important art events of the past season and a proposal for an article about any of them. The editor hired Pach to write a three-part series, titled "The Approach to Modern Art," for the early months of 1920.[32] In his essays, Pach summarized his aesthetic credo. His statement that "the hot discussions of our time are merely the echo of those of the past generations" contained the germ of his argument in favor of an evolutionary interpretation of art.[33] He expressed his belief that the artist's true mission was "the expression through form and color of ideas called forth in him by the visible universe." Modernists differed from their predecessors because they rejected the imitation of nature as the basis for creation and chose instead to produce works in which "an equivalent for certain mental impressions" was given through form and color alone.[34] Pach accepted and promoted the idea that the function of art was no longer merely mimetic. Finally, he professed that art, like music and literature, was a living thing. To be a vital force in the world, it needed to reveal essential truths in a language that expressed

not only the spirit of its day but also the soul of the universe. These ideas were not new; however, the journal reached readers who were not necessarily conversant with modern art and thus helped spread the word further afield and to a new audience.

In June 1920, Pach began writing for the *Freeman,* and over the course of the next three years, he wrote thirty-one articles for the periodical. The original *Freeman* was a short-lived journal published from 1920 to 1924.[35] Among its founders and on its editorial board were Suzanne La Follette—an early feminist and libertarian and a relative of the renowned Progressive Wisconsin senator Robert M. La Follette—as well as writer Albert Jay Nock, literary historian Van Wyck Brooks, and Francis Neilson. Noted American publishing entrepreneur Benjamin W. Huebsch was the publisher, and the financial backing came from Neilson's wife, Helen Swift Morris Neilson (of Chicago's Swift and Morris meat industry families). The magazine was libertarian and humanistic with content devoted to social, political, and cultural issues and criticisms. Although Pach consistently stated that he had no interest in politics of any kind, he was certainly aware of political developments at home and abroad. He firmly sided with the liberal camp and was a humanist at heart.

Many of Pach's writings for the *Freeman* were exhibition reviews, but in others he focused on larger art issues, as in his two-part "Art in America," in which he set forth his attitude toward art in the United States and its place in the society of his time. In part 1, he argued that only a small segment of the American people was interested in art; the public as a whole did not understand or appreciate it. The reasons for this lack of enthusiasm were twofold. First, there were few public collections in the country that contained masterpieces from which individuals could learn the value of great art; second, "America does not yet possess a sufficiently settled body of ideas out of which to create an art of its own, the appreciation of which would not depend on a knowledge of the classics."[36] He believed that the solution to the problem would come gradually when those with sympathy for art encouraged others to pursue similar interests. The public needed to be educated to the belief that art was the province of each individual, not merely for the privileged rich. In stating these beliefs Pach echoed those of his mentors and colleagues and reflected the teachings of the Ethical Culture Society, Robert Henri, and the philosophical ideologies of Puteaux Group artists.

In part 2, Pach discussed the development of American art. For centuries, he argued, artists in the United States had borrowed ideas and forms from the European schools of painting and sculpture and had failed to create a language of their own. In the skyscrapers of Manhattan and in the automobiles and machines of the industrial age, Pach saw the raw materials for a truly American art: "When we get harmony and co-operation between the workman unconscious of the larger significance of his product, and the artist who sees the slight additions of emphasis, of gesture, of clarity that make the work an expression of the characteristic ideal of its time, then we shall at last have turned our fine material into fine art." "It is American life itself," he declared, "that must move on to the mature individuality out of which will naturally grow self-realization, style—art."[37] Inextricably linked to its time and place, art was an expression and product of its era. Pach perceived and appreciated the connection between art and the industrial age, his friendship with the Duchamp brothers and others of the Puteaux Group undoubtedly helping to foster this outlook.

Through the exhibition reviews he wrote for the *Freeman,* the *Dial,* and other outlets, Pach helped shape Americans' views on art, thus becoming a tastemaker. Pach was usually not overly critical and found something favorable to say about all the shows he visited. He saw in them true growth and the latest tendencies in American and European art and asserted, much to the dismay of conservative critics, that modern art had not only come through the war but was moving forward with vigor.

Some of these writings were quite inventive. A critique of a photography show curated by Alfred Stieglitz at the Anderson Galleries, for example, was cast in dialogue form, as if Pach were reporting a conversation. In this one-act play, Pach played the part of a skeptic who viewed photographs as "matters of our physical experience rather than of our mental life."[38] Stieglitz was not impressed by Pach's lack of support and understanding for photography as a fine art. Pach did, however, commend Stieglitz for his role in the exhibition of contemporary art on view at the Pennsylvania Academy of the Fine Arts in Philadelphia. Pach was encouraged by the new developments in American art he saw at the show, which he felt marked "the first time that American artists have been engaged on the living idea while it still possesses its generating capacity."[39] He wholeheartedly threw his support behind many of the artists who participated and those who organized the event.

Through his work for these periodicals, Pach met some of the leading New York literati and developed lifelong friendships with several of them, including architectural critic and historian Lewis Mumford, Van Wyck Brooks, and Suzanne La Follette.[40] Through Brooks, Pach met Harold Stearns; invited to Stearns's home, Pach participated there in discussions about art, life, and contemporary culture. At one of these gatherings Pach met Joel Spingarn, who had been a professor of comparative literature at Columbia University, and the two became fast friends. Joel Spingarn and his brother, Arthur, were among the early leaders of the National Association for the Advancement of Colored People (NAACP), and Pach, a believer in equal rights for African Americans, was a strong supporter of their efforts. The relationships Pach formed with these liberal-minded individuals sustained him emotionally, psychologically, and intellectually in the years to come.

In 1922, Stearns asked Pach to participate in a literary venture. Stearns was editing *Civilization in the*

United States: An Inquiry by Thirty Americans, which would contain essays by the leading authors, critics, social historians, sociologists, and philosophers of the day. As Stearns wrote in the preface, "The book has been an adventure in intellectual co-operation[,] . . . the deliberate and organized outgrowth of the common efforts of like-minded men and women to see the problem of modern American civilization as a whole, and to illuminate by careful criticism the special aspect of that civilization with which the individual is most familiar."[41] Among the contributors were H. L. Mencken, poet Conrad Aiken, Mumford, Joel Spingarn, and cultural anthropologist Elsie Clews Parsons. This group, referred to by Pach as the "Civilizers of America," met at one another's homes every two weeks or so for almost a year to discuss various aspects of American life and culture.[42] Pach's inclusion in this elite group attests to his stature among the intelligentsia of the United States.

In his essay "Art," Pach argued that the United States was still groping toward a full appreciation of the necessity of art in an advanced society. The United States, he observed, had no real history or tradition of art, unlike Europe, where it had been created and appreciated for centuries. He felt that in Europe "the exceptional individual, born with a strong instinct toward art, has surroundings and a foundation that are lacking" in the United States. Art, and its appreciation, Pach argued, had not been highly regarded in the country until recently, and then only by a relatively few people compared to the size of the population. "A striking proof of the difference between the two continents is the effect of the war on art-interest," he noted. "Whereas in America public attention has been turned away from art to a most marked degree, Europe is producing and buying art with a fervour that can only be explained by a desire to get back to essentials after years in which people were deprived of them." On the Continent, Pach observed, art was vital to everyday life; in the United States, it remained a luxury. Pach believed that art would never reach maturity in the United States until it was integrated in daily life, becoming a necessity, not an extravagance. The country had to create an art of its own, but without denying the lessons of past masters. Americans must learn from the Europeans, but build from them an art unique to their nation and their time. Toward the end of his essay Pach observed, "The steel bridges, the steel buildings, the newly designed machines, and utensils of all kinds we are bringing forth show an adaptation to function that is recognized as one of the great elements of art."[43] In the modern cities of the United States, Pach saw hope for the future of art in the country.

In the spring of 1923, *The Arts* magazine printed an article by Pach on Georges Seurat, on which Pach based his monograph on the artist, also published that year. Pach had written about Seurat's work as early as 1916, when the artist's *Study for "A Sunday on La Grande Jatte"* was exhibited at the Bourgeois Galleries in New York. He was among the earliest critics to hail Seurat as one of the greatest painters of his time and as having had a profound impact on generations of artists who followed him. Reiterating his evolutionary idea of art, Pach promoted Seurat as a painter who represented the classic line in art, which found its contemporary expression in the art of the cubists. In a 1920 article in the *Christian Science Monitor,* Pach wrote,

Seurat made haste, but instead of the furious rush of van Gogh's painting, we have an art where logic laid the sure basis on which the master built. . . . He enters the line of the great investigators, which includes Uccello, da Vinci, and Dürer, through his precise observation of the effect of the various combinations of lines and colors. To this he adds an interest in life so strong that he seems a realist of the highest order almost as often as a searcher for the laws of aesthetic. No one could dream of calling his work passionless, but neither could anything but perfect control have permitted the man to hold the astoundingly diverse elements of his art in their classic balance.[44]

In reviewing the 1921 exhibition of modern art at the Metropolitan Museum of Art, in which paintings by Seurat were on view, Pach remarked, "To find the other dominant figure of the past ten years, we must turn back to Seurat. He is usually spoken of with Signac as a neoimpressionist, an investigator of colour; but we see to-day that the chief lesson he gave the men who came after him was in bringing the idea of structure into painting. It is not simply design; and it is freer than architecture, because it deals only with things as they exist on the plane of the mind. From this conception to a system of counterpoint like that of music was the next step—which we get in cubism."[45]

In the 1920s, as noted scholar Robert L. Herbert observed, "Seurat was being hailed by French painter and critic André Lhote as the 'beacon' for modern artists. . . . At issue was the view that artists of modern persuasion had moved in the direction of structure and order, and thus away from the freely brushed, seemingly spontaneous vision of the Impressionists."[46] Pach, Herbert wrote, was "one of the several voices—including Gustave Coquiot, Lhote, and André Salmon—responsible for constructing this history and for identifying Seurat as one of the four canonical Postimpressionists, along with Cézanne, Gauguin, and Van Gogh."[47] In his writings on Seurat, Pach admitted his debt to critics who had evaluated the painter's work before him: George Moore, Clive Bell, Roger Fry, Felix Fénéon, Jules Christophe, Julius Meier-Graefe, Élie Faure, and Lucie Cousturier. Many of Pach's ideas were derived from these authors' texts; however, his was the first substantial book written in English about this seminal figure in the history of modern art. It helped popularize Seurat's art among English-speaking people and laid the foundation for future studies on him. The article and book were well received by the press; Pach, by contrast, had a few complaints for Forbes Watson,

editor of the *Arts.* For one thing, Pach did not appreciate the "bad Englishing" of the titles, translated from the French, that Watson had given to the paintings.[48] Further, an important fact that Pach had uncovered about Seurat's teacher Henri Lehmann, who was in fact a pupil of Ingres, had been omitted from the essay. Pach often complained bitterly when alterations were made to his writings.

In 1923 and 1924, Pach made his most definitive statements to date on his philosophy of modern art in a series of eight articles for the *Freeman* and in his book *The Masters of Modern Art.* The *Freeman* articles were commissioned by Suzanne La Follette, who felt they "would be admirable for the summer, when there isn't much on that is of current interest."[49] In these writings, Pach presented his concept of the evolutionary development of modern art from the French Revolution of 1789 through World War I and reasserted his belief that French art, with a few minor exceptions, was the fountainhead of modernism. As he admitted, "In giving to this book its title, I am aware that there can be nothing definitive in any attempt to follow the course of mastery in a period to which we still belong. The consideration of the modern development which I present here is sure to be revised by time."[50] Yet many of the masters whom Pach identified retain that title today. While he avowed that "modern art is, if not exclusively French, at least an art having Paris as its hearth and focus," he did rank the American Maurice Prendergast and the Mexican Diego Rivera among the leaders of the modern field—with the stipulation, however, that they achieved their stature because they had learned and studied in Paris.[51] From Jacques-Louis David and Ingres; through Corot and the Barbizon school; to the poles of the modern movement exemplified by Cézanne and Redon; to the postimpressionists, fauves, and finally cubists, Pach traced an unbroken line that connected the past to the present and the future. Fully acknowledging the need of critics for labels and categories, Pach ended his book with the statement,

"We divide off a certain period and call it modern so that we may, for the moment, study it for itself."[52]

Reviews of the book were mixed. In advertising material, praise was given by Faure; William Rose Benét, of the *Saturday Review of Literature;* La Follette, writing for the *New York Herald-Tribune;* and Leigh Mitchell Hodges, of the Philadelphia journal the *North American.* A *New York Times* editorial read, "Walter Pach writes about modern art as no other has written about it, with a clarity and reasonableness, an understanding, a benignant breadth learned from none."[53] Negative reviews came from Guy Eglington, who wrote that the volume "gives such a definite expression to accepted modern esthetic theory, one is tempted to wonder whether the theory has not seen its best days," and from Robert Allerton Parker, associate editor of the *Arts,* who also criticized Pach's methodology: "Art today is crying out for a fresher, more vital type of appreciation than this pseudo-archaeology of the contemporaneous, with its unilluminating comparisons, its pigeon-holing and placing of works of art in their historical sequence, its insistence upon the temporal order of past, present, and future, its fatal preoccupation with the dissection of living art with the clumsy instrument of evolutionary determinism."[54] Pach's approach was considered "obsolete" by Parker and others and he was called upon to reevaluate his criticism and address the pressing needs of the day by presenting more critical analysis of the work of living artists.

Among the other books of the time devoted to such a topic were Katherine Dreier's *Western Art and the New Era* and Sheldon Cheney's *Primer of Modern Art.* Susan Noyes Platt argues in her *Modernism in the 1920s: Interpretations of Modern Art in New York from Expressionism to Constructivism* that "Cheney's book was the first survey of modernism published in this country that attempted a complete historical overview and combined the theoretical premises of formalism and expressionism." "Pach's book," she continues, "is biased toward an intellectual formalism that is based on his close affiliations to the French Cubists."[55] While some of Pach's contemporaries were highly critical of his writings, as are some art historians of today, many readers of the time admired his book for its clarity and enjoyed it because of his familiarity with the artists about whom he wrote.

Pach's essays and book were well received by his friends and colleagues; Mumford, Brooks, La Follette, Julius Meier-Graefe, Jacques Villon, and Diego Rivera had positive reactions.[56] Mumford wrote, "Just a breathless note to congratulate you on the opening article on Modern Art. It is far & away the best piece of criticism we've had in America, to my knowledge—a really profound analysis. If the rest of the series goes on at this level you'll have left nothing for the rest of us to say! I am delighted—and other people are too."[57] Other admirers were Brooks and Ida Guggenheimer, who, Pach reported, "bucked me up about the articles."[58] Perhaps the most rewarding response came from teachers Xavier Martínez and Paul Sachs from Harvard. The former—one of the most influential artists in California, particularly in the San Francisco Bay Area, in the early twentieth century and an art professor at the California College of Arts and Crafts in Oakland— told his pupils and friends who were interested in art about Pach's book, "the most authentic and significant on modern art," as he put it.[59] Sachs regarded *The Masters of Modern Art* as a perfect text for the classroom and highly recommended it to his students at Harvard University. Pach's articles and book shaped the American perception and understanding of modernism for decades; the book was assigned in college classrooms, becoming a standard for early art history courses devoted to modern art.

Pach had another work published in 1924, the long-awaited *Raymond Duchamp-Villon, Sculpteur, 1876–1918,* which had taken nearly four years to complete. The journey to publication began in August 1920. Pach had secured the assistance of Duchamp-Villon's brother Jacques Villon and felt sure that John Quinn would back his idea to bring out a publication on Duchamp-Villon. Pach broached the subject with Quinn, who in turn consulted Walt Kuhn and Ezra Pound before he gave his assent to his involvement with the project. To ensure the success of the undertaking in the United States, Pach talked with the print dealer/bookshop owner Weyhe, who estimated "twenty-five as the number of copies of the Duchamp-Villon book he could sell at $12 a copy."[60] Pach worked tirelessly with Villon and Yvonne Duchamp-Villon, Raymond's widow, on the manuscript. This book, which appeared only in French, was the first monograph ever devoted to this important sculptor.

Among the leading contemporary scholars on Raymond Duchamp-Villon are George Heard Hamilton, William C. Agee, and Judith C. Zilczer.[61] Hamilton's and Agee's 1967 book, *Raymond Duchamp-Villon, 1876–1918,* published on the occasion of the exhibition at M. Knoedler and Company, was, after Pach's work, among the earliest devoted to the artist. Zilczer has done extensive research on the sculptor, publishing articles and mounting several groundbreaking exhibitions—at the Philadelphia Museum of Art in 1980, the Hirshhorn Museum and Sculpture Garden in 1997–98, and the Musée des Beaux-Arts de Rouen in 1999. Pach's book, nevertheless, continues to be the most significant primary source on the artist. Pach not only wrote the biography but also transcribed several of Duchamp-Villon's letters for inclusion in the book. Understandably proud of his accomplishment, Pach sent a copy to several friends, among them Matisse and Mumford, whose reactions were positive. The book was well received by artists, critics, and writers alike, much to Pach's relief and pleasure.

In the mid- to late 1920s, Pach's output on the subject of modern art declined, probably out of a feeling that the battle for its acceptance had been won; in his few pieces during this period he reiterated his familiar concept of the evolutionary aspect of modern art. In "Is Cubism Pure Art?—a Debate; Picasso's Achievement," he asserted that "there are those [artists] who are so conscious of the movement of the time that they enter into every struggle that it makes for readjustment, and are of those who most actively bring to birth the new era. Picasso is this type. His restlessness is of our time." "The Cubist," he went on, "breaks with literal representation for the sake of an expression not to be obtained—at least by him—through the depicting of objects as they exist before his eye. . . . Picasso and his group count as men who have accepted every risk in order to preserve for themselves and for us the vital force of all art."[62] Pach was among those who early on recognized the enormous breadth of Picasso's genius, and he remained a great admirer and promoter of Picasso's work into the future.

In the fall of 1928, John Kraushaar, a prominent dealer in New York who represented many contemporary American artists, asked Pach to write a foreword and essay for an exhibition catalog of modern American art to be held at Kraushaar's gallery. This was Pach's only book devoted exclusively to American art and artists. In it Pach explained that he had "endeavored to keep these pages free from the nationalism which today finds too many misplaced expressions in exaggerated claims for our art; free also from the reverse defect of underestimating the value of a culture that is as old and as rich in achievement as our own." Pach was keenly aware of the heated debate raging in New York art circles in the late 1920s about the place and promotion of American versus European art in the United States. He remained convinced that France was still the fountainhead out of which all avant-garde art flowed but conceded that several American artists had made "significant and permanent contributions" to modernism.[63] Among the Americans he singled out for recognition in his essay were Winslow Homer, John Twachtman, John Sloan, Robert Henri, Max Weber, John Marin, Alfred Maurer, Charles Sheeler, Morton L. Schamberg, Charles Demuth, Edward Hopper, Preston

Dickinson, Georgia O'Keeffe, Niles Spencer, William Zorach, and Gaston Lachaise. Pach, who knew many of these artists personally, praised them for "making a courageous and idealistic effort" under unfavorable conditions. American artists, Pach observed, "are not offered such rewards in public appreciation or even in financial support as await their fellows in Europe. But they know that their work is of fundamental importance, for they are giving to the country a consciousness of idea and of aspiration that it could not have without them."[64] Art, regardless of nationality, should be an essential element of daily life, Pach said, but artists in the United States still struggled in a country where most of the population was preoccupied with material problems. As a painter, Pach understood the myriad difficulties encountered by American artists, from acquiring patrons and making sales to finding venues to show their work and appropriate studio space, and he commended them for their valiant efforts in the face of indifference.

Pach's most ambitious, and time-consuming, literary undertaking in 1928 was his text *Ananias, or the False Artist.* This was an expansion of an article he had written in the spring of 1927 for *Harper's Magazine* titled "What Passes for Art," which had caused much furor. "Walter Pach is about to drop another bomb into the art world," C. J. Bulliet of the *Chicago Evening Post* predicted. "The author of 'The Masters of Modern Art' and the translator of Elie Faure's 'History of Art,' tells just how bad the bad artists of today really are. 'What Passes for Art,' the bombshell is entitled. . . . Anyone knowing Walter Pach can scent trouble from the title."[65] In this essay, Pach explored some of the ideas about bad pictures that he had been working on since the previous summer. In scathing remarks, he lambasted academic artists such as Kenyon Cox for their artistic deadness and attacked the Metropolitan Museum of Art for its acquisition policies, which he believed favored bad art. *Ananias* would reiterate these themes.

Pach shared his thoughts on this manuscript with several artists, writers, and collectors. After he spoke with José Clemente Orozco, who was living in New York at the time, Orozco related to fellow artist Jean Charlot, who was in Mexico, "Walter Pach: I had to visit him and he told me he is writing a book that will be called: *Ananias or the False Artist,* because Ananias was a man in the Bible who gave only half of his wealth to Saint Peter and hid the other half, and the false artists of today are like Ananias, they want to be with the moderns with whom they strive for beauty, etc., but they make their underhanded deals and curry favor with the critics."[66] This concept remained the basic thrust of Pach's book: many artists were giving only a small percentage of their effort to their work and expecting the critics and the public to praise them.

To complete his manuscript, Pach knew he needed a quiet space away from the constant demands placed on him in New York. The Pach family left the city in the summer of 1928 for the country estate of Joel and Amy Spingarn and Joel's younger brother, Arthur, in Amenia, Dutchess County. The Spingarns' summer home was a haven for the Pachs and allowed Walter the time and freedom from obligations to work on his book. Pach invited Orozco to visit him in Amenia, an invitation the latter accepted. Orozco recounted several details of the day to Charlot:

I saw Pach yesterday, he invited me to come to the place where he is spending the summer . . . owned by some very rich people, the Spingarns. . . . He read me the translation of the part of his book *Ananias* that refers to Mexico. . . . He showed me the illustrations, which are photographs of the principal monstrosities "produced" by American artists who earn the most money. He thinks that they may accuse him of slander, because this is a very delicate matter here and it's not possible simply to say that a picture or an artist is bad, each day he has conferences with two lawyers, one his and the other his publisher's.[67]

Pach's lawyer was Arthur Spingarn, who was one of the most highly regarded attorneys in New York. Pach knew that his book would cause controversy and asked Spingarn to help represent him in the matter. He dedicated the volume to Spingarn, a "friend of all true artists." Spingarn was quite moved by the dedication and was proud to be associated with the book, which he called a "solid . . . contribution to human culture," and told Pach how deeply he valued their friendship.[68]

Soon after *Ananias* appeared in print, in November 1928, the publisher forwarded a copy to Orozco, requesting his opinion. Given Orozco's previous unfavorable views of Pach—described in many a letter to Charlot—he surprisingly complied with this request. He even mailed Pach a copy of the letter he sent to Ruth Raphael at Harper and Brothers in which he wrote,

> I found this work so interesting and courageous that I was compelled to read it in one sitting. Truly I did not believe that it were possible to publish such opinions in this great but conservative country, since that which Mr. Pach preaches, very likely without thinking about it, is at bottom, a complete social revolution of the most radical type. . . . Mr. Pach's book will work real miracles; it will disinfect the atmosphere, purify the public mind, provoke many examinations of conscience, arouse enthusiasm among the true elect—in a word, it will surely be recognized as a great tribute to Truth and to Justice, in these days of fraud and of shameless mistification [*sic*].[69]

Pach had bluntly denounced the art of many popular painters and sculptors of the day: John Singer Sargent (his last society portraits in particular), Daniel Chester French, Lorado Taft, and Paul Manship, among others. He attacked the collecting practices of museums such as the Metropolitan, the Museum of Fine Arts in Boston, and the Art Institute of Chicago. For Pach to make such an assault on these institutions was quite bold, for much of his livelihood depended on lectures at these very museums and on dealings with their curators and directors. As Orozco astutely observed, the book was a "social revolution of the most radical type."

From the moment *Ananias* was published it sparked enormous controversy. Artists, critics, writers, dealers, collectors, and museum people took sides for and against its author and his opinions. The press, ever eager for good copy, had a field day with the story. Pearl Gross of the *Washington Herald* wrote, "Because Pach's scalpel falls alike on moderns and eminently respected masters of the past, a whirlwind of controversy has arisen in local art circles."[70] News of a lecture that Pach was to deliver on Delacroix at the Cleveland Museum of Art was overshadowed by the "furore caused by [his] latest and most interesting book, 'Ananias or the False Artist,' in which he flays the insincere creators of bad but popular art."[71] After the talk at the museum, Grace V. Kelly, the art critic for the *Cleveland Plain Dealer,* interviewed Pach about his book, which, she wrote, "had disrupted our world, just recovering from the effects of the World War." Pach explained that he had not intended to disrupt any world and "had only said in his book what artists had been saying in their studios right along." His book, he insisted, was merely a "report of the regret felt by artists, that some of their number had debased their great ability by pandering to the faddy tastes of the markets."[72] In the *New York Times Book Review,* Edward Alden Jewell noted that the work had created "considerable ruction among devotees of art," and he credited it for "startling us, as it cannot but do, out of our complacent attitude toward painting and causing great searchings of heart." He thanked Pach for offering "an eclectic platform that may be accepted or rejected" and praised the "clear, trenchant style" of his writing and his "shockingly delightful plea for clear vision."[73]

Others, however, were not impressed. Lee Simonson, editor of *Creative Art* magazine, warned Pach that he was going to publish a rather hard-hitting review of the book and offered space in his regular "Palette Knife" column for rebuttal. His criticisms, he claimed, "had the specific approval and enthusiastic co-operation of such men as Alfred Stieglitz and Leo Stein," as if that bit of information would somehow impress or intimidate Pach.[74] In his essay, "God and the Esthetic Prig," Simonson compared Pach's writing to that of conservative artist and critic Kenyon Cox, one of Pach's nemeses. "It is a pity," Simonson wrote, "that so earnest a painter, and, up to the present moment, so intelligent a champion of certain modern schools as Mr. Pach, should give way to this kind of esthetic demagoguery. . . . His book is even more damaging to the development of sound, modern criticism than the worst academic painting could conceivably be to the cause of modern art."[75] William Howe Downes, writing in the *American Magazine of Art,* likened Pach to nineteenth-century British critic John Ruskin and criticized both for being partisan, arrogant, and self-righteous. "Is it not strange that he, with the advantage of a twentieth century background, should be as unable to perceive any good in his *false artists* as he is to see any defects in his favorites?"[76] Downes also denounced Pach for the overly moral tone of his book. *Ananias* reignited the long-simmering debate over whether one could define art as good or bad, true or false. This battle raged on, with Pach and his book at the center of the maelstrom, for months, and it is quite probable that the uproar was partially to blame for Pach's self-imposed exile in Paris for the next three years.

Pach's main literary achievements in the 1930s were his *Vincent van Gogh, 1853–1890: A Study of the Artist and His Work in Relation to His Times* (1936) and *Queer Thing, Painting: Forty Years in the World of Art* (1938). The dust jacket of the van Gogh biography claimed that "Mr. Pach was probably the first man in America to lecture and write about van Gogh. His friendship with van Gogh's family enables him to add a warmth and personal enthusiasm concerning van Gogh the man, to his sound knowledge and accurate evaluation of van Gogh, the artist."[77] Since noticing his work in that shop window in Haarlem in 1906, Pach had written about the artist in several articles, where the ideas he expressed were similar to those of other critics. In a 1920 article in the *Christian Science Monitor,* Pach observed, "Light and color have always been dealt with by art, but van Gogh's use of them as an independent means of expression instead of depicting what he saw, constitutes a step that had not been taken before."[78] Also that year, in a review of the van Gogh exhibition at the Montross Gallery, which Pach had helped organize, he promoted van Gogh's art as "the great things of a great century," asserting that "we must look to van Gogh, more than anyone else, for the conception of colour on which great artists of to-day, like Matisse and Derain, built. . . . Van Gogh, while carrying our knowledge of the relation of colour to light as far as any one of his time, had a special faculty of firing the imagination of the young men."[79] In his 1936 book, Pach chronicled van Gogh's life and art and reiterated his earlier ideas on and criticisms of the artist. The art of van Gogh, observed Pach, traversed national and political boundaries, as Pach believed all great art should. The artist had created a "community of men's efforts," which was "the reverse of the isolationist idea" that was so very prevalent in American art and politics in the 1930s.[80]

In his review, Edward Alden Jewell wrote, "Mr. Pach, one feels, has used the biographical material chiefly as a framework upon which may be hung his own analysis of the painter's character and work. To such evaluations as have been arrived at in the course of his study must be said to attach to the book's principal value."[81] The traveling exhibition of van Gogh's work that opened at the Museum of Modern Art in New York undoubtedly prompted a flurry of interest in Pach's book. This was not the first book on van Gogh to appear in the United States. In 1913, Katherine S. Dreier, an avid collector of modern art, had translated into English and written an introduction to Elisabeth Huberta du Quesne-Van Gogh's *Persönliche Erinnerungen an Vincent Van Gogh,* published in Munich two years earlier. Yet Pach's articles and 1936 biography reached a much wider audience and were vital in firmly establishing van Gogh as a master of modern art. Pach's volume proved to be hugely successful in the United States, and by May 1936 the text was in its sixth printing.

In October 1938, *Queer Thing, Painting: Forty Years in the World of Art* was published by Harper and Brothers. Many have referred to this book as an autobiography, but the author did not see it in that light, and although it contains many biographical aspects, it is more a series of reminiscences. It is mainly chronological, but the time frame is not precise in many passages. In a very lively and personal manner, Pach recounted his meetings and relationships with the foremost artists, critics, dealers, collectors, and museum personnel in the Parisian, American, and Mexican art worlds of the early twentieth century.

In general, the book received much acclaim from friends, colleagues, and critics in art circles and beyond. The first letter Pach received was from his friend Van Wyck Brooks, who wrote, "It has moved me more than anything I have read this year. . . . You haven't written one sentence of gossip, in even the great good sense of the word. . . . Your record of art-history, which no one can re-write without you as a basis. You have followed more nerves and arteries in the *corpus* of modern art and revealed the arterial structure as no one else (known, that is, to me)." With these accolades given, Brooks then criticized some ideas in the book, but "only in a kindred spirit."[82] He felt that his friend did not give nineteenth-century Americans enough credit for their knowledge and understanding of Italian art. He also disagreed with Pach's assessment of collectors J. P. Morgan and John Quinn and his enthusiasm for the Duchamp-Villon brothers. In his response, Pach

admitted that he deliberately ignored the unpleasant personal qualities of some collectors. "I hope I never have to tell anyone the rotten, downright rotten things I know about John Quinn," he told Brooks.[83] He did, however, vigorously defend his praise of Marcel Duchamp, Jacques Villon, and Raymond Duchamp-Villon.

Of the book, Edward Alden Jewell opined, "This is certainly not a dull book, but one instead that is of quietly absorbing interest throughout; mellow with winnowed wisdom; gentle but substantial and often very illuminating in its expansive mood of reminiscence."[84] He detailed at length the organization of the book and listed many of the individuals Pach wrote about. Jewell's appraisal was positive and he encouraged his audience to read the work. Oliver Larkin, by contrast, writing for the *Saturday Review,* rebuked Pach for his narrative approach and wrote that in his recollection of the events surrounding the controversy over Diego Rivera's murals at Rockefeller Center Pach was "floundering in deep water," implying that he was out of his element.[85] Despite such criticism, Pach was pleased with the book's reception as well as the royalties he received.

In the 1940s and 1950s, Pach published fewer articles on modern art and in them restated the basic aesthetic and philosophical beliefs that he had formulated over the years. For example, in "The Role of Modern Art," published in the *Virginia Quarterly Review* in 1945, he placed modern art within the context of the contemporary world and its tragic events. Pach felt that humans were more interconnected than ever before in history and that life and art, although dimmed by the specter of war, would recover and move forward as they had always done. He singled out Henry Moore, Joan Miró, and Piet Mondrian as heralds of the future of art. At the same time, he reiterated his belief in a distinctly American character, as evidenced in the ancient sculptures found in the soil of Ohio, Georgia, and Oklahoma, as well as Mexico and Peru. He also took the opportunity to denounce Adolf Hitler's view of modern art as degenerate. In May 1950, Pach's article "Art Must Be Modern" was published by the *Atlantic Monthly.* In it he expressed his long-held belief that "art must be modern because life must be modern. You may reverence the past for its great works, but you can neither live in the past nor produce its art. What you do today, if art at all, is modern art." Pach condemned the approach to contemporary art espoused in the writings of Leo Stein; Bernard Berenson; and Francis Henry Taylor, then director of the Metropolitan Museum. He felt that these men, all of them friends or acquaintances, failed to see the living vitality of contemporary art. Pach did not see "the spiritual breakdown, the sterility, and the intellectual vacuum" that his fellow critics saw in the art of their time.[86] Instead, he found hope for the future of painting in artists such as Picasso, Matisse, and Derain.

Throughout the 1940s and 1950s, Pach tried to keep abreast of the latest developments in art, but he readily admitted his own shortcomings when it came to accepting some contemporary works. Although the surrealists did not move him very much, he recognized that he might "need to modernize" his ideas on art. "I don't think one has to run after the 'dernier cri,'" he wrote his son, "but I bitterly regret the time I lost in Paris at the beginning, when I was unresponsive to the great things going on around me. At first I did not even know they existed."[87] Trying never to repeat this mistake, Pach frequented the galleries in New York and scoured the pages of numerous American and European art magazines to keep informed of the newest developments. He visited Pierre Matisse in his gallery from time to time and reported to Henri Matisse that he was developing an appreciation for the paintings of the surrealist painters Matta, Marc Chagall, and Yves Tanguy and for the recent sculptures of Jacques Lipchitz.

It was during and immediately after a trip to Paris in the spring of 1948 that Pach began to seriously contem-plate the best way to respond to recent developments in painting. He told his good friend John Sloan that when he had arrived in Paris "it was with the idea that non-realistic art had run its course, though of course still producing great results at the hand of the men who created it—Picasso, Braque, Villon, and a few others of lesser calibre." However, he confessed that he "had to change that idea" as there was "a whole group of men, a generation or more younger, who are going on with work of an anti-realistic quality, and who are doing important things." He had hoped to see "a new outcropping of realistic art," but, as he told Sloan, "all that I saw of talent was in the 'abstract' camp, so that tendency is apparently in the saddle for some time yet."[88] Obviously, Pach was going to have to rethink his attitude toward contemporary art as a result of this sojourn.

In the 1950s, Pach responded to what he perceived as a disconcerting trend toward complete abstraction. "I'm quite sure," he wrote Brooks, "that the 'modern decadents,' as I call them will dislike it, but I've waited long enough about saying these things, and I just needed to."[89] To Villon he declared, "I broke my silence on abstract painting. It certainly has its raison d'être, and it has provided excellent discipline, but it has been shamefully abused, and our museums and collectors have been fooled on the matter."[90] Pach felt that a great deal of so-called modern art was the "decadence of what Picasso, Braque, and, above all, Marcel Duchamp did about 1912."[91] While he could admire some of the work of the European surrealists, he still would not, or could not, grasp the significance of the new art being created by Jackson Pollock, Mark Rothko, Adolph Gottlieb, and other abstract expressionists and members of the New York school. It was his belief that only Paris could produce the next great movement in art, maintaining the prominence it had held since 1789. He hailed French artists for their "vivacity and penetration" and lambasted Americans for falling short of the former's "intelligence, finesse and creativeness."

Upon moving to its new building at 22 West

Fifty-fourth Street in 1954, the Whitney Museum of American Art held an exhibition of its collection of recent American art, and the work on view left Pach "to wonder, all over again, at the ignorance or effrontery of those writers here who claim that we have overhauled Paris in the 'contest of art' (the words are bad enough in themselves), or even that we have left the French behind." He supposed that this show was "another manifestation of the isolationism-chauvinism one sees among political personages—who may lead us into another war."[92] Nationalism, felt Pach, had no place in the world of art. He was even more appalled at what he perceived to be a lack of understanding and appreciation of the Old Masters, especially his beloved Delacroix, among the contemporary painters. This was a sacrilege he simply could not tolerate. These views on art, and his inability to accept the new developments taking place in his own backyard, were among the reasons that Pach and his ideology fell out of favor rather quickly in the 1950s.

Artists and critics have been divided in their opinion of Pach's criticism. Friends such as Élie Faure, Lewis Mumford, Van Wyck Brooks, Suzanne La Follette, and Bernard Berenson admired and agreed with his philosophy of art. Other contemporaries, among them the conservative critics and artists Royal Cortissoz and Kenyon Cox and even progressives such as Katherine Dreier, Paul Strand, and Alfred Stieglitz, were far from enthusiastic about his approach and methodology. Dreier found his style of writing to be rather dry and dull, though she did not necessarily disagree with its content. Strand and others saw his method of criticism as excessively subjective. Stieglitz found abhorrent Pach's view of photography as something less than fine art, but he applauded Pach's work in educating Americans on modern art. Susan Noyes Platt points out, in her *Modernism in the 1920s: Interpretations of Modern Art in New York from Expressionism to Constructivism,* "By the mid twenties Pach's combination of formalism and evolutionary determinism was considered obsolete as a method of analysis of modern art by the more up-to-date commentators."[93] Sandra Phillips wrote in her article on Pach's criticism that his "written work is important mainly as a barometer of the cultural awareness of the times rather than for its ideas."[94] Differences aside, all agreed that Walter Pach was one of the leading authorities on modern art in his day.

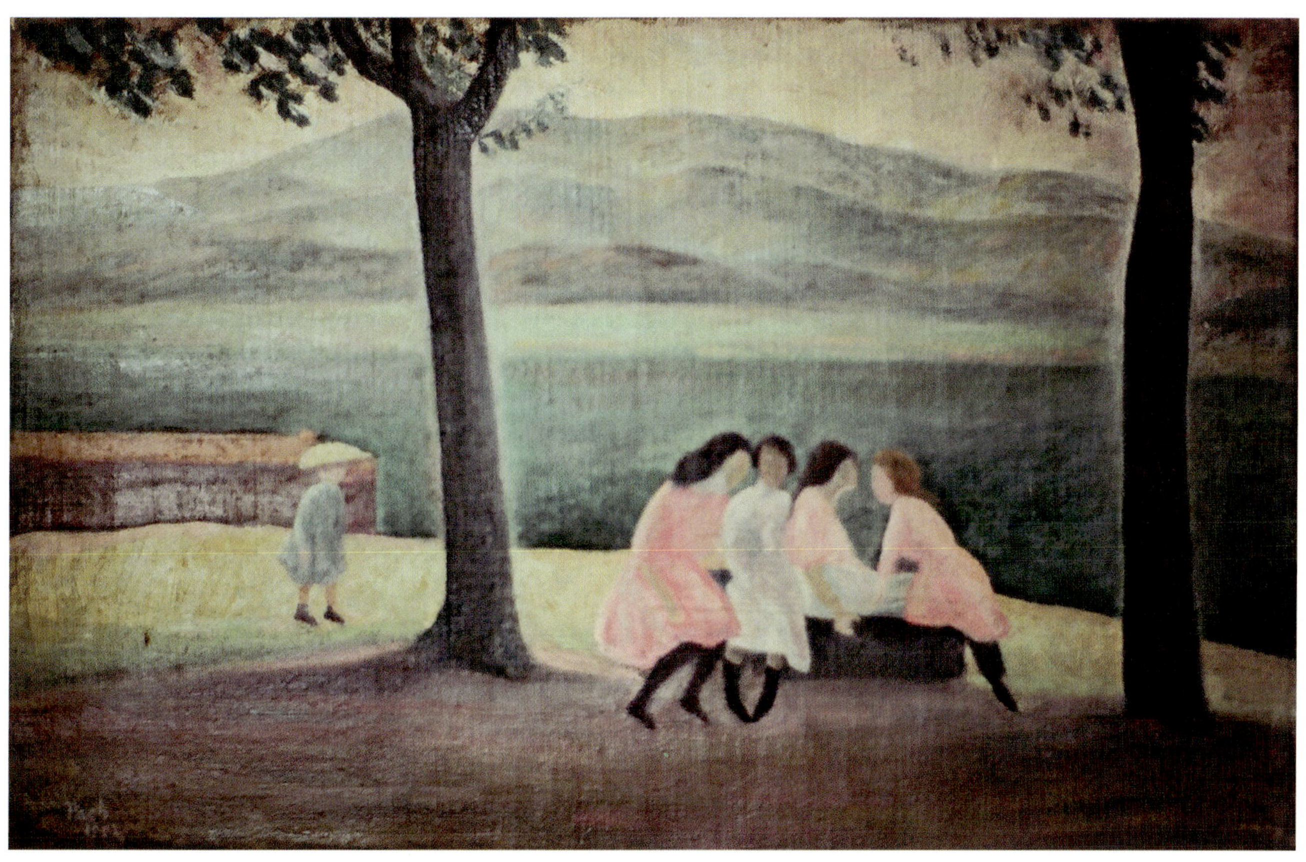

Plate 1

Walter Pach, *Casentino Mountains,* 1912, oil on canvas. Collection of Mrs. Nikifora N. Iliopoulos.

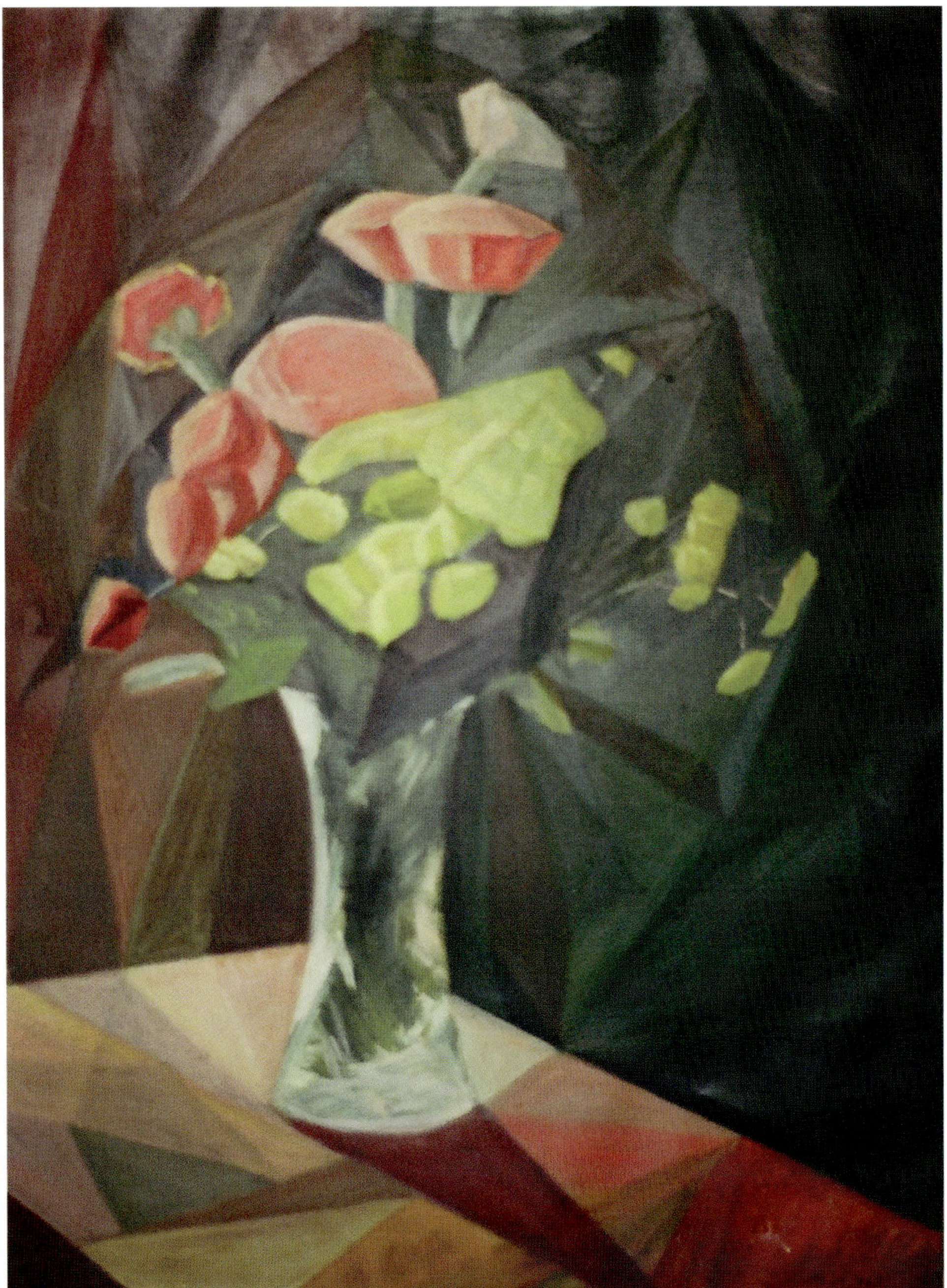

Plate 2
Walter Pach, *Progression No. 1 (Flowers)*, 1913, oil on canvas. Collection of Mrs. Nikifora N. Iliopoulos.

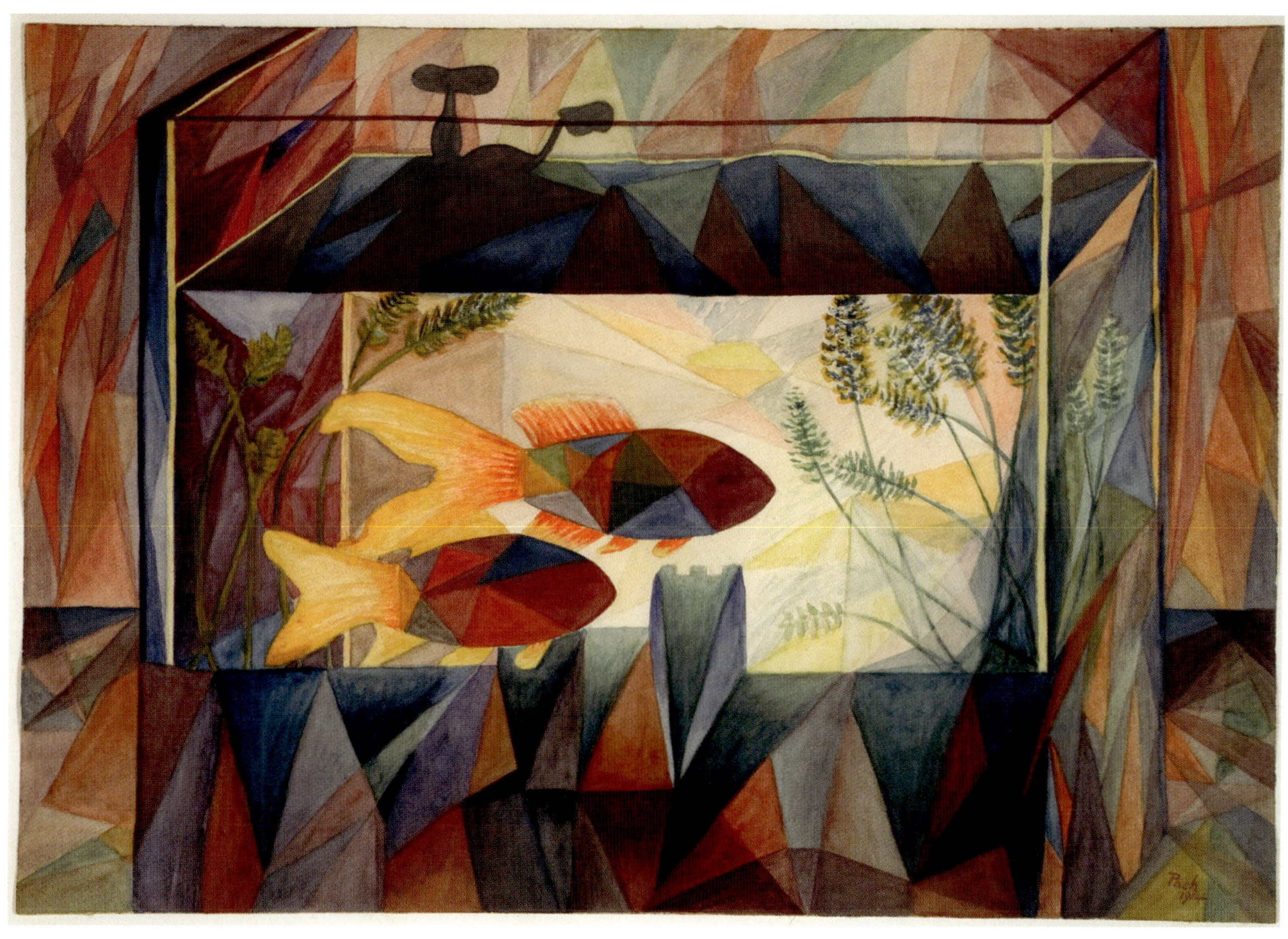

Plate 3
Walter Pach, *Progression No. 3 (Aquarium)*, 1914, watercolor, 10 × 14 in. (25.4 × 36.6 cm). Private collection.

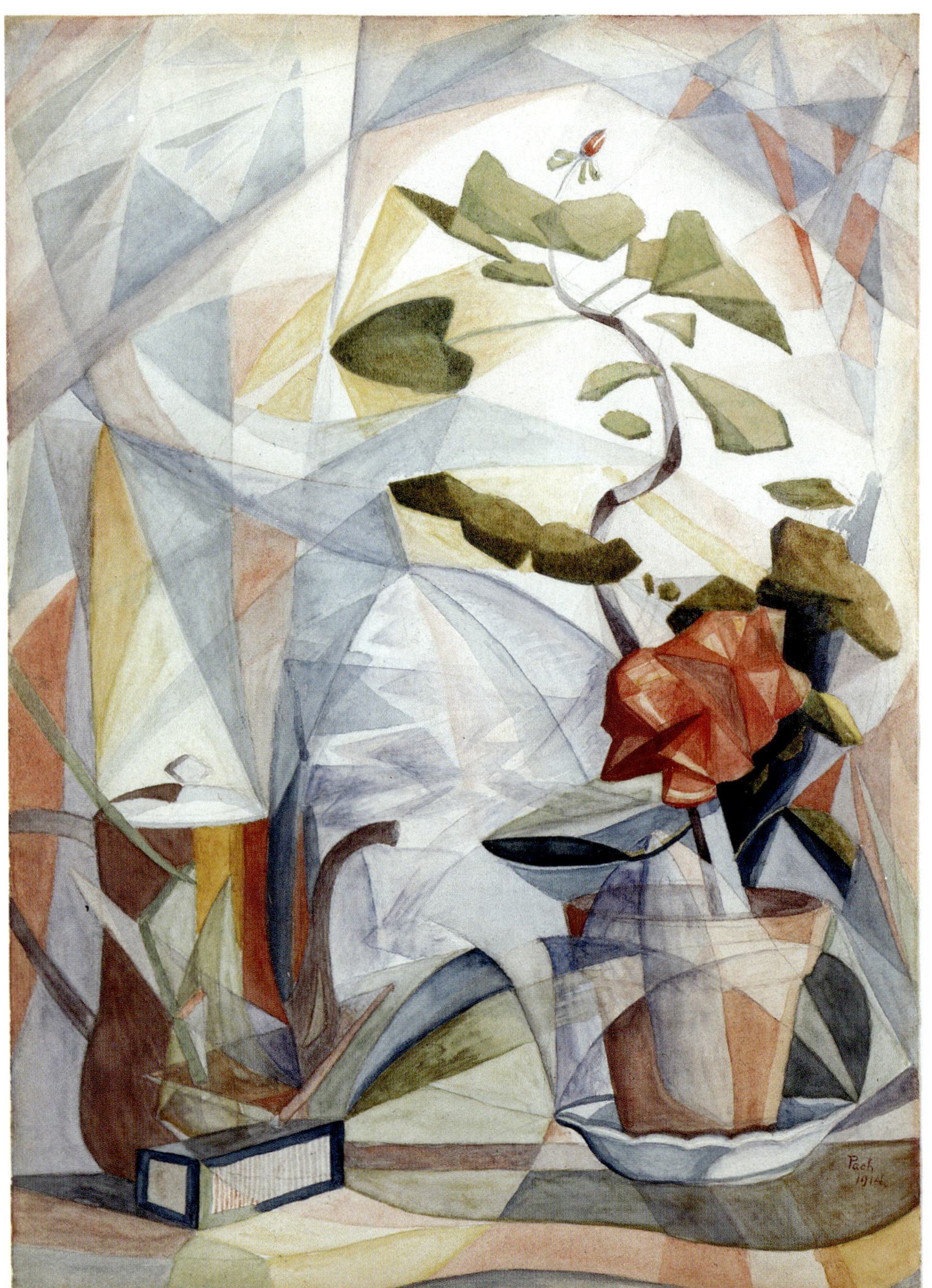

Plate 4
Walter Pach, *Untitled (Cubist Still Life),* 1914, watercolor and graphite pencil on paper, sheet 14 × 10 in. (35.6 × 25.4 cm). Whitney Museum of American Art, New York, Gift of Francis Steegmuller in memory of Gerda and Beatrice Stein, 85.22.

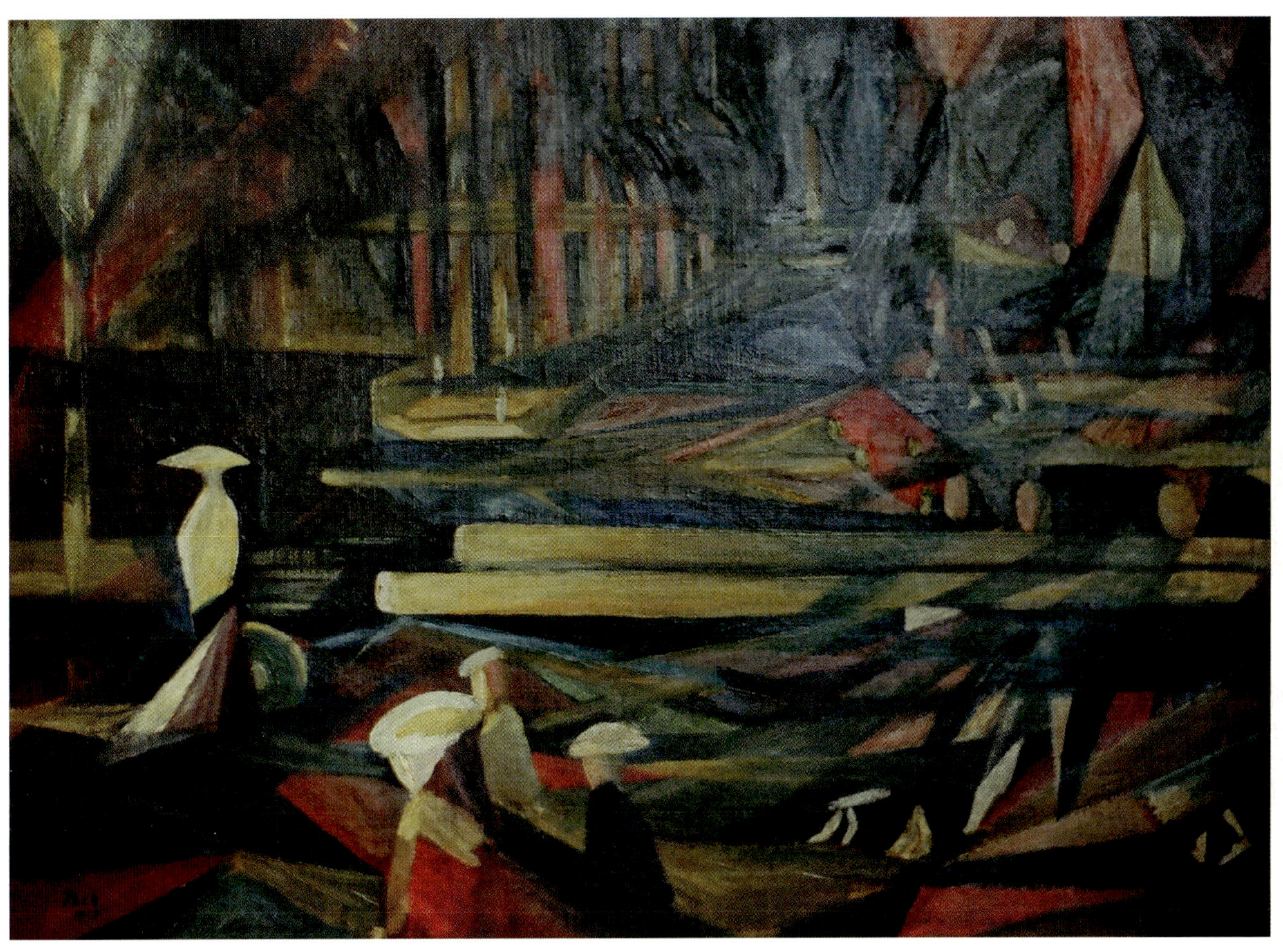

Plate 5
Walter Pach, *Sunday Night (St. Patrick's at Night)*, 1916, oil on canvas, 18 × 24 in. Collection of Mrs. Nikifora N. Iliopoulos.

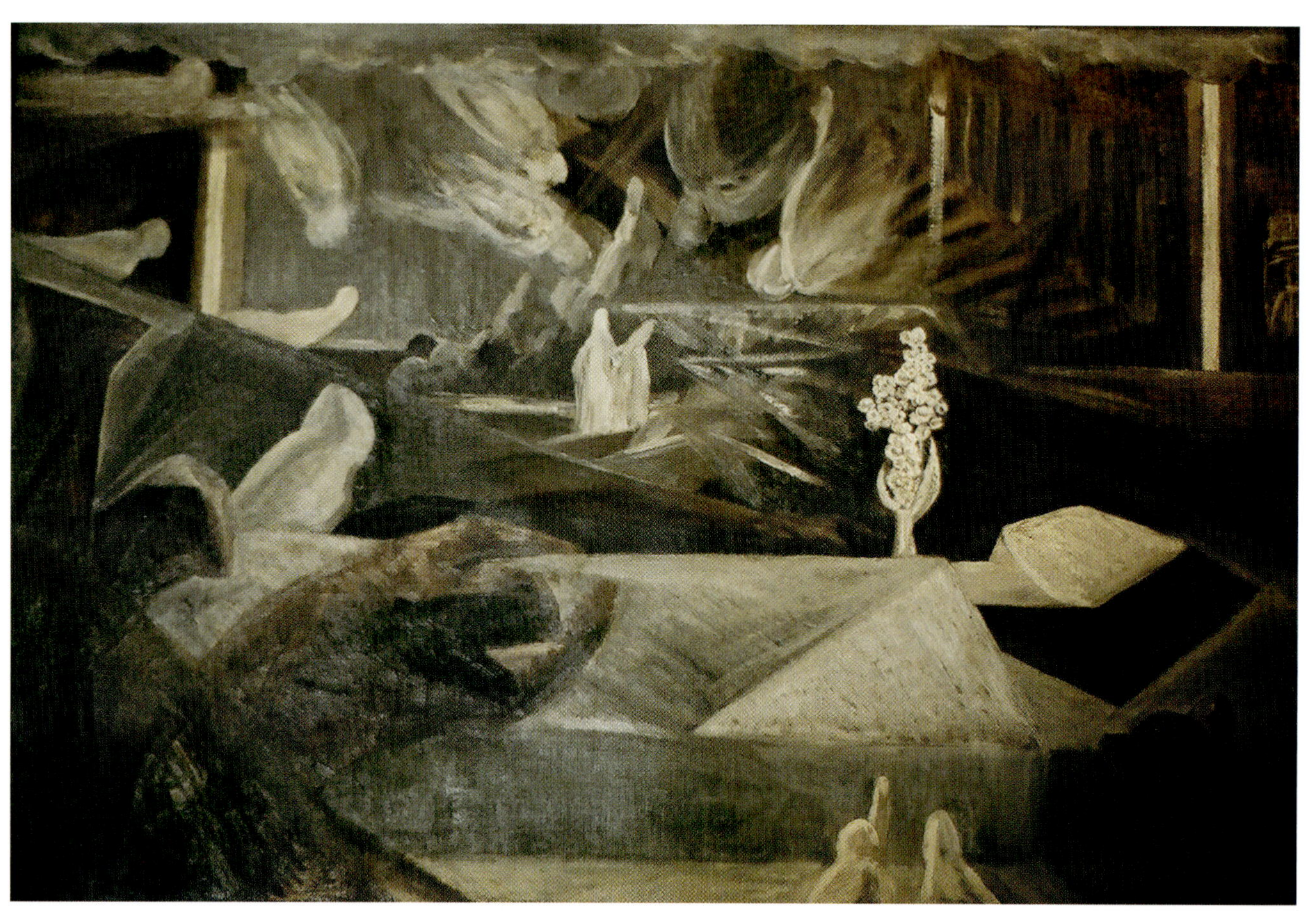

Plate 6
Walter Pach, *The Lily of the Valley,* 1917, oil on canvas. Collection of Mrs. Nikifora N. Iliopoulos.

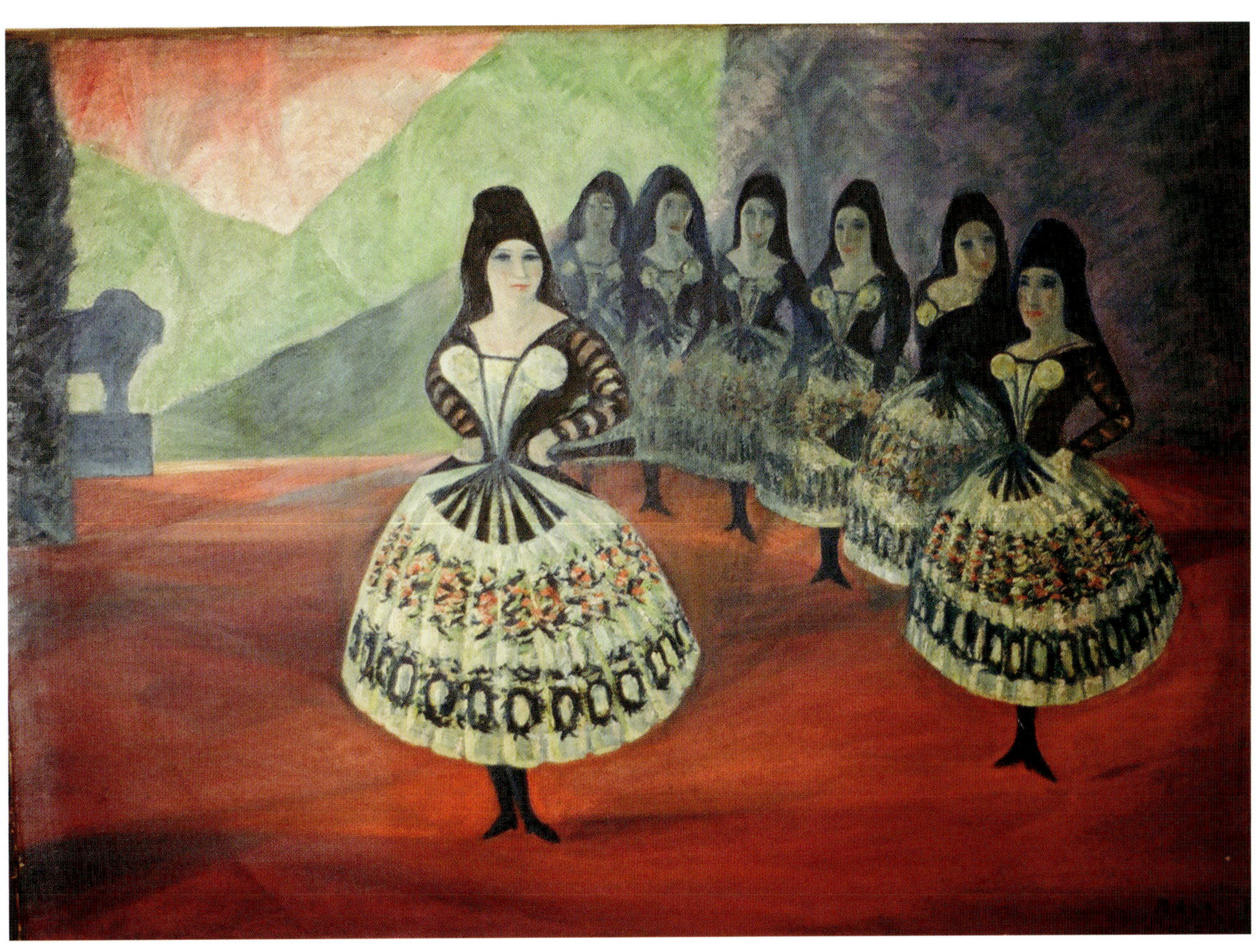

Plate 7
Walter Pach, *"La Maja de Goya,"* 1918, oil on canvas. Collection of Mrs. Nikifora N. Iliopoulos.

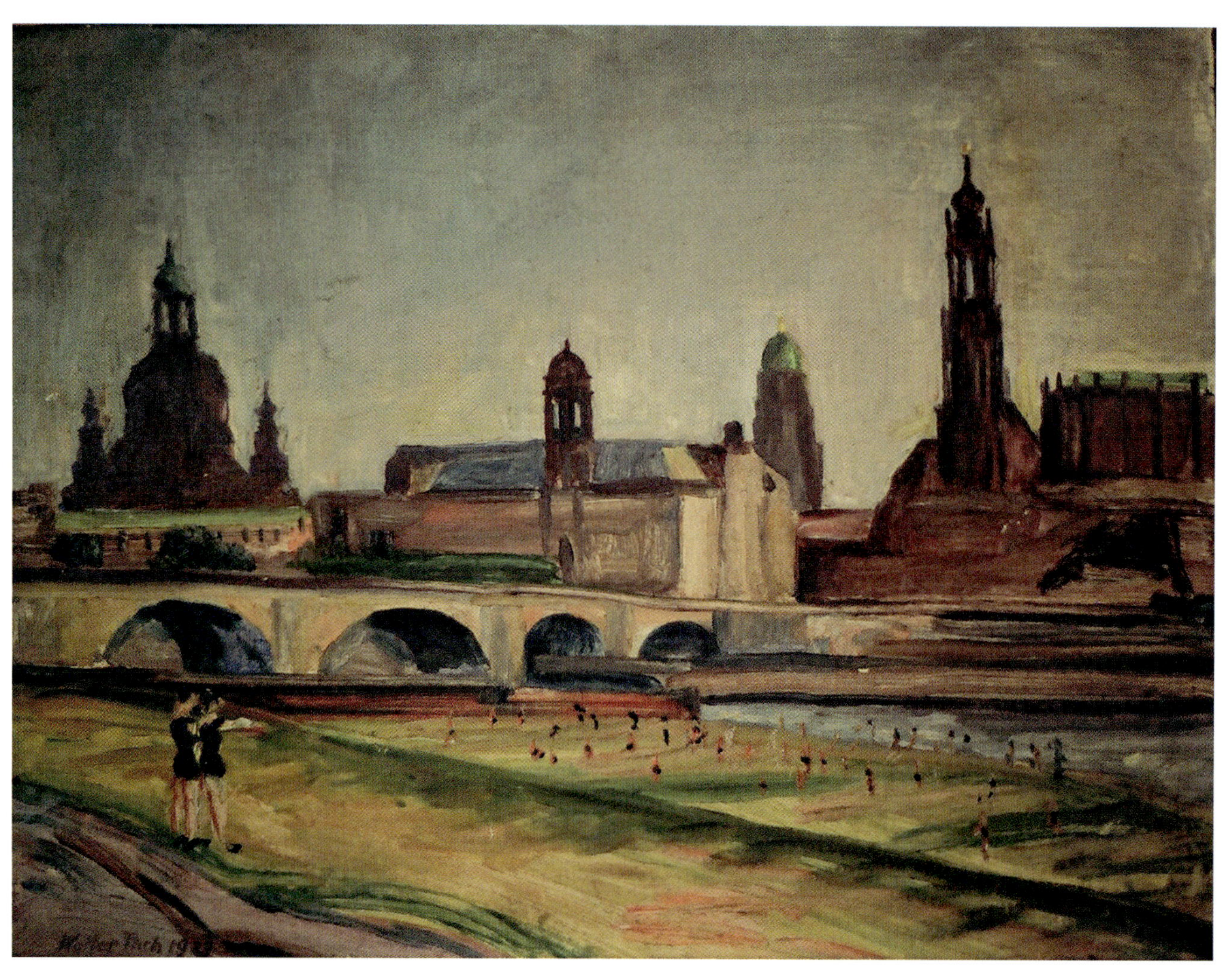

Plate 8

Walter Pach, *Dresde (Dresden Palace),* 1929, oil on panel. Collection of Mrs. Nikifora N. Iliopoulos.

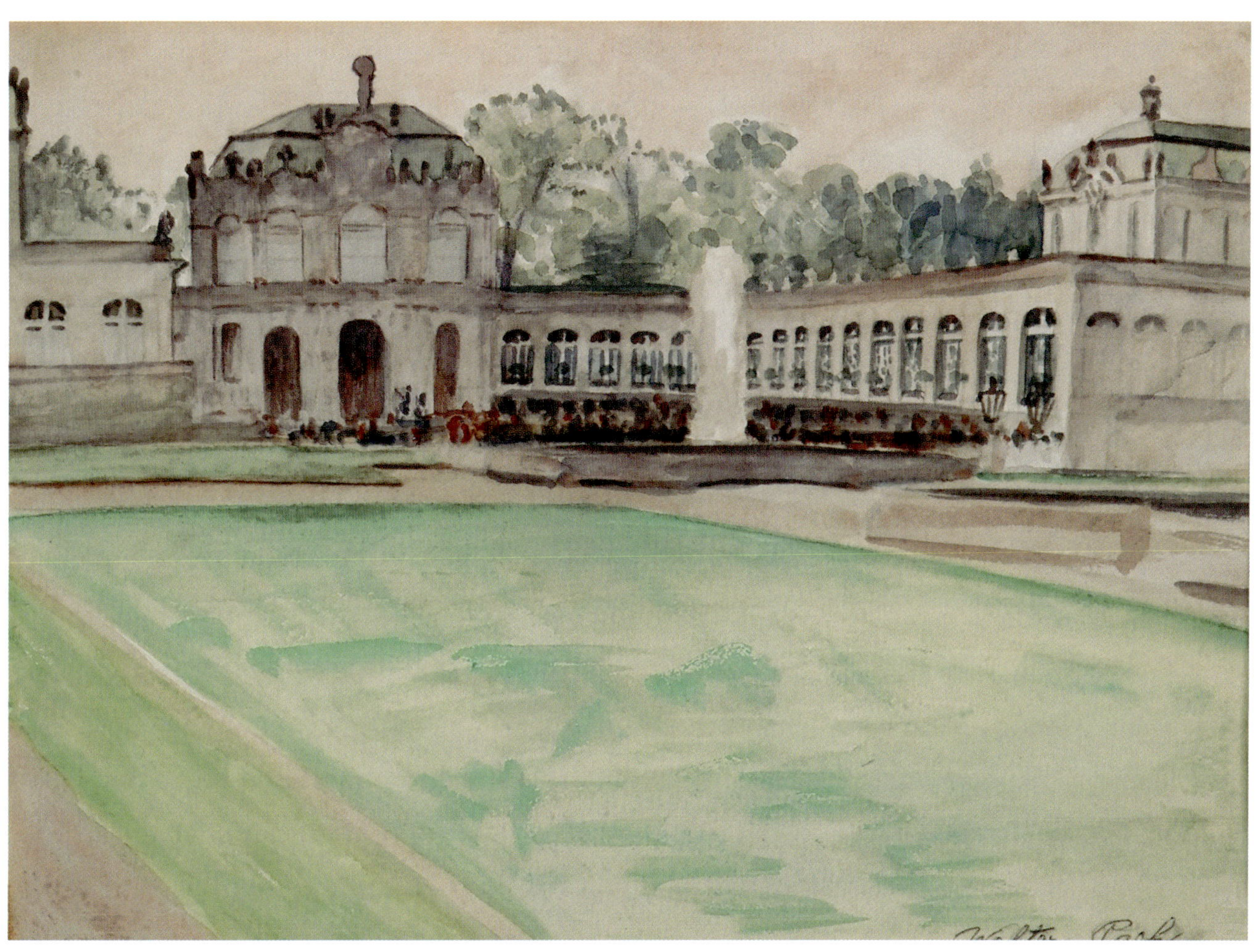

Plate 9

Walter Pach, *Dresden Gardens, the Zwinger,* 1929, watercolor on paper. Raymond P. Pach Collection.

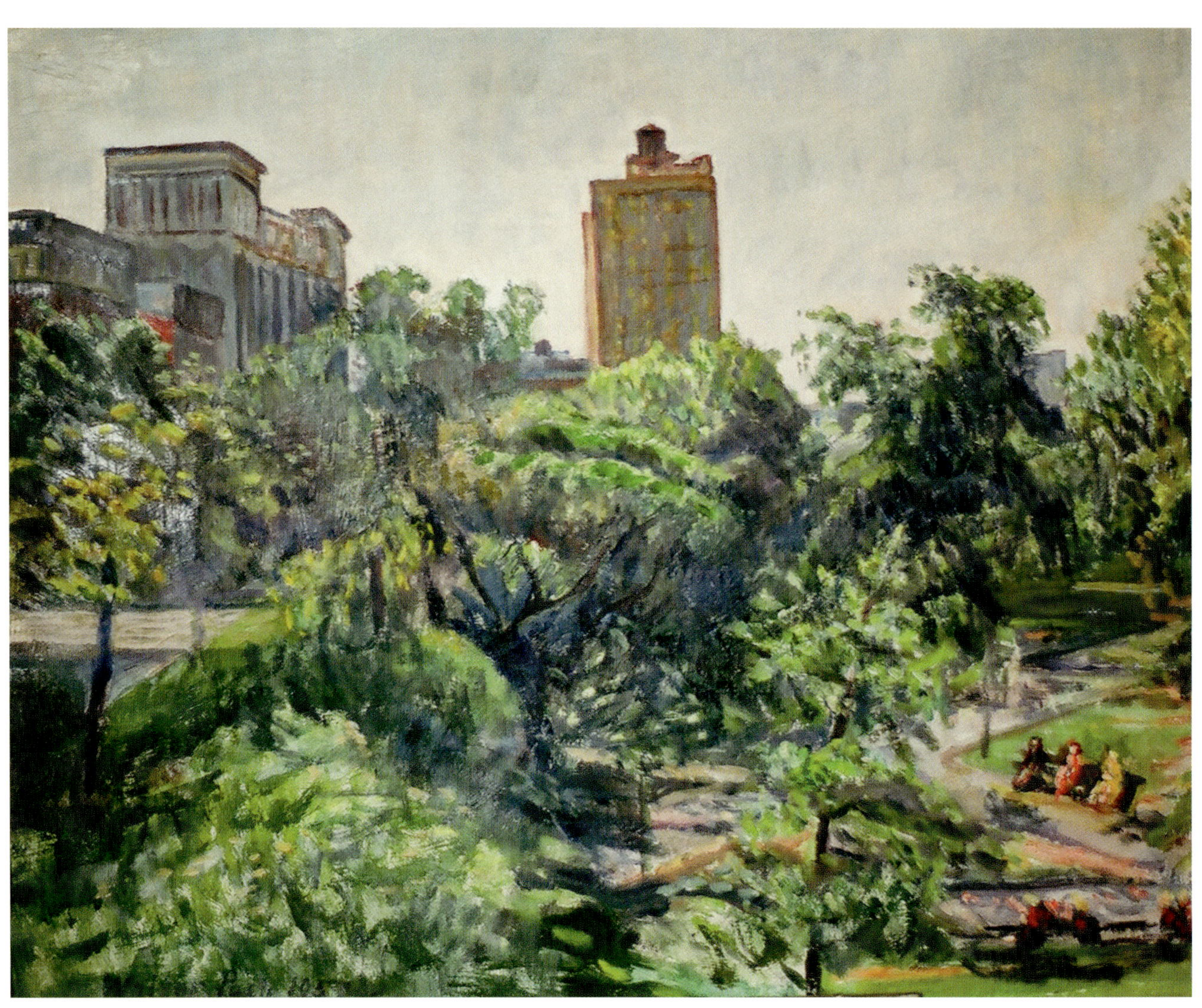

Plate 10
Walter Pach, *Washington Square,* 1957, oil on canvas. Collection of Mrs. Nikifora N. Iliopoulos.

10
Lectures on Modern European and American Art

From the Armory Show of 1913 until his death in 1958, Pach delivered dozens of lectures on modern art to diverse audiences across the United States and in Canada, and though he often complained that these activities infringed on his career as an artist, he understood the importance of his task. Pach's understanding of the theories of art on which works by the postimpressionists, fauves, cubists, and futurists, among others, were based and his personal relationships with the most advanced artists and thinkers of his day made him the ideal candidate to promote modernism in the United States. He recognized that the acceptance of contemporary art depended on an understanding of its connection with the past and used the theory of the evolution of art to win converts to the cause. To appeal to a broad section of the populace, Pach gave lectures at women's clubs, galleries, museums, colleges and universities, and art institutions, reaching a wider and more diverse audience than did his contemporaries such as critics Henry McBride and Christian Brinton and collector and author Katherine Dreier. Pach's ideas on modern art were not revolutionary in content; however, they were perceived as authoritative and therefore had a great impact on the understanding, appreciation, and acceptance of modern art on the North American continent.

Pach's influence as a speaker on modern art was at its height beginning with the Armory Show of 1913 and running through the 1930s, during which time he crisscrossed the country. Although the specific content of most of Pach's speeches is not known, the drafts of his lectures on modern art delivered at the University of California at Berkeley, where he taught in the summer of 1918, contain themes similar to those presented in his published writings, which can be seen as representative of the ideas he probably presented in other talks.[1] In his class, Pach focused on nineteenth- and early twentieth-century French art. This was, as far as the records show, the first course on modern art taught at Berkeley, and perhaps at any American college or university. Pach became rather ill on the train trip west and had virtually no time to organize his lectures

beforehand. Faced with this dilemma, he quickly jotted notes for his next day's lecture the night before, or sometimes in the afternoon prior to an evening lecture. In these abbreviated writings, Pach set goals for his students and explained his philosophy of art.

In his opening remarks to the students Pach stated his fundamental belief that "there is probably no study that admits of such freedom of approach or such individuality of treatment as the subject of Art. . . . We can not give exact definitions of art. It is a force, submissive doubtless to certain laws which are beyond our ken, but to be judged in its effects, in its products, and not to be grasped by itself."[2] His main objective was to help his pupils develop the ability "to recognize art and to enjoy it." Although readings were assigned for each class, and the students were asked to keep notebooks, Pach told them, "I don't care whether you take notes on my talks or whether you don't. . . . In looking over the books [the students' notebooks] I shall give far more credit for original work, your own observations and impressions about the arts, than for a faithful following of my own words." He was not interested in reading his own thoughts regurgitated; rather, he wanted the students to think critically and for themselves. Since there were very few original works of art for them to examine, Pach used lantern slides to illustrate his points. He also advised his classes to study his collection of "etchings, water colors, paintings and lithographs" that was exhibited in July that year at the university.[3] He suggested that the students further supplement their knowledge of art by consulting reproductions of paintings and sculptures in the books he recommended to them.

One of Pach's main goals in the course was to reveal and clarify "the relation of art to life and show how the two forces act one upon the other." Art was inextricably connected with every aspect of life, he felt. Although he said that he was "not very deep in sociological matters and still less in politics," Pach revealed his political awareness and allegiance when he proclaimed that the battles waged by the soldiers on the Continent during World War I were echoed in artists' struggles for release from the tyranny of the academy and for freedom of artistic expression. He encouraged the same autonomy in his students and exhorted them to think independently and approach works of art with an open mind.

The students thoroughly enjoyed the course, and many had words of high praise for Pach and his teachings. Said one, "Mr. Pach lectures with charm and spontaneity; his observations come from profound and sober study of the art he is enthusiastically interested in."[4] A visitor to the modern art class was San Francisco dealer Frederick Torrey, who had bought Duchamp's *Nude Descending a Staircase, No. 2* from the Armory Show and whom Pach had known, at least by name, before he arrived in California. Torrey wrote Dean

Hart, head of the university, "It is a joy to listen to a man who knows—and more important still—really FEELS."[5] Pach was undoubtedly thrilled by the enthusiastic response he received to his lectures.

Throughout the 1920s, Pach was in great demand as a lecturer on modern art. During this period he undertook several lengthy lecture tours, particularly in the midwestern and western states. He visited Denver, Omaha, St. Louis, Des Moines, Milwaukee, Chicago, and Cleveland as well as cities in Kansas and Minnesota. He spoke at art societies, museums, women's groups, and colleges and universities—the Omaha Society of Artists, the St. Louis Art Museum, the Milwaukee Art Institute, the Cleveland Museum of Art, the Des Moines Women's Club, and other venues. Closer to home, Pach spoke in New York, Boston, Worcester, Hartford, Philadelphia, and Toronto. In the east his lectures were sponsored by New York University; Harvard University; Vassar College; the Worcester Art Museum; the Art Gallery of Toronto; the Metropolitan Museum of Art; the Boston Art Club; the Société Anonyme; and the Ixia Society, an organization composed of women art teachers in the New York City public schools. Pach began lecturing for New York University in 1923; in 1926 he was named an assistant professor of fine arts, a post he held for three years. As he explained to Edward Duff Belkan, acting director of the Carnegie Institute, many of his engagements were return invitations, and though he really did not want to leave his studio, it was, he admitted, "nice to be asked a second time."[6] He wrote Matisse that most of these lectures were on modern art and confessed modestly that he had earned "a little" reputation for his opinions on the subject.

In the spring of 1926, New York University asked Pach to lead a class of undergraduates on a summer art program at the Louvre in Paris. Early in June, he and his family set sail for France, where they would remain for several months. Seventy students attended the course, which ran from July 12 through August 21. Pach taught one class called Nineteenth-Century and Modern French Painting and Sculpture and another called Methods of Art Study for the Traveling Student in Europe. Each course met twice a week, so there were twelve lectures in all, which Pach illustrated with lantern slides. There were also five field trips on the weekends, for which both short and extended excursions were arranged. At the end of the program all pupils were required to take a four-day tour south to châteaux in the Loire Valley, after which most of the class sailed for home on August 25 aboard the SS *Rotterdam.*

In a description recalling the ideas Pach set forth in his 1918 Berkeley class, in his 1923 *Freeman* articles, and in his *Masters of Modern Art* of 1924, the announcement for the summer session was given as follows: "While France had for centuries been producing art of the greatest importance, the French school of the 19th and 20th centuries enjoys a unique position as the truest continuer of the classic traditions at a time when but a few isolated masters appear in other countries. It is in Paris alone that the full significance of the rich and sustained production of the school is to be realized, and in Paris alone can a thorough insight into the direction of recent movements be obtained." The course reiterated Pach's ideology of the evolutionary aspect of art and traced the development of modern art from nineteenth-century France to the present. It began with an examination of "the modern period and its relation to the past" and ended with "cubism and its successors." Pach continued to teach this subject for New York University, in conjunction with and at the Metropolitan Museum of Art, for the next two years.[7]

While in Paris from the fall of 1929 to the summer of 1932, Pach does not appear to have given any formal lectures; however, toward the end of his sojourn he began corresponding with colleagues back home to inquire about such employment opportunities upon his return. Henry W. Kent, the secretary of the Metropolitan Museum, had written Pach that there was "great

interest in modern art and few to speak of it with understanding." Kent felt that Pach was eminently qualified to speak on the topic and encouraged him in his pursuit of work in this arena. As Pach explained to Paul Sachs of the Fogg Museum of Art, one of the reasons he had settled in Paris for so long was to "get a better grasp" of modern art, and it was from the viewpoint of Parisian modernism that Pach wished to discuss the subject when he began lecturing again in the United States. Pach kept abreast of the art news in the United States when he was overseas, noticing that the country was "gobbling down modern art shows in great numbers." He was convinced, however, that most people did not fully understand what they were viewing and thought he could help remedy that situation. He confessed to Sachs, "Though I don't pretend I can offer an infallible ingredient for making them [modern art exhibitions] sit right within the body artistic, I do think I can be of some use. I don't pretend either that I can prophesy the future (though I have seen a few interesting directions in the work of the younger men), but I believe I can offer some parallels with various phases of the past which can help to clarify judgement." Pach was once more promoting the concept of the evolutionary development of modern art, with Parisian art as the fountainhead from which the best in contemporary art flowed. Not all American artists shared this opinion, and Pach knew that there was "a strong 'America First' movement at home now." While, as a painter himself, he was relieved that there was "no prejudice against home products," he still firmly believed that there was "urgent need of perspective" and admitted that "even if it may not be popular in all quarters if I say that not all American pictures are good and that the central tradition is still here (even when obscure), I think those things should be said."[8] Pach was keenly aware that the controversy ignited in 1928 by his book *Ananias, or the False Artist* was still raging and that his Francophile, Eurocentric views were at odds with the outlook of a growing number of American artists. Undeterred by the specter of criticism from his fellow artists and the possibility of rejection from museum officials, universities, and art associations, Pach wrote dozens of letters in the hope of finding lecture engagements that would allow him to spread his message to as wide an audience as possible.

The economic situation in the United States was dismal when the Pachs returned from France, with the stock market crash of 1929 continuing to affect all aspects of life. Especially hard hit was the art world; nevertheless, throughout the 1930s Pach lectured regularly on modern, mainly modern French, art. The ideas he espoused in his talks mirrored those in his writings, as he traced the beginning of the modern period to Cézanne and usually ended his discussions with cubism and the European artists Picasso, Matisse, and Derain. The types of venues at which he spoke were the same as in previous years—museums, art associations, and colleges and universities—but he now reached different listeners by traveling to new locations in the United States and Canada, including the Baltimore Museum of Art, the Joslyn Memorial Art Museum in Omaha, the Philadelphia Art Alliance, the Art Association of Montreal, McMaster University in Ontario, Skidmore College, Bowdoin College, the John Herron Art Institute in Indianapolis, and Howard University in Washington, D.C. He also branched out into a new medium, radio, through which he was able to reach his largest group of listeners to date. In the fall of 1932, he spoke on the Columbia Broadcasting System (CBS) and tried to convince his friend Van Wyck Brooks to join him and a musician friend in proposing a series of broadcasts on literature, music, and art.

Two prestigious events at which Pach was invited to present a paper in the 1930s were at the Worcester Art Museum and the Whitney Museum of American Art. He was the premier guest lecturer for the opening of the Worcester Art Museum's new building and its inaugural show of contemporary painting, the 1933 International Exhibition of Contemporary Art,

assembled by the College Art Association. The museum's director, Francis Henry Taylor, as well as Edward Forbes, then director of the Fogg Art Museum at Harvard University, were the other speakers for the evening. In his address, Pach explained the importance of the role of museums in a society and the complexity of their missions. A city or country would "be judged to a great extent by the quality, by the standard of the work shown" in its museums. "The very existence of a museum," he added, "is an affirmation that there are certain enduring principles in art which render valid for all time the things which attain the level of true mastery."[9] Museums should house objects that reflected universal truths and ideas, Pach felt, and museum officials were responsible for determining which objects fit this criterion. Later in life, Pach would formulate these ideas on art museums in a book.

In the spring of 1935, Pach participated in a symposium at the Whitney Museum, "The Problem of Subject Matter and Abstract Esthetics in Painting." Sculptor Jo Davidson and painter Leo Katz also spoke, with Lloyd Goodrich as moderator. The symposium coincided with the museum's groundbreaking exhibition Abstract Painting in America. Pach's inclusion on this panel reveals that many in the New York art world regarded his opinion on the subject as important and valid, although they might not necessarily agree with him. Pach announced to his audience,

The problem of contemporary art, as it is faced by artists and art-lovers today, may be defined by the exclusion in terms of two types of pictures to be condemned: first those in which the imitation of nature has eliminated all aesthetic values, as in the "official" portraits, second, those in which the opposite mistake occurs—the omission of all human interest through a too narrow preoccupation with form and color. . . . True work of today does not stand between these two extremes, it stands above them. Its human values unite with its aesthetic values to engender a life that is absent from work which tries to exist without such a union.

He also spoke out against Vladimir Lenin, Leo Tolstoy, and others who condemned modern, nonrealistic painting as antisocial and who promoted art with an overtly social and political message that glorified "scenes of the Revolution, the life of the worker, etc." For Pach, this type of art was merely illustrative, devoid of any artistic or aesthetic value as fine art. Furthermore, "the influence of government or other bodies which inculcate the idea that such things are art is truly anti-social influence for it is poisoning the minds of the masses."[10] Pach was fully aware of the United States' primary political stance of isolationism in the 1930s and was cognizant of the popularity of social realist and regionalist movements in American art of the period. He was adamant that politics should not influence the content of art, or be any part of it. This view was at odds with much of the art prevalent in the United States in the 1930s and, as Pach fully admitted, was one of the reasons he was lambasted by many American artists, whose work was infused with social and political content. Pach was, however, in agreement with many artists who felt that democracy was the most favorable system of government under which art could flourish.

In the depths of the Great Depression, Pach found it very difficult to find work as a lecturer; to increase his chances he composed his own circular to advertise his services. The small card specified the types of talks he was available to give, which included "Modern Art (either the subject as a whole or special phases of it; the Classical School, the Romantic School, the Impressionists, the Post-Impressionists, the Cubists). Also individual masters of the modern period, like Delacroix, Courbet, Manet, Renoir, Cézanne, van Gogh, Matisse, Picasso, Derain, etc.; American Art, Mexican Art, Ancient, Colonial and Modern; The Revival of Mural Painting, The Collector of Small Means. Also certain phases of the older arts of Europe, to be discussed on application." This was quite a broad array of topics, and the diversity was designed to ensure he would be steadily in demand as a speaker. That Pach, for the first time, felt the need to market himself in such a manner reveals his growing concern with earning a living, as well as with trying to find new ways to reach newer and larger audiences. Magda was his agent, and inquiries were directed to their West Seventy-second Street home. Pach soon realized, however, that the lecture circuit in the United States, especially for specialized topics such as art, had grown more sophisticated. Therefore, in 1936 he contracted with the College Art Association and the Bralans Lecture Bureau for them to advertise and book engagements for him. Hiring professional representatives proved to be prudent, and Pach was kept quite busy throughout the 1930s.

Friends also assisted Pach in finding work. In 1937, Arthur Strasser, Frederick P. Keppel (president of the Carnegie Corporation), Belle Greene (director of the Morgan Library), and Frederick Clapp (director of the Frick Collection) raised a subscription for him to present a series of "ten illustrated lectures based on the important exhibitions to be held in New York during the months of November, 1937, to March, 1938, inclusive."[11] The talks were to be given at Columbia University and were open mainly to students and young artists. By late September, Pach was able to report with great relief that "people had begun to join up for the lectures."[12] This association with Columbia, which had begun the previous summer when he had been hired to teach a painting class, would continue for several years.

In the early to mid-1940s, Pach remained a highly sought-after speaker on modern art, but by the late 1940s his influence within this sphere began fading rapidly. At the beginning of the decade, Pach undertook a lengthy lecture circuit along the Pacific Coast, from Seattle to San Diego and then back east via the southern route. Among the cities he visited were Bozeman in Montana, Seattle, San Francisco, Los Angeles, Santa Barbara, San Diego, San Antonio, Houston, New

Orleans, and Detroit. His talks—mainly on modern art—were presented at venues such as Montana State College, the de Young Museum, the Stendahl Gallery, the Museum of Fine Arts in Houston, the Isaac Delgado Museum in New Orleans, and the Detroit Institute of Arts. Also during this period, Pach lectured at Atlanta University and at Fisk University in Nashville, Tennessee, two prominent black colleges. As noted elsewhere, Pach was an early and ardent admirer and supporter of African American art and artists. His friend and colleague Paul Sachs arranged for his 1945 talk in Atlanta, given in connection with the Fourth Annual Exhibition of Paintings, Sculptures, and Prints by Negro Artists. In his lecture he tried to connect older arts—Greek, Gothic, Mexican, and African—with one another. Pach admitted that he was "a shade anxious" about doing a good job, yet his concerns about the audience's response were quelled when, as he wrote Sachs, he "was assured by several colored people that my hearers liked what I said."[13] A few years later, Aaron Douglas invited Pach to return to Fisk to speak on modern art. Douglas, painter, muralist, illustrator, and member of the Harlem Renaissance, was the chairman of Fisk's art department from 1937 until 1966. Pach was concerned about choosing an appropriate topic for this talk and asked Douglas if he should include references to the university's new acquisitions, such as those from the Alfred Stieglitz collection that had recently been donated by Stieglitz's widow, Georgia O'Keeffe. Pach explained to Douglas that for such an audience he felt it was best to approach modern art by following a chronological format in which the evolution of art could be expressed in a logical fashion.

Pach's views on modern art had not altered dramatically in decades. This failure to change with the times and to recognize the importance of some of the newer movements in American art was the primary reason why Pach's influence within the contemporary art world had waned significantly by this time.

Arguably Pach's last significant lectures on modern art were in the series "The Pioneers of Modern Art," given in conjunction with the exhibition of the same name that opened at the Whitney Museum in 1946 and traveled to the Columbus Museum of Art in Ohio in 1947 under the auspices of the American Federation of Arts. Pach spoke at both venues. The inclusion of three of his paintings in the show attests to his recognized place as one of the earliest American artists to adopt modernism—though it could also be construed as signaling Pach's relegation to historical status.

Advertisements, letters, and other archival materials reveal the specific topics on which Pach lectured and the technology he used for his presentations—lantern slides—yet it is a letter from his friend Wallace Stevens after a 1928 lecture on modern art in Hartford, Connecticut, that affords a rare insight into Pach's manner of lecturing. Although Stevens found the speech to be "surpassingly good," he also remarked,

I had thought it was too much of an outline on art, as you went along. But the lovely and unexpected denouement of the floppy Matisse, the one in white with the big hat, justified your process. And yet I doubt too if the long pedagogical preface should be there. The particular doubt relates to the fact that it obscures you. That is the part of the lecture that seems to be a little like preaching. Unquestionably it is the paler part. The essential part of it comes when you are showing the slides and when the mere nervousness of talking is changed into the concentration and excitement of discussing those things for which you have a positive passion.[14]

Pach undoubtedly read from prepared notes at the beginning of his talk and then switched to a more impromptu style. His didactic opening remarks struck his friend as a bit too stuffy and preachy, a frequent criticism launched against Pach. The formal approach, Stevens felt, did not allow Pach's personality to come through. It was vital, Stevens believed, for the audience to see and hear the passion Pach had for art. Pach welcomed his friend's candid comments: "Thanks ever so much for your letter on my modern art lecture at Hartford. If you knew how hard it is for me to get any intelligent opinion on my writing and lecturing you would feel that it was amiss for me to have braced you for an expression of it." He went on, "You gave me the most helpful idea of how it sounded that I've had in years. Mere praise is no more helpful than straight disparagement—and I've had both. I can see that the first part must have had a pedagogical flavor; I am a partisan, and am usually facing prejudiced audiences. Too much enthusiasm, without a measure of the didactic and explanatory would, it seemed to me, strike most hearers as panegyrics; but I think I can watch myself better and give a person beyond the *Philister* class a better time of it than I managed last week."[15]

Although Pach lectured and taught extensively throughout his career, Stevens noted his friend's "nervousness of talking," and indeed he was always ill at ease with public speaking. Pach confessed to Raymond, his son, in 1946, "I remember from twenty-two years ago, a lecture I gave in Milwaukee when I was so sick that I feared I was going to cave in on the platform. I used to take a pill of pain-killer just before I began to speak, each time, and that evening I felt the effect of it wearing off before I finished my lecture. By an effort of will, I fought the thing off, and went to the end of my talk."[16] Clearly suffering from stage fright, Pach nevertheless knew that his work in this vein, like his writing and his roles as exhibition organizer, liaison, agent, and advisor, was essential in the battle for the acceptance of modern art in the United States.

11
Latin American Art and Artists

Walter Pach was among the first twentieth-century artists and critics to recognize and promote Mexican art and artists, both ancient and contemporary, and his enthusiastic support for the arts of Mexico lasted a lifetime. He helped organize several exhibitions of Mexican art in the United States. In addition, he wrote influential articles on Mexican art and artists for American, French, and Mexican newspapers and periodicals, including the *Freeman, Harper's Monthly Magazine, Creative Art, Parnassus, Art News, Art in America, Virginia Quarterly Review,* the *Nation,* the *New York Times, L'Amour et l'Art, Gazette des Beaux-Arts, Cuadernos Americanos, Letras de Mexico, El Hijo Pródigo,* and *México Moderno.* He also included references to Mexican artists Diego Rivera and José Clemente Orozco in his books *The Masters of Modern Art; Ananias;* and *Queer Thing, Painting.* Finally, he contributed a short piece, "Relaciones entre la cultura notreamericana y la obra de Diego Rivera," for the book *50 años de su labór artistica,* published in 1951. Pach was a vitally important figure in the introduction and dissemination of Mexican art to international audiences from the 1920s through the early 1950s. Indeed, art historian Margarita Nieto ascribed "the enthusiasm for Mexican culture" to "two phenomena, one being the overall American cultural climate" and the other "the presence in Mexico of an American intellectual who has only recently been 'rediscovered' by the United States, Walter Pach," who "served as a bridge between the School of Mexico artists—indeed, Mexican art in general—and the North American art institutions."[1]

Pach noted in *Queer Thing, Painting* that he began his studies of ancient Mexican art at the American Museum of Natural History in New York City, and Nieto claims that it was Élie Faure who stimulated Pach's curiosity about Mexican art, but it was during his trip to Berkeley, California, in the summer of 1918 and on two lengthy trips to Mexico City in 1922 and the 1940s that Pach really developed a deep appreciation for the art and artists of Mexico and established lifelong friendships with many of the leading Mexican painters. Remarkably, Pach and Diego Rivera never met in Paris when both were living there between 1911 and January 1913, even though they knew the same artists and both were very good friends with Faure. Pach recalled that the first time he saw works by Rivera was at Marius de Zayas's Modern Gallery in Manhattan in 1916. He would also have seen Rivera's art in various exhibitions in which both participated, including the 1917 and 1918 Society of Independent Artists shows, the Modern Art Exhibition at the People's Art Guild in 1917, the Exhibition of Paintings by the "Moderns" at Vassar College in 1917, and the Exhibition of Contemporary Art at the Penguin Club in 1918. Rivera said that he had actually heard of Pach many years before the two met, when

Rivera was in Spain. Luis de la Rocha, a Spanish artist Pach had met in Madrid in the summer of 1905 while with the Chase program, showed Rivera a letter he had received from Pach (dated 1907 or 1908, according to Pach's version of the story), who wrote from Paris about Cézanne, Picasso, and Matisse and the whole modern movement taking place there and urging de la Rocha to come to the city. Rivera's biographer, Bertram D. Wolfe, also observed that it was Pach's letter that inspired the artist to travel to Paris. Pach himself noted in *Queer Thing, Painting* that Rivera went to Paris "incited. . . . by the phrases of an unknown man."[2]

When Pach was teaching art history at Berkeley in 1918, he met Xavier Martínez and Pedro Henriquez-Ureña, who helped further his interest in Mexican art and culture. Martínez, Mexican by birth, was a pivotal figure in the California art scene and knew many of the leading artists, literary figures, and social critics in Mexico, the United States, and France. He had studied art at the California School of Design, also known as the Mark Hopkins Institute of Art, as well at the École des Beaux-Arts in Paris. His home and studio in Piedmont, California, was a gathering place for artists and writers, among them Maynard Dixon and Jack London. Henriquez-Ureña was a visiting professor of Spanish literature who was living in the same apartment building as the Pachs. These three men became fast friends and shared a passion for art, literature, and culture.

In 1922, Henriquez-Ureña asked Pach to teach a course on modern art for the summer session at the Universidad Nacional de México in Mexico City. The friendship between the two was undoubtedly a driving force behind the invitation, yet Pach's reputation as a leading authority on modern art and as a lecturer, in addition to the fact that he spoke Spanish almost fluently, was also essential for this appointment. Henriquez-Ureña, who had become director of the Exchange University and its secretary, made all the arrangements. Pach was to be paid approximately seven dollars and fifty cents a day plus living expenses and was to lecture two or three times a week. The subject of the three-to-four-month course would be similar to that of the class on modern art Pach taught at Berkeley, where Henriquez-Ureña had attended some of the sessions. Pach confessed that he was a bit nervous about the job, as he had "never spoken publicly in a foreign language before," but despite this trepidation, he was quite excited by the prospect.[3] The Pachs rented their apartment for the summer and departed for Mexico, by boat, near the end of June.

Through his course at the university and through introductions from Henriquez-Ureña, Pach met many of the foremost figures in the fields of art, literature, archaeology, business, and politics in Mexico City: Diego Rivera, José Clemente Orozco, Jean Charlot, Rufino Tamayo, Carlos Mérida, Ramón Mena, Porfirio Aguirre of the Museo Nacional, Octavio G. Barreda, and director of the Bank of Mexico Eduardo Villaseñor. Orozco and Rivera attended some of his classes at the university; so did Charles Thompson, future chief of the Latin American division of the State Department. The main thing they gained from Pach's lectures, as Orozco wrote, was a better understanding of many aspects of contemporary art. In addition to the slide lectures he gave, Pach exhibited a small selection of etchings by Jacques Villon while he was in Mexico City. Pach also encouraged his colleagues in Mexico to form a Society of Independent Artists like the ones in Paris and New York and, before he returned to Manhattan, began arrangements for the painters to show their work at the SIA back home. The friendships Pach formed with Rivera, Orozco, and Charlot would prove vital for the advancement of modern Mexican art in the United States.

The land, the people, and the art of Mexico enchanted Pach. As he wrote Sloan, "We are having a fine time—climate perfect, people friendly and the city just wonderful. It is a very live town—gay streets, fine University crowd and modern. My lectures are well received and I am not afraid of the language anymore. And I'm painting!"[4] He also wrote glowingly of his time in Mexico to Yvonne Duchamp-Villon: "For us it was a pure enchantment with the beauty of the countryside, the grandeur of the ancient art, and the endlessly new fascination of the inhabitants who are for the most part Indians—which we don't know about in the United States, at least not in the east. They are very close to the old indigenous races in their character and their artistic talent. They welcomed my conferences very cordially and with a rapid intelligence."[5] Perhaps the best compliment to Mexico was expressed to Quinn: "I will say only that it has been a delightful time from the first day of our visit. . . . I think Mexico is more different from the United States than any place I know in Europe. It is endlessly beautiful and the people are an inexhaustible mine of interest. . . . There is the most remarkable art instinct here I ever saw anywhere."[6] Pach fell in love with the beauty and strength of the Mexican people and their art.

While in Mexico, Pach bought several ancient sculptures and tried to buy some pieces he felt would fit with Quinn's collection. This latter task proved particularly difficult. He reported his frustrations to the collector: "Mexico is a paradise for artists but hell for art collectors or business men. People here are simply not interested in doing business."[7] The obstacles he encountered trying to buy art multiplied. He confessed that the possibility of obtaining a forgery was a real problem, as was getting the objects out of the country without government officials confiscating them. Nevertheless, he persevered and sent Quinn photographs and lists of objects for sale. Upon his return to New York, Pach corresponded with Jean Charlot, Professor Palacios of the Museo Nacional, and Dr. Hugo Brehme (a German friend of Weyhe's that he met in Mexico) and, eventually, acquired several pieces for Quinn.

Pach stayed in Mexico until mid-October, during which time he "had quite a good chance to paint," though, in the end, he had few paintings to show for his efforts.[8] One canvas begun during this summer was *Street in Mexico* (fig. 27). Although it is hard to tell from the reproduction, the pictures of Rivera, Orozco, and other Mexican muralists—whose realistic style and down-to-earth subject matter Pach admired—served as the inspiration for this painting. Pach's approach, like that of his Mexican colleagues, is representational, and he captures the air of a bustling and active street scene. His figures, however, appear a bit insubstantial and the perspective is not quite right. Nevertheless, Charlot told Pach that "Diego called it more Mexican than their own contributions."[9] Rivera also wrote in praise of the painting and said it "showed the character of our country, not a picturesque character but one intimate and powerful."[10] Pach undoubtedly received these compliments with great satisfaction.

Throughout the fall of 1922 and early months of 1923, Pach was preparing for the Society of Independent Artists annual exhibition, an event with which he had become inextricably linked. Through a series of letters and other communications, particularly with Rivera and Charlot, he arranged for a group of works by many of Mexico's leading painters to be shown at the 1923 show. Rivera wrote on December 7, 1922, with a list of artists he wished to be represented: Orozco, Charlot, Fermín Revueltas, David Alfaro Siqueiros, Fernando Leal, Emilio Garcia Cahero, Mateo Bolaños, Enrique Ugarte, A. Cano, Nahui Olin, Dr. Atl (Gerardo Murillo), Alba, and himself, in addition to drawings by Mexican schoolchildren. He discussed the space and hanging requirements for the works and suggested a possible installation arrangement. Soon after Pach received this letter, a *New York Times* headline announced, "Mexican Independents Accept Local Society's Invitation."[11] The artists whose works were actually shown were Siqueiros, Emilio Amero, Abraham Angel, Adolfo Best de Maugard, A. Cano, Charlot, Carlos Mérida, Orozco, Manuel Martinez Pintao, Rivera, Manuel Rodriguez Lozano, Rufino Tamayo, Rosario Cabrera, and Nahui Olin (or Carmen

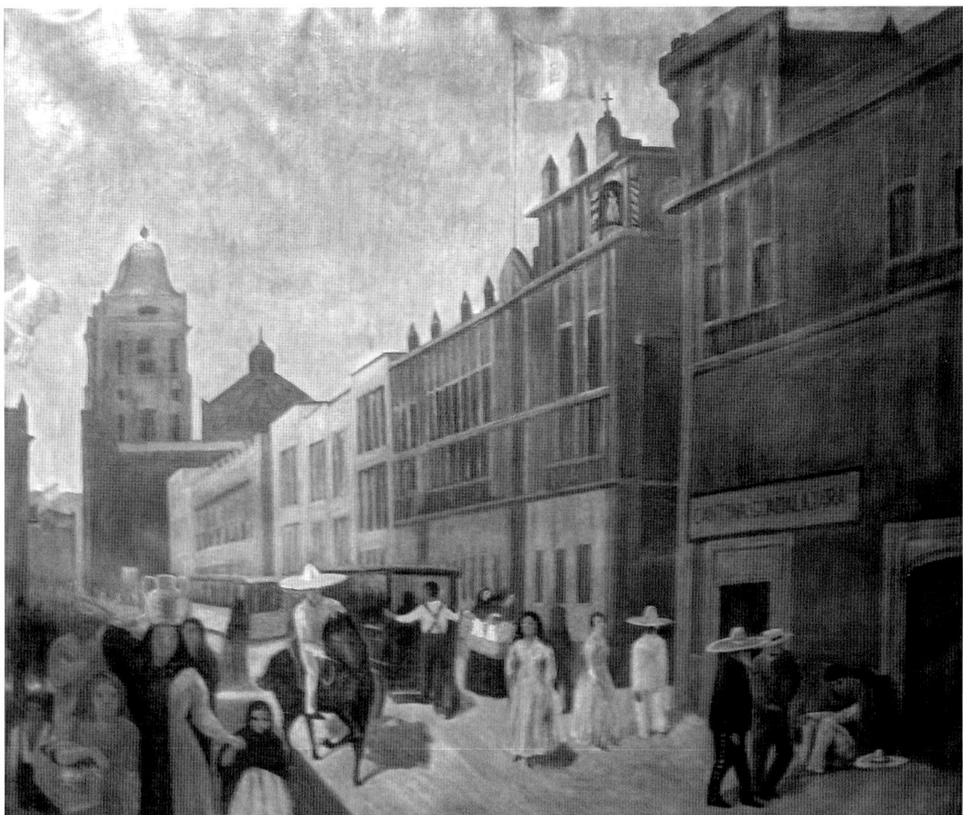

Mondragón, wife of Manuel Rodriguez Lozano).[12] Pach had met many of these artists the previous summer. Only Rivera and de Maugard had exhibited at the SIA previously, Rivera at the inaugural show in 1917 and in 1918, and de Maugard in 1920. In the 1923 show, thirty-nine works by Mexican artists were displayed. Rivera had the most works on view—two paintings, two studies of details for frescoes, and seven drawings—followed by Orozco, with five paintings. This was the first exhibition of its kind by these artists in the United States, and it was a historic event. The fact that two women artists were represented at such an early date is also quite remarkable.

Pach not only made all the arrangements for shipping, insuring, and so on, but also praised the artists and their works in his review of the show. "The collection displayed here," Pach wrote, "showed a very high level of talent, and it was conspicuously character-istic of its country in that it contained the various elements that go to make up the Mexican national life."[13] In the paintings, drawings, and sculptures of these artists, Pach saw a blend of indigenous, Spanish, and modern art; he singled out Rivera for his synthesis of these various influences. The painters were under-standably elated and thanked Pach profusely for his efforts on their behalf, as did José Vasconceles, then president of the Universidad Nacional de México and Mexico's secretary of education.

Pach's interest in and promotion of contemporary and ancient Mexican art grew throughout the 1920s. He regularly corresponded with the artists, especially Rivera, Charlot, and Orozco, and the level of intimacy that developed between these individuals is clear from the tone of their letters. These artists kept Pach apprised of their daily activities in Mexico, especially the progress of their mural painting. Pach, in turn, kept them informed of the events and news in the New York art world. He sent them catalogs of the SIA exhibition and contemporary art periodicals. He also helped coordinate the exhibition and sale of the artists' works in the United States. In his December 7, 1922, letter to Pach, Rivera thanked him for introducing him, via mail, to a Miss Porter who was connected with the Wanamaker department store's exhibitions of art and who had sent Rivera a letter regarding a possible show of his drawings. It is unclear whether this show ever materialized, but Rivera wrote Pach again in 1923 and asked him to thank "the other entities that cared to invite us to exhibit at a later time."[14] In October 1925, Charlot sent Pach fifty paintings and ninety-one drawings by parcel post from Mexico with the hope that Pach could sell the works; subsequently, Pach arranged for the Exhibition of Art Work by Mexican School Children and Jean Charlot at the Art Center of New York in April 1926. When Rufino Tamayo arrived in New York in 1926, he contacted Pach, who brought him to the Weyhe Gallery, where Tamayo had his first one-person show in the United States. Pach also arranged for Tamayo's solo exhibition at the Art Center in 1927. In the fall of 1927, Pach wrote Rivera about the show of his work being organized for the Weyhe Gallery by his good friend Carl Zigrosser and asked the artist to send additional works, a request he accepted. When Rivera arrived in New York en route to the Soviet Union on October 17, 1927, Pach took him to the Weyhe Gallery, where several of the drawings Rivera had in hand were purchased by the dealer.[15] Pach served as Rivera's escort for the one day Rivera was in Manhattan and recalled in *Queer Thing, Painting,* "The first time he [Rivera] was in New York—it was only for a day—I insisted on his taking time for at least a brief visit to our museum [Metropolitan]."[16]

Pach probably also introduced Orozco to Weyhe and Zigrosser when the artist arrived in Manhattan from Mexico in the late fall of 1927. He may also have introduced Emilio Amero, who lived in New York from

1924 to 1930, to the gallery. During this period, Pach's colleagues introduced him to other Mexican and Latin and South American artists and writers. For example, Henriquez-Ureña asked Pach to see if he could assist Argentine painter Emilio Pettoruti with a show in New York. Rivera sent his friend Miguel Covarrubias to Manhattan with a letter of introduction to Pach and asked the latter to review the young artist's works. Pach became a vital link between these artists and the New York art world.

Beginning in 1920 and throughout the decade, several Mexican and Latin and South American artists came to the United States and to New York City in particular, and all were befriended by Walter Pach. As in the 1910s with the French émigrés, Pach opened his home and studio to his friends and colleagues. In the summer of 1920, the Pachs rented their apartment to Uruguayan painter Joaquin Torres-Garcia. He had arrived in New York from Paris and was probably given Pach's name by artists and dealers in the French city. He could also have been introduced to Pach in Manhattan by Marcel Duchamp. Among the artists who frequently came to the Pachs' were Rufino Tamayo, who arrived in June 1926, and Orozco, who arrived toward the end of 1927 and was one of Pach's most frequent guests. Orozco described one of his visits to Pach's studio in a letter to Jean Charlot:

In the evening I visited W. Pach. Very pleasant. Magnificent studio. He gives lectures at the Metropolitan Museum. He does NOT take me very seriously as a painter. A passionate admirer of Picasso. He didn't like what I said. He showed me his own works and asked my opinion of them. He did NOT like my frankness. His wife as a *china poblana*! /Wonderful picture/ He took me to visit the/independents/. A nude model for 1 dollar an hour. In his house he has some very good pictures: a head by Derain-very fine!—lithographs by Cézanne, Signorelli, etc. There wasn't time to see them all.[17]

Obviously Orozco and Pach had different ideas about art, yet Pach was ever the gracious host. He took Orozco under his wing and introduced him to his friends and colleagues in the art business.

Reading other letters from Orozco to Charlot from this particular period makes it clear that Orozco's opinion of Pach had changed dramatically since Pach's visit to Mexico in 1922. Orozco did not think very highly of Pach and criticized him for his support and praise of Rivera. He complained bitterly to Charlot, "In everything he says, he seems to infer, 'Let us, the failures, bow down before the masters.' And he intimates that Rivera is on the same level as Picasso and that the latter esteems the former highly. . . . Let us bow down before the masters! Hosanna!"[18] Orozco was clearly angered by Pach's support of Rivera's work. He also attacked the SIA and, in the process, Pach: "'The Independents': 2,000,000 'paintings' or something like that, sculpture with wire, called very 'daring' and 'the latest thing' (50 years ago), perhaps an imitation of the 'independents' of Paris. W. Pach, very interested, asked me if I had seen it—yes, indeed Mr. Pach! Extraordinary, isn't it? Yes, indeed Mr. Pach!" At the same time that Pach was helping Orozco, the latter lambasted his colleague's relationships with the very dealers he was hoping would represent him. Orozco wrote Charlot about "the dirty tricks played by the dealers and their panderers, the critics, to get rich at the expense of the unfortunate artists. . . . W.P. [Walter Pach] is one of the panderers."[19] Orozco was one of several artists who felt that Pach was too familiar with the dealers and, therefore, biased in his view of art. Despite his dislike of Pach's views on art and on Rivera, Orozco took advantage of his American colleague's numerous connections. Pach advised Orozco to approach Kraushaar Galleries about selling his drawings from *Horrores de la Revolución,* but the dealer found the works rather strange. Toward the end of 1928, Pach selected Orozco's lithograph version of *Requiem* from *Horrores* for the 1928 Fifty Prints of the Year exhibition presented by the American Institute of Graphic Arts.[20]

Throughout the 1920s, Pach promoted contemporary Mexican art and artists by means of his writings. Before he left Mexico in the fall of 1922, he wrote his first essay in Spanish, "Impresiones sobre el arte actual de México," published in the October issue of *México Moderno.* This was one of the first writings in any language to discuss the work of Rivera, Orozco, and other contemporary Mexican artists and as such was seminal to the history of the literature in the field. Pach wrote of the works that Orozco had shown him when he was in Mexico City,

The Mexican types of José Clemente Orozco are of an expression so definitive that it is tempting to believe that his art has reached full maturity. But if one looks under the surface of his output, one comes to realize that the most important work of the artist is still ahead of him in time. His drawings, his watercolors possess the hard texture of a spring soil. The forms—physical and psychological—recorded by the painter have the preciseness of the primitive, that is of art in such a state of intensity that, when it divides and recombines its components, it still gains in richness. . . . The Mexican artist has produced a work that is part of the great modern expression, as much in its idea of life as in its handling of the abstract properties of art.[21]

Pach was particularly struck by the power of Orozco's draftsmanship and saw in his work the blending of the past and present that he felt was the hallmark of all truly great art. He saw this synthesis in the paintings and murals of other Mexican artists as well and was impressed by the passion and dignity that he found in their works.

Pach also praised Mexican painters in his English writings. In his series of articles on modern art for the *Freeman* in 1923 and in his book *The Masters of Modern Art,* Pach placed Rivera's cubist paintings on par with those of Jean Metzinger, Albert Gleizes, Fernand Léger, and Jacques Villon, thus canonizing Rivera among the masters of his era. He furthermore praised Rivera for the beautiful art of his mural decoration, for the directness of his vision, and for its connection to the past. Rivera was, understandably, thrilled by Pach's critique of his work and tried to have a Spanish translation of the text published, but to no avail. In his 1928 book, *Ananias, or the False Artist,* Pach observed that Rivera was "already known and admired in the United States" and that "when we know more of Orozco it seems certain that we shall add his name to the roll of great men of our time."[22] Pach also contributed a short piece on Rivera to the January 1929 issue of *Creative Arts,* an edition devoted to "the phenomenal development of art in Mexico." Rivera wrote "The Revolution in Painting"; Orozco outlined his artistic and aesthetic credo in "New World, New Races, and New Art"; Tina Modotti provided photographs of Rivera's murals; Anita Brenner's article on Mexican colonial art was accompanied by photographs by Edward Weston; and Lewis Mumford and Emily Hamblem, who was writing a book on Orozco, were also contributors. Pach's contribution, "The Evolution of Diego Rivera," discussed Rivera's development from his early academic days through cubism to his latest work. He saw Rivera's work through the same lens of evolutionary determinism that he espoused in his description of modern French art from the time of David to the present, and Rivera as part of the same art-historical tradition as the leading avant-garde French painters he had championed for more than a decade. In the contemporary art of Mexico, particularly in the work of Diego Rivera, Pach saw the classic traditions of the past alive and well.

During this period, Pach also wrote about ancient Mexican art in articles for the *Freeman, Harper's Monthly Magazine,* and *L'Amour de l'Art.* For his short piece in the *Freeman,* Pach focused his attention on the artisans who made pottery, glassware, basketry, blankets, and other utilitarian goods in which Pach found true beauty and art. In his essays for *Harper's* and *L'Amour de l'Art* he discussed the ancient art of Mexico—of the Aztecs, Mayans, and Toltecs—asserting that their work belonged in art museums, not in the natural history museums of New York, London, and Paris where he had seen them. Pach found in the sculptures and pottery of the ancient peoples of Mexico similarities to the art of the ancient tribes of Egypt and discerned connections between the art of South America and that of North America; the world, he hoped, would see "the essential oneness of the whole Western Hemisphere."[23] His view of Mexican art and his adherence to the concept of a Pan-American region were ideals that Pach shared with his fellow artists from Mexico, and he championed these beliefs for decades.

During the 1930s, Pach not only continued to support and promote the art of Rivera and Orozco—he devoted a chapter of his *Queer Thing, Painting* to the artists—but also championed the work of Frida Kahlo. He was kept informed of Rivera's activities in the United States while he was in Paris between 1929 and 1932 by friends and colleagues such as Allen Tucker and Ida Guggenheimer. Once the Pachs returned to New York, the friendships with these artists were revived. Pach recalled in *Queer Thing, Painting* that during the period when Rivera and Kahlo were in Detroit and New York, "the grand evenings of talk and songs and picture-seeing that we used to have in Mexico City in 1922, were renewed." Pach visited Rivera in Detroit in January 1933, when the artist was working on his mural series *Detroit Industry* for the Detroit Institute of Arts and "had a chance to mount on the scaffolding with him and see a fresco in progress."[24] While Pach was in town, Wilhelm Valentiner, director of the museum, sent him on a "pacifist mission to the architect of the Detroit Museum, who was disturbed by the Rivera murals," to assure the architect that the "building had gained by the painting of the decorations."[25] When Rivera and Kahlo arrived in Manhattan for Rivera to work on his next commission, they naturally contacted their good friend Walter Pach, who soon thereafter found himself at the center of yet another artistic maelstrom.

The topic that made front-page news in the New York art world in the spring of 1933 was the controversy surrounding Rivera's mural for Rockefeller Center, and Pach placed himself at the center of the fray. This scandal has been discussed in detail in the literature, with several authors mentioning Pach's role.[26] While Rivera's portrait of Lenin is generally given as the impetus behind the destruction of his mural, Pach wrote of another troubling image in the work that disturbed the Rockefellers: "The real reason, as the officials stated privately, was that he had painted syphilis germs in his scene of the bridge-playing society folk (only a few years ago, the dread word could not be uttered in public)." Pach, however, felt that this explanation was not accurate either: "You may doubt my statement, if you like, but from two persons who were in a position to get the facts, I know that underneath both of the assigned reasons was the real one: quite simply, a dislike of Rivera's painting as art."[27]

The true cause of the uproar may never be fully known. In any event, Pach naturally sided with Rivera and attempted to intervene on his behalf with the Rockefellers, particularly with Abby Rockefeller, whom he knew quite well. He first wrote to her on May 10:

All day long I have been having visits and 'phone calls about the Rivera matter, and now at 9:30 at night a really good friend gives me the most sensible suggestion—that I write you and send the letter at once to ask to see you as early as possible, for you, to-morrow.

The point is that if the incident is not closed promptly, the professional trouble-makers who are always hungry for an opportunity to take up a "cause" will have an excuse for propaganda that will continue not only during the misunderstanding about the decoration but on every occasion when the Modern Museum or any other art-activity of yours or Mr. Rockefeller's is to the fore. I am not an opponent of Communism, but I do object to the use of art as a pretext to further communistic interests, and so my one desire is to see this matter arranged and Rivera's fine work carried out as it deserves to be.

Since Mr. Rockefeller has not been quoted in the papers so far, the way is open for him to override the objections that have been made and simply deflate the whole business—which will then sink from notice as so many baseless things in the past have done. If the matter is embittered by controversy it will only increase the difficulty of getting rid of it—and that, I am sure, is the desire of the people who are already planning protests of a disagreeable character which—as they are ostensibly in Rivera's interest—he can not easily disavow.

As an admirer of his art, I said in my first talk with him on the 'phone this morning, that I should be glad to serve on a committee that would support his work. I am in favor of it, and so take this means to further his interest—which I believe to coincide exactly with your own. I shall be glad to come to you on receipt of a 'phone call tomorrow (Susquehanna 7-3417 the number is in the book) and I am sure that a dignified and satisfactory solution can be arrived at.[28]

Ever the diplomat, Pach was trying to find an amicable middle ground for both parties. Like most of his contemporaries, Pach felt it essential that the artist be allowed to complete his work, "whatever the difficulty of dealing with him as to treatment and subject." He suggested that Mr. Rockefeller "step in to remedy a mistake" and allow the work to be finished and viewed before making a final decision on its possible destruction.[29] Unfortunately, Pach's powers of persuasion did not work this time. His requests for a meeting with the Rockefellers were rebuffed; he received a curt reply informing him that his letters had been referred to the managing directors of Rockefeller Center.

Disappointed by the Rockefellers' actions, Pach joined dozens of other artists in a protest against the dismissal of Rivera and the fate of his mural. Pach's was the first name on a telegram sent to the Rockefellers asking them to discuss the "questions raised by the dismissal of Diego Rivera."[30] Other signers of the telegram were John Sloan, Suzanne La Follette, Alexander Brook, and Peggy Bacon. This group was joined by Niles Spencer, George Biddle, Lewis Gannett, A. S. Baylinson, and Lou Block and they sent a letter to collectors and museum personnel, among them Duncan Phillips and Fiske Kimball, and asked for their support. Pach, Sloan, and La Follette did meet with "the Rockefeller Center people" over dinner, an event that lasted until one o'clock in the morning. Unfortunately, they made very little progress toward changing their minds.

The Rivera controversy proved a very delicate matter for Pach, who was caught between the artist and the Rockefeller camp, patrons whose goodwill he could ill afford to loose. He described this dilemma to his friend Ida Guggenheimer:

I want to write an article on the business. Within a week I have spoken to three men who are against me in my idea about the fresco. One is an important art-collector, the other two are prominent on the staff of the Metropolitan Museum. All three are friends of mine who would stand by me in other matters, but the way they are against me in this case shows how I should run into danger if I wrote imprudently on this Rivera business. I hate to count such risks, but, in the first place, my future is too insecure to allow myself to be classed as a Bolshevist; in the second place, it would make me useless for service that I might render in future causes. . . . I think I have a line to begin the article (that is usually the hardest part), but it's going to be a case of 'watch your step,' there being just as much danger of pussy footing as of going wrong the other way. It's my job to rush in where fools fear to tread (fools and liars), and I don't think I am quite enough of an angel for the requirements. However, I'll do my best.[31]

Pach felt morally and aesthetically obligated to address this situation in print so that he might reach a wide audience, but, having experienced the controversial reception of *Ananias* just a few years earlier, he was understandably hesitant. He struggled with this problem for several weeks and finally submitted a draft of his manuscript in July. His initial title for the essay was "The Artist Tells the Truth," but it was changed to "Rockefeller, Rivera, and Art" before it reached publication in *Harper's Weekly* in September 1933. In this article, Pach summarized the problem as a fight between "art and the counterfeit of art" and defended the artist's right to complete his design.[32]

In September 1933, Pach again involved himself directly in the controversy of Rivera's Rockefeller Center mural. The artists' appeal to the managing directors to save the work had been ignored. Once more Pach tried to persuade Mrs. Rockefeller to intervene. Rivera was preparing to leave for Mexico and a decision had to be made on the fate of the mural. Pach sent Mrs. Rockefeller a copy of "Rockefeller, Rivera, and Art," upon which he received another terse reply, from Anna L. Kelly, secretary, on behalf of Mrs. Rockefeller, effectively stopping any further correspondence on the issue. The course had been determined.

Early in 1934, the six-month controversy over Rivera's fresco at Rockefeller Center finally reached a conclusion, much to the dismay of Pach and others. Although many had explained how the mural could be removed without any damage to the painting or the wall, it was utterly destroyed the weekend of February 10–11. In protest, dozens of artists who were to participate in the Municipal Art Exhibition at Radio City, including Pach, withdrew from the show. He was one of the speakers at a demonstration of some one thousand people at Irving Plaza. In addition, he wrote a letter of protest to the *New York Times* denouncing the destruction of the mural; in "destroying the Rivera mural," he lamented, "the directors of the Rockefeller Center show that they have no sense of the importance of art, or else no respect for it. Whoever remains silent in the presence of such vandalism condones the act."[33] Ever the cautious diplomat, Pach was careful in his wording and did not mention his friends Abby or John Rockefeller directly in his condemnation.

For the brief period that Rivera and Kahlo remained in New York after the Rockefeller debacle, they saw the Pachs regularly. Pach painted a portrait of Kahlo, complaining that she frequently left the sittings unexpectedly. Rivera asked for Pach's assistance in getting some of his friends' work into exhibitions in New York. He gave Pach lessons in the fresco technique, lending him his best assistant to prepare several panels for Pach's experiments. Pach visited Rivera while the latter worked on his *Portrait of America* murals at the New Workers' School on West Fourteenth Street and wrote glowingly of them in an article for the *Nation* in September 1933.

Pach remained close friends with the couple, reviewing Kahlo's first one-person show, at the Julien Levy Gallery, for the November 1938 issue of *Art News.* He was among the first critics to discuss Kahlo's art, and he did so in one of the leading art journals of the time. In his piece, "Frida Rivera: Gifted Canvases by an Unselfconscious Surrealist," Pach wrote, "The exhibition of Frida Kahlo (Frida Rivera) . . . gives us the art of a woman, a Mexican and a modern," revealing his belief that gender played a significant role in an artist's work. He went on, "This painter, who did not know the word surrealist till told she was one, is poignantly of her time. . . . Her work goes beyond the trial stage of a young artist's first show; it is, definitively, a beautiful achievement."[34] Pach was certainly aware of the surrealist movement and saw in some of Kahlo's pictures aspects

of this style, as did André Breton, who had arranged the exhibition. In addition to praising the pictures in the exhibition, Pach purchased a work from the show, a tiny oil painting titled *Survivor.*

Throughout the 1940s, Pach stayed in contact with his colleagues from Mexico and elsewhere in Latin America as he continued to be a cultural ambassador between the United States and her neighbors to the south. Toward the end of spring 1942, he received a financial godsend in the form of an invitation to return to Mexico City to give a series of lectures for the Universidad Nacional de México, the invitation issued by a former colleague from the university who was "now an important man in the Mexican government."[35] It is most likely that this friend was Octavio G. Barreda, who was in the Department of Commerce in Mexico and had been the Mexican consul in New York and London. Pach had known him since the former's first visit to Mexico in 1922 and felt "much closer" to Barreda "than to anyone else in Mexico."[36] Most of his lectures, which were on modern art, were to be given in Spanish at the university; others were also to be presented at the Palacio de Bellas Artes (Palace of Fine Arts). Pach borrowed lantern slides from the library at the Metropolitan Museum of Art to illustrate these talks.

The Pachs' departure was scheduled for the end of July, and to ready themselves they began to sell some items and put others in storage. They would give up their lease on their apartment. At the beginning of the month, Magda Pach asked Carl Zigrosser if he knew of anyone who might want to acquire their "full-size etching press with a 300 lb. roller."[37] Another item they let go was a much more prized possession, Marcel Duchamp's *Sad Young Man on a Train.* Some time before they left for Mexico, Pach sold the painting to Peggy Guggenheim, much to the chagrin of the artist and the Arensbergs.

The Pachs traveled via Laredo, Texas, to Mexico City "in a fine, government car and with charming Mexican friends" and arrived in July 1942.[38] When the couple first got to the capital they stayed with Barreda but soon found "a peach of an apartment, with a fine studio" in the heart of the city.[39] Both were pleased by the fact that expenses in Mexico City were "from a fourth to a third of what they were in New York." Pach was elated at being reacquainted with Rivera and Kahlo, who "were most cordial in their welcome," and with Orozco.[40] He found among these artists and other friends and acquaintances in Mexico City great intellectual activity. Pach was not, however, as politicized as his Mexican colleagues, and he was dismayed at the amount of time spent discussing politics and the war. He was especially frustrated with Rivera, who, as he told Brooks, "has the whole war doped out—insists that it is all a war of Fascism versus mankind, which, he says, is why the Allies refuse to open a second front— their purpose being to have Russia eliminated as a menace."[41] Pach complained to Brooks, "The politics— of every kind—here just drives me to drink."[42] This was probably an exaggeration, but reveals his lack of interest in the topic. Nonetheless, he enjoyed the camaraderie and intellectual furor of the city.

Soon after his arrival, Pach immersed himself in the artistic and literary circles of the city. As he told Brooks, one of his hosts at the university was Alfonso Reyes, a "professor—philosopher—poet who is very highly regarded throughout the Spanish-speaking world."[43] Pach also made the acquaintance of artist Roberto Montenegro, art historian Fernando Gamboa, and *Cuadernos Americanos* secretary Juan Larrea and renewed his friendship with Barreda. Reyes, Larrea, Barreda, and others helped Pach obtain writing assignments for numerous journals, among them *Cuadernos Americanos, Letras de Mexico, Hoy,* and *El Hijo Pródigo,* during his stay in Mexico. Pach's first publication was an article on the self-taught Mexican artist Hermenegildo Bustos. Francisco Orozco Muñoz, of the Museo Nacional, had introduced Pach to Bustos's paintings, which reminded Pach of the work of primitive portraitists in the United States. Appearing in the November–

December 1942 edition of *Cuadernos Americanos,* this was the first piece on Bustos by a foreign critic and an important contribution to awareness among Spanish-speaking audiences of the artistic heritage of Mexico. In the fall of 1942, Carlos Mérida broadcast a portion of this article over the radio from North Texas State Teachers College (now the University of North Texas) in Denton, Texas, where he was teaching, spreading the word farther afield. Pach had initially proposed the topic to Jean Lipman, editor of *Art in America,* and the English version of the article was published in the January 1943 issue of that periodical.

In this essay, and virtually all his writings about Mexican art, Pach stressed the work's connection with the art of its northern neighbor. He believed that the countries shared a common ancestry, and he supported a Pan-American vision that saw America as "a far bigger place than the United States."[44] He fully agreed with Rivera's notion that "the New World is essentially one place—and one whose special need is greater recognition of its own tradition and genius."[45] In his writings, Pach promoted the concept of "Hemisphere Solidarity," an ideal that he regarded as a great need of the period. He felt there was an innate bond among all the peoples and art of the Western Hemisphere, "whether we call it North America or South America, Canada or Mexico," and he consistently emphasized the relevance of the ancient arts of the Americas to contemporary artists and audiences.[46]

During this trip to Mexico, Pach helped organize several exhibitions in the capital and gave lectures outside the university setting. He visited local galleries and other art establishments and became quite close with Alberto G. Misrachi, director of the Central Art Gallery, and Inés Amor, director of the Gallery of Mexican Art. In September and October 1942, Pach arranged a display of paintings and prints by contemporary Mexicans for the University Club in Mexico City. Among the artists represented were Raúl Anguiano, Federico Cantú, Fernando Castillo, Miguel Covarrubias,

Francisco Gutiérrez, Maria Izquierdo, Frida Kahlo, Roberto Montenegro, José Clemente Orozco, Diego Rivera, Rosa Rolando, David Siqueiros, and Rufino Tamayo. Pach spoke at the opening, wrote a foreword for the catalog, and penned an article for the Spanish magazine *Hoy.* During this time he also attempted to organize an exhibition of Rivera's work at the Arts Club of Chicago, but this did not come to fruition. In Mexico City, Pach gave a presentation, in Spanish, in conjunction with the exhibition 100 Years of Mexican Portraits, which was held at the Benjamin Franklin Library, now part of the U.S. Embassy; his lecture, titled in English "Bustos and the Mexican Portrait," undoubtedly reflected the thoughts from his essay on this artist. As a result of these activities, Pach was "drafted for other lectures, organizing of exhibitions, and writing," including participation in a symposium on the artist José Posada at the National Museum.[47] Through his shows and lectures, Pach became one of the premier cultural liaisons between Mexican artists and Americans in Mexico City.

The officials at the Universidad Nacional de México were so pleased with the response to Pach's classes that they wanted him to stay another term. Money, however, was an issue, and officials at the school asked for Pach's assistance in obtaining funds for his position. On behalf of the rector, Rudolfo Brito Foucher, Pach contacted, in Manhattan, Henry Allen Moe, director of the Committee for Inter-American Artistic and Intellectual Relations, part of the John Simon Guggenheim Memorial Foundation, with a request for a grant. The committee paid the Pachs $250 dollars a month to cover the couple's living expenses while they were in Mexico, an insurance premium, and their return railroad fare to New York. The grant from the committee extended Pach's assignment at the university from January through June 1943. Pach shared this news with a former classmate from CCNY, Stephen Duggan, who was the director of the Institute of International Education in New York. Duggan was delighted by his colleague's

success in Mexico. Both organizations were actively engaged in promoting cultural exchanges between Mexico and the United States as part of the American government's Good Neighbor policy. Pach was not only well acquainted with their missions, but was one of their ambassadors. Because of the grant, Pach was able to deliver a group of lectures in Carso de Inverno at Mascarones and to offer a course at San Carlos, the university's art school, from March through July 1943.

While in Mexico, reversing the usual flow of cultural exchange, Pach helped introduce an American artist to Mexican audiences. In December 1942, Zigrosser sent Pach *Letters of John B. Flannagan,* published by their mutual friend Curt Valentin in New York and edited by another colleague, Wilhelm Valentiner. Flannagan was one of the foremost modernist sculptors in the United States. When Pach showed this small volume to the editors at *Cuadernos Americanos,* "they ordered an article."[48] This essay, the first substantial text on Flannagan, was published in Spanish in the March–April issue of the journal and was printed in English in the summer 1943 volume of the *Kenyon Review.* Pach arranged for Diego Rivera and Carlos Mérida to write articles on Flannagan, too—for *El Hijo Pródigo* and *Tiras de Color,* respectively. Pach saw in Flannagan's work an affinity with the ancient sculpture of Mexico and felt that the sculptor participated in "orienting our course toward a vision representative of the American continent as a whole."[49]

Although the Pachs were enchanted by Mexico's landscape and people and wished to stay longer, they felt compelled to go home; with their future yet to be planned, Pach wrote museum officials across the country to inquire after any available positions. He asked Paul Sachs of Harvard, "Will it be harder (or impossible?) to find anything to do at home? Such support as I have previously had from people who buy paintings or pay for writing is not to be counted on in a period like this; so it seems to me I must look for a job in some college, museum, or other institution. Could you perhaps suggest such a possibility for me?"[50] Sachs replied that Pach might "give a summer course to North American students, particularly those interested in Latin America, at some such Summer School as the Summer Language School at Middlebury, Vermont, or the Summer School of Inter-American Affairs, which has functioned recently at Williams College under Dean Haldam Gregersen."[51] He suggested that Pach place his name on the list of speakers on Latin American subjects that was being compiled by Annette Cottrell in the Office of the Coordinator of Inter-American Affairs in Washington, D.C. Pach had many ideas for lectures, magazine articles, and brochures that would bring Latin American culture to American audiences. He took Sachs's advice to heart and immediately wrote to Cottrell and Gregersen and contacted several other individuals and organizations involved with relations between the United States and Latin America. He sent a letter to Robert C. Smith, director of the Hispanic Foundation at the Library of Congress, and applied for a substitute teaching license so he could teach Spanish either in an adult evening course or at the junior high or high school level in the New York public school system upon his return.

Pach felt strongly that he could turn his experience in Mexico into a position in the United States and hoped to be "the cultural ambassador from Mexico." He told Sloan, "I have important credentials from friends in the government there, and shall shortly present them in Washington."[52] He had already contacted Henry Allen Moe regarding a book and opportunities in government service. Moe in turn put him in touch with Charles A. Thompson of the State Department, and Pach also wrote to Laurence Duggan, a State Department advisor on political relations; later he went to the nation's capital to speak with these individuals. Pach certainly was well connected and knew whom to contact, but government moves slowly, and he had to wait weeks for a response to his overtures for work. He wrote Sloan, "I am being kept waiting for news by the

State Department in Washington. You see, for the last six months in Mexico, I was working for them, or more directly for the Inter-American Committee (Nelson Rockefeller's outfit). Now I have what seem to me splendid plans for carrying on the work from this side of the border, and I have written Washington about it—and the really wonderful endorsement I have from the Mexican government."[53] This endorsement came in the form of a letter of support from several prominent individuals: Inés Amor; Francisco Orozco Muñoz; Eduardo Villaseñor; Alfonso Noriega Jr., secretary of the Universidad Nacional; and Rivera, Orozco, and Barreda. They endorsed any endeavors on behalf of Latin American art that Pach would be engaged on in the United States, and they attested to his understanding of their cultures and his fluency in their language. This letter was presented to minister counselor Rafael de la Colina and to Ezequiel Padilla, secretary of exterior relations for Mexico, by Eugenio de Anzorena, secretary of the Mexican Embassy in Washington. Pach was poised to dive into the world of politics. Unfortunately, his ideals and plans were too lofty and elaborate for the reality of everyday life in the contemporary political world, and nothing came of his quest.

Walter Pach's enthusiastic support and promotion of Mexican art, both contemporary and ancient, was invaluable for its acceptance in the United States and beyond. He was among the first to write about Diego Rivera, José Clemente Orozco, and others and because his essays appeared in journals in the United States, Mexico, and France, he reached a wide international audience. Through his efforts many Mexican artists were able to exhibit at some of the most prestigious galleries in the United States. As MacKinley Helm noted in his 1941 book, *Modern Mexican Painters,* Pach was "the most *simpatico* of Americans in the eyes of Mexican artists."[54] In him they found a steady ally and a true believer in the power and beauty of their art.

12
Historian

While Walter Pach is most recognized for his promotion of modern art, he was also a well-regarded art historian. His knowledge of the history of art was encyclopedic, although he preferred European and American art history. Pach believed that art historians should not specialize but rather should address the major problems of art and discuss the broad issues that related every phase of art to every other. He strove to achieve this goal in his career as a historian, which formally began with a lecture in 1906 and lasted a lifetime. Pach made his greatest impact in the field of art history through his lectures, teachings, translations, and writings. In addition, he was the director general for the monumental 1940 Masterpieces of Art exhibition for the New York World's Fair. This show, comprising 373 European and American paintings ranging from the sixteenth to the nineteenth centuries, was among Pach's last statements on the evolution of Western art from the Renaissance to the early modern era, the latter being, by 1940, indeed historical art.

Pach delivered dozens of lectures (fig. 28) and taught numerous courses on nonmodern art across the United States and in Canada. Many of his speeches were freelance assignments, talks delivered at women's clubs, galleries, museums, and art institutions, such as the Arts Club of Chicago, the Milwaukee Art Institute, the Omaha Society of Fine Arts, the Art Association of Montreal (now the Montreal Museum of Art), the Stendhal Gallery in Los Angeles, and the Phillips Collection. In the 1930s and 1940s, Pach presented lectures under the auspices of the College Art Association. Among their titles were "Greek Art," "Greek Sculpture Before Phidias and Greek Sculpture from Phidias to End," "Ancient Art Through Modern Eyes," "Gothic Sculpture," Mexican Art: Ancient, Colonial, and Modern," "The Romantic School: Figure and Landscape Painting," and "Ancient Answers to Modern Problems." During William Merritt Chase's European summer schools in Italy in 1907 and 1910, Pach gave a

lecture titled "History of Art, Architecture, Sculpture, and Painting." Although he reached hundreds of students and others through these talks, arguably his greatest influence on the field of art history was through his more formal work as a university professor.

From 1918 to 1956, Pach taught courses on art history not of the modern period at important colleges and universities. At Berkeley in the summer of 1918, he gave a survey course beginning with Egyptian art and ending with the early nineteenth century, including a brief discussion of India, Japan, and China. Two years later, he was "invited to speak in the [Metropolitan] Museum's special courses on Saturdays and Sundays," offered in cooperation with New York University. Using the museum's collection as well as lantern slides from its library, Pach lectured at the Metropolitan for more than two decades. Among his lectures were "A Renaissance Master and Pupil—Piero della Francesco and Signorelli;" "Pompeiian Painting"; "Three Great

Americans: Eakins, Ryder, and Prendergast"; "Classical and Romantic Art"; "Mexican Ceramics in the Metropolitan Museum"; "Realism, the Art of the European Race"; "Jacques-Louis David and His Successors"; and "The Classicism of Delacroix." Other talks were on Theodore Géricault, Winslow Homer, and Antoine-Louis Barye.

In 1923, Pach "participated in reviving the art courses of N.Y.U." along with Fiske Kimball, Richard Offner, and others.[1] He was appointed assistant professor and taught at the school through 1929. In 1926, he conducted New York University's first European summer school, offered in conjunction with the Louvre. Seventy students attended the course, which ran from July 12 through August 21. One of the two classes that Pach taught was "Methods of Art Study for the Traveling Student in Europe." Its purpose, as the brochure (hence Pach) described it, was "to acquaint

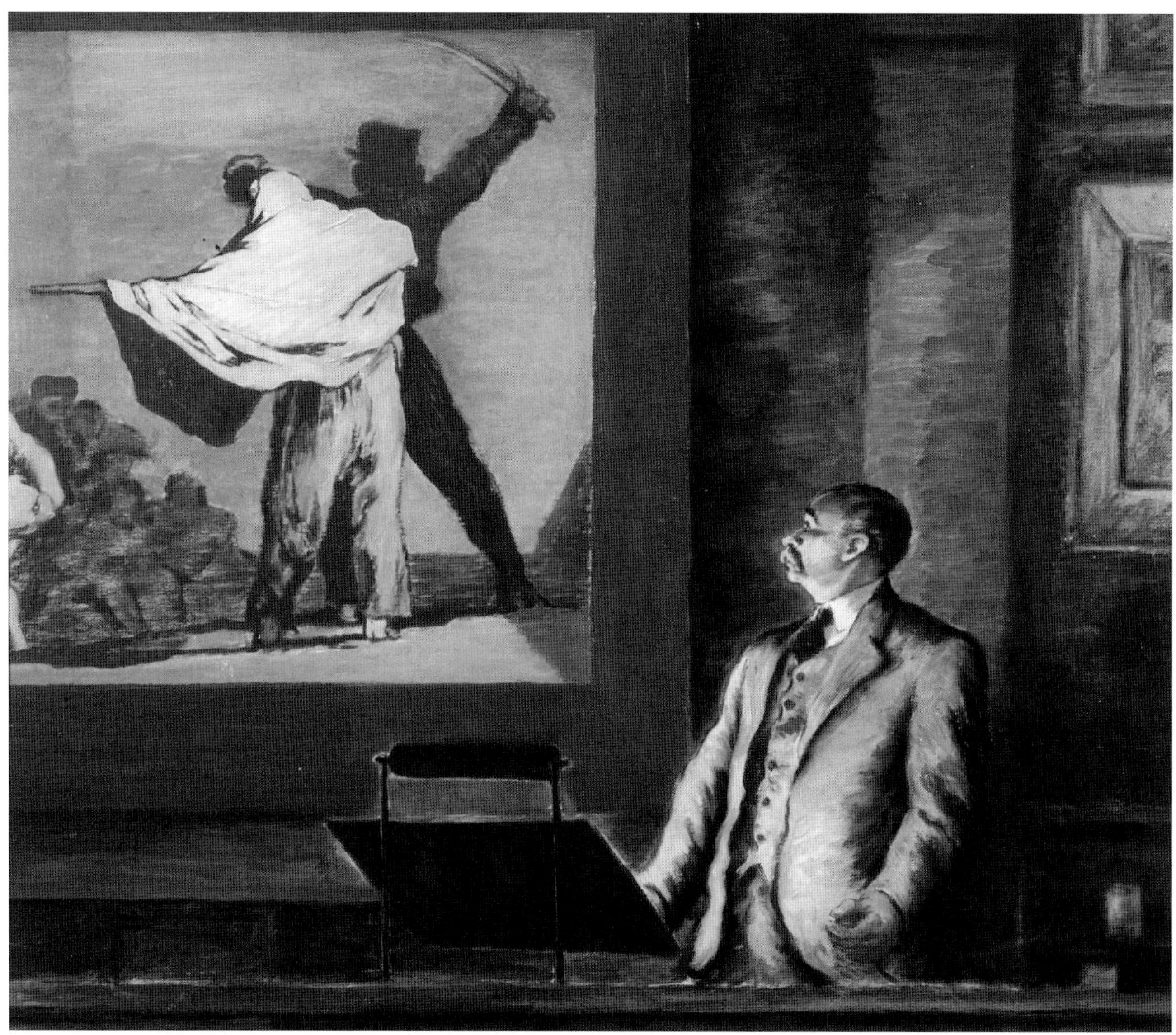

Fig. 28
Grant Reynard, *Walter Pach Lecturing,* 1938, oil on canvas. Gift of Jane Wilcox, Museum of Nebraska Art, Kearney, Nebraska.

the student with what he will find in the principal centers of artistic interest outside France, and to follow out the historical and cultural relations of the French schools with those of the rest of Europe."[2] For several years beginning in 1932, Pach was engaged by Teachers College, Columbia University, to teach "Seventeenth- and Eighteenth-Century French Painting" and other art history courses at the Institute of Arts and Sciences and in summer sessions. From 1951 until 1956, Pach was a professor at his alma mater, City College of New York.

Many of the classes Pach taught at these institutions were survey courses, in which he strove to connect the past with the present. "While I was convinced of the greatness of the best modern men and, above all, of the necessity of grasping the ideas that expressed so large a part of the essential character of the time," he wrote, "I went on with my studies in the older arts, and know that it was often because of my work in clarifying the relationship between the ancient and the modern that I was asked to . . . speak."[3] Pach was confident in his vision of art history and that his knowledge and experience would be beneficial to his students. Through his numerous lectures and courses, Pach had a profound influence on the next generation of budding art historians.

Pach also reached a wide and diverse audience through his translation of Élie Faure's monumental *History of Art.* He translated its five volumes, *Ancient Art, Medieval Art, Renaissance Art, Modern Art,* and *The Spirit of Forms,* over a nine-year period, 1921–30. Pach had tried to get the first four volumes published as early as 1913; as he told Alfred Stieglitz, "I worked for seven years—off and on—from the first weeks I was back in America, when I ran up to Scribner's from the great old Armory—trying to get the work published here."[4] He could not convince the publisher, however, to take on the project. In 1920, Faure approached Pach again, more emphatic this time in his requests. He not only asked his friend to translate all the volumes into English, but he also wanted Pach to help him find a publisher in

the United States. The French writer could have chosen anyone to translate his books, but he preferred Pach, whose translations were highly regarded in France and would soon become just as appreciated in the United States.

Between 1921 and 1924, Pach and Faure worked with Harper and Brothers to publish the first four volumes. The books were a success. Stieglitz wrote Pach that he and O'Keeffe very much enjoyed his translations of the Faure books and felt they went a long way toward filling the need to educate Americans about the history of art. Pach replied that there was "a capacity for educating in those books that exactly fills the need of this country." "Last season," he wrote, "while out West on a lecture tour, I had the chance to see that the thing was working right: they had the book everywhere—in libraries, clubs and private houses—they were reading it and it was thawing away at the frozen mass, which has its cracks in it in not a few places. . . . It is surely something of a good sign when those Faure books have sold in the remarkable way they have."[5] Pach was understandably pleased that these texts were so well received by audiences across the country and felt they had met a burning need for information on the history of art. As a firm believer in the idea that art was the province of all peoples, he was also thrilled that the art spirit contained in these volumes was reaching individuals in households across the country. Through his and Faure's efforts, art was becoming democratized. Pach was thrilled to report "the sale of the Faure 'History' which broke all records for a book of its kind and, within a year, had repaid the high cost of its production."[6] Harpers had taken a gamble on publishing this series, since art books were usually not best sellers. Undoubtedly, Pach's name and reputation had helped propel sales.

The books eventually became so well known, not only in the United States but also in American circles in Paris, that Henry Miller mentioned them in *Tropic of Cancer:*

At four-thirty I dash out of the hotel, resolved to make a last minute stab at it [the American Express office]. Just as I turn the corner I brush against Walter Pach. Since he doesn't recognize me, and since I have nothing to say to him, I make no attempt to arrest him. Later, when I am stretching my legs in the Tuileries his figure reverts to my mind. He was a little stooped, pensive, with a sort of serene yet reserved smile on his face. . . . I wonder what goes on in the mind of this man who translated the four thick volumes of the *History of Art* when he takes in this blissful cosmos with his drooping eye.[7]

Whether Pach read Miller's book is unknown; however, Miller's reference to him and his translation may well have influenced the sale of the volumes both at home and abroad.

While in Paris between 1929 and 1932, Pach undertook the rigorous study of several nineteenth-century French artists, particularly Delacroix and Ingres, and the results of these investigations were two significant contributions to the field: an English translation of *The Journal of Eugène Delacroix* and the first book in English on Ingres. Pach relied on two previous French editions of Delacroix's journal for the basis of his translation, but he reduced the number of pages from fifteen hundred to just over seven hundred. Nevertheless, and although he was assisted by his wife and Wallace Brockway, the translation was a grueling process, and a long one, as he reported to Ida Guggenheimer: "We had put every moment into translating,—and three or four hundred pages of manuscript had accumulated—and had to be revised; in some spots re-written." One of the most difficult parts, Pach admitted, was that "Delacroix mixes up his tenses, on occasion, begins a passage in the past, jumps to the present, then back—then forward." Pach "hammered out so many kinks in this gnarled thing" until it was completed to his and the editor's satisfaction.[8] In his introduction, he stated, "For many years

artists and art lovers have been urging an English edition of the *Journal.* I was finally led to undertake it by Mrs. J. Caesar Guggenheimer's interest in the great painter and his book."[9] Since this was the first American translation of the journal, it became an invaluable source of information on Delacroix for fellow artists, collectors, dealers, and the general public with an interest in art. Naturally, Pach received rave reviews from friends such as Guggenheimer and from Arthur Strasser and Joel Spingarn, who read the book before its publication. Allen Tucker wrote Pach, "You have made another great contribution to civilization," and Van Wyck Brooks hailed Pach's achievement: "The translation is masterly. . . . In all your writing, I don't remember *anything* more wholly satisfying than your introduction. . . . The book is truly a great book and you've done it in a noble fashion and every writer & artist must thank you everlastingly for it."[10] In the *New York Times Book Review,* Frances Winwar applauded the translation and Pach's editing of the journal, claiming that "there are not two tedious pages in the 731 which comprise the present volume," although she admonished him for not including Delacroix's lists of colors and similar notations.[11] Herbert Read, editor of the *Burlington Magazine,* complained that "Mr. Pach's translation of the *Journal* suffers from two defects: it is not complete, and it has no index," but also admitted that the translation, though "sometimes American in its phraseology," was "otherwise very fluent."[12]

Despite the favorable reviews, the book was not a financial success. Undeterred, Pach began planning another art book, a biography of Ingres. In the spring of 1939, he was hard at work "morning, noon, and night" on the manuscript. He told Mumford, "It will be the first in English and there is a big need for it. Here's hoping the public is aware of that fact."[13] He wrote Bernard Berenson that he viewed the book not only as a history and biography of the artist but also as "an essay on the Classical and the Romantic, and an inquiry into their functions."[14] Almost immediately upon its release Pach received praise from his friends and colleagues. Brooks, one of the first to give his congratulations, was effusive: "Well, it's a glorious achievement, and, dear Walter, I think by far your best book. . . . You never wrote before with such a *masterful* clarity and directness. . . . The book is magnificent in all aspects, and I am lost in the wonder of it, that you can write books like this,—and in six months too."[15] Margery Ryerson, in the *New York Times Book Review,* praised Pach for the "very many quotations from the words of Ingres himself." She wished, however, he "had written less and translated more." She rebuked his methodology and chastised him for allotting too much space to "placing Ingres's work in the development of French art and to a discussion of his difference with Delacroix."[16] This criticism cut to the very core of Pach's style of writing and his evolutionary philosophy of art. It was also a consistent complaint against Pach's outdated approach to the discussion and analysis of art and art history.

While Pach's writings on Delacroix and Ingres brought him recognition, neither garnered much money, and with the United States still in the grip of the Great Depression, the economic situation did not bode well for job prospects; however, toward the end of 1939, Pach landed a full-time, temporary position as the director general of the Masterpieces of Art exhibition at the New York World's Fair of 1940. He inherited the job from his dear friend Wilhelm Valentiner, who organized the 1939 show. Soon after he was hired, Pach sent a lengthy letter to Germain Seligmann, the man in charge of organizing the fair, which included a detailed account of his life and a narrative that spanned the years from his childhood in the Metropolitan with his father to his present circumstances. He named the important critics he knew; listed his books and lecture topics; and recounted his involvement with numerous exhibitions, including the Armory Show and those of the SIA. He spoke of his work in the "journalistic, legal (custom house) and educational fields of art," told of

his experience with American and European collections, and described his role as an agent for various museums and collectors.[17] This served as proof of his abilities to serve as director general, a post that would occupy most of Pach's energies throughout the next year, and more.

The task of curating the Masterpieces of Art exhibition was a formidable one, but Pach welcomed the challenge and, in fact, thrived upon it. Other individuals with whom he would work very closely on the exhibition were A. Hamilton Rice (president of Art Associates, Inc., organizers of the show), Millard J. Bloomer Jr. (vice president), J. Arthur Leve (vice president and treasurer), Francisco Borrell (secretary), Rolf H. Waegen (executive secretary), the marquis and marquise de Cuevas (financial backers of the project), Alfred M. Frankfurter, Charles R. Henschel, and Stephen S. Pichetto and William Suhr (conservators). Magda Pach headed the office staff during the operations and was her husband's right-hand assistant throughout the entire project. Early on a committee was formed that met regularly at Seligmann's gallery to discuss potential loans. Before the first meeting of its key members, Pach sent Seligmann a preliminary list of the galleries to be included along with a short list of pictures for the coming exhibition. He told his friend Brooks that he was going to organize the show "on wholly new lines."[18] Pach envisioned the show as a survey of Western European and American art ranging from the Renaissance to late nineteenth-century France.

Being a veteran of the exhibition game, Pach knew all too well that it was crucial to act as quickly as possible to secure loans before they were promised elsewhere. The New York fair was, in many ways, in competition with the fair taking shape in San Francisco that was scheduled to open around the same time. Pach understood that it was vital to have key individuals as their allies and urged his colleagues to seek support from collectors such as Joseph Widener and Philip and

Robert Lehman. Among those whom Pach approached personally were Drs. Harry and Ruth Bakwin, a Dr. Oppenheimer in San Antonio, Duncan Phillips, A. E. Gallatin, Paul Sachs, and John and Abby Rockefeller. Magda Pach wrote to Etta Cone on behalf of the association that was organizing the exhibition. In his letters to lenders, Pach appealed to their generous nature and to their patriotic duty in a time of war. "I realize that, in undertaking a work for the benefit of the country as a whole," he wrote Abby Rockefeller, "the burden falls on the individual. But the country as a whole cannot furnish the works, we are cut off from the aid of Europe, and we, who are giving our time to this undertaking, hope that it may appeal to the generous spirit you have shown on other occasions. Please feel assured that the help and instruction your pictures would offer to the hundreds of thousands of visitors to our Exhibition will be deeply appreciated not only by those direct recipients of your kindness but also by the group of public spirited persons who have subscribed the expenses of the showing."[19]

While Pach had a tremendous amount of energy and enthusiasm, the overwhelming tasks of the fair did take a toll. He confided to Brooks, "It is a grueling business—the time allowed us is too short, and there have been moments when I thought I'd cave in under the strain."[20] There were quite a few disappointments from collectors who refused to lend their works, including Francis Neilson and Helen Swift Morris Neilson and Grenville Winthrop, and many headaches with the installation and lighting. It was Pach's job as director general to ask lenders for additional funds to pay for the catalog that art fair officials wished to produce—a task with which he was never comfortable. The booklet, as well as a small army of docents, was needed, Pach felt, to "let our visitors get the full benefit of the great art treasures at the fair" and to "make the meaning of our exhibition more accessible to a greater number of people."[21] Pach intended the exhibition to be an uplifting educational experience for the vast numbers of

visitors expected from all parts of the country. Unfortunately, "49 successive days of rain," followed by oppressive heat, kept the hoped-for throngs of visitors away from the fairgrounds.[22] Further, and much to Pach's chagrin, most people were more concerned with the war raging on the Continent than with art. Because income from ticket sales was lower than expected and insurance on the paintings was high, the committee overseeing the art fair reduced the number of pieces in the show. The committee considered closing the galleries ahead of schedule but instead allowed them to remain open for the duration of the fair, which closed on October 27.

As director general, Pach was expected to be at the fair on a regular basis to see to all the details concerning the show. He was in attendance every Tuesday from eleven o'clock until five and by appointment and conducted tours of the galleries. "Even when I am not there officially," he wrote Guggenheimer, "they phone for me to come out and attend to one thing or another, I have letters to write for it, short articles, interviews, phones, etc., etc., etc."[23] He gave a special lecture on June 26 and delivered radio addresses, and it was Pach who wrote the essays for the exhibition catalog.

In the final decade of his life, Pach published two books, the culmination of his career as an art historian: *The Art Museum in America* and *The Classical Tradition in Modern Art.* In July 1944, Pach wrote his old friend Ben Huebsch, founder of and senior editor at the Viking Press, with preliminary ideas for a book on the history of museums in the United States, and the two colleagues discussed the project at length. Work on this manuscript would occupy Pach for the next four years. He informed Berenson that the text was "ordered (or subsidized) by the Rockefeller Foundation."[24] In connection with this project, Pach traveled a great deal during the spring and summer of 1945, visiting institutions large and small and calling on directors and curators, most of whom were personal friends. At the beginning of July 1945, Pach wrote his son Raymond, "After a lot of work at the libraries, I finished gathering the notes I need for my summer of writing at the book; I now have hope of pushing it through to completion, so as to return to painting in the fall.”[25] Pach worked on his book every day “from breakfast time (or before that) till evening.”[26] He was assisted by Henry W. Kent, who acted as a consultant at the request of the Rockefeller Foundation. Toward the end of July 1945, Pach happily reported to his son that he had written “some 46,000 words” and was “well past the half-way mark” of the manuscript.[27] Soon thereafter, he asked Brooks for his opinion on the introduction, which Brooks was glad to read. Pach finally completed the manuscript on September 20. Then began the editing, a process that would take three more years. Over this period, Pantheon, the publisher, made numerous “corrections” to the text, changes that the press felt “all serve[d] the purpose of suppressing less important passages, of clarifying the essential meaning of your ideas, and of putting the whole into a more concentrated shape.”[28] Some of these criticisms, as Pach noted, accused him of “blatant flag-waving” and “excessive kindness to businessmen (the trustees of the museums).” Pach was none too pleased with the “over 2000 ‘suggestions’” for changes to his manuscript.[29] To add insult to injury, he was informed that the whole thing would have to be retyped at his expense.

Work on *The American Art Museum: Its History and Achievement* continued through the first part of 1948. In addition to working on the numerous revisions and edits, he had the task of writing colleagues in museums across the country to request photographs of works in their collections for reproduction in his text. The book was finally published in November 1948. Its most important theme, Pach felt, was the concept that “the museum and what it stands for are needed to give us a better world.”[30] Pach never wavered in his conviction that art was a powerful social force that could uplift, educate, and enlighten the world and bring about peace and universal understanding among peoples around the globe.

Early in 1958, Pach was commissioned to write a “study of the classicism of the great modern painters.”[31] By this date, artists of the late nineteenth and early twentieth centuries whom Pach championed as “great modern painters” were no longer avant-garde but had long ago entered the canon of accepted masters and become part of the mainstream of traditional Western art history. Pach spent the better part of the summer preparing this manuscript, several chapters of which had been written as early as 1930 and 1932. In the book, he summarized his belief that there were certain “fundamentals, permanent truths,” upon which all masters built their art. He ended his text by noting, “I am happy to have such confirmation of my own conception of art. Its symbol is the Phoenix, that bird in which the Greeks and other ancient peoples saw the continuance of true ideas. Their form would burn to ashes, from time to time, but always there was something indestructible which arose again, spreading its wings with new life.”[32] Pach saw art as a powerful, ever renewing force whose spirit could never be extinguished but lived from generation to generation.

As an art historian, Walter Pach was not in the forefront of the field; many professionals felt his ideas were not progressive enough. Opinions on his writings were divided, with friends and colleagues like Brooks and Mumford praising his work and other art critics and historians denouncing his style and methodology. The most consistent criticism leveled against Pach was his lack of rigorous analysis; his approach was seen as too subjective and thus deemed old-fashioned. Nonetheless, some of his works, especially his translations of Delacroix’s *Journal* and Faure’s *History of Art,* and his book on Ingres, were deemed significant by his peers. These contributions alone rank Walter Pach among the important art historians of his era.

13
Return to Naturalism, 1919–1958

Although today he is not well known for his paintings and prints, Pach always considered himself primarily an artist, and for much of his career, his work was well received by colleagues, the press, and the art community. Pach's shift away from cubist elements in his art was a gradual process, but by 1919, his return to naturalism was complete. He explained later in life that in "going back (or, as I think, forward) to a renewal of naturalistic art, I believe I have remained modern."[1] While his art was representational, from the 1920s through the 1950s his style was diverse, incorporating academicism, impressionism, and postimpressionism. His subject matter ranged from American themes to landscapes, portraits, still lifes, and animals. Oil paintings predominated, but Pach also made many watercolors and etchings. From the 1920s until 1947, he participated in numerous group exhibitions and had many solo shows at prestigious galleries in New York and Paris. During this period, several of his works were purchased by collectors and friends, and others entered museum collections.

In 1919–20, as Pach's style became more decidedly naturalistic, his subject matter became specifically American. His interest in American topics and his return to realism were consistent with art trends in the United States at this time. "It is American life itself," Pach believed, "that must move on to the mature individuality out of which will naturally grow self-realization, style—art." He asserted, "We are moving steadily on the way towards [a truly American art]. This is clearly indicated in our bridges, our steel buildings . . . in our locomotives, automobiles, tools and utensils. Such things are often commented on as outward signs of our modern American life; but they are rarely mentioned, unless by foreigners, as the material of American art. It is as raw material that I believe they must, in fact, be regarded."[2] Pach heeded his own advice and turned to these materials as sources for his art.

Among the objects of American life that Pach chose to depict was the Brooklyn Bridge. He may have been influenced in this choice by his friend Joseph Stella, whose work *Brooklyn Bridge* Pach probably knew. Yet Pach's print of the bridge (fig. 29) was markedly different from Stella's rendition of the theme. Pach's image did not celebrate the magnificence of the steel and cable construction but compared the modern marvel of engineering to the antiquated wooden buildings of the nearby fish market. The focus of Pach's etching was not the structure itself but its relation to its surroundings, a juxtaposition that commented on the old and new aspects of the urban environment. In addition, the bridge by itself could be understood as a symbol of the connection between the past and the future. Carl Zigrosser included this work in the show *Twelve Prints by Contemporary American Artists* held at Weyhe Gallery in 1919. Other participants were Rockwell Kent, Jerome Myers, Boardman Robinson, John Sloan, Albert Sterner, and Mahonri Young. While the inclusion of Pach's prints was no doubt influenced

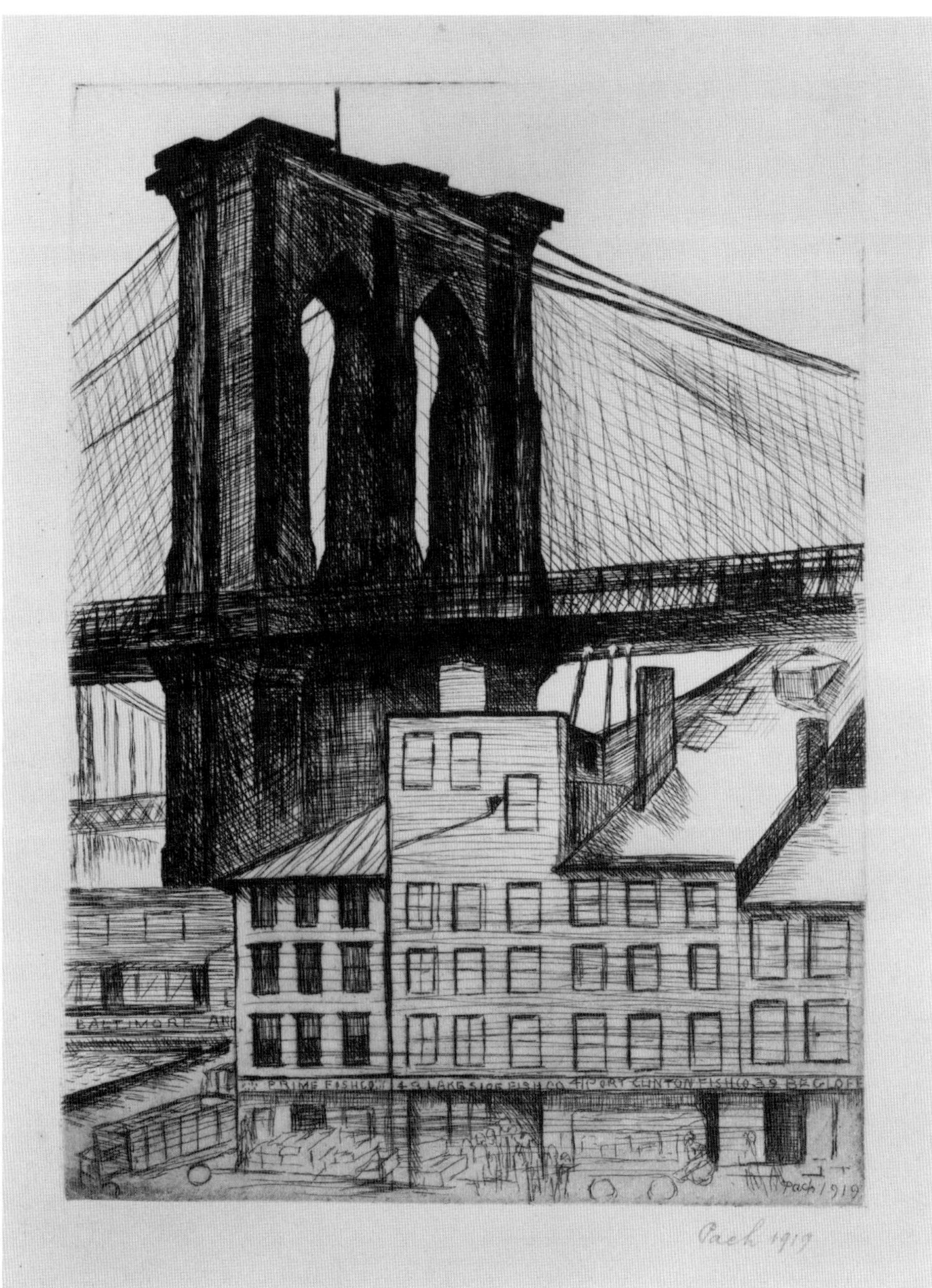

Fig. 29

Walter Pach, *Brooklyn Bridge,* 1919, etching, sheet 17 ¹³⁄₁₆ × 13 ³⁄₈ in. (45.24 × 33.97 cm), plate 6 ¹⁵⁄₁₆ × 4 ⅞ in. Whitney Museum of American Art, New York, Gift of Gertrude Vanderbilt Whitney, 31.694.5

by his friendship with Zigrosser and Weyhe, it nonetheless placed Pach in good company; these were some of the foremost printmakers of the day.

Another work created by Pach in 1919 that addressed the changes that were taking place in New York City as the United States and the world entered the modern era was an oil painting, *The Subway* (fig. 30). In this picture, he depicted a diverse group of individuals aboard one of Manhattan's elevated trains. As one can see from the sign in the train, the station shown in the painting was the Eighth Street station.[3] New York and other municipalities in the United States grew dramatically after World War I, and their demographic and physical characteristics were altered. Pach noted this development in his work. For example, appearing prominently among the riders on the subway is an African American soldier. The artist's inclusion of this figure showed his awareness of the presence of servicemen who were returning from overseas, settling in urban centers such as Manhattan, and looking for peacetime employment. Working women and businessmen also appear in the painting. People, especially single females, from other parts of the country flocked to the city in search of work. This painting reveals Pach's keen consciousness of the dramatic changes that took place in American cities and society after the European conflict.

Pach depicted the soaring skyline of lower Manhattan in his etching *New York from Governor's Island* (fig. 31). Located off the southern tip of Manhattan, Governors Island was one of the oldest and most strategic ports in the United States.[4] It had served as a U.S. military base since 1800, and during the early days of the war it functioned as a training ground for soldiers and as an airfield. In this view of New York's skyscrapers from the island, Pach could have been remarking on the economic and physical growth of the city that resulted from the United States' emergence as a world power after World War I. Since the skyscraper was invented in the United States, Pach's use of this structure as a

subject for his work shows him heeding the call to use the steel buildings as raw material for a truly American art. Duchamp, who was fascinated with the American skyscraper, certainly would have approved of Pach's choice of subject matter.

In his etching *The Shot Tower* (fig. 32), Pach may also have been indirectly commenting upon the landscape of the city after the war. Gunshot and cannonballs were manufactured in this structure, built in 1823.[5] The tower was operational when Pach made his print and had probably been active during World War I. Pach's print, produced after that conflict, could be construed as a commentary on the war's carnage inflicted on humankind. Pach may also have used the image of the shot tower to contrast the old and new aspects of twentieth-century New York.

These and other prints appeared in an exhibition held at the Weyhe Gallery in the summer of 1920. In her review in the *New York Times Book Review and Magazine,* Elizabeth Cary remarked, "Mr. Pach has got out of cubism an agreeable contempt for romanticism and sentimentality. He approaches his subjects with sincerity and strives for precision of execution. Each plate is endowed with a personal style that differentiates it from anything in the contemporary field. One feels that the artist had made his way toward his goal through a thousand scruples, has pondered his theme with many rejections and revisions, has been long in making up his mind, but finally has arrived at a rather unusual clarity and certainty."[6]

Cary singled out and included an illustration of *The Shot Tower,* "the most important etching of the group." She admired the composition and structure of the piece and particularly Pach's ability to make a "strictly objective portrait" of the tower without romanticizing it. Pach was quite pleased with the "nice article" about his etchings but also understood that one favorable review would not bring "fame and fortune."[7]

Pach's foray into American subject matter was rather limited, and beginning in the early 1920s, he returned to the more general themes of portraits, landscapes, still lifes, and classical and mythological subjects in his paintings, watercolors, and prints. Early in 1924, he sent photographs of at least three oil paintings—a portrait of Raymond; one of Magda; and a depiction of a mythological subject, most probably *The Birth of Venus (Venus Anadyomene)* (fig. 33)—to his friends Élie Faure and Jacques Villon, soliciting their opinions. He also sent Jean Charlot photographs of this work, and Charlot, in turn, showed them to Diego Rivera.

In *The Birth of Venus,* Pach deliberately distorted the proportions of the figures, especially that of Venus, and skewed their relationship to the painting as a whole. Perhaps this was meant to emphasize the fantastical aspect of the subject matter. Faure generously wrote that he was "enchanted by the firmness of your painting" and praised the "harmony" of the mythological painting, the intelligence of its composition, and the exceptional synthetic quality.[8] Villon remained silent about the work but admired the balance and harmony

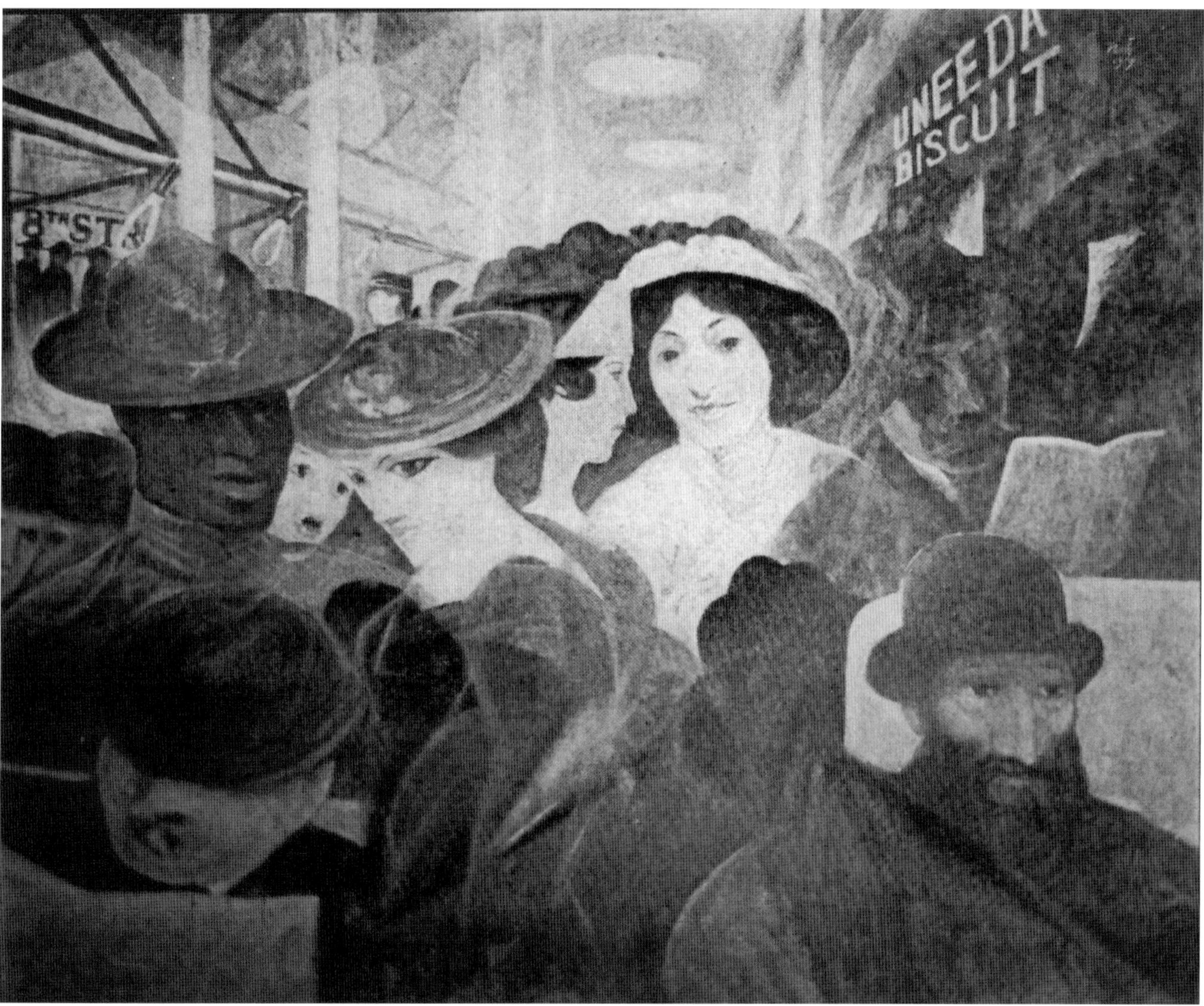

Fig. 30
Walter Pach, *The Subway,* 1919, oil on canvas. Collection of Mrs. Nikifora N. Iliopoulos.

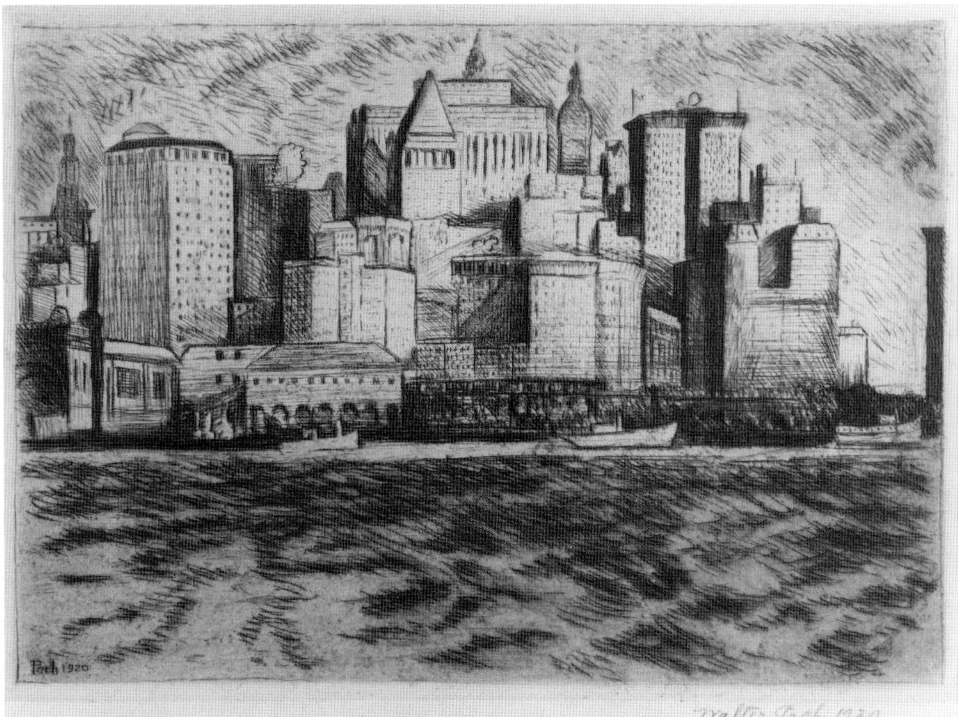

Fig. 31
Walter Pach, *New York from Governor's Island*, 1920, etching, sheet 9 ⅛ × 11 %₆ in. (23.18 × 29.37 cm), plate 4 ¹⁵⁄₁₆ × 6 ⅞ in. Whitney Museum of American Art, New York, purchase, 31.798.

of Magda's portrait. Rivera found in *The Birth of Venus* "excellent execution, very fine sentiment, a compound of realism and perfectly achieved style."[9] Pach greatly valued the input of his colleagues, whom he felt could and would be completely objective about his art.

The Birth of Venus was included in Pach's first one-person show, held early 1925 at his friend Joseph Brummer's gallery at 27 East Fifty-seventh Street. The exhibition contained twenty-two paintings and ten drawings and was intended as a retrospective of Pach's career since 1915; however, the majority of works were rather recent. Understandably, Pach was anxious for a good showing, as this was the most comprehensive display of his work that had ever been held, and he was hoping to find some supporters and one or two buyers. His friends were enthusiastic, but not everyone was so appreciative of his art, as Pach knew, and reviews were mixed. As he told Mumford, "Forbes Watson roasted the show in the *World* this morning. . . . Cortissoz, on the other hand, is friendly and speaks of careful

drawing and a couple of other things he finds good, though at the end his recollection of my critical heresies makes him take back some of his approval. But I had discounted those articles before the pictures were hung, and what I was, and still am eager for is the opinion of some half a dozen persons like yourself and Bryson Burroughs and [William] Ivins who can see the work in comparison with other things of our time."[10] One critic whom Pach admired, Henry McBride, observed, "The color has extraordinary purity, his blues are those of clear water reflecting clear skies. His color makes the itinerant visitor to the gallery draw a long, reviving breath, as though country had come to town." McBride praised the "strong individuality of the exhibition as a whole," finding that "only when one comes to the fancy and the rococo does Mr. Pach betray limitations. Out of his own orbit of simple seriousness he is in danger."[11] This latter criticism probably applied to paintings such as *The Birth of Venus*. While the critics may not have said what Pach wanted to hear, they had nonetheless visited the show and had therefore taken him seriously as an artist whose works they needed to review.

Pach must have felt that *The Birth of Venus* was one of his best and most representative paintings to date, for when he was invited by Katherine Dreier to submit works for "a very important Exhibition of Modern Art" to be held at the Brooklyn Museum under the auspices of the Société Anonyme in 1926, he sent this painting and a still life.[12] Dreier asked Pach to write some articles about the exhibition, but because of other literary engagements, he declined. The International Exhibition of Modern Art included more than three hundred works by artists from nineteen countries. Most of the major art movements of the early twentieth century—cubism, German expressionism, surrealism, Dada, De Stijl, and Russian constructivism—were represented. The show was mainly composed of European artists; Pach was one of the twenty-eight Americans selected. Inclusion in this event was quite an honor, and it reveals that Pach and his contributions to the international modern art movement were still highly regarded among many in the avant-garde art circles of New York. According to Dreier, the show had an attendance of

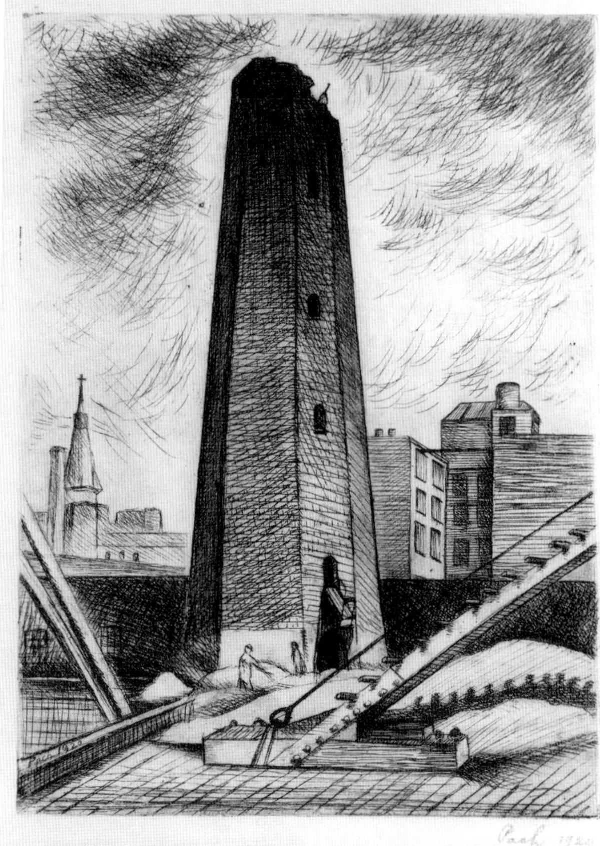

Fig. 32
Walter Pach, *The Shot Tower*, 1920, etching, sheet irregular 10 ¹³⁄₁₆ × 6 ⅝ in. (27.46 × 16.83 cm), plate 6 ⅞ × 4 ⅞ in. Whitney Museum of American Art, New York, purchase, 31.799.

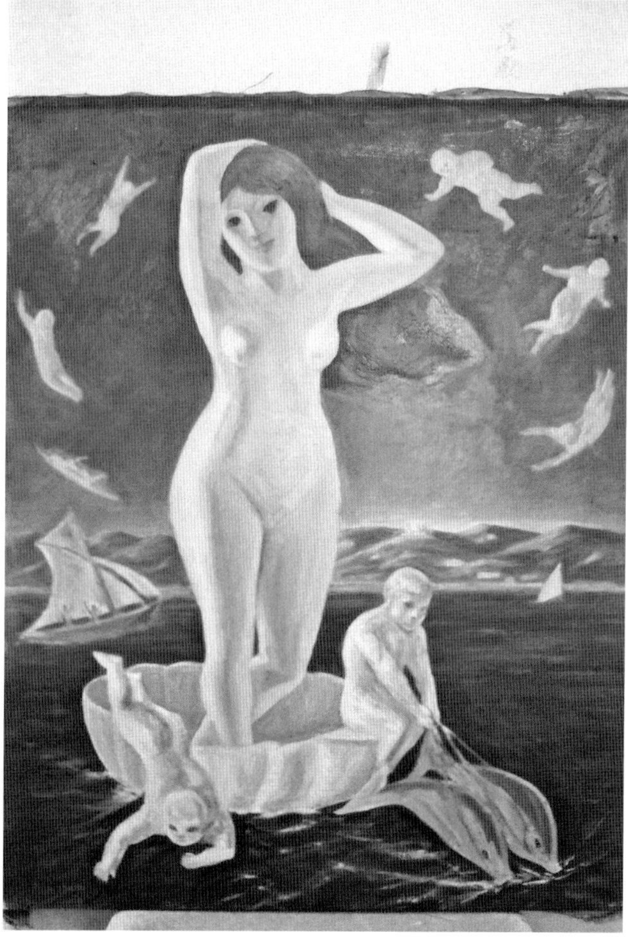

Fig. 33
Walter Pach, *The Birth of Venus (Venus Anadyomene),* 1924, oil on canvas. Collection of Mrs. Nikifora N. Iliopoulos.

"52,000 during the period of the Exhibition."[13] Pach went to the Brooklyn Museum twice and was stimulated "in the extreme," even though he "did not agree with every exhibit in it."[14] For him, seeing his pictures among the other artists' works was "helpful" to his own progress in painting.[15]

In founding the Société Anonyme in 1920, Dreier and Marcel Duchamp aimed "to bring European art to America to join progressive native art, and they would do it as artists showing the work of their colleagues, rather than as dealers tied to commercial interests or historians who cluttered museums and books with the sanctioned art of the past." Unlike Pach, who felt that the postimpressionists and cubists were in the avant-garde in 1920, Dreier and Duchamp believed they were "already part of the past." They wanted to "single out significant trends and individuals and let the viewing public experience some of the latest expressions of the new spirit."[16] Dreier explained that the organization was not like traditional museums that collected and conserved art; rather, it was "a circulating museum where the movements in contemporary art may be studied."[17] Through an ambitious schedule of exhibitions, lectures, concerts, and symposia, the Société Anonyme brought some of the most vanguard art to American audiences throughout the 1920s and 1930s. While it may have begun as a noncollecting organization, the Société Anonyme became such, and through numerous acquisitions and gifts it grew into one of the most significant collections of modern art in the United States. It was bequeathed to Yale University in 1941.

In the late 1920s, Pach had the distinction of being represented by two exhibitions at C. W. Kraushaar Art Galleries in New York City, which was quite a coup, since the gallery handled many of the most advanced American painters of the day. The 1927 and 1928 shows consisted of recent and older works, most of which were for sale and ranged in price from one hundred dollars for a small watercolor to nine hundred dollars for a large oil painting. Among the paintings displayed that have been identified and located is *Miss Eda Puckhaber* (fig. 34). This work reveals that Pach's manner of painting remained representational and fairly traditional. The style, coloration, and pose of Eda Puckhaber are reminiscent of Auguste Renoir's portraits that Pach so admired. The bust-length figure is shown against an unadorned background. Puckhaber is placed close to the front of the picture plane and at a slight angle to the viewer. The fullness of the figure and the solidity of its shape fills the small, shallow space of the picture plane, almost to the bursting point. It is as if she could move out of the frame of the picture at any moment, or, certainly, after the sitter is through posing for the day. Her eyes do not meet ours but glance away as if deep in thought as Pach captures the pensive and dreamlike mood of the sitter. When he had the time, he could create quite lovely paintings.

Reviews of the 1928 show, which were plentiful, were mixed. Edward Jewell of the *New York Times* wrote, "Mr. Pach confesses rather a preoccupation with pure form. Neither in color nor in texture of his volume does he more than approximate or suggest the human body. There is a solidity (which is not a matter of surface hardness) that makes one doubt whether this form would meet the touch with the soft resistance that resides in flesh. On the other hand, as form it brilliantly convinces." Although he was somewhat disparaging, Jewell praised Pach for his "earnest search for the form and for the design that inhabits an ideal graphic plane" and admired his brushwork, which was "always careful, but not so studied as to create an atmosphere of midnight oil and technical hairsplitting." He added, "A glance at the drawings and etchings . . . proves that in Mr. Pach's hands draftsmanship unaided is fully competent to express the thought he wishes to convey."[18] McBride felt Pach was "honest enough, and tries hard enough," but that many of the paintings were "dry."[19] *Art News* noted that "several of the watercolors date back fifteen years or more and afford a most interesting comparison." Among these works from 1913

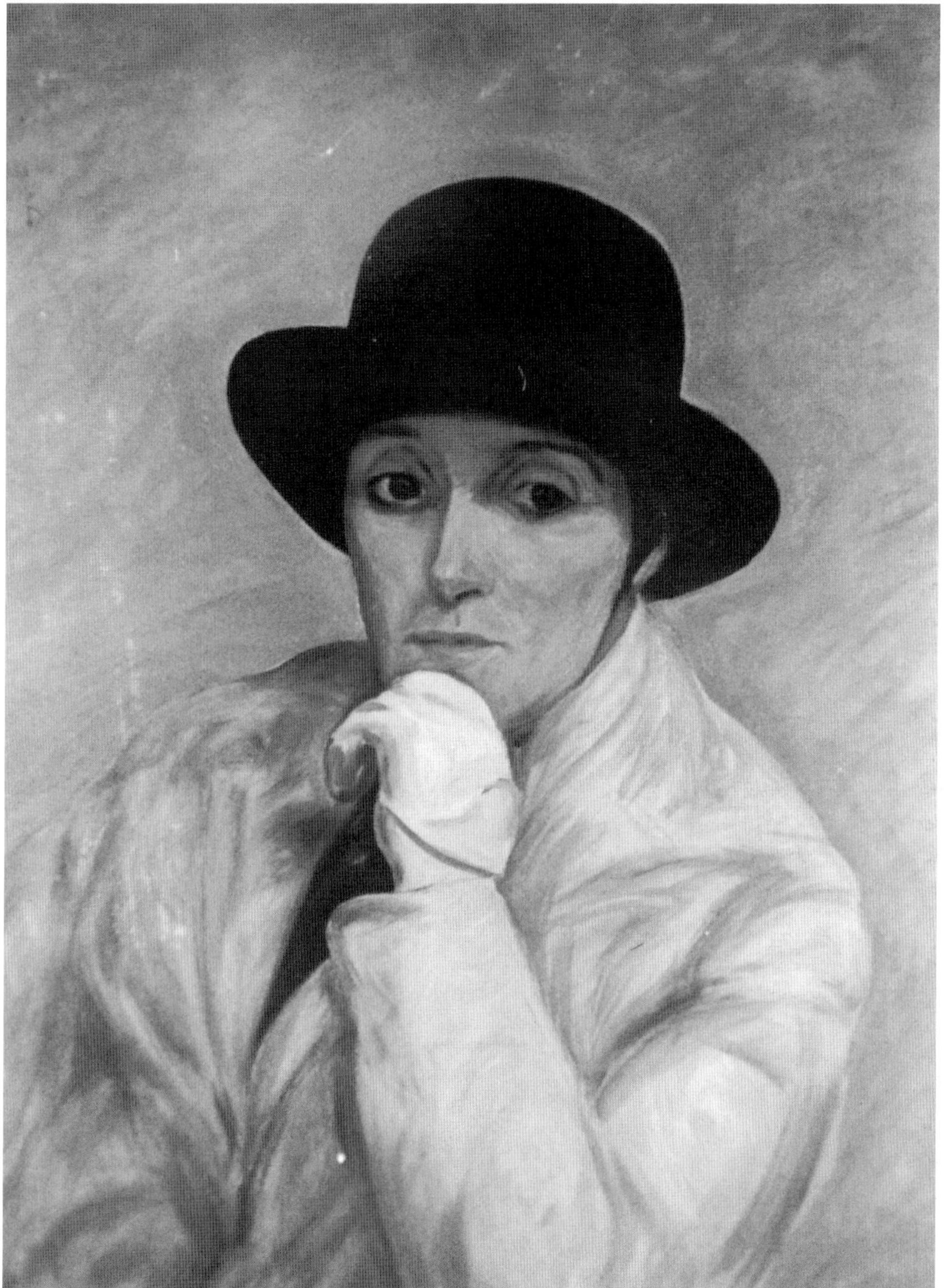

Fig. 34
Walter Pach, *Miss Eda Puckhaber,* 1927, oil on canvas. Raymond P. Pach Collection.

and before, some were probably Pach's cubist pictures painted immediately after the Armory Show. This same critic found the show to be "the best which Pach has had."[20] All reviewers agreed that the portraits were among his best works and that there was more fluency and spontaneity of approach in his watercolors than in his oils. Pach was happy enough with the reviews of his show but disappointed that there were not many sales.

Throughout his life, Pach experienced bursts of artistic activity, which inevitably coincided with periods of time he spent away from his work as a critic, agent, dealer, and teacher and which usually involved travel overseas. From 1929 to 1932, Pach was in Europe, where he had the time and leisure to make numerous paintings, watercolors, drawings, and prints—one of the most productive periods of his artistic career. While visiting with Magda's family in Dresden in the early fall of 1929, Pach was inspired to paint *Dresde (Dresden Palace)* (plate 8), an oil painting, and *Dresden Gardens, the Zwinger* (plate 9), a watercolor. Though the style in both is representational, they differ in appearance, probably owing to the variety of the media used. In *Dresde (Dresden Palace)* the oil paint is laid on the canvas in broad, thick strokes. The buildings are not rendered in any great detail, and the figures are not realistic but rather generalized. In *Dresden Gardens, The Zwinger,* the individual panes of glass are delineated, as are the arches and roofline of the building. The fluidity of the watercolor medium fosters a feeling of vibrancy and liveliness in *Dresden Gardens, The Zwinger,* whereas the density and somber hues of the pigments in *Dresde (Dresden Palace)* create a sense of stasis.

Pach and his wife spent the majority of these years in Paris, and indeed one of the main reasons for going abroad was for Walter to drink in the rich, intoxicating atmosphere of the Parisian art world and revive his career as a painter. He felt that he and Paris were "a marriage made in Heaven" and was "as happy as the day is long" in the city, especially after he felt settled into his new home and studio and could concentrate on his

painting.[21] At first, the style in which he worked was—as he himself described it—a renewal of his "'abstract' work of ten or fifteen years ago."[22] Yet the extant works from these years are not abstract but are very traditional and representational in style. While he may have been "deeply impressed with Picasso's new form of Cubism," as he told Guggenheimer in the fall of 1929, he was more influenced and inspired by nineteenth-century French painters, including Delacroix, Géricault, and Barye, and by the late works of Auguste Renoir.[23]

Besides being able to indulge in painting virtually full time while abroad, Pach had quite a bit of success in selling and exhibiting his art during these three years. Alexander Bing, head of a family of New York real estate developers, visited Pach in Paris and bought six of his recent watercolors. When Bing returned to New York, he offered four of these works to the Metropolitan Museum as a gift.[24] Unfortunately, there was a bit of a mix-up with the works and hence a delay in their acceptance by the museum board. Confident of its approval, however, curator Bryson Burroughs wrote Pach, "They are excellent water-colors I think and represent you very well indeed. One can see that you did them with great pleasure and spontaneity. Your foreign stay is certainly doing a lot for you and I congratulate you on these works. . . . The modern style has not the bitter enemies it used to have."[25] Pach was a bit baffled by having these particular works referred to as in "the modern style," for, as he wrote Guggenheimer, he thought of them as "looking like 1887 or thereabout."[26] In the end, all four were accepted by the museum, an honor with which Pach was thrilled.

Another coup for Pach in his artistic career at this time was his solo exhibition at Kraushaar Gallery in New York—his third in four years—which opened in the spring of 1931. Fifteen oil paintings and a collection of watercolors were displayed. The show received favorable reviews from friends, colleagues, and the critics. The *Art News* reviewer felt that "Mr. Pach's

painting gains with each appearance, gains in individuality and attack."[27] There was a mixed review from the
New York Times critic, who found fault with the
"woodenness" of the figural works but admired the
"convincingly 'first-hand' quality in the still-life pictures
. . . that contain beautifully painted figurines" and the
"charming" flower pictures.[28] The exhibition was not a
huge financial success, but Pach did sell two works—an
oil painting, *Anemones,* to noted collector Abby
Rockefeller, and a watercolor, *Paris Autumn,* that Pach
judged "to be about the best" he had done, to his dear
friends the lawyer Arthur Strasser and his wife, Edna.

Buoyed by the positive response to his show,
particularly to his watercolors, Pach engrossed himself
in his art. He told Guggenheimer that after he finished
his work for the Kraushaar exhibition he was going to
"try some very different work, probably working from
animals for a while. I have always loved animals and I
have found a man who has a small menagerie for
artists."[29] In May, he proudly reported, "I had a month
of animal painting, and I think it is my best performance of the season. I hope to do more."[30] Pach did at
least a dozen watercolors of animals in 1931, and the few
that survive are among the most charming and beautiful of his paintings. Sarah Stein "thought so well of
them as to suggest their publication in a book," a
project that did not come to fruition.[31] In *The Fox* (fig.
35), we see Pach's love of animals manifested. He
captures the beauty of the creature in delicate washes of
bright, pure colors. The fox is lovingly rendered with a
real sense of depth and proportion, and there is an
anthropomorphic sweetness in the face of the animal.
This picture was bought by Etta Cone on a springtime
visit to Paris in 1931 and is now in the Cone Collection
at the Baltimore Museum of Art.

In the summer of 1931, the Pachs took a long-antici-
pated trip to Africa and Spain. Pach was enthralled by
Morocco and raved about it as the place where he
discovered Delacroix's subjects, which he had been
studying intensely since he had arrived in Paris in the

fall of 1929. He saw the master's inspiration firsthand in
the people and places of northern Africa, especially
Morocco and Tangiers. This voyage was extremely
inspirational for Pach and he created numerous oil
paintings and watercolors based on his experiences.

Following his wave of good fortune of sales to Bing
and Rockefeller, and the exhibition at Kraushaar, Pach
was invited to have a one-person show at Galerie Dru
Bourgeat et Van Gelder in Paris in the spring of 1932.
Although he was thrilled by the prospect of the exhibition, Pach was exhausted by the amount of work it
entailed. He complained to Guggenheimer that he had
to write the preface to the catalog at the "eleventh hour"
and had to hang the paintings himself—things usually
taken care of by the dealers in New York galleries.[32]
Nevertheless, there was quite a crowd at the opening,
including artists and dealers such as Jacques Villon,
Jean Marchand, Gino Severini, and Roland Knoedler.
Pach showed seventeen oil paintings, thirty-one
watercolors, and various drawings and etchings, all
done on his journey abroad and several inspired by his
trip to Morocco and Tangiers. Many of the watercolors
of animals that he had painted the previous spring were
also included. This was, by far, the largest showing of
his work to date. He was quite pleased with the turnout
and told Guggenheimer, "For a first encounter with a
one-man show in Paris, we thought we had come
off well—and M. [Charles] Bourgeat thanked me for
showing."[33] All those involved with the show were
optimistic about sales; unfortunately, they did
not materialize.

After three years abroad, Pach returned to New York
in the summer of 1932, and throughout the remainder
of the 1930s, he met with some degree of success as an
artist. He was invited to submit a painting to the First
Biennial Exhibition of Contemporary American
Painting to open at the Whitney Museum of American
Art in New York in November 1932. It was quite an
honor to be asked to participate in this groundbreaking
exhibition, and clearly those in charge at the Whitney

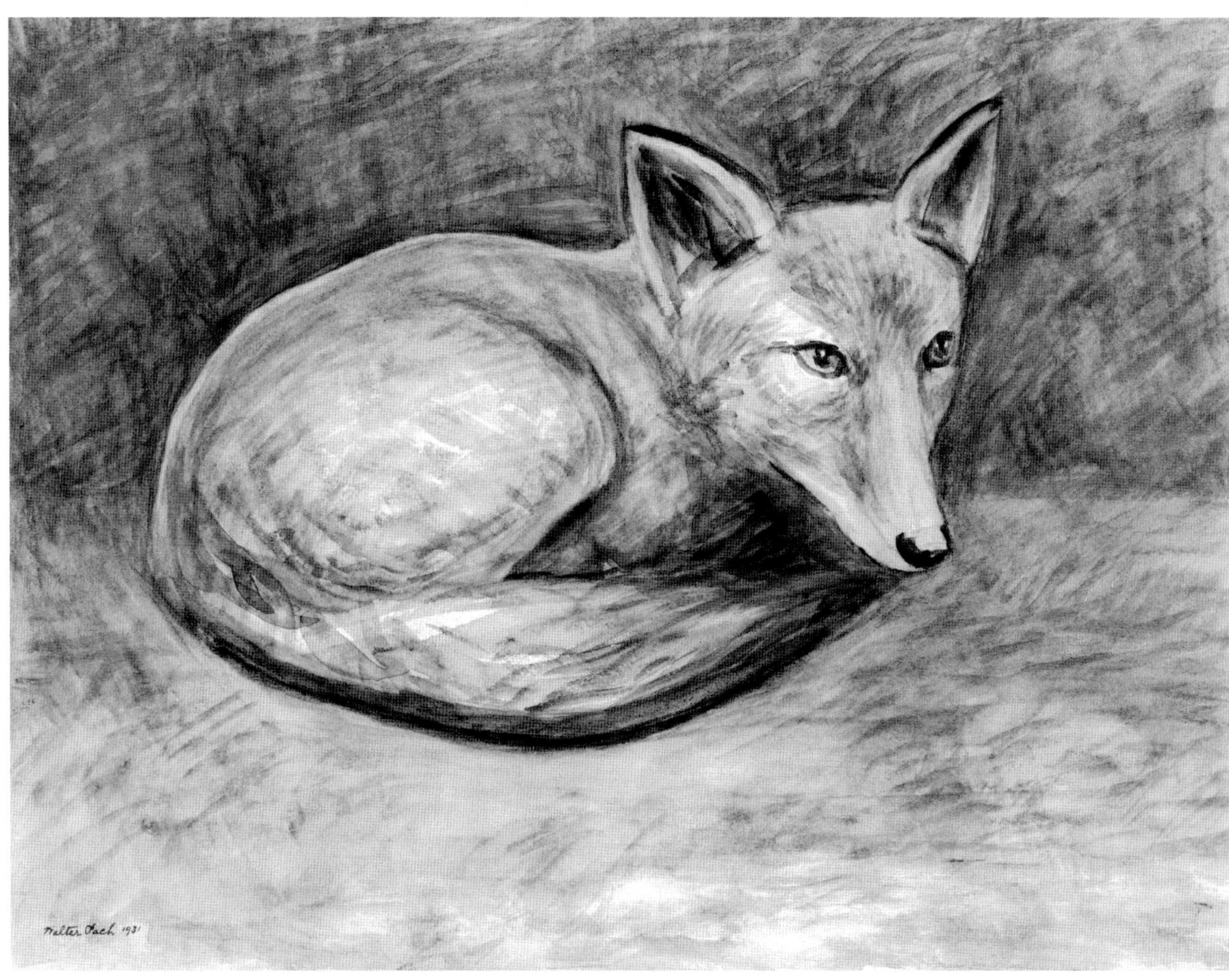

Walter Pach (1883–1958)

recognized the significance of Pach's work, though it may not have been very original. In 1933, there was a retrospective exhibition of Pach's paintings and watercolors at the Modern Galleries in Philadelphia. The twenty-four oil paintings and six watercolors spanned his career from 1913 to 1933 and included mainly works that had been displayed before. While there was not extensive coverage in the press, Pach was nonetheless pleased with the show and the support he received from those who sponsored it, which included most of the leading figures in Philadelphia's art world, among them his friend Fiske Kimball.

The mid- to late 1930s were a particularly active time for Pach as an artist. He participated in the Whitney annuals in 1933, 1934, and 1938. In February 1934, nine of his etchings were included in an exhibition at the Weyhe Gallery, and in the spring he opened his studio for a showing of his work—not an unusual thing for an artist to do, since finding gallery representation was often difficult. In the same year, Pach approached his alma mater, City College of New York, about creating a fresco for one of its buildings. Since the summer of 1933, when his friend and colleague Ida Guggenheimer invited him to paint a mural for her summer home in Canada, Pach had been experimenting with the fresco technique, undoubtedly inspired to do so by his friend Diego Rivera's work on the Rockefeller Center mural. Although the university's decision was delayed, Pach moved forward with the project and prepared four panels for fresco with the help of Rivera's "best assistant." These panels were included, along with five other frescoes and numerous watercolors, in his solo show at the prestigious M. Knoedler Gallery, which opened in 1935 and received mixed reviews. Many felt, as previous reviewers had, that Pach was at his best "in the smaller works, such as the watercolors." The writer for *Art News* noted how these works glowed "with a fine intensity" and observed, "The studies of animals . . . reveal a great sensitiveness, allied with a highly sophisticated use of color and design."[34] As critics and fellow artists noted,

Pach's watercolors have a spontaneity and lightness of touch that make them much more appealing than his oils and frescoes, which can be somewhat dry and overworked. Also in 1935, Pach was recognized by his peers as a significant force in the early avant-garde movement in the United States through the inclusion of two of his early works, *The Lily of the Valley* (plate 6) and *Sunday Night (St. Patrick's at Night)* (plate 5), in Abstract Painting in America, an exhibition organized by the Whitney Museum of American Art. The following year, Beatrice Stein facilitated the gift of one of Pach's paintings to the Brooklyn Museum of Art, and he had a one-person show of his watercolors at the Kleemann Galleries in the fall. All these events greatly bolstered Pach's morale and convinced him of the merit of his artistic abilities.

Toward the end of August 1936, Pach made his "début as a teacher of painting—save for a few pupils in my studio—with a newly founded school at Columbia University, an outgrowth of the School of Architecture there."[35] He told Paul Sachs, "When the School of Architecture decided to give its work in drawing and modelling to an independent (but related) faculty and to add courses in painting, I was selected to found that studio, which I conducted during the two terms 1936–1937."[36] He wrote Berenson, "It is a big step for Columbia, where Dr. Butler has always been doubtful of art work. For me it is a chance to try out some theories of art teaching."[37] This was quite an honor for any artist and testifies to the esteem in which Pach was held by the higher education community in New York. The course, which met four times a week throughout the fall, was an adaptation of one he had taught in 1932 at the Art Students League of New York. This earlier course entailed a series of lantern slide "demonstrations" that were designed to show the pupils the "approach to drawing, modelling, composition, expression, and other matters as handled by the masters both the modern and the older ones of classical and romantic art" and "make the students feel the accessibility of the great things which formed the masters in the old schools and which must still form them, for the classics are directly applicable to the tangled problems of modern art." Pach envisioned the class as being "as practical as [Thomas] Anshutz's demonstrations of anatomy."[38] The course, which ran for six weeks at the Art Students League in the autumn of 1932, was the first that Pach had taught to practicing artists—though it was not a studio class. In his 1936 classes at Columbia, Pach conducted technical, hands-on demonstrations, putting into practice the ideas he had taught in his previous slide lectures. Understandably, Pach was thrilled to have the privilege of initiating such a class at one of the United States' most prestigious universities. He was even more excited that he was going to earn part of his living as an artist.

Beginning in the 1940s, Pach had difficulty finding places to show his art, and with the demise of the Society of Independent Artists in 1944, he lost a key exhibition arena. Still, he participated in several group exhibitions in the mid- to late 1940s and had his final solo show during this decade. He was invited to send works to the exhibition Pictures for Peace: A Retrospective Exhibition Organized from the Armory Show of 1913, which was put together by the Cincinnati Art Museum in 1944. In addition, he exhibited at the Whitney annual in 1944 and in a show held at the Mortimer Brandt Gallery in April of that year called 5 Americans: Baylinson, Constant, Walter Pach, Tricca, John Sloan: Oils, Watercolors, Drawings. He was asked to lend an oil painting to the 140th Annual Exhibition of the Pennsylvania Academy of the Fine Arts in 1945 and sent another work the following year. Also in 1945, a painting of his was accepted into the Nineteenth Biennial Exhibition of Contemporary American Oil Paintings at the Corcoran Gallery of Art in Washington, D.C. In addition, Paul Sachs of the Fogg Art Museum acquired two of his drawings, one for his own personal collection and one for the museum. While Pach was understandably pleased with the acknowledgments of

his artistic abilities, his traditional style of painting was rapidly falling out of favor.

In the spring of 1947, Pach had what would be his last one-person exhibition at a New York gallery, Walter Pach: Oils and Water Colors. Held at the Laurel Gallery, it consisted of sixteen oil paintings and seventeen watercolors. Some of these pictures had been exhibited before, and many were not recent productions. In the introduction to the catalog, which Pach wrote, he defended his artistic and aesthetic decision to return to a representational style. He believed that many misunderstood "the essential point of modern art. And that is its constant self-renewal, achieved by turning to always new aspects of the pictorial problem."[39] For him, this new experiment led to realistic and naturalistic representations. The reviewer for *Art News* felt that "his portraits and still lifes are sensitive, conservatively realistic works, executed in a competent if somewhat laborious technique. There are occasional lapses of taste. . . . But for the most part, especially in the portraits and in a studio interior, Pach has his medium well under control, and creates a quiet poetry."[40] Edward Alden Jewell of the *New York Times* observed, "Pach, a very astute and learned critic, allies himself with those who 'accept the full range of natural appearances.' And that, of course, is all right, only Walter Pach's painting is somehow so wooden and dry and tight. He is at his most persuasive in the self-portrait."[41] Fellow artist James Daugherty told Pach, "It seems to me that your work has grown simpler and broader and more unified and you have achieved a solidity of form which I enjoyed especially and which must be very gratifying to you. The watercolors were especially fine in their clear and transparent tones."[42] Public response was reasonably good, and, according to the Laurel Gallery records, three works sold.

In the 1950s, the last decade of his life, Pach spent more time in his studio than at any other period in his career, and there are dozens of paintings that date from these years. As he told Berenson, he had reached the age and stage in his life where he was "free to paint nearly all the time" and was convinced that he was improving in his work.[43] Pach thought of his art as a balance between the classical and the modern and told Berenson,

> I myself (if I may refer to my own work as an example) am not immune to doubt as to the rightness of my persisting with a naturalistic formula, especially when I see—as I did this week—a talented man almost as old as I who has gone over to "abstractions." . . . Perhaps he'll do masterpieces in his new method. . . . But anyhow it's not for me—though Picasso, Braque and Villon do masterpieces (which are not abstract like those of these dress-goods-designers.) I do even admire one of those last named fellows, but only for his patterns and surfaces—the decorator's field.[44]

The subjects of Pach's late works are portraits, landscapes, still lifes, and cityscapes, and while the style is representational, his approach oscillates between overt realism and impressionism. *Washington Square* (plate 10) is typical of several canvases from this period in Pach's career in which the palette and technique are impressionistic. In this view from the Pachs' Washington Square studio, the application of paint in short, thick brushstrokes and the bright sunlight enliven the surface of the canvas.

Although Pach remained naturalistic in his manner, he could and did admire the abstractions of his French friends, but he simply could not abide the bold, daring experimentations being carried on by American artists Jackson Pollock, Willem de Kooning, and others in New York in the late 1940s and early 1950s. He confided in his son,

> Painting and sculpture—are being bombarded by a kind of modernism which seems to me quite alien to the kind which I defended at the Armory Show

of 1913, and at later times. Villon has gone the limit on "abstraction," but it has the most logical connection with the older schools and the classics. I fear I can see the majority of new things today only as a decadence of what Picasso, for example, did supremely forty or more years ago. The few times I have heard certain "modern" composers I have thought also they have gotten away from everything solid in their art. . . . A painter *is* a composer, so the problem of the validity in these latter-day forms does concern me. However, I can be good, even if "old school," so I just plug along as best I can.[45]

Pach was always a staunch supporter of his Parisian colleagues and remained a Francophile to the end. The work of the new generation of American artists was too revolutionary for him; it signaled a complete break with his beloved masters, which was a schism he could not and would not bridge.

Walter Pach's art was not revolutionary in style or content, but it did, until the mid-1940s, develop in accordance with the larger art movements of his day, and as such much of his art remained current. However, by failing to grasp, or accept, the significance of the newest developments in American art in the 1940s and 1950s, he fell woefully out of tune with the contemporary art world. Because he had to earn a living through his work as an agent, dealer, critic, and historian, Pach could not devote substantial time to his art, and therefore his work was inconsistent and never developed to its full potential. When he had, or took, the time, he made paintings and prints that were skillfully rendered and, in some cases, quite striking and beautiful.

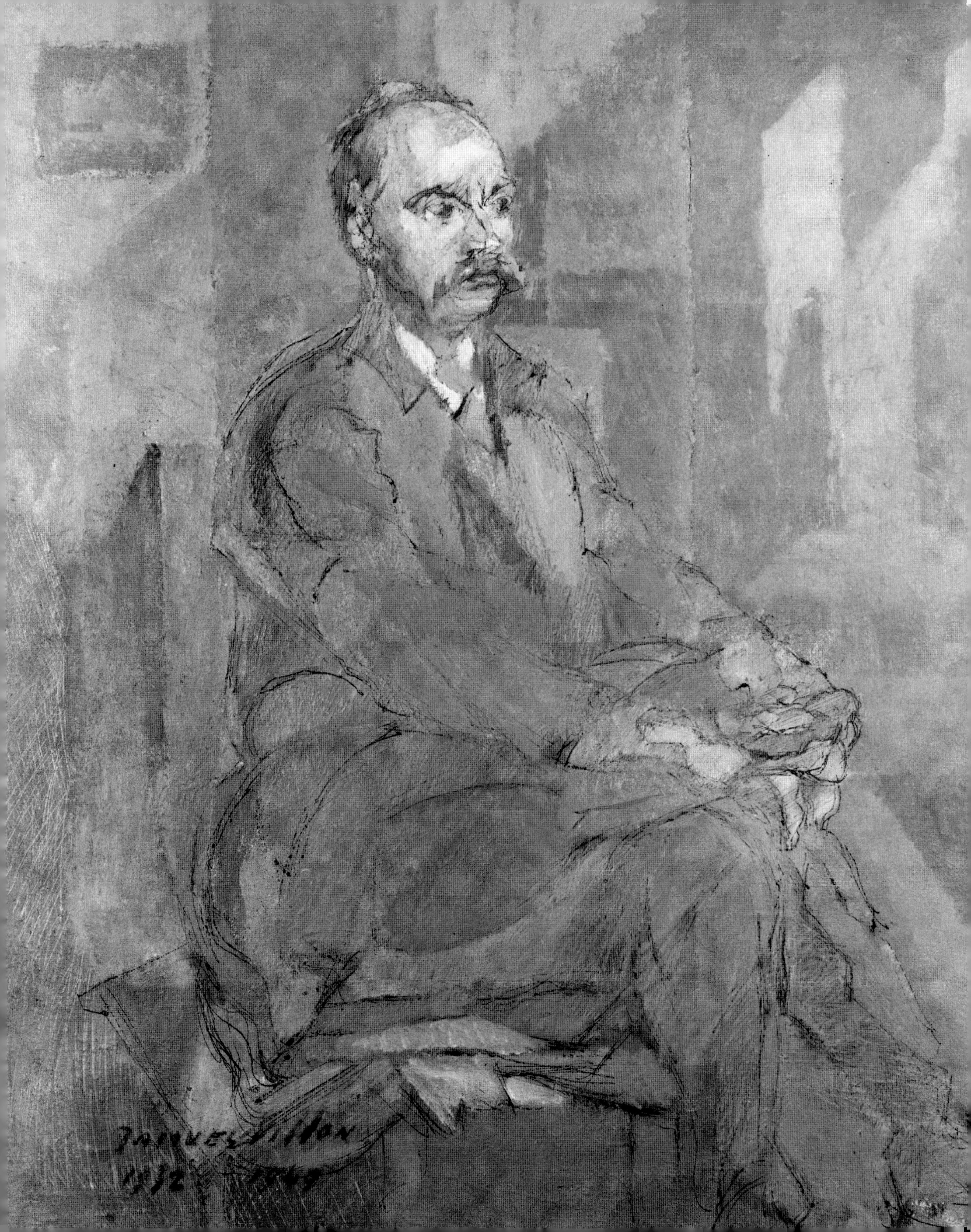

14
Final Decade

Toward the beginning of September 1950, Pach's world began to fall apart; Magda was taken seriously ill. She underwent a battery of tests to determine the cause of her sickness. She had suffered from bursitis, anemia, and gallstones intermittently for several years, but this was something different. She remained at the cottage in Brewster, New York, that she had had built in 1939, but eventually was taken to the Neustadter Home, where she could have around-the-clock nursing care; Pach could no longer tend to her. Her condition, which still had not been diagnosed, deteriorated further and in October, she was admitted to Saint Vincent's Hospital in New York for further tests. The devastating news, that a brain tumor had been discovered, came on October 28. Pach immediately contacted Raymond, who was in Italy, to inform him of his mother's condition. Magda underwent an operation to remove the tumor, but despite optimistic predictions, "her great heart gave out" and she died on November 9, 1950, at Saint Vincent's Hospital. Funeral services were held at Frank E. Campbell's in Manhattan. She was cremated at Ferncliff Cemetery and Pach scattered her ashes at her beloved cottage in Brewster.

Pach was devastated by his wife's death, but he stoically accepted her absence. He confided in Guggenheimer, "As I had the incomparable privilege of being united to her—during the forty-three years since we first met—by the strongest of bonds, I feel . . . that they can not be severed, and that she is still with us."[1] Sympathy poured in from Mrs. Allen Tucker, Van Wyck and Gladys Brooks, René and Sarah d'Harnoncourt, Fanny and Ralph Ellison, Carl Zigrosser, and Paul Sachs, among others. With the loving support of friends such as the Sloans, Guggenheimer, the Mumfords, Zigrosser, and especially the Brookses, with whom he spent the Christmas holidays, Pach managed to hold his world together and "go on living."

After the death of his wife, Pach remained in a daze for months and felt crushed by the mundane details of life. He complained to his son—who had remained in Italy—"You don't know my physical and mental condition, you don't know what my duties and jobs are, you don't know how I am trying to look forward to some kind of future when I can crawl out from under the load of work that has fallen on me—and that no one can do."[2] Among his obligations and responsibilities was his course at CCNY, with classes twice a week.

In addition, he had taken on "a couple of literary jobs" before his wife died and had to finish them as well.[3] Pach thought a great deal about returning to Europe; he told his son that his mind was "very unsettled" and he often thought of going back to Paris where he felt most at home and centered.[4] By early January 1951, he had decided to leave for Europe at the end of March and stay overseas for several months. Between the beginning of the year and his departure, Pach tried to resume his regular routine and found comfort in the friendships of the Brookses and Mumford.

After weeks of planning and organizing, Pach set off for the Continent for an adventure that would change his life. After a brief visit to Brussels and Antwerp, he arrived in Athens on April 2, for his first trip to Greece, a place he had always wanted to see. Gloria Radus, one of his painting students in New York, was Greek and had given him the names and addresses of her family in Athens. George Constant, a Greek American painter and friend of Pach, also furnished him with contacts in Greece, and Pach was met at the airport by these individuals. Pach was overwhelmed by Greece and sent a postcard of the Parthenon to Brooks that read, "Everything I'd heard about Greece was an understatement. You have to see this building to realize what it is."[5] He met a good number of Greeks; he wrote his friend Julius Rauzin, "Gloria Radus's family were simply a joy, and other people I met through George Constant or his friend Mr. Lecatis gave me such a good feeling about the country."[6] Radus's uncle was a distinguished writer, but it was her aunt who really captured Pach's attention. She was a Greek beauty more than thirty years his junior named Nikifora Loutsi, with whom he fell in love.

Pach tried to continue with his European trip as planned, but was not very successful. He flew to Italy on April 27 and stayed for a month, spending time with his son and daughter-in-law, who were then living in Rome. He went to Florence, where he finally had the opportunity to visit with his dear old colleague Bernard Berenson. He also met with Guggenheimer's daughter Clara, but he could not concentrate on his surroundings or the miles of art in Italy—he had a decision to make about his future. Pach had left Athens earlier than he had anticipated because of the intensity of his feelings for Nikifora Loutsi. He grappled with his emotions for almost two weeks before he asked her to marry him. "With my age, my one-track preoccupation with art, the differences in our backgrounds, and—above all—the ever present image of Magda, I do not think it is a sign of weakness that I needed twelve days of reflecting before I could write a letter to Nikifora. I wrote asking her to marry me," he told Guggenheimer. Her initial response was "perhaps" and then, after Pach returned to Athens to speak with her again, she agreed to his proposal. Pach was "radiant with a happiness" that he "should have thought impossible . . . even a short time ago."[7] At the end of May, he wrote his son to share his news. Understandably, Raymond Pach was very surprised by this sudden turn of events, but certainly wished to see his father happy and he eventually gave "his full consent."[8] After making all the necessary arrangements, Walter Pach and Nikifora Loutsi were married in a Greek Orthodox church in Athens on June 19. The couple remained in the city for several weeks and overseas for almost four months. They flew to Rome, traveled through Italy on their honeymoon, and arrived in Paris on July 13, where they remained until mid-September. While in Paris, they visited with Pach's friends, among them Jacques Villon and the Jean Crottis, and spent much of their time, not surprisingly, in the museums. While overseas, Pach received the dreadful news that John Sloan had died. Once again he was thrown into deep despair at the loss of a loved one and wrote Helen Sloan immediately upon reading the news in the papers. He was heartbroken not to be able to pay his respects in person and say his final farewell to a dear friend of forty-five years. This sad event made Pach anxious to get home. The Pachs were delayed almost two months in the French capital, mainly because of a continuing problem with Nikifora Pach's visa. Fortunately, his new wife's passport came through in mid-September and the couple flew to New York on September 18.

Back in New York in the fall of 1951, the couple began a new life together and Pach quickly fell back into his regular routine. He resumed his weekly speaking schedule at CCNY, which was going "very well indeed" in spite of the fact that it was "a chore to get up there at the rush hour."[9] No matter how strenuous the task, the job did make him feel useful and needed. Pach was invited to speak at the Museum of Modern Art in November, though the exact topic is not known. In addition, he quickly returned to his studio and to painting, inspired by Sloan's example and by works he had restudied in the Louvre.

For Pach, there was never enough time in a day to accomplish all he wished and he complained to his son, "All I need is a 48-hour day—and another thirty years."[10] Throughout the 1950s, teaching at CCNY engaged much of his time and energy, as did writing and painting. Also, early in the spring of 1952, Pach's nephew, Alfred Pach, approached him with a new venture: a print shop run by Pach Brothers Studio in connection with B. Altman's department store. The photography studio was located at 5 East Fifty-seventh Street; Altman's was on Fifth Avenue. Pach was to be responsible for purchasing the prints and other art for the shop, but Alfred Pach would basically run the store with the assistance of one or two employees. The gallery opened on May 9, 1952, "in very splendid quarters"[11] in the store in Manhattan. The business then expanded to include "a new place in the suburbs (a rich place)," and was eventually located in several of Altman's stores.[12]

Lack of correspondence makes it difficult to reconstruct the last years of Pach's life, but in 1957 he wrote Villon, "I have finally pulled away from all the jobs which wasted my time in the past; for one reason: I no longer have the energy to do all the various works

which I did before, and I need to paint every day, even if it means sacrificing some sources of revenue." With this attitude Pach abandoned almost all his work outside his painting. He relinquished his position at CCNY and concentrated on his art, convinced that his paintings showed "the effects of this new, rapt attention."[13]

Several times during his life, Pach had suffered from kidney stones and other medical conditions and now his health was beginning to deteriorate. In July 1954, he wrote his son that he "needed some medical attention" for an undisclosed problem.[14] He was told to quit smoking, a habit in which he had indulged since his twenties. He was probably also diagnosed at this time with ulcers and was undoubtedly told to slow down, advice he chose to ignore. He complained of the "considerable shots of pain from the stomach ulcer" that had been bothering him.[15] This problem would not only persist, but worsen. In the early months of 1958, Pach's doctor put him on a strict regimen of diet and medicine that kept him in "admirable condition"; however, by the fall his stomach problems worsened rapidly and the end was not far off.[16] Happily, he read his friend Brooks's latest book and sent him a congratulatory note. He also climbed the stairs to his studio a few more times to paint, but two weeks after an operation for gastric ulcers, his heart failed, and Walter Pach died on November 27, 1958. After a small semiprivate ceremony, his body was cremated and his ashes were given to Nikifora Pach.

When Walter Pach died he left the bulk of his "personal property, household effects, some paintings and four-fifths of the residuary" to his second wife, Nikifora Loutsi Pach Iliopoulos.[17] Raymond Pach, his only child, received more than sixty of Walter's paintings, watercolors, and prints as well as several works from his considerable collection. Pach had drawn up his will late in the summer of 1952 and filed the papers with Arthur Strasser, who had been his attorney for years. Pach told his son, "With my will, at Mr. Strasser's office and in my safe deposit box is a list of the more important works in the collection, with a suggested division of them between Nikifora and you. Among my papers is a complete list of art works I own, with very tentative valuations, as a guide in your disposing of them, you and Nikifora, after my death."[18] Although the will survives, neither of the lists mentioned in the letter has been located. A complete and accurate compilation of the Walter Pach collection is therefore impossible. Raymond Pach objected to the will submitted for probate and through his lawyers charged "lack of testamentary capacity" on his father's part. For probate purposes the estate was valued at "over $20,000."[19] The suit was settled out of court for an undisclosed sum. Nikifora Pach retained the bulk of the art. She has sold some paintings, prints, and other objects over the years. Raymond Pach sold some works and generously donated others to museums. Neither party spoke to the other after the court settlement in 1958.

Epilogue

Walter Pach was a seminal figure in the history of modern art. Through his remarkably energetic efforts, hundreds of paintings, prints, and sculptures by his contemporaries from Europe, America, and Mexico were exhibited in the United States, and while most were put on display in New York City, others were shown from the Midwest to California. He helped organize some of the major groundbreaking exhibitions in the United States, among them the Amory Show and the first significant shows of the art of Paul Cézanne, Henri Matisse, and the Mexican modernists. Pach sold numerous paintings, prints, and sculptures in the United States and was responsible for cultivating a taste for modern art among American collectors. While he was an intermediary for major collectors such as John Quinn and Walter and Louise Arensberg, he also advised friends and colleagues on the formation of their more modest collections. Through his intercession, the Metropolitan Museum of Art acquired its first painting by Cézanne, *View of the Domaine Saint-Joseph.* By means of his position with the Shilling Fund, Pach orchestrated the donation of dozens of pieces by contemporary American artists to museums across the country. Although he received some compensation for his work, either monetary or in gifts of art, Pach was motivated mainly by his love of art and his admiration of the artists he assisted. His assiduous efforts to place works with collectors and museums had far-reaching consequences for American taste.

From the 1910s through the early 1940s, Pach also promoted modern art through his writings, lectures, and teaching assignments and helped formulate the foundation upon which the traditional history of modern art was based. Many of his articles and essays—written in English, French, and Spanish—

appeared in the popular press, as well as in more specialized, art-related journals in the United States, France, and Mexico, thus reaching a wide and diverse international audience. Unlike many other critics of the day, Pach lectured extensively on modern art at museums, art associations, libraries, and colleges in the United States, Canada, and Mexico, becoming more recognized, internationally, than most other writers on modern art. Through his teachings at Berkeley, the Universidad Nacional in Mexico City, New York University, the City College of New York, Bowdoin College in Maine, and Columbia University, Pach influenced a generation of art students and budding art historians.

Walter Pach, a cultural ambassador extraordinaire, was extremely well known in his time, yet, before the present study, his complete life, work, and contributions had never been fully examined—although in the past twenty-eight years, several art historians and other authors have contributed to the scholarship on Pach.[1] In the 1980s and early 1990s, and again in 2004, Raymond Pach organized an exhibition of his parents' work that traveled to several museums in the United States, but only a small brochure was produced for the show. A catalogue raisonné of Walter Pach's paintings, watercolors, and prints has never been undertaken. The goals of this book have been to give a more complete accounting of Walter Pach's multifaceted careers and fascinating life and to help restore him to his rightful place as one of the most important figures in the history of twentieth-century art and culture.

Appendix: Chronology

1883

Born, July 11. Father: Gotthelf Pach, born Berlin, October 9, 1851, age thirty-two, photographer. Mother: Frances Wise, born Milwaukee, January 29, 1857, age twenty-six. Father runs Pach Brothers Studio photography firm in New York, one of the oldest studios in the United States. Semiofficial photographers for the Metropolitan Museum of Art. Family lives at 1631 Park Avenue, New York City.

1894

Summer, Pach at Willey House in Essex County, New York. Pach's first painting.

1895

Pach attends the Ethical Culture Society of New York's Workingman's School, 109 West Fifty-fourth Street. Enrolls in PS 6 at Madison Avenue and Eighty-fifth Street.

1898

June 24, graduates from PS 6. Fall, enrolls in City College of New York (CCNY).

1900

Summer at Pyramid Lake House, Essex County, New York.

1902

August–September, studies with William Merritt Chase at Shinnecock for eight weeks.

1903

Senior oration subject, "Aesthetic Tendencies in the Nineteenth Century." Graduates from CCNY June 18. Studies with Leigh Hunt.

Chase Summer School in Haarlem, the Netherlands. Morton Schamberg is his roommate.

1904

Chase Summer School in London. Schamberg is roommate again. Meets Charles Sheeler. July 27, travels to Germany. August, visits art exhibition in Dresden and sees many French impressionist paintings. August 17–31, first trip to Paris.

1905

Summer, Chase Summer School in Madrid. Autumn in Paris, sees Salon d'Automne, but does not recall seeing any of the fauve paintings on view. First museum exhibition, *The Toledo Bridge* accepted into the Sixth Annual Exhibition of the Fellowship of the Pennsylvania Academy of the Fine Arts.

1906

January 15, gives his first art history lecture at Westfield State Normal School. March, meets John Sloan. Summer, agent for Robert Henri summer class in Madrid. Fall, travels to Paris, Brussels, Bruges, Antwerp, London, and Haarlem. First sees drawings by Vincent van Gogh. Fall, opens own studio at 935 Broadway, in his father's business. December, *Open-Air Restaurant, Bombilla*, accepted into the Winter Exhibition of the National Academy of Design.

1907

April, four paintings included in the Exhibition of Paintings at the New York School of Art, New York. Summer, Chase Summer School in Florence. Pach is an agent for the class and teaches art history classes. Meets Magdalene Frohberg at a bookstore in Florence. Meets Charles Loeser. Meets

Henri Matisse through Leo, Gertrude, Michael, and Sarah Stein. July, publishes "The 'Memoria' of Velazquez," in *Scribner's Magazine*, his first article. October, living at 9 rue Campagne première. Becomes a regular guest at the Stein families' salons. Writes article on Matisse, but it never gets published.

1908

February, Pach in the Netherlands. March, six works, including *Silhouette of Florence*, accepted into the 24 exposition de la Société des artistes indépendants, Salon des indépendants, Paris. June, "At the Studio of Claude Monet," *Scribner's Magazine* published. June in Brussels, July–September 10, in Italy. November 5, Pach's address 1135 Park Avenue, New York, his parents' apartment. December, "Cézanne: An Introduction," *Scribner's Magazine*, first serious article on Cézanne published in an American journal. December, *Silhouette of Florence* accepted into the Second Exhibition: Oil Paintings by Contemporary American Artists at the Corcoran Gallery of Art, Washington, D.C.

1909

January or February, lecture on art in Springfield, Massachusetts. Meets Professor Alfred Vance Churchill of Smith College, future director of the Smith College Museum of Art. Summer, exhibition of works at Smith College Museum of Art, and the museum acquires at least one painting. Gertrude Stein writes "Portrait of Walter Pach." "Quelques notes sur les peintres américains" published in *Gazette des Beaux-Arts*, first of several articles on American artists that Pach writes for foreign journals.

1910

February, two articles published: "Manet and Modern American Art," in the *Craftsman,* and "New York as an Art Centre," in *Harper's Weekly*. April, participates in the Exhibition of Independent Artists, New York. Summer, Chase Summer School in Florence. Pach is agent for the class and teaches art history classes. Fall, Pach's address, 3 bis rue des Beaux-Arts. Attends the Lycée Charlemagne in Paris. Meets Élie Faure at the Association polytechnique, Paris.

1911

January, "On Albert P. Ryder," published in *Scribner's Magazine*. June, interviews Renoir. November 16, 1911–March 21, 1912, attends Henry Marx's lectures on aesthetics at Lycée Charlemagne. "M. J. Alden-Weir," published in *Gazette des Beaux-Arts*. Around this time meets Marcel Duchamp, Jacques Villon, and Raymond Duchamp-Villon and becomes part of the Puteaux Group.

1912

February, "The Morgan Collection," published in the *Outlook*. June–August, Florence, Arezzo, and Perugia, Italy. Writes Arthur B. Davies and offers his assistance with the Armory Show. September, address, 83 boulevard Montparnasse; "Pierre Auguste Renoir," published in *Scribner's Magazine*. "Le mouvement artistique a l'étranger: Etats-Unis" published in *L'Art et les Artistes,* which announces Arthur B. Davies's upcoming trip to select art for the Armory Show. October, Walt Kuhn arrives in Paris. November, Arthur B. Davies arrives in Paris. November, "Winslow Homer," published in *Gazette des Beaux-Arts*.

1913

January, address, 1 rue de Beaux-Arts. Returns to New York for the opening of the Armory Show. February, addresses, 1135 Park Avenue and 935 Broadway, New York. February–May, International Exhibition of Modern Art (The Armory Show). Meets John Quinn; Walter Arensberg; Carl Zigrosser; and, perhaps, Wallace Stevens in New York. Visits with Walter and Louise Arensberg in Cambridge, Massachusetts. (Pach exhibited five paintings and five etchings at the Armory Show.) December, engaged to Magdalene Frohberg. Helps organize exhibition of modern American art for the Detroit Museum of Art (now the Detroit Institute of Arts), the Cincinnati Art Museum, and the Peabody Art Gallery in Baltimore. Participates in the exhibition.

1914

February, marries Magdalene Frohberg. New address, 17 West Ninth Street, New York. April, "The Point of View of the 'Moderns,'" published in the *Century* magazine. August, in Round Top, New York. John Quinn helps establish Carroll Galleries with Harriet Bryant as proprietor. Pach becomes main agent and advisor for the gallery and for John Quinn. October–November, Pach goes to France to secure works for important modern art shows for the Carroll Galleries and Montross Gallery in New York. December 26, Raymond, only child, born, New York.

1915

January 20, Henri Matisse show opens at Montross Gallery. February, "Why Matisse?" published in the *Century* magazine. February, Maurice Prendergast show opens at the Carroll Galleries. June 15, Marcel Duchamp arrives in the United States; Pach meets him at the dock. Pach introduces Duchamp to Walter and Louise Arensberg, who had moved to New York. Pach begins advising Arensbergs on their collection. Summer, Gape Clark, Harriman, New York. October, Pach and dealer Stéphan Bourgeois begin planning exhibitions of modern art for the following year. October, participates in the Autumn Exhibition at Montross Gallery.

1916

Cézanne exhibition and the Exhibition of Pictures by Jean Crotti, Marcel Duchamp, Albert Gleizes, and Jean Metzinger open at Montross Gallery. The Exhibition of Modern Art Arranged by a Group of European and American Artists in New York opens at Bourgeois Galleries. February, participates in show Fifty Pictures by Fifty Artists at Montross Gallery. May, participates in Philadelphia's First Exhibition of Advanced Modern Art at McClees Galleries, Philadelphia. Summer, Harriman and Ashokan, New York. Fall, Duchamp, Pach, Arensberg, and others meet at the Arensbergs' apartment on West Sixty-seventh Street and found the Society of Independent Artists. Pach to be treasurer. October, participates in the Opening Exhibition, Montross Gallery.

1917

January, participates in the Modern Art Exhibition at the People's Art Guild, Parish House of the Church of the Ascension, New York. February, participates in the Exhibition of Modern Art at Bourgeois Galleries, New York. April, first Annual Exhibition of the Society of Independent Artists. Pach exhibits two paintings, including *Sunday Night (St. Patrick's at Night)*. May 9, Pach's mother, Frances Wise Pach, dies at home at 1135 Park Avenue. Summer at Valhalla, New York, and Edgemere, near Far Rockaway, Long Island, where the Pachs meet Johanna van Gogh-Bonger and her family. Pach designs stage sets for Wallace Stevens's play *Bowl, Cat, and Broomstick* at the Neighborhood Playhouse in Greenwich Village. Arranges an exhibition of Gino Severini's work at 291. Toward the end of 1917, Pach participates in at least three group exhibitions: Opening Exhibition at Montross Gallery, for its new season; Exhibition of Watercolors by American Artists at Montross Gallery; and Exhibition of Paintings by the "Moderns," at Vassar College.

1918

New address, 13 East Fourteenth Street, New York. January, participates in the Special Exhibition of Paintings at Montross Gallery. February, "Universality in Art" published in the *Modern School*. March, participates in the Exhibition of Contemporary Art at the Penguin Club, New York. Summer, teaches two classes, including "Modern Art," at the University of California, Berkeley; lives at 1637 Euclid Avenue, Berkeley, California. Meets Xavier Martínez, professor at the California School of Art and Design, and Pedro Henriquez-Ureña, a visiting professor of Spanish at Berkeley. Also meets Frederick Torrey, a San Francisco dealer who bought Marcel Duchamp's *Nude Descending a Staircase, No. 2* from the Armory Show. October, "Jean Le Roy," published in the *Modern School*.

1919

February, "The Significance of Redon," published in the *Dial*. March, participates in the Exhibition of Unusual Monotypes by Contemporary Artists at the Ehrich Print Gallery, New York. May, "The Schamberg Exhibition," published in the *Dial*. May, participates in Exhibition: Paintings: Drawings: Watercolors: Etchings at the "Call" Bazaar, New York Starr Casino. Pach becomes closely acquainted with Paul Sachs, future director of the Fogg Art Museum at Harvard University, whom he had met at the Armory Show. Meets Bernard Berenson. Summer, Joseph Cottage in Scroon Lake, New York.

1920

January, "Art of the American Indian," and March, "Notes on the Indian Water-Colours," published in the *Dial*. January, series of articles, "The Approach to Modern Art," published in the *Christian Science Monitor*. April, participates in the Exhibition of Modern Art by Contemporary Artists at the Worcester Art Museum, Massachusetts.

May, participates in the Special Exhibition: Works by Eighteen American Artists at Montross Gallery. Summer, Pachs rent their apartment to the Uruguayan artist Joaquin Torres-Garcia and go to East Pittson in Gardiner, Maine. June, Pach begins writing for the *Freeman*. Meets Suzanne La Follette, Van Wyck Brooks, and Lewis Mumford. Publishes two articles on Vincent van Gogh and the exhibition of his work at Montross Gallery: "Vincent van Gogh," in the *International Studio* (November), and "A Modern Artist," the *Freeman* (December).

1921

January, participates in the Exhibition of Paintings by Contemporary American Artists at the Art Gallery of Toronto. April, participates in the Exhibition of Paintings and Drawings Showing the Later Tendencies in Art at the Pennsylvania Academy of the Fine Arts, Philadelphia. Begins translation of Élie Faure's five-volume *History of Art* (project will take nine years). May, participates in the Exhibition of Works by French and American Artists, including a collective exhibition of paintings by Jennie Van Fleet Cowdery, at the Joseph Brummer Galleries, New York. Summer, address, 15 rue Louis-Phillipe, Neuilly, outside Paris. Visits Matisse and his family at Issy. Begins work on a catalogue raisonné project for Camille Redon. Fall, renews his acquaintance with Bernard Berenson and hereafter the two men correspond regularly until the 1950s. November, participates in A Selected Group of American and French Paintings, at the Arts Club of Chicago.

1922

Summer, invited by Henriquez-Ureña to teach at the Universidad Nacional in Mexico City. Meets Diego Rivera, José Clemente Orozco, Jean Charlot, and other Mexican artists. October, "Impresiones sobre el arte actual de México," published in *México Moderno*, first serious article on Mexican artists to be published. Starts planning for an

exhibition of modern Mexican artists at the Society of Independent Artists exhibition for 1923. "Art," published in *Civilization in the United States: An Inquiry by Thirty Americans*.

1923

January, "The Popular Arts of Mexico," published in the *Freeman*. March, "Georges Seurat," published in *The Arts*. *Georges Seurat* published by Duffield, New York, first substantial book in English on the artist. Summer, Westport, Connecticut. Commissioned by La Follette to write a series of articles for the *Freeman* on modern art. Fall, Pach begins his affiliation with New York University.

1924

January, "The Greatest American Artist," published in *Harper's Magazine*. February, begins a fifteen-week lecture series on modern art in conjunction with New York University and the Metropolitan Museum of Art. May–September in Saint-Tropez. September, Paris, Giverny, and Dresden. *The Masters of Modern Art* and *Raymond Duchamp-Villon, Sculpteur, 1876–1918* published.

1925

February, first one-person show, Exhibition of Paintings and Drawings by Walter Pach at Joseph Brummer Galleries, New York. April 17, Gotthelf Pach, Walter's father, dies. June, "Is Cubism Pure Art? A Debate; Picasso's Achievement," published in the *Forum*. Summer, Hurricane, Adirondack Mountains, Essex County, New York. Exhibits two etchings at the Tenth Annual Exhibition of the Brooklyn Society of Etchers.

1926

January, Paintings, Watercolors, and Sculptures Selected from the John Quinn Collection exhibition on view at the Art Center in New York. Pach writes the introduction to the catalog and an article for the *Art Center Bulletin*. March, Exhibition of Etchings by Walter Pach and Paintings by Magda F. Pach at Weyhe Gallery, New York. April, An Exhibition of Art by Mexican Schoolchildren and Jean Charlot opens at the Art Center, New York. May, new address, 48 West Fifty-sixth Street, New York. Summer, conducts European summer school program for New York University at the Louvre. Fall 1926, assistant professor of fine arts for New York University. September, article by Leon Rosenthal, "Graveur American," on Pach's graphic works published in *Byblis, Mirror des Arts du Livre et de l'Estaque*. Rufino Tamayo arrives from Mexico and Pach introduces him to dealer Erhard Weyhe, who gives him his first one-person show in the United States. November, participates in the International Exhibition of Modern Art organized by the Société Anonyme at the Brooklyn Museum of Art.

1927

Spring, assistant professor of fine arts for New York University. April, Exhibition of Paintings, Drawings, and Etchings by Walter Pach, C. W. Kraushaar Art Galleries, New York. June, "What Passes for Art," published in *Harper's Magazine*, prelude to his book *Ananias, or the False Artist*. December, Orozco arrives in New York and Pach introduces him to dealers, including Kraushaar.

1928

April or May, lectures on modern art in Hartford, Connecticut. Summer, Amenia, New York, at home of Joel Spingarn. Fall, *Ananias, or the False Artist* published. *Modern Art in America*, published by C. W. Kraushaar Art Galleries. Fall, assistant professor of fine arts at New York University. December, Exhibition of Paintings, Drawings and Etchings by Walter Pach at C. W. Kraushaar Art Galleries.

1929

January, "The Evolution of Diego Rivera," published in *Creative Arts*. Spring, assistant professor of fine arts at New York University. Fall, address, 20 rue Jacob, Paris.

1930

January, "Notes sur le classicisme de Delacroix," published in *L'Amour de l'Art*. *An Hour of Art* published. August, south of France.

1931

March, Paintings and Water Colors by Walter Pach at C. W. Kraushaar Art Galleries. May, "Raymond Duchamp-Villon," published in *Formes*. July–August, Tangiers and Morocco.

1932

March, first one-person show in Paris, Peintures, Aquarelles, Dessins et Eaux-fortes de Walter Pach at Galerie Dru Bourgeat et Van Gelde. July, returns to the United States with his family. November, "Le classicisme de Barye," published in *L'Amour de l'Art*. New address, 39 West Sixty-seventh Street, apartment 2, New York. November, participates in the First Biennial Exhibition of Contemporary American Painting at the Whitney Museum of American Art, New York.

1933

January, gives speech at the Worcester Opening of the International 1933 at the Worcester Art Museum, Worcester, Massachusetts. May, Exhibition of Paintings 1913 to 1933 by Walter Pach at Modern Galleries, Philadelphia. Summer, accepts invitation from Ida Guggenheimer to visit with her in Westport, Ontario, Canada, and paint a mural for her summer home, Green Shingles. September, "Diego Rivera at Work," published in the *Nation* and "Rockefeller, Rivera, and Art," published in *Harper's Magazine*. December, participates in the First Biennial of

Contemporary American Sculpture, Watercolors, and Prints at the Whitney Museum of American Art.

1934

February, "The Rivera Mural. Letter to the Editor," published in the *New York Times*. August, new address, 148 West Seventy-second Street, New York. Summer, Westport, Connecticut. Organizes Maurice Prendergast retrospective for the Whitney Museum of American Art. November, Water Colours by Walter Pach at McMaster University, Hamilton, Ontario, Canada. December, Water Colours by Walter Pach at the Montreal Art Gallery, Canada.

1935

May, Walter Pach, Exhibition at Knoedler Galleries, New York. Summer, Dobbs Ferry, New York.

1936

August, Westport, Connecticut. Fall, begins teaching a painting class at Columbia University. *Vincent van Gogh, 1853–1890: A Study of the Artist and His Work in Relation to His Times* published. November, An Exhibition of Water Colors by Walter Pach, Kleemann Galleries, New York.

1937

Shilling Fund established; becomes main advisor. Pach's translation of *The Journal of Eugène Delacroix* published. August–September, Gaylordsville, Connecticut.

1938

Queer Thing, Painting: Forty Years in the World of Art, published. November, "Frida Rivera: Gifted Canvas by an Unselfconscious Surrealist," published in *Art News*. Review of Frida Kahlo's first one-person show in the United States.

1939

July, Magda buys land and builds a small house at RFD 3, Brewster. *Ingres* published. Pach made director general of the Master-pieces of Art exhibition at New York World's Fair.

1940

Masterpieces of Art exhibition at the New York World's Fair. Asked to help plan and organize Origins of Modern Art for the Arts Club of Chicago. Participates in the Golden Gate International Exposition, Palace of Fine Arts, San Francisco.

1941

April, Recent Paintings by Walter Pach, Schneider-Gabriel Galleries, New York.

1942

Participates in "Conference on Science, Philosophy and Religion and Their Relation to the Democratic Way of Life" and publishes "The Artist and the Democratic Way of Life." July, teaches again at the Universidad Nacional in Mexico City. "Descubrimiento de un pintor americano," published in *Cuadernos Americanos* with the English version, "A Newly Found American Painter: Hermenigildo Bustos" published by *Art in America* the following year.

1943

March, "John B. Flannagan" published in *Cuadernos Americanos* with an English version published in the *Kenyon Review* in the summer. Returns to New York in July. New address, 3 Washington Square North, New York. Edward and Jo Hopper are upstairs neighbors.

1944

March, participates in the Pictures for Peace exhibition at the Cincinnati Art Museum.

1946-1947

Participates in the Pioneers of Modern Art in America at the Whitney Museum of American Art and the Columbus Museum of Art, Columbus, Ohio, March, 1947.

1947

March, Walter Pach: Oils and Water Colors at Laurel Gallery, New York, last one-person exhibition. Approached by Curt Valentin of Buchholz Gallery to assist in a translation of Mexican author Juan Larrea's book *Guernica, Picasso*.

1948

Spring of 1948, invited to present a paper to the "Congress of Art Critics," in Paris. Around mid-October, gives a radio address on art on the Columbia Broadcasting System. This talk was part of a "series of conversations" with noted authors conducted by the station on Sundays at noon. *The Art Museum in America* published. Introduction to book on Renoir published.

1950

March 7, receives the Medal of Chevalier of the Légion d'honneur. Spring, asked to serve on the Advisory Board of the Art Book Guild of America. July, brother Alfred dies. November 9, Magda dies.

1951

Visits his son in Italy; goes to Greece. Meets Nikifora Loutsi. June 9 marries Nikifora Loutsi. Fall, professor of fine art at CCNY. "Relaciones entre la cultura notreamericana y la obra de Diego Rivera," published in *Diego Rivera, 50 años de su labór artistica, exposition de normenaje nacional*.

1952

Nephew Alfred Pach asks Walter to be an advisor to a new venture, the Altman-Pach Fine Print Shop in B. Altman and Company at Thirty-fourth Street and Fifth Avenue, New York. Pach elected president of CCNY's chapter of Phi Beta Kappa.

1953

Autumn, "A Modernist Visits Greece," published in *Archaeology*.

1958

November 27, dies.

1959

The Classical Tradition in Modern Art published.

1983

March, Sandra Phillips, "The Art Criticism of Walter Pach" published in the *Art Bulletin*.

1986

Walter Pach, A Retrospective, Asheville Art Museum, North Carolina.

1988

Walter Pach Papers, sold by Nikifora Loutsi Pach to Salander-O'Reilly Galleries, New York, acquired by the Archives of American Art, Washington, D.C., with the assistance of the Brown Foundation; William C. Agee, "Walter Pach and Modernism: A Sampler from New York, Paris, and Mexico City," published in *Archives of American Art Journal*; Bennard B. Perlman, "Walter Pach (1883–1958) and Magda Pach (1884–1950)," published in *Exhibition of the Art of Walter and Magda Pach*.

1988-91

Exhibition of the Art of Walter and Magda Pach, the Butler Institute of American Art, Youngstown, Ohio, September 4–October 2, 1988; Minnesota Museum of American Art, St. Paul, July–September 10, 1989; the Gertrude Herbert Institute of Art, Augusta, Georgia, February 23–March 30, 1990; the Albrecht-Kemper Museum of Art, St. Joseph, Missouri, October 10–December 1, 1991.

1990

Discovering Modernism: Selections from
the Walter Pach Papers, on view at the
Archives of American Art, New York.

1991

The Paintings of Walter Pach, exhibition at
Forum Gallery, New York.

1997

Laurette E. McCarthy, "Modernists on Tour:
A New Look at an Historic Show," published
in *Archives of American Art Journal*.

2002

*American Artists, Authors, and Collectors:
The Walter Pach Letters, 1906–1958,* edited by
Bennard B. Perlman, published.

2004

The Art of Walter and Magda Pach, Old
Dominion University Gallery, September
12–October 10, 2004; Laurette E. McCarthy,
"The 'Truths' About the Armory Show:
Walter Pach's Side of the Story," published in
Archives of American Art Journal.

2008

October 2, Raymond Pach, Walter and
Magdalene Pach's only child, dies.

Notes

Most of the biographical information about Walter Pach may be found in his papers: Walter Pach Papers, Archives of American Art, Smithsonian Institution, Washington, D.C., reels 4216–21 (hereinafter Pach Papers, AAA). Further biographical information was obtained from Walter Pach, *Queer Thing, Painting: Forty Years in the Art World* (New York: Harper and Brothers, 1938), and from Pach's unpublished autobiography in the Walter Pach Collection, City College of New York, Archives and Special Collections Division, City College Libraries (hereinafter CCNY). Additional information was provided by Walter Pach's son, the late Raymond Pach (1914–2008), and Walter Pach's widow, Mrs. Nikifora N. Iliopoulos, who has graciously granted permission to quote from all of Walter Pach's unpublished archives, letters, manuscripts, and writings located worldwide. I wish to express my deepest appreciation for their generous support of this project.

Chapter 1

1. Walter Pach to Paul J. Sachs, October 26, 1939, Paul J. Sachs Papers, Harvard University Archives, Harvard Archives HUG 4764.12 [Miscellaneous Correspondence] (hereinafter Sachs File). Also quoted in Bennard B. Perlman, ed., *American Artists, Authors, and Collectors: The Walter Pach Letters, 1906–1958* (Albany: State University of New York Press, 2002), 1, 346.

2. For more biographical information about Pach, see "Pach in Paint," *Time Magazine,* June 3, 1935, and "Walter Pach Hasn't Got Really Mad for 13 Years: Enfant Terrible of Art World Is Now the Kind and Gentle Critic," *New York Post,* April 29, 1941.

3. "Pach in Paint."

4. See "Gotthelf Pach, 73, Dies in His Sleep," *New York Times,* April 18, 1925, and Walter Pach, *Queer Thing, Painting: Forty Years in the Art World* (New York: Harper and Brothers, 1938), 6. See also United States Department of Commerce, Bureau of the Census, Twelfth Census of the United States, Borough of Manhattan, New York City, June 14, 1900, vol. 169, E.D. 798, sheet 20, lines 37–40 (National Archives, Washington, D.C.).

5. For more on Frances Wise, see United States Department of Commerce, Bureau of the Census, Eighth Census of the United States, County of Milwaukee, State of Wisconsin, June 13, 1860, 1:95, State Historical Society of Wisconsin, Madison and United States Department of Commerce, Bureau of the Census, Twelfth Census of the United States, Borough of Manhattan, New York City, June 14, 1900, vol. 169, E.D. 798, sheet 20, lines 37–40 (National Archives, Washington, D.C.).

6. Information on Frances Wise and Gotthelf Pach's involvement with the New York Society of Ethical Culture courtesy of e-mail correspondence with Marc Bernstein, archivist, New York Society for Ethical Culture, July 13, 2004.

7. For the history of the Ethical Culture Society in New York, see Horace L. Friess, *Felix Adler and Ethical Culture: Memories and Studies,* ed. Fannia Weingartner (New York: Columbia University Press, 1981) and Percival Chubb, *The Origin and Growth of the Ethical Movement* (New York: New York Society for Ethical Culture, n.d.).

8. For the Pach Brothers Studios, see "Gotthelf Pach, 73, Dies in His Sleep"; undated and untitled article from the archives of Oscar White, last owner of Pach Brothers Studio; *Trow's New York City Directory* (New York: Trow Directory, Printing, and Bookbinding, 1866–1867), 90:782; *Portrait* 4 (August 1916), Pach Papers, AAA, reel 4216, frame 51; and Oscar White, interviews by the author, June 20, 1995, and August 7, 2001.

9. Pach, *Queer Thing, Painting,* 6.

10. Pach, *Queer Thing, Painting,* 9.

11. When Pach was born, the family's address was 1631 Park Avenue; in 1890 the street numbers were changed and the address became 1135 Park Avenue. I wish to thank Eileen Morales of the Museum of the City of New York for this information.

12. Walter Pach to Lewis Mumford, August 23, 1931, folder 3764, Lewis Mumford Papers, Rare Book and Manuscript Library, University of Pennsylvania, Philadelphia (hereinafter Mumford Papers). Also quoted in Perlman, *American Artists, Authors, and Collectors,* 217.

13. Chubb taught English in New York City high schools for several years before becoming an instructor at, and head of, the Ethical Culture Society's Manhattan secondary school division. See Chubb, *The Origin and Growth of the Ethical Movement.* Percival Chubb quotation from Chubb, *The Origin and Growth of the Ethical Movement,* 2.

14. Friess, *Felix Adler and Ethical Culture,* 100.

15. Ann J. Dunn to Gotthelf Pach, undated, but either December 1894 or January 1895, Pach Papers, AAA, reel 4216, frame 151.

16. Gotthelf to Walter Pach, July 30, 1894, Pach Papers, AAA, reel 4216, frames 144–45. Since Mr. and Mrs. Pach were involved with the society and Walter and Alfred attended the schools, it seems probable that Percival Chubb is the gentleman mentioned.

17. For the Adirondack area where the Pachs summered, see Federal Writers Project, *New York: A Guide to the Empire State* (New York: Oxford University Press, 1940), 511. Davidson founded the Glenmore Summer School for his Concord School of Philosophy in Keene Valley. See Friess, *Felix Adler and Ethical Culture,* 6, 10, 122 and Seneca Roy Stoddard, *The Adirondacks Illustrated* (Glen Falls, N.Y.: The Author, 1895), 128, 141, 173-B, 263.

18. For CCNY, see Solomon Willis Rudy, *The College of the City of New York: A History, 1847–1947* (New York: Arno Press, 1977); *The College of the City of New York, Fifty-Third Annual Register, 1901–1902* (New York: Knickerbocker Press, 1902). While at college Pach was a member of the Athena Club, a ten-person fraternity at CCNY. See Mrs. Elias Lieberman to Sandra Phillips, July 8, 1979, Sandra Phillips Research Materials on Walter Pach, Archives of American Art, Smithsonian Institution, Washington, D.C., unmicrofilmed.

19. Walter Pach, "Aesthetic Tendencies in the Nineteenth Century," senior oration, Pach Papers, AAA, reel 4220, frame 362.

20. Pach, unpublished autobiography, CCNY.

Chapter 2

1. Pach, unpublished autobiography, CCNY.

2. Pach, unpublished autobiography, CCNY.

3. For a complete discussion of Chase's Shinnecock Summer School of Art, see Ronald G. Pisano, *A Leading Spirit in American Art: William Merritt Chase, 1849–1916* (Seattle: Henry Gallery Association, 1983), 121–26.

4. Pach, *Queer Thing, Painting,* 41.

5. Frances to Walter Pach, August 16, 1902, Pach Papers, AAA, reel 4216, frames 175–76.

6. Pach, unpublished biography, CCNY.

7. Walter Pach, New York–Haarlem logbook, June 24–September 14, 1903, Pach Papers, AAA, reel 4216, frames 73–102. All references to and quotes from this 1903 journey were recorded in this logbook. For a discussion of the Chase schools abroad, see Pisano, *A Leading Spirit* and Keith L. Bryant Jr., *William Merritt Chase: A Genteel Bohemian* (Columbia: University of Missouri Press, 1991).

8. Pach, *Queer Thing, Painting,* 77. Pach did teach himself some Japanese, but he was not as adept at this language as he was with German, French, Spanish, and Italian.

9. Pach's manuscript "Aesthetics" is not among his papers at the Archives of American Art and I have been unable to locate it.

10. William Merritt Chase to his wife, Alice Chase, August 18, 1903, William Merritt Chase Papers, Archives of American Art, Smithsonian Institution, Washington, D.C., reel N69–137, frame 644.

11. Pach's logbook, September 5, 1903, Pach Papers, AAA.

12. For Pach's studies with Henri, see Pach, unpublished autobiography, CCNY and Pach, *Queer Thing, Painting,* 42–48. For Henri's teachings, see William Innes Homer, *Robert Henri and His Circle* (Ithaca: Cornell University Press, 1969) and Helen Evelyn Goodman, "Robert Henri: The Teacher" (Ph.D. diss., New York University, 1975).

13. Robert Henri, *The Art Spirit* (1923; reprint, New York: Harper and Row, 1984), 16.

14. Pach, *Queer Thing, Painting,* 42.

15. Henri, *The Art Spirit,* 111.

16. Pach, *Queer Thing, Painting,* 77.

17. For this Chase summer school, see Ronald G. Pisano, *William Merritt Chase in the Company of Friends* (Southampton, N.Y.: Parrish Art Museum, 1979) and Pisano, *A Leading Spirit.*

18. Walter Pach, New York–London (Berlin) log-book, June 14–August 2, 1904, Walter Pach Papers, AAA, reel 4216, frames 103–36, and diary, August 3–September 27, 1904, AAA, reel 4220, frames 581–604. Unless noted otherwise, all reference to and quotes from this 1904 journey were recorded either in Pach's logbook or in his diary.

19. Harmony in Blue and Gold: The Peacock Room was sold to Obach and Company Galleries of Bond Street in 1904. It was erected in Obach's galleries and opened to the public in June 1904. See Susan Hobbs, *The Whistler Peacock Room* (Washington, D.C.: Freer Gallery of Art, Smithsonian Institution, 1980), 18, 30.

20. For his trip to Germany and Paris, see Pach, diary, August 3–September 27, 1904, Pach Papers, AAA, reel 4220, frames 581–604. Pach seems not to have taken his logbook with him on this trip, but kept a separate diary. All quotations related to this trip are from this diary.

21. Walter Pach to Ida Guggenheimer, April 24, 1931, Ida Guggenheimer Papers, Archives of American Art, Smithsonian Institution, Washington, D.C. (hereinafter Guggenheimer Papers). Pach wrote, "My father and mother went there [Nauheim] every summer from 1904 to 1914 inclusive, and it did my father no end of good. He had advice from Dr. Schott."

22. Pach wrote a slightly different version of this event in his book *Queer Thing, Painting:* "At an exhibition of modern art in Dresden, I came upon a picture that appealed to me strongly. In the diary I kept at the time I noted down 'superb work by Buzenne(?),' the question mark meaning that I was not sure of the name. I had no catalogue and the spelling I used was the best I could do in reading the signature in the paint. It was many years afterward that the sight of a similar work led me to look up that notation,

when I found that my 'Buzenne' was Cézanne, and I had the satisfaction of knowing that I had first liked the great man for his art alone, and not for his fame, which was unknown to me," Pach, *Queer Thing, Painting,* 12. However, recent research suggests that the painting Pach actually saw was not a Cézanne, but most probably a work by Eugène Antoine Durenne. The *Offizieller Katalog der grossen Kunstausstellung Dresden 1904* lists a work by Durenne in the same room as five paintings by Degas as well as the other artists Pach mentions in his diary. I want to thank Norman Köhler, archivist, Staatliche Kunstammlungen Dresden, for his assistance in this research. E-mail correspondence with Köhler, August 29, 2008.

23. Stephen Duggan, director, Institute of International Education to Walter Pach, November 30, 1942, Pach Papers, AAA, reel 4218, frame 750.

24. For the Chase program in Spain, see Bryant, *William Merritt Chase, a Genteel Bohemian* and Pisano, *A Leading Spirit.*

25. Pach, *Queer Thing, Painting,* 117.

26. Pennsylvania Academy of the Fine Arts, *Catalogue of the Sixth Annual Exhibition of the Pennsylvania Academy of the Fine Arts* (Philadelphia, 1905), 9, no. 217. The show ran November 16–30, 1905.

27. John Sloan, *John Sloan's New York Scene, from the Diaries, Notes, and Correspondence, 1906–1913,* ed. Bruce St. John, introduction by Helen Farr Sloan (New York: Harper & Row, 1965), 23–24.

28. Walter Pach to Ezra Pound, February 9, 1918, Ezra Pound Papers, Yale Collection of American Literature, Beinecke Rare Book and Manuscript Library. Pach wrote Pound, "I wonder whether, by any chance, you may remember our meeting in Madrid in 1906. You were working at Lope de Vega then. We met at the house of Senora Carmona and spent an evening at a dance-café where the pianist told us of his concertising ambitions."

29. Walter Pach to Robert Henri, August 27, 1906, Robert Henri Papers, Yale Collection of American Literature, Beinecke Rare Book and Manuscript Library (hereinafter Henri Papers). Also quoted in Perlman, *American Artists, Authors, and Collectors,* 178.

30. Pach to Henri, September 14, 1906, Henri Papers. Also quoted in Perlman, *American Artists, Authors, and Collectors,* 179.

31. Pach to Henri, September 14, 1906, Henri Papers. Also quoted in Perlman, *American Artists, Authors, and Collectors,* 179.

32. On Pach's paintings done in Haarlem at this time, see Pach to Henri, September 30, 1906, Henri Papers. Also quoted in Perlman, *American Artists, Authors, and Collectors,* 179. See also Edna Strasser to Walter Pach, October 26, 1935, Pach Papers, AAA, reel 4218, frame 531.

33. Pach, *Queer Thing, Painting,* 12–13.

34. For Pach's studio, see Walter Pach to Alice Klauber, April 22, 1907, the Klauber Collection, Archives of the San Diego Museum of Art. Also located in the Archives of American Art, reel 583, frame 544 (hereinafter Klauber Papers). Pach wrote, "I should be glad to see you in my studio (above address)." The address on the letterhead was 935 Broadway, where Pach Brothers Studio had their business. Also quoted in Perlman, *American Artists, Authors, and Collectors,* 194.

35. *Open-Air Restaurant, Bombilla,* oil on canvas, present location unknown. *The Annual Exhibition Record of the National Academy of Design, 1901–1950,* ed. Peter Hastings Falk (Madison, Conn.: Sound View Press, 1990), 12, 395.

Chapter 3

1. Walter to Raymond Pach, October 17, 1945, Walter Pach Papers, Helen Farr Sloan Library and Archives, Delaware Art Museum (hereinafter Pach Papers, DAM).

2. Pach, unpublished autobiography, CCNY.

3. Pach, unpublished autobiography, CCNY.

4. For the Chase program in Florence, see Pisano, *A Leading Spirit.*

5. Pach to Klauber, March 4, 1907, Klauber Papers, AAA, reel 583, frames 538–42. Also quoted in Perlman, *American Artists, Authors, and Collectors,* 193.

6. See circular in the Klauber Papers, AAA, reel 583, frames 538–40.

7. Information about Magdalene Frohberg from a letter from Walter to Raymond Pach, October 27, 1945, Pach Papers, DAM and Raymond Pach interview with the author, April 26, 1994, Newport News, Virginia.

8. For information on Charles Loeser, see John Rewald, *Cézanne and America: Dealers, Collectors, Artists, and Critics, 1891–1921* (Princeton: Princeton University Press, 1989), 20, 29, and Pach, *Queer Thing, Painting,* 88–94.

9. For Pach's meetings with the Stein families, see Pach, *Queer Thing, Painting,* 116, and James R. Mellow, *A Charmed Circle: Gertrude Stein and Company* (Boston: Houghton Mifflin, 1974), 122.

10. Aline Saarinen, interview with Walter Pach, February 1956, Aline Saarinen Papers, AAA, reel 2071, frame 1487. See also Aline Saarinen, *The Proud Possessors: The Lives, Times, and Tastes of Some Adventurous American Art Collectors* (New York: Random House, 1958).

11. Begun in 1905, Picasso's *Portrait of Gertrude Stein* was completed late in the summer of 1906. See Pierre Daix, "Portraiture in Picasso's Primitivism and Cubism," in *Picasso and Portraiture: Representation and Transformation,* ed. William Rubin (New York: Museum of Modern Art, 1996), 257, 268.

12. For Pach's first meeting with Matisse, see Pach, *Queer Thing, Painting,* 116, and Walter Pach to Henri Matisse, March 24, 1946, Henri Matisse Archives, Les Héritiers Matisse, Issy-les-Moulineaux, France (hereinafter Matisse Archives). Unless noted

otherwise, all letters from Pach to Madame and Henri Matisse are located in this repository. Pach's letters to Madame and Henri Matisse are written in French; translations are mine with additional translations by Susan Berger. I wish to thank M. Claude Duthuit, Wanda de Guibriant, Georges Matisse, and Les Héritiers Matisse (Matisse Archives) for granting me access to these valuable materials. See also John Cauman, "Henri Matisse's Letters to Walter Pach," *Archives of American Art Journal* 31 (1991): 2–14, and John H. Cauman, "Matisse and America, 1905–1933" (Ph.D. diss., City University of New York, 2000), 3, 37.

13. Pach, unpublished autobiography, CCNY. See also Pach to Klauber, November 2, 1907, Klauber Papers, AAA, reel 583, frame 561. Pach must have gotten to Paris sometime before this date, for he wrote Klauber, "When I got back here and found I missed you."

14. Pach to Klauber, November 16, 1907, Klauber Papers, AAA, reel 583, frame 557.

15. For Ogihara, see Pach, *Queer Thing, Painting,* 77–87.

16. Cauman, "Matisse and America," 37–38. Cauman states that Pach had gone to the Steins early in 1907; however, Pach was not in Paris until the fall of that year. See also Pach to Klauber, November 16, 1907, Klauber Papers, AAA, reel 583, frame 557. Also quoted in Perlman, *American Artists, Authors, and Collectors,* 196. Pach wrote, "I felt easier—even about the big still-life [by Matisse] in rue Madame." Clearly he had been to Michael and Sarah Stein's apartment.

17. Pach, *Queer Thing, Painting,* 124.

18. Jack Flam, *Matisse and Picasso: The Story of Their Rivalry and Friendship* (Cambridge, Mass.: Westview Press, 2003), 42, 233.

19. Pach, *Queer Thing, Painting,* 118. See also Cauman, "Matisse and America," 39.

20. Pach, *Queer Thing, Painting,* 118.

21. Cauman, "Matisse and America," 40.

22. Pach to Klauber, January 3, 1908, Pach Papers, AAA, reel 4219, frame 401.

23. Moriye Ogihara to Walter Pach, January 22, 1908, Pach Papers, AAA, reel 4216, frame 796.

24. Pach to Klauber, February 8, 1908, Klauber Papers, AAA, reel 583, frame 563. Also quoted in Perlman, *American Artists, Authors, and Collectors,* 197.

25. Pach to Klauber, March 9, 1908, Klauber Papers, AAA, reel 583, frame 570. Also quoted in Perlman, *American Artists, Authors, and Collectors,* 198.

26. Pach, *Queer Thing, Painting,* 15.

27. Pach to Klauber, November 16, 1907, Klauber Papers, AAA, reel 583, frame 558.

28. Pach, *Queer Thing, Painting,* 117.

29. Pach to Klauber, November 16, 1907, Klauber Papers, AAA, reel 583, frame 556. Also quoted in Perlman, *American Artists, Authors, and Collectors,* 196. See also Cauman, "Matisse and America," 40.

30. Pach to Klauber, November 16, 1907, Klauber Papers, AAA, reel 583, frame 556. Also quoted in Perlman, *American Artists, Authors, and Collectors,* 196.

31. Pach to Klauber, November 16, 1907, Klauber Papers, AAA, reel 583, frame 557. Also quoted in Perlman, *American Artists, Authors, and Collectors,* 196.

32. Pach to Klauber, March 9, 1908, Klauber Papers, AAA, 583, frame 571. Also quoted in Perlman, *American Artists, Authors, and Collectors,* 198.

33. Pach, *Queer Thing, Painting,* 119.

34. Pach to Klauber, February 8, 1908, Klauber Papers, AAA, reel 583, frame 563. Also quoted in Perlman, *American Artists, Authors, and Collectors,* 197.

35. Pach to Klauber, June 20, 1908, Klauber Papers, AAA, reel 583, frame 573.

36. Pach, *Queer Thing, Painting,* 15.

37. Pach, *Queer Thing, Painting,* 20.

38. Pach to Klauber, February 8, 1908, Klauber Papers, AAA, reel 583, frame 564. Also quoted in Perlman, *American Artists, Authors, and Collectors,* 197.

39. Pach to Klauber, February 8, 1908, Klauber Papers, AAA, reel 583, frame 564. Also quoted in Perlman, *American Artists, Authors, and Collectors,* 197.

40. Pach, unpublished autobiography, CCNY.

41. Pach to Klauber, June 20, 1908, Klauber Papers, AAA, reel 583, frame 573.

42. Pach to Klauber, November 16, 1907, Klauber Papers, AAA, reel 583, frame 558. Also quoted in Perlman, *American Artists, Authors, and Collectors,* 196.

43. Pach to Klauber, February 8, 1908, Klauber Papers, AAA, reel 583, frame 563. Also quoted in Perlman, *American Artists, Authors, and Collectors,* 197.

44. Pach, "Cézanne: An Introduction." *Scribner's Magazine* 44 (December 1908): 768.

45. Pach stated in his essay that he had read Emile Bernard's articles on Cézanne in the July 1904 issue of *L'Occident* and the October 1907 number of *Mercure de France.* It is possible that he was also aware of Maurice Denis's piece in a 1907 issue of *L'Occident.* In his article on Cézanne, Pach referred to Julius Meier-Graefe's "spirited essay" on Cézanne, which he read and admired.

46. Sandra S. Phillips, "The Art Criticism of Walter Pach," *Art Bulletin* 65 (March 1983): 106.

47. Pach to Klauber, June 20, 1908, Klauber Papers, AAA, reel 583, frames 573–74.

48. Pach to Klauber, March 9, 1908, Klauber Papers, AAA, reel 583, frame 570.

49. Pach to Klauber, August 19, 1908, Klauber Papers, AAA, reel 583, frame 578. Also quoted in Perlman, *American Artists, Authors, and Collectors,* 199.

50. Pach to Klauber, November 2, 1908, Klauber Papers, AAA, reel 583, frames

583–84. Also quoted in Perlman, *American Artists, Authors, and Collectors,* 199.

51. Pach to Klauber, November 2, 1908, Klauber Papers, AAA, reel 583, frame 584. Also quoted in Perlman, *American Artists, Authors, and Collectors,* 200.

52. Pach to Klauber, November 2, 1908, Klauber Papers, AAA, reel 583, frame 584. Also quoted in Perlman, *American Artists, Authors, and Collectors,* 200. See also Walter Pach to August F. Jaccaci, December 13, 1909, and February 27, 1910, August F. Jaccaci Papers, AAA, reel D-121, frames 1470, 1472.

53. "Walter Pach Hasn't Got Really Mad for 13 Years: Enfant Terrible of Art World Is Now the Kind and Gentle Critic," *New York Post,* April 29, 1941. See also Rewald, *Cézanne and America,* 121, 128n33. Rewald states that there is no way to substantiate this anecdote.

54. Pach to Klauber, June 9, 1909, Klauber Papers, AAA, reel 583, frame 593. Also quoted in Perlman, *American Artists, Authors, and Collectors,* 200.

55. Pach to Klauber, November 13, 1909, Klauber Papers, AAA, reel 583, frames 602–4. Also quoted in Perlman, *American Artists, Authors, and Collectors,* 202.

56. Walter Pach, "Quelques notes sur les peintres américains," *Gazette des Beaux-Arts* 2 (1909): 324–35.

57. John Sloan, *John Sloan's New York Scenes,* ed. Helen Farr Sloan and Bruce St. John (New York: Harper and Row, 1965), 254, 299.

58. Sloan, *New York Scenes,* 348.

59. Pach, "Manet and Modern American Art," *Craftsman* 17 (February 1910): 483.

60. Sloan, *New York Scenes,* 373–74. For a detailed account of the First Independent Exhibition, see Sloan, *New York Scenes,* 373–409.

61. Sloan, *New York Scenes,* 398–99.

62. Sloan, *New York Scenes,* 402.

63. For information on Chase's 1910 summer school in Florence, see Pisano, *A Leading Spirit.*

64. Walter Pach to John Sloan, September 25, 1910, John Sloan Archives, Helen Farr Sloan Library and Archives, Delaware Art Museum, Wilmington (hereinafter Sloan Archives).

65. M. C. Benthall to Walter Pach, May 21, 1911 or 1912, Pach Papers, AAA, reel 4219, frame 309.

66. Pach to Sachs, October 26, 1939, Sachs file. Also quoted in Perlman, *American Artists, Authors, and Collectors,* 347.

67. Maurice Denis, "Definition of Neotraditionism," quoted in Herschel B. Chipp, ed., *Theories of Modern Art: A Source Book by Artists and Critics* (Berkeley and Los Angeles: University of California Press, 1968), 94.

68. Pach, *Queer Thing, Painting,* 133–34.

69. Gertrude Stein, *Two: Gertrude Stein and Her Brother and Other Early Portraits* (1951; reprint, Freeport, N.Y.: Books for Libraries Press, 1969), 338–40.

70. For Toklas's editing of Pach's essays, see Walter Pach to Alice B. Toklas, December 31, 1910, Gertrude Stein and Alice B. Toklas Papers, Yale Collection of American Literature, the Beinecke Rare Book and Manuscript Library (hereinafter Gertrude Stein Manuscript Collection).

71. Pach to Toklas, February 14, 1911, Gertrude Stein Manuscript Collection. See also Barbara Haskell, *Joseph Stella* (New York: Whitney Museum of American Art, 1994), 58, 190.

72. Pach, *Queer Thing, Painting,* 135.

73. Pach met Amadeo de Souza-Cardoso in 1911 at the home of Italian artist Umberto Brunelleschi, at 23 rue Boissonade. See Laura Coyle, "Amadeo and America," in *At the Edge: A Portuguese Futurist, Amadeo de Souza Cardoso* (Lisbon: Textype Artes Graficas, Gabibete das Relações Internacio-

nais, 1999), 80–81 and appendix C, 187–88, Walter Pach to Madame de Souza Cardoso, March 2, 1958.

74. For discussions of Pach's affiliation with the Puteaux Group, see Pach, *Queer Thing, Painting,* 139–63; Allan Antliff, *Anarchist Modernism: Art, Politics, and the First American Avant-Garde* (Chicago: University of Chicago Press, 2001), 167, 172–82; Mark Antliff, *Inventing Bergson: Cultural Politics and the Parisian Avant-Garde* (Princeton: Princeton University Press, 1993), 39.

75. R. Stanley Johnson, *Cubism and La Section d'Or* (Chicago: Klees/Gustorf, 1991), 7.

76. Robert Rosenblum, *Cubism and Twentieth-Century Art* (New York: Harry N. Abrams, 1976), 180–81.

77. Antliff, *Anarchist Modernism,* 178.

78. Antliff, *Anarchist Modernism,* 169.

79. John Golding, *Cubism: A History and Analysis, 1907–1914,* 3rd ed. (Cambridge: Belknap Press of Harvard University Press, 1988), 16.

80. Pach, *Queer Thing, Painting,* 159.

81. For Faure, see Martine Courtois and Jean-Paul Morel, *Élie Faure, biographie* (Paris: Librairie Séguier, 1989).

82. Pach, *Queer Thing, Painting,* 261.

83. Pach, *Queer Thing, Painting,* 262.

84. For more on Fabbri, see Pach, *Queer Thing, Painting,* 94–97, and Rewald, *Cézanne and America,* 22–26.

85. Pach, *Queer Thing, Painting,* 94.

86. Walter Pach, "Journal of the Un cours de bonheur (reconnu d'utilité publique)," Pach Papers, AAA, reel 4220, frames 387–430. The journal is written in French; translations are mine. Unless noted otherwise, all quotations related to this class come from this journal.

87. Walter Pach, "Winslow Homer," *L'Art et les Artistes* 16 (November 1912): 79; translation mine.

88. Pach to Klauber, June 20, 1908, Klauber Papers, AAA, reel 583, frame 577. See also Pach's notes from interview with Auguste Renoir, June 2, 1908, Pach Papers, AAA, reel 4220, frame 566.

89. Walter Pach, "Pierre Auguste Renoir," *Scribner's Magazine* 51 (May 1912): 607.

90. Walter Pach, "A Recollection of Arthur B. Davies," published posthumously in *Arthur B. Davies (1862–1928): A Centennial Exhibition* (Utica, N.Y.: Munson-Williams-Proctor Institute, 1962), 4. See also Rewald, *Cézanne and America,* 151, and Perlman, *American Artists, Authors, and Collectors,* 139–40.

91. Charles Loeser to Walter Pach, April 28, 1911, Pach Papers, AAA, reel 4217, frames 23–25.

Chapter 4

1. Much of this chapter is derived from my "The 'Truths' About the Armory Show: Walter Pach's Side of the Story," *Archives of American Art Journal* 44, no. 3–4 (2004): 2–13. All parts from the article are quoted by permission of the *Archives of American Art Journal,* Smithsonian Institution. The main accounts of the Armory Show are Pach, *Queer Thing, Painting,* 192–203; Walt Kuhn, *The Story of the Armory Show* (New York: [Printed privately], 1938); Frank Anderson Trapp, *The 1913 Armory Show in Retrospect* (Amherst: Amherst College, 1958); Milton W. Brown, introduction to *Armory Show 50th Anniversary Exhibition, 1913–1963* (New York: Henry Street Settlement and the Munson-Williams-Proctor Institute, 1963); Milton W. Brown, *The Story of the Armory Show* (New York: Joseph H. Hirshhorn Foundation, 1963); Ian Dunlop, *The Shock of the New: Seven Historic Exhibitions of Modern Art* (London: Weidenfeld and Nicholson, 1972), 163–97; Judith K. Zilczer, "The Armory Show and the American Avant-Garde: A Reevaluation," *Arts Magazine* 53 (September 1978): 126–44; "The Seventy-fifth Anniver-sary of the Armory Show," *Archives of American Art Journal* 27 (1987); Milton W. Brown, *The Story of the Armory Show,* 2nd ed. (New York: Abbeville Press and Joseph H. Hirshhorn Foundation, 1988); Andrew Martinez, "A Mixed Reception for Modern-ism: The 1913 Armory Show at the Art Institute of Chicago," *Museum Studies* 19 (1993): 31–57, 102–5; Moira McLoughlin, "Negotiating the Critical Discourse: The Armory Show Revisited," in *On the Margins of the Art Worlds,* ed. Larry Gross (Boulder, Colo.: Westview Press, 1995): 17–37; and J. M. Mancini, "'One Term Is as Fatuous as Another': Responses to the Armory Show Reconsidered," *American Quarterly* 51 (December 1999): 833–71.

2. Pach, "A Recollection of Arthur B. Davies," 4.

3. Arthur B. Davies to Walter Pach, October 1912, Pach Papers, reel 4217, frames 95–96. Also quoted in Perlman, *American Artists, Authors, and Collectors,* 140.

4. Arthur B. Davies to Walt Kuhn, undated, fall 1912, Archives of American Art, Smithsonian Institution, Washington, D.C. (hereinafter Kuhn Papers, AAA), reel D-240, frame 415.

5. Davies to Kuhn, October 1, 1912, Kuhn Papers, AAA, reel D-240, frame 391.

6. Walt Kuhn to Mr. de Bois, Artz and de Bois, The Hague, Netherlands, November 20, 1912, Armory Show Papers, AAA, reel D-72, frames 363–64. Kuhn informed de Bois, "*Mr. Walter Pach 83 Boulevard Montparnasse, Paris* will be our authorized representative for the Exhibition, as we leave to-morrow morning for America."

7. Walt to Vera Kuhn, October 28 and 29, 1912, Kuhn Papers, AAA, reel D-240, frames 423, 429.

8. Pach, *Queer Thing, Painting,* 178.

9. Pach, *Queer Thing, Painting,* 118.

10. Walt Kuhn to Walter Pach, November 19, 1912, Archives of American Art, Smithsonian Institution, Washington, D.C. (hereinafter Armory Show Papers, AAA), reel D-72, frame 468.

11. Kuhn to Pach, November 19, 1912, Armory Show Papers, AAA, reel D-72, frames 468–74.

12. Alexander Archipenko in *Armory Show 50th Anniversary Exhibition, 1913–1963,* 93.

13. For Picabia's version of coming to the United States, see Gabrielle Buffet-Picabia, "Introduction à l'art moderne aux Etats-Unis," *XXe siècle* 40 (June 1973): 63–64.

14. Pierre Cabanne, *Dialogues with Marcel Duchamp,* translated from the French by Ron Pladget (New York: Viking Press, 1971), 43–44.

15. Walt Kuhn to Theodore E. Butler, December 21, 1912, Armory Show Papers, AAA, reel D-72, frame 296.

16. Walt to Vera Kuhn, October 31 and November 6, 1912, Kuhn Papers, AAA, reel D-240, frames 434, 445.

17. Some primary sources simply state that the futurists were not included, without specifying the reason. See Frank Jewett Mather Jr., "Art: Old and New," *Nation* 96 (March 6, 1913): 242; Kenyon Cox, "The 'Modern' Spirit in Art," *Harper's Weekly* 57 (March 15, 1913): 10; and "Cubists Con-demned by Clergyman and Praised by Artist," *Minneapolis Journal,* April 12, 1913, 4. Other secondary sources that discuss the futurists' absence include Milton W. Brown, *American Painting from the Armory Show to the Depression* (Princeton: Princeton University Press, 1955), 49; Trapp, *The 1913 Armory Show in Retrospect,* 8; Frank Anderson Trapp, "The Armory Show Revived by Amherst," *Art in America* 46 (Spring 1958): 66; "The Glorious Affair," 67; Brown, *The Story of the Armory Show* (1963), 57–58; *Decade of the Armory Show: New Direction in American Art, 1910–1920* (New York: Whitney Museum of American Art, 1963), 30; Frank Anderson Trapp, "The

Armory Show: A Review," *Art Journal* 23 (Fall 1963): 6; Tillim, "Dissent on the Armory Show," 101; Zilczer, "The Armory Show and the American Avant-Garde,"129; Constance H. Schwartz, *The Shock of Modernism in America: The Eight and the Artists of the Armory Show* (Roslyn Harbor, N.Y.: Nassau County Museum of Fine Art, 1984), 68; Milton W. Brown, "Walt Kuhn's Armory Show," in *Archives of American Art Journal* 27 (1987): 10; McLoughlin, "Negotiating the Critical Discourse," 20.

18. Brown, *The Story of the Armory Show* (1988), 79.

19. See Bennard Perlman, *The Lives, Loves, and Art of Arthur B. Davies* (Albany: State University of New York Press, 1999), 219.

20. *The Armory Show International Exhibition of Modern Art,* 3 vols. (New York: Arno Press, 1972). Most of the writings published for the show by the AAPS and other primary sources were reprinted in these volumes.

21. Walter Pach, "As to Futurists," in *For and Against: Views on the International Exhibition Held in New York and Chicago,* ed. Frederick James Gregg (New York: Association of American Painters and Sculptors, 1913), reprinted in *The Armory Show International Exhibition of Modern Art,* 3 vols. (New York: Arno Press, 1972).

22. Walter Pach to Katherine S. Dreier, December 21, 1920, the Katherine S. Dreier Papers/Société Anonyme Archives, Yale Collection of American Literature, Beinecke Rare Book and Manuscript Library (hereinafter Dreier Papers). Also quoted in Perlman, *American Artists, Authors, and Collectors,* 145.

23. Kuhn to Pach, December 12, 1912, Armory Show Papers, AAA, reel D-72, frame 343.

24. Pach, "A Recollection of Arthur B. Davies," 7.

25. Walter Pach to Ambroise Vollard, March 8, 1913, Armory Show Papers, AAA, reel D-72, frame 1455.

26. For information on John Quinn, see Benjamin L. Reid, *The Man from New York: John Quinn and His Friends* (New York: Oxford University Press, 1968) and Judith Zilczer, *"The Noble Buyer": John Quinn, Patron of the Avant-Garde* (Washington, D.C.: Smithsonian Institution Press, 1978).

27. Walter Conrad Arensberg to Elmer L. MacRae, March 14, 1913, MacRae Papers, AAA, reel 4131, frame 991. For a biography of Walter Conrad Arensberg, see Francis Naumann, "Walter Conrad Arensberg: Poet, Patron, and Participant in the New York Avant-Garde, 1915–20," *Philadelphia Museum of Art Bulletin* 76 (Spring 1980): 3–33.

28. Walter Pach to Michael Stein, March 30, 1913, Gertrude Stein Manuscript Collection. Also quoted in Perlman, *American Artists, Authors, and Collectors,* 384.

29. Carl Zigrosser, *A World of Art and Museums* (Philadelphia: Art Alliance Press and Associated University Presses, 1975), 28–29.

30. Zigrosser, *A World of Art and Museums,* 29.

31. For Wallace Stevens, see Alan Filreis, *Wallace Stevens and the Actual World* (Princeton: Princeton University Press, 1991), 5, and Joan Richardson, *Wallace Stevens: The Early Years, 1879–1923* (New York: Beech Tree Books, William Morrow, 1986), 400. This latter source states that Stevens met Pach through Walter Arensberg. Walter Pach first met Walter Arensberg at the New York venue of the show. It is possible that Arensberg introduced Stevens to Pach at the exhibition; however, Pach did not become close with Arensberg until the show went to Boston.

32. Walt to Vera Kuhn, March 23, 1913, Kuhn Papers, AAA, reel D-240, frame 483.

33. Kuhn to Davies, undated, MacRae Papers, AAA, reel 4131, frame 875.

34. Manierre Dawson, journal, March 25, 1913, Manierre Dawson Papers, AAA, reel 64, frame 955 (hereinafter Dawson Papers). Permission to publish from the Dawson papers courtesy of Peter Lockwood.

35. Pach, *Queer Thing, Painting,* 195.

36. "Cubists Depart, Students Joyful," *Chicago Daily Tribune,* April 17, 1913.

37. Walt Kuhn to Elmer L. MacRae, March 24, 1913, quoted in Brown, *The Story of the Armory Show* (1963), 172.

38. Unsigned, but probably Kuhn to Pach, April 5, 1913, Armory Show Papers, reel D-73, frame 21.

39. Pach to Michael Stein, March 30, 1913, Gertrude Stein Manuscript Collection. Also quoted in Perlman, *American Artists, Authors, and Collectors,* 387.

40. Walter Pach to Koehler, April 26, 1913, Armory Show Papers, AAA, reel D-72, frame 792.

41. Pach to Michael Stein, March 30, 1913, Gertrude Stein Manuscript Collection. Also quoted in Perlman, *American Artists, Authors, and Collectors,* 383–84, 387.

42. *Thirty-fourth Annual Report of the Copley Society of Boston* (Boston: Industrial School for Crippled and Deformed Children, 1913), 4–5.

43. Walter Pach, "The Politer, the Cutt'n'er," Arensberg Archives, Philadelphia Museum of Art, Archives, Philadelphia, Pennsylvania (hereinafter Arensberg Archives © PMA). This draft of Pach's review of the exhibition of the Arensberg Collection at the Art Institute of Chicago in 1949 was unpublished.

44. Pach to Kuhn, May 15, 1913, Armory Show Papers, AAA, reel D-73, frame 49.

45. Walter Pach, *The Art of Odilon Redon* (New York: Association of American Painters and Sculptors, 1913), 8.

46. Walter Pach, *A Sculptor's Architecture* (New York: Association of American Painters and Sculptors, 1913), 18.

47. Walter Pach, "The Cubist Room," in *For and Against: Views on the International Exhibition Held in New York and Chicago,* ed. Frederick James Gregg (New York: Association of American Painters and Sculptors, 1913), 51–52, 54.

48. See Pach to AAPS, May 29, 1913, MacRae Papers, AAA, reel 4131, frame 880. Pach wrote, "Received from the Association of American Painters and Sculptors Inc. the sum of $1200 for services rendered."

Chapter 5

1. *The Toledo Bridge* was shown at the Sixth Annual Exhibition of the Fellowship of the Pennsylvania Academy of the Fine Arts, which opened November 16, 1905. *Open-Air Restaurant, Bombilla* was shown at the National Academy of Design, Winter Exhibition, 1906–1907. *Hay-Bilt, Haarlem* and *Dutch Lowlands* were shown at the Exhibition of Paintings, held at the Gallery of the New York School of Art, 2237–2239 Broadway (corner of Eightieth Street), April 22–May 4, 1907. See Peter Hastings Falk, ed., *The Annual Exhibition Record of the National Academy of Design, 1901–1950* (Madison, Conn.: Sound View Press, 1990), 12, 395, and *Catalogue of the Exhibition of Paintings* (New York: New York School of Art, 1907), Pach Papers, reel 4221, frames 14–15. None of these paintings has been located.

2. Elizabeth Cary, "The World of Art: Etchings in Variety," *New York Times Book Review and Magazine,* July 18, 1920.

3. Pach to Klauber, March 9, 1908, Klauber Papers, AAA, reel 583, frame 571. Also quoted in Perlman, *American Artists, Authors, and Collectors,* 198. The show actually opened on March 20. See *Catalogue de la 24 exposition de la Société des artistes indépendants, Salon des indépendants* (Paris, 1908). A copy of this catalog is in the National Gallery of Art, Washington, D.C.

4. Walter Pach, quoted in Trapp, *The 1913 Armory Show in Retrospect* (Amherst: Amherst College, 1958), 27.

5. Pach to Dawson, November 24, 1913, Dawson Papers, AAA, reel 64, frame 877.

6. W. K. Kelsey, "You'll Swear You've Got 'Em If You See Futurists' Display," *Detroit Times,* March 2, 1914.

7. "Cubist Art Now Museum Feature," *Detroit Journal,* March 3, 1914.

8. Mary L. Alexander, "Bewilderment May Strike Viewers of the Canvases," *Cincinnati Times Star,* March 28, 1914. A photograph of *Progression No. 1* appeared in the Montross Gallery catalog. This picture, along with the description of *Progression No. 2* in the *Cincinnati Commercial Tribune,* leads to the identification of *Progression No. 3* as the "Gold Fish" referred to in the article by Mary L. Alexander in the *Cincinnati Times Star,* March 28, 1914. I believe that the work now known as *Aquarium* is *Progression No. 3.*

9. "Weird Futurist Paintings Exhibited at Art Museum," *Cincinnati Commercial Tribune,* March 29, 1914.

10. J. O. L., "The Three Arts," *Baltimore Evening Sun,* May 8, 1914.

11. Walter Arensberg to Walter Pach, March 1, 1914, Pach Papers, AAA, reel 4217, frame 173. Also quoted in Perlman, *American Artists, Authors, and Collectors,* 33–34 (mistakenly dated March 2, 1914).

12. Pach to Matisse, October 21, 1915, Matisse Archives.

13. Matisse to Pach, November 20, 1915, Pach Papers, AAA, reel 4217, frames 255–60, and Cauman, "Henri Matisse's Letters to Walter Pach," 4–5. Permission to publish the Matisse letters courtesy of Les Héritiers Matisse.

14. Pach to Matisse, May 16, 1916, Matisse Archives.

15. Pach to Matisse, July 7, 1916, Matisse Archives and Cauman, "Matisse and America," 285.

16. Antliff, *Anarchist Modernism,* 178.

17. Antliff, *Anarchist Modernism,* 177.

18. Antliff, *Anarchist Modernism,* 169.

19. Antliff, *Anarchist Modernism,* 177.

20. Frank Jewett Mather Jr., "The Society of Independent Artists," *Nation* 104 (May 10, 1917): 574.

21. Pach to Matisse, September 15, 1916, Matisse Archives.

22. This date for *Petrouchka* differs from that given in my previous writings. The dance was first performed in Paris in 1911 by Diaghilev's Ballets Russes with Vaslav Nijinsky dancing the lead role. See also Barbara Naomi Cohen-Stratyner, *Biographical Dictionary of Dance* (New York: Schirmer Books, 1982), 659.

23. Quoted in Alexandre Tansman, *Igor Stravinsky, the Man and His Music,* trans. Therese Bleefield and Charles Bleefield (New York: G. P. Putnam's Sons, 1949), 164. Quotation taken from Stravinsky's *Chronique de ma vie.*

24. Tansman, *Igor Stravinsky,* 177.

25. Pach exhibited *Petrouchka* at the annual exhibition of the Society of Independent Artists in 1918. It was criticized by the art writer of the *New York Evening World,* who observed, "One of the boys explained it this way: the canvas portrays a little stage with three figures holding their hands straight out, resembling 'T's.' Moving toward them is an old man dragging two small forms like dolls. Streaks of light and rays of red flash across the picture. It is the symbol revealed to the artist after having seen the ballet 'Petruska.' No one else knows it." "Independent Art Closes Exhibit with Big Feast," *New York Evening World,* May 10, 1918.

26. *Modern Art Exhibition* (New York: People's Art Guild, 1917), AAA, reel 4856, frame 982. The exhibition was held throughout January and February 1917. For more information on John Weichsel and the People's Art Guild, see Gail Stavitsky, "John Weichsel and the People's Art Guild," *Archives of American Art Journal* 31 (1991): 12–19.

27. Walter Pach to Robert Harshe, December 15, 1917, Papers of the Museum of Art, Carnegie Institute, Pittsburgh, PA, AAA, reel 32, file 4050, "P." Regrettably, none of these ceramics has been located.

Chapter 6

1. Kuhn to Pach, May 2, 1913, Armory Show Papers, AAA, reel D-73, frame 32.

2. Walt to Vera Kuhn, after July 31, 1913, Kuhn Papers, AAA, reel D-240, frame 573–74.

3. Although Pach was not raised in the Jewish faith, his family was Jewish. Kuhn, who was an anti-Semite, railed against Pach's heritage when he wrote, for example, to Vera in 1912, "I had Joe Davidson with me to-day. . . . As the day went on he grew more and more 'jewy' and no doubt if he went with me much more, I'd have a run in with him. After all its all up to me, Pach is easier to handle but they all have their ax to grind." Kuhn to Vera, October 31, 1912, Kuhn Papers, AAA, reel D-240, frame 433.

4. For a more complete discussion of this exhibition, see Aaron Sheon, "1913: Pittsburgh in the Cubist Avant-Garde," *Carnegie Magazine* 56 (July/August 1982): 12–17, 38–39, and "1913: Forgotten Cubist Exhibitions in America," *Arts Magazine* 57 (March 1983): 93–107. Sheon stated, "Pach, it should be noted, had relatives who were associated with New York Department Stores; he may have suggested the showing of the paintings in such stores." While Pach knew Benjamin Altman of department store fame, most likely through Pach Brothers Studio, no Pach family member was affiliated with any department store until the 1950s. Bennard B. Perlman wrote that Davies was approached "to help organize an exhibition of cubist works to be shown between June and August, 1913, at department stores in Cleveland, Pittsburgh and Philadelphia," Perlman, *The Lives, Loves, and Art of Arthur B. Davies,* 237. Since Davies did not personally know any of the artists who participated in this show, it seems highly unlikely that he could have arranged such an exhibition.

5. See Raymond Duchamp-Villon to Walter Pach, April 18, 1913, Pach Papers, AAA, reel 4217, frames 132–33.

6. For a complete account of the American modernist show, see Laurette E. McCarthy, "Modernists on Tour: A New Look at a Historic Show," *Archives of American Art Journal* 37 (1997): 2–16. All excerpts from this article are quoted by permission of the *Archives of American Art Journal*, Smithsonian Institution.

7. Walter Pach to the director of the Museum of Fine Arts, Cincinnati, Ohio, December 5, 1913, Cincinnati Art Museum Archives. I wish to express my sincere gratitude to William K. Clark, Volunteer Archivist at the Cincinnati Art Museum, for sending me a copy of this letter.

8. Walter Pach to Clyde H. Burroughs, director, Detroit Museum of Arts, December 14, 1913, Museum Archives of the Detroit Institute of Arts. I wish to thank Mrs. Betty J. Davis for sending me copies of the correspondence between Pach and Burroughs.

9. Ruth Edelstein of the Fine Arts Department, the Carnegie Museum of Art, kindly sent the checklist of the Pittsburgh show.

10. *Exhibition of Paintings and Drawings,* Montross Gallery, New York, February 2–23, 1914, Pach Papers, AAA, reel 4221, frames 16–31. On the cover, in Pach's handwriting, is written "Priced Catalogue." Prices are noted next to the works, and additional pieces, with titles and prices, are also listed.

11. "Weird Futurist Paintings Exhibited at Art Museum," *Cincinnati Commercial Tribune,* March 29, 1914.

12. John H. Gest to Walter Pach, April 8, 1914, Cincinnati Art Museum Records, AAA, reel 2512, frame 562.

13. Louis H. Dielman to Walter Pach, April 18, 1914, Peabody Gallery of Art Records, AAA, reel 3312, frame 338.

14. Walt to Vera Kuhn, February 4, 1914, Kuhn Papers, AAA, reel D-240, frame 700. Kuhn reported, "Sold 2 paintings by Of and a Pach watercolor."

15. Arensberg wrote Pach, "If you have been married since I saw you or if you are still waiting to be married, you will scarcely have time for even a word from me." Arensberg to Pach, March 1, 1914, Pach Papers, AAA, reel 4217, frame 173. Also quoted in Perlman, *American Artists, Authors, and Collectors,* 33. Perlman states that the couple wed on February 26, 1914, but I have found no record of their wedding.

16. Pach to Dielman, March 15, 1914, Peabody Gallery of Art Records, AAA, reel 3312, frame 317. Pach wrote, "new address 33 Beekman Place, New York."

17. Pach to Dawson, April 5, 1914, Dawson Papers, AAA, reel 64, frame 884.

18. Walter to Raymond Pach, October 17, 1945, Pach Papers, Helen Farr Sloan Library and Archives, Delaware Art Museum (hereinafter Pach Papers, DAM).

19. Pach, *Queer Thing, Painting,* 218.

20. Zilczer, *"The Noble Buyer,"* 31.

21. John Quinn to Mrs. Charles C. Rumsey, November 1, 1913, quoted in Zilczer, *"The Noble Buyer,"* 31.

22. Pach to Matisse, April 27, 1914, Matisse Archives. For more on Matisse's exhibition at Montross, see Cauman, "Matisse and America," 188, 252–77.

23. Pach, *Queer Thing, Painting,* 218.

24. Pach to Matisse, October 16, 1914, Matisse Archives. Pach wrote, "I arrived in Paris yesterday." The association he referred to was the AAPS. See also Cauman, "Matisse and America," 253.

25. Walter Pach to Walter Arensberg, February 8, 1940, Arensberg Archives ©

PMA. Also quoted in Perlman, *American Artists, Authors, and Collectors,* 36.

26. Pach, *Queer Thing, Painting,* 222.

27. Walter Pach to Homer Saint-Gaudens, Director of the Carnegie Institute, November 28, 1939, Carnegie Papers, AAA, reel 32.

28. Frances to Walter Pach, November 3, 1914, Pach Papers, AAA, reel 4216, frames 204–5.

29. Birth certificate, Raymond Pach, December 26, 1914, Pach Papers, AAA, reel 4216, frame 68.

30. Walter to Raymond Pach, October 27, 1945, Pach Papers, DAM.

31. For Matisse's loan of the Gauguin, see Pach to Matisse, March 9, 1915, Matisse Archives. Pach wrote, "Your Gauguin is, since yesterday [March 8] in an exhibition at the Carroll Galleries." Pach later informed Matisse that he was responsible for the sale of this painting. Pach to Matisse, May 5, 1915, Matisse Archives.

32. For Druet's loan, see Druet to Pach, May 22, 1915, Pach Papers, AAA, reel 4217, frames 229–30.

33. Cauman, "Matisse and America, 1905–1933," 188. See also Pach to Matisse, January 19, 1915, Matisse Archives.

34. For Pach's correspondence with Matisse, see Pach to Matisse, January 19, 22, 29; February 5, 14, 26; and March 9, 1915, Matisse Archives. For more on Matisse's exhibition at Montross, see Cauman, "Matisse and America," 261–77.

35. Pach to Matisse, January 29, 1915, Matisse Archives.

36. Pach to Matisse, March 5, 1915, Matisse Archives.

37. Pach to Matisse, March 5, 1915, Matisse Archives.

38. Pach, *Queer Thing, Painting,* 223.

39. Pach to Matisse, October 21, 1915, Matisse Archives.

40. Matisse to Pach, November 20, 1915, Pach Papers, AAA, reel 4217, frames 255–60, and Cauman, "Henri Matisse's Letters to Walter Pach," 4.

41. For the Cézanne show, see Rewald, *Cézanne and America,* 288–89, and for the show at Bourgeois, see Francis Naumann, *New York Dada, 1915–23* (New York: Harry N. Abrams, 1994), 233–34n2.

42. Pach to Matisse, March 30, 1916, Matisse Archives and Cauman, "Matisse and America," 84.

43. Pach to Matisse, May 26, 1916, and November 13, 1916, Matisse Archives. For more on this exhibition, see Cauman, "Matisse and America," 308–11.

44. For a discussion of Pach's role in the Severini exhibition, see John M. Lukach, "Severini's 1917 Exhibition at Stieglitz's '291,'" *Burlington Magazine* 113 (April 1971): 196–206.

45. Pach to Matisse, September 15, 1916, Matisse Archives.

46. Pach to Matisse, November 13, 1916, Matisse Archives.

47. Pach to Matisse, November 22, 1916, Matisse Archives and Cauman, "Matisse and America," 285.

48. Walter Pach, "The Weyhe Book and Print Shop," *Publisher's Weekly* 65 (March 16, 1929): 1396.

49. Pach to Sloan, May 24, 1943, Sloan Archives.

50. Schamberg thanked Pach for "that Indian tile which has given me so much pleasure" and told his friend, "I selected the one with the big round face. Sheeler as anticipated preferred the other one so it worked out beautifully." See Morton Schamberg to Walter Pach, September 30, 1918, Pach Papers, AAA, reel 4217, frame 420. Also quoted in Perlman, *American Artists, Authors, and Collectors,* 364.

51. Walter Pach to Edgar Hewett, October 25, 1918, Pach Papers, AAA, reel 3292, frames 70–72.

52. Walter Pach to John Quinn, October 29, 1918, John Quinn Papers. Manuscripts and Archives Division. The New York Public Library, Astor, Lenox, and Tilden Foundations, New York (hereinafter Quinn Collection). Also available at the AAA on reel 2017L and quoted in Perlman, *American Artists, Authors, and Collectors,* 294.

53. Pach to Quinn, October 4, 1918, Quinn Collection.

54. Pach to Quinn, October 4, 1918, Quinn Collection.

55. Preface to "Catalogue of an Exhibition of Paintings by Contemporary American Artists at the Art Gallery of Toronto, Jan. 8th to Feb. 6th, 1921," Pach Papers, AAA, unmicrofilmed.

56. For Pach's meeting of van Gogh-Bonger, see Johanna van Gogh-Bonger to Walter Pach, August 20, 1918, Pach Papers, AAA, reel 4217, frame 417. I wish to thank Claire Rifelg of the Armand Hammer Museum for providing me with the provenance of *The Sower.* See also Walter Pach to Fiske Kimball, March 17, 1928, "They [the two van Gogh paintings] were two of the finest in the exhibition at Montross's in 1920," General Correspondence, Fiske Kimball Records, Philadelphia Museum of Art, Archives (hereinafter Kimball Records). For the exhibition of van Gogh in 1923, see Johanna van Gogh-Bonger to Pach, June 27, 1923, in which she writes, "Yes, the pictures have come back, that is to say the Steamer has arrived, But I have not yet received them. I am glad they have been shown in America. Time must work the rest. I repeat your words 'the future is sure.'" Gogh-Bonger to Pach, June 27, 1923, Pach Papers, AAA, reel 4217, frame 731. I wish to thank Patricia Schuil of Research and Documentation at the Van Gogh Museum for sharing information about this exhibition with me.

57. For information on the exhibition at Des Moines, see Lester Carl Walker, "Art in Average America: The Cultural Pattern of Des Moines, Iowa" (Ph.D. diss., Ohio State University, 1951), 290–91.

58. For the exhibition of Quinn's collection, see Walter Pach, *Paintings, Watercolors, and Sculptures Selected from the John Quinn Collection* (New York: Art Center, 1926). See also Judith Zilczer, "The Dispersal of the John Quinn Collection," *Archives of American Art Journal* 19 (1979): 15–20, and Cauman, "Matisse and America," 395–96.

59. Walter Pach, "Importance of the John Quinn Collection," *Art Center Bulletin* 4 (January 1926): 140–41.

60. Walter Pach to Fiske Kimball, March 6, 1928, Kimball Records.

61. Fiske Kimball to Walter Pach, March 9, 1928, Kimball Records.

62. Quoted in Denys Sutton, ed., *Letters of Roger Fry,* vol. 2 (New York: Random House, 1972), 560. The letter was dated September 27, 1924. Pach met Roger Fry sometime between 1906 and 1910, when Fry was the curator of paintings at the Metropolitan Museum of Art. See Pach, *Queer Thing, Painting,* 256. Pach does not give the specific date when he met Fry, but the critic was the curator of paintings, then the European advisor to the department in 1906–10. See William Innes Homer and Lloyd Goodrich, *Albert Pinkham Ryder, Painter of Dreams* (New York: Harry N. Abrams, 1989), 98. Pach may have been introduced to Fry by his father, Gotthelf Pach, who was the semiofficial photographer for the institution.

63. Walter Pach to Carl Zigrosser, October 3, 1916, Carl Zigrosser Papers, AAA, reel 4636, frame 466, and Carl Zigrosser Papers, Rare Book and Manuscript Library, University of Pennsylvania, Philadelphia.

Chapter 7

1. Pach, *Queer Thing, Painting,* 231. For more on the gatherings at the Arensbergs' apartment, see Naumann, *New York Dada,* 22–33.

2. For a description of Pach's involvement with the SIA from 1916 to 1920, see Laurette E. McCarthy, "Walter Pach: Artist, Critic, Historian, and Agent of Modernism" (Ph.D. diss., University of Delaware, 1996), chap. 6. For a full account of the first SIA show, see Francis Naumann, "The Big Show: The First Exhibition of the Society of Independent Artists, Part I," *Artforum* 17 (February 1979): 34–39, and "The Big Show: The First Exhibition of the Society of Independent Artists, Part II: The Critical Response," *Artforum* 17 (April 1979): 49–53. For the association's exhibition record, see Clark S. Marlor, *The Society of Independent Artists: The Exhibition Record, 1917–1944* (Park Ridge, N.J.: Noyes Press, 1984).

3. For the certificate of incorporation, see unpublished typescript in the Records of the Society of Independent Artists (Incorporated), John Sloan Collection, Helen Farr Sloan Library and Archives, Delaware Art Museum, Wilmington (hereinafter SIA Records). The existence of the organization was officially recognized on December 16, 1916.

4. For Quinn's assistance with the legal issue, see John Quinn to Marcel Duchamp, September 27, 1916, Quinn Collection. Quinn wrote, "One night when Pach was in my office working with me on the bylaws of the Independent Society."

5. Pach to Quinn, October 9, 1916, Quinn Collection. Also quoted in Perlman, *American Artists, Authors, and Collectors,* 279.

6. Pach to Quinn, January 30, 1917, Quinn Collection.

7. Typescript of the foreword to the 1917 catalog, on which is handwritten "Introduction to Catalogue—by Walter Pach." SIA Records. Since this introduction is almost identical to the flyer, one can assume that Pach wrote the preliminary announcement. *Announcement, the Society of Independent Artists (Incorporated),* 1917, unpaginated, SIA Records.

8. Circular for SIA 1917 exhibition, SIA Records.

9. Walter Pach to Henry McBride, January 24, 1917, Henry McBride Papers, Yale Collection of American Literature, Beinecke Rare Book and Manuscript Library.

10. Pach to Quinn, January 30, 1917, Quinn Collection. Also quoted in Perlman, *American Artists, Authors, and Collectors,* 279.

11. For a complete study concerning the *Fountain* and its history, see William A. Camfield, *Marcel Duchamp Fountain* (Houston: Houston Fine Art Press, 1989).

12. Zigrosser, *A World of Art and Museums,* 179.

13. Walter Pach to Alfred H. Barr Jr., former director of the Museum of Modern Art in New York, undated, SIA Records. Although the official, typed letter to Barr dated January 18, 1937, was signed by John Sloan, the original letter was handwritten by Walter Pach. This letter was penned in protest against a statement about the SIA that appeared in the literature connected with MoMA's exhibition Fantastic Art, Dada, and Surrealism that was held in 1936. See also Camfield, *Marcel Duchamp Fountain,* 26. According to Camfield, "There was not time enough to assemble the entire board of directors, but a group of about ten was gathered to decide the issue."

14. Marcel Duchamp to Katherine S. Dreier, April 11, 1917, Dreier Papers. All letters of Marcel Duchamp © Succession Marcel Duchamp, 2011 Artists Rights Society (ARS) New York/ADAGP, Paris.

15. William Ivins to Fiske Kimball, March 15, 1954, William Mills Ivins Papers, AAA, unmicrofilmed. Ivins, former curator of prints at the Metropolitan Museum of Art, recalled, "Walter Pach for a while came [to the Arensbergs] quite regularly, but he had his celebrated falling down or out with Duchamp and as Duchamp was there all the time Walter Pach rather faded away." See also Duchamp-Villon to Pach, May 20, 1918, AAA, reel 4217, frames 408–9. Duchamp-Villon wrote that he was glad the rift

between Pach and his brother was mended. It is my belief that this refers to the rift caused by the rejection of Duchamp's *Fountain* from the 1917 SIA.

16. "Foreword," *Catalogue of the First Annual Exhibition of the Society of Independent Artists (Incorporated),* 1917, unpaginated, SIA Records.

17. Walter Pach, "Speech for an SIA dinner honoring John Sloan," April 7, 1941, Pach Papers, AAA, reel 4220, frames 434–35.

18. Pach to Mr. [John] Marin, April 24, 1917, Dreier Papers.

19. Pach to Dreier, May 2, 1917, Dreier Papers.

20. Pach to Dreier, May 2, 1917, Dreier Papers.

21. Pach to Quinn, April 8, 1918, Quinn Collection. Also quoted in Perlman, *American Artists, Authors, and Collectors,* 291.

22. "Foreword," *Catalogue of the Second Annual Exhibition of the Society of Independent Artists (Incorporated),* 1918, unpaginated, SIA Records.

23. Pach to Matisse, March 19, 1918, Matisse Archives.

24. *Announcement of the Third Annual Exhibition of the Society of Independent Artists (Incorporated),* 1918, unpaginated, SIA Records.

25. Pach to McBride, March 8, 1919, McBride Papers, Yale Collection of American Literature, Beinecke Rare Book and Manuscript Library.

26. Walter Pach, "The Independents," *Dial 66* (March 22, 1919): 307–8.

27. Walter Pach to James N. Rosenberg, February 6, 1920, James N. Rosenberg Papers, Archives of American Art, reel 674, frame 68.

28. James N. Rosenberg to Walter Pach, February 19, 1920, James N. Rosenberg Papers, AAA, reel 674, frame 70.

29. Edgar Hewett to Walter Pach, February 2, 1920, Pach Papers, AAA, reel 4217, frame 505.

30. For Field's attack on Pach and Pach's response, see Hamilton Easter Field, "The Opening of the Independent Show," *Brooklyn Daily Eagle,* March 14, 1920; Walter Pach, "Mr. Pach Replies to Mr. Field," *Brooklyn Daily Eagle,* March 14, 1920; and Hamilton Easter Field, "An Answer to Walter Pach," *Brooklyn Daily Eagle,* March 21, 1920. See also Marlor, *The Society of Independent Artists,* 16–18.

31. Helen Farr Sloan, interview by the author, April 6, 1994, Wilmington, Del.

32. The 1920 audit shows a surplus of $1,986.15. See SIA Records.

33. Pach to Rosenberg, April 7, 1920, James N. Rosenberg Papers, AAA, reel 674, frame 74.

34. *Announcement of the Fourth Annual Exhibition of the Society of Independent Artists (Incorporated),* 1920, unpaginated, SIA Records.

35. For the dispute and Field's founding of the Salons of America, see "Artists Squabble on Eve of Show," *New York Times,* February 24, 1922, and Clark Marlor, *The Salons of America, 1922–1936* (Madison, Conn.: Sound View Press, 1991), 9.

36. For the show of Mexican artists, see Diego Rivera to Walter Pach, December 7, 1922, Pach Papers, AAA, reel 4217, frames 682–85; Maragarita Nieto, "Mexican Art and Los Angeles, 1920–1940," in *On the Edge of America: California Modernist Artists, 1900–1950* (Berkeley and Los Angeles: University of California Press, 1996), 124; and Marlor, *The Society of Independent Artists,* 16 .

37. Marlor, *The Society of Independent Artists,* 20. For more on this event, the trials, and Sloan's participation in the SIA, see John Loughery, *John Sloan: Painter and Rebel* (New York: Henry Holt, 1995), 231, 233–35, 242–44, 249, 256–57, 266–67, 275–79, 318, 343, 346, 369.

38. Marlor, *The Society of Independent Artists,* 20.

39. For further history on the SIA, see Marlor, *The Society of Independent Artists,* 22–52.

Chapter 8

1. Pach to Matisse, October 21, 1915, Matisse Archives. Matisse thanked him for the sale and the money. Matisse to Pach, November 20, 1915, AAA, reel 4217, frames 255–60, and Cauman, "Henri Matisse's Letters to Walter Pach," 5.

2. Pach to Matisse, March 30, 1916, Matisse Archives. The Arensbergs paid four thousand francs for the work. See also Cauman, "Matisse and America," 283–85.

3. Pach to Matisse, March 30, 1916, Matisse Archives.

4. Matisse to Pach, April 28, 1916, AAA, reel 4217, frames 289–90, and Cauman, "Henri Matisse's Letters to Walter Pach," 6.

5. For Pach's relationship with Quinn, see Zilczer, *"The Noble Buyer,"* and Cauman, "Matisse and America," 314–408.

6. For the sale of the *Nude Descending a Staircase, No. 1,* see Quinn to Pach, August 30 and October 8, 1915, and Pach to Quinn, September 27 and October 4 and 5, 1915, Quinn Collection, and Perlman, *American Artists, Authors, and Collectors,* 267, 269, 270. See also Francis M. Naumann, ed., *Affectionately, Marcel: The Selected Correspondence of Marcel Duchamp* (Ghent: Ludion Press, 2000), 42; Calvin Tomkins, *Duchamp: A Biography* (New York: Henry Holt), 148; and Cauman, "Matisse and America," 286, 330–31.

7. For the sale of the Brancusis, see Walter Pach to Constantin Brancusi, September 23, 1915, quoted in Pontus Hulten, Natalia Dumitresco, and Alexandre Istrati, *Brancusi* (New York: Harry N. Abrams, 1987), 100. Brancusi gave the Pachs the cast of *The Kiss,* displayed at the Armory Show, as a wedding

gift. See Anna C. Chave, *Constantin Brancusi: Shifting the Bases of Art* (New Haven: Yale University Press, 1993), 205.

8. Pach to Quinn, July 14, 1915, Quinn Collection. Also quoted in Perlman, *American Artists, Authors, and Collectors,* 261.

9. Albert Gleizes, "Unpublished Incidents and Letters Showing the Spirit of Workers in Various Arts Now on the Firing Line," Pach Papers, AAA, reel 4220, frame 73.

10. Pach to Quinn, April 15, 1915, Quinn Collection. Also quoted in Perlman, *American Artists, Authors, and Collectors,* 252–53.

11. Pach to Quinn, September 27, 1915, Quinn Collection. Also quoted in Perlman, *American Artists, Authors, and Collectors,* 269. Belle Greene had been the librarian of the J. Pierpont Morgan library.

12. Quinn to Pach, October 8, 1915, Quinn Collection. Also quoted in Perlman, *American Artists, Authors, and Collectors,* 270.

13. Pach to Quinn, October 10, 1915, Quinn Collection. Also quoted in Perlman, *American Artists, Authors, and Collectors,* 271. Pach's father knew Belle Greene from having photographed J. P. Morgan and having been a frequent visitor to the Morgan household.

14. Marcel Duchamp to John Quinn, November 5, 1915, Quinn Collection. All letters of Marcel Duchamp © Succession Marcel Duchamp, 2011 Artists Rights Society (ARS) New York/ADAGP, Paris.

15. Pach to Quinn, May 29, 1915, Quinn Collection. Also quoted in Perlman, *American Artists, Authors, and Collectors,* 256. For more on the Arensbergs and their collection, see Naumann, "Walter Conrad Arensberg," 3–33.

16. Duchamp sent two paintings and a drawing to Pach in April 1915: *The Nude Descending a Staircase, No. 1, The Passage from the Virgin to the Bride,* and a large drawing on board. Duchamp to Pach, April 2, 1915, AAA, reel, 4219, frames 332–35. See also Naumann,

"Amicalement, Marcel: Fourteen Letters from Marcel Duchamp to Walter Pach," *Archives of American Art Journal* 29 (1989): 39, 48n25. Pach kept *The Passage from the Virgin to the Bride.*

17. Walter Pach to Henry McBride, November 2, 1915, McBride Papers, Yale Collection of American Literature, Beinecke Rare Book and Manuscript Library.

18. John Quinn to Raymond Duchamp-Villon, January 17, 1916, Quinn Collection.

19. Quinn to Pach, July 13, 1917, Quinn Collection.

20. Quinn to Pach, August 1, 1917, Quinn Collection. Also quoted in Perlman, *American Artists, Authors, and Collectors,* 287.

21. Harriet C. Bryant to John Quinn, September 13, 1917, Quinn Collection. Emphasis in the original.

22. John Quinn to Harriet C. Bryant, September 14, 1917, Quinn Collection.

23. Pach to Quinn, December 6, 1918, Quinn Collection.

24. As far as I can determine, Quinn paid Pach only $120.00 in commission on the purchase of four landscape paintings by André Derain obtained through Ambroise Vollard. Pach used eighty-three dollars of these funds to cover the cost of shipping the remaining inventory from the Carroll Galleries to France in 1919.

25. Pach to Dawson, February 4, 1919, Dawson Papers, AAA, reel 64, frame 692.

26. Frederick Torrey to Walter Pach, January 3, 1919, Pach Papers, AAA, reel 417, frame 453. See also Francis M. Naumann, "Frederick C. Torrey and Duchamp's *Nude Descending a Staircase,*" in *West Coast Duchamp,* ed. Bonnie Clearwater (Miami Beach, Fla.: Grassfield Press, 1991).

27. Torrey to Pach, February 3, 1919, Pach Papers, AAA, reel 4217, frames 456–57.

28. For Pach and Quinn's letter to Matisse, Derain, and Picasso, see "Letter from Walter Pach to Matisse, Derain and Picasso,—Final

Form," enclosed in Pach to Quinn, June 15, 1919, Quinn Collection. Also quoted in Perlman, *American Artists, Authors, and Collectors,* 297–98. See also Cauman, "Matisse and America," 331–32.

29. Pach to Matisse, June 14, 1919, Matisse Archives.

30. "Letter from Walter Pach to Matisse, Derain, and Picasso,—Final Form," enclosed in Pach to Quinn, June 15, 1919, Quinn Collection. Also quoted in Perlman, *American Artists, Authors, and Collectors,* 298. See also Cauman, "Matisse and America," 331–32. Through Quinn's legal efforts the custom duty on contemporary art imported to the United States was lifted. See Zilczer, *"The Noble Buyer,"* 30–31.

31. "Letter from Walter Pach to Matisse, Derain, and Picasso,—Final Form," enclosed in Pach to Quinn, June 15, 1919, Quinn Collection. Also quoted in Perlman, *American Artists, Authors, and Collectors,* 298. See also Cauman, "Matisse and America," 331–32.

32. Pach to Quinn, April 6 and May 18, 1920, Quinn Collection. Also quoted in Perlman, *American Artists, Authors, and Collectors,* 304, 305.

33. Pach to Quinn, December 23, 1923, Quinn Collection. Also quoted in Perlman, *American Artists, Authors, and Collectors,* 316. See also Cauman, "Matisse and America," 388–89.

34. Walter Pach to Thomas Curtin, August 3, 1924, Quinn Collection. Also quoted in Perlman, *American Artists, Authors, and Collectors,* 319.

35. Pach to Curtin, October 15, 1924, Quinn Collection. Also quoted in Perlman, *American Artists, Authors, and Collectors,* 321.

36. For the sale of the Quinn Collection, see Zilczer, "The Dispersal of the John Quinn Collection," 15–20, and Cauman, "Matisse and America," 395–96.

37. Douglas W. Druick and Gloria Groom, "'Almost by a Miracle': *La Grande Jatte* at the Art Institute of Chicago," in Robert L. Herbert, ed., *Seurat and the Making of "La Grande Jatte"* (Chicago: Art Institute of Chicago in association with University of Chicago Press, 2004). As noted in the essay, "Bartlett's address book includes the New York residence of critic Walter Pach" (15).

38. For the sale of the *Study for "A Sunday on La Grande Jatte"* to Adolph Lewisohn, see Félix Fénéon to Walter Pach, May 19, 1919. On the envelope in Pach's writing is Fénéon receipt for Seurat check. Pach Papers, AAA, reel 4217, frame 466. Lewisohn bought the work in 1919 from Bourgeois Gallery, where it had been since its 1916 showing.

39. For Pach and Tovell, see Harold Tovell to Walter Pach, October 25, 1929, Pach Papers, AAA, reel 4218, frames 252–55.

40. Marcel Duchamp to Dr. Harold Tovell, September 13, 1926, enclosed in a letter from Pach to Arensberg, summer or fall 1950, Arensberg Archives © PMA. Also quoted in Perlman, *American Artists, Authors, and Collectors,* 51. See also Zilczer, *"The Noble Buyer,"* 85. All letters of Marcel Duchamp © Succession Marcel Duchamp, 2011 Artists Rights Society (ARS) New York/ADAGP, Paris.

41. For the relationship between Pach and the Bakwins, see Ruth Bakwin, "Unpublished Memoirs of Ruth Bakwin." I wish to express my sincere appreciation to Mr. Gregory Selch, grandson of the Bakwins, for providing me with a copy of this writing.

42. Bakwin, "Unpublished Memoirs of Ruth Bakwin," 53–55.

43. Bakwin, "Unpublished Memoirs of Ruth Bakwin," 60.

44. Pach to Kimball, January 30, 1929, Kimball Papers. Also quoted in Perlman, *American Artists, Authors, and Collectors,* 189.

45. Walter Pach to Bryson Burroughs, January 20, 1931, the Metropolitan Museum of Art Archives, New York. Also quoted in Perlman, *American Artists, Authors, and Collectors,* 123–24.

46. Burroughs to Pach, February 6, 1931, the Metropolitan Museum of Art Archives, New York. Also quoted in Perlman, *American Artists, Authors, and Collectors,* 124.

47. Burroughs to Pach, March 28, 1931, Pach Papers, AAA, reel 4218, frame 329. Also quoted in Perlman, *American Artists, Authors, and Collectors,* 126.

48. Burroughs to Pach, March 31, 1931, Pach Papers, AAA, reel 4218, frame 331. Also quoted in Perlman, *American Artists, Authors, and Collectors,* 127.

49. Susan Eakins to Pach, January 25, 1931, Pach Papers, AAA, reel 4218, frame 310. Also quoted in Perlman, *American Artists, Authors, and Collectors,* 161.

50. Burroughs to Pach, April 14, 1931, Pach Papers, AAA, reel 4218, frame 333. Also quoted in Perlman, *American Artists, Authors, and Collectors,* 128.

51. Several letters were exchanged before the painting was actually shipped to Paris.

52. Pach to Quinn, October 19, 1919, Quinn Collection. Also quoted in Perlman, *American Artists, Authors, and Collectors,* 301.

53. For Pach and Matisse's meeting and business arrangements, see Cauman, "Henri Matisse's Letters to Walter Pach," 6–10. See also Matisse to Pach, September 7, 1921, Pach Papers, AAA, reel 4217, frames 598–99; Pach, *Queer Thing, Painting,* 166; and Walter Pach to Erhard Weyhe, October 19, 1921, Carl Zigrosser Papers, Rare Book and Manuscript Library, University of Pennsylvania, Philadelphia (hereinafter Zigrosser Papers).

54. Jean Metzinger to Walter Pach, May 19, 1925, Pach Papers, AAA, reel 4218, frames 39–40.

55. Pach to Sloan, February 22, 1931, Sloan Archives. Also quoted in Perlman, *American Artists, Authors, and Collectors,* 373.

56. Walter Pach, "The Shilling Fund," *The New Republic* 114 (February 4, 1946): 159. See also Perlman, introduction to *American Artists, Authors, and Collectors,* 23.

57. Fred Stein and Arthur L. Strasser to Walter Pach, March 21, 1942, Pach Papers, AAA, reel 4218, frame 679. This letter states that "the Shilling Fund has been in existence since March 15, 1937."

58. Strasser and Stein to Pach, February 8, 1946, Pach Papers, AAA, reel 4219, frame 146.

59. M. M. Pochapin, managing director, Art Appreciation Movement, to Walter Pach, May 6, 1942, Pach Papers, AAA, reel 4218, frames 680–81.

60. Pochapin to Magda Pach, May 13, 1942, Pach Papers, AAA, reel 4218, frames 682–83.

61. Marcel Duchamp to Walter Pach, September 28, 1937, Pach Papers, AAA, reel 4216, frames 569–70. All letters of Marcel Duchamp © Succession Marcel Duchamp, 2011 Artists Rights Society (ARS) New York/ADAGP, Paris. See also Naumann, *Affectionately, Marcel,* 215–16. For more on the sale of this painting, see Tompkins, *Duchamp,* 310–11. As of July 20, 1942, the Pachs had their property from 148 West Seventy-second Street removed to the Beverly Storage Warehouse at 304 East Sixty-first Street, New York. Duchamp's *Sad Young Man on a Train* is not listed on the insurance policy for works of art that the Pachs placed in storage when they departed for Mexico. See Raymond B. Humphrey, director, Brown, Crosby and Co., Inc., Insurance to Pach, September 3, 1942, Pach Papers, AAA, reel 4218, frames 706–12. It is highly unlikely that they brought Duchamp's painting to Mexico and probably sold it to Peggy Guggenheim before their departure. In October 1942, dealer Robert Lebel wrote Pach that "the famous Peggy Guggenheim Museum comes to be inaugurated and we have reviewed the Duchamp that one had to tear away from you." Robert Lebel to Walter

Pach, October 22, 1942, Pach Papers, AAA, reel 4218, frame 734.

62. Pach to Arensberg, June 21, 1950, Arensberg Archives © PMA. Also quoted in Perlman, *American Artists, Authors, and Collectors,* 44.

63. Arensberg to Pach, June 29, 1950, Arensberg Archives © PMA. Also quoted in Perlman, *American Artists, Authors, and Collectors,* 46.

64. Pach to Arensberg, May 28, 1949, Arensberg Archives © PMA. Also quoted in Perlman, *American Artists, Authors, and Collectors,* 44.

65. For Matisse's son coming to the United States, see Matisse to Pach, November 18 and December 5, 1924, Pach Papers, AAA, reel 4217, frames 827–30, Cauman, "Matisse and America," 397–403, and John Russell, *Matisse: Father & Son* (New York: Harry N. Abrams, 1999), 34–40.

66. Matisse to Pach, November 18 and December 5, 1924, Pach Papers, AAA, reel 4217, frames 827–30. See also Cauman, "Henri Matisse's Letters to Walter Pach," 11.

67. For the show at Weyhe, see Russell, *Matisse: Father and Son,* 37. The show ran March 25–April 6, 1925.

68. Pach to Guggenheimer, August 29, 1930, Guggenheimer Papers.

69. Pach to Mumford, May 17, 1930, folder 3764, Mumford Papers.

70. Pach to Guggenheimer, November 1, 1929, Guggenheimer Papers.

71. Pach to Guggenheimer, January 30, 1930, Guggenheimer Papers.

72. Mumford to Pach, March 12, 1930, Pach Papers, AAA, reel 4218, frames 271–72, Courtesy of Lewis and Sophia Mumford. Also quoted in Perlman, *American Artists, Authors, and Collectors,* 215.

73. Pach to Mumford, May 17, 1930, folder 3764, Mumford Papers.

Chapter 9

1. Thomas H. Goetz, *Taine and the Fine Arts* (Madrid: Coleccion Scholar Universal, 1973), 20.

2. Walter Pach, notebooks from his lectures delivered at the University of California, Berkeley, June 26, 1918, Pach Papers, AAA, reel 4220, frame 286. Pach, Notebooks, July 2, 1918, Pach Papers, AAA, reel 4220, frame 291.

3. Walter Pach to Mr. Leonard, December 13, 1919, Sidney C. Woodward Collection of Nineteenth and Twentieth Century American, English and some European Artists' Letters, Archives of American Art, Smithsonian Institution, Washington, D.C., reel D194, frame 329.

4. Walter Pach, "Winslow Homer," *L'Art et les Artistes* 16 (November 1912): 73–79, and "L'art de John Sloan," *L'Art et les Artistes* 18 (October 1913–March 1914): 222–26; translation mine.

5. Pach, "Winslow Homer," 77.

6. Pach to Quinn, February 3, 1915, Quinn Collection.

7. Pach to Dawson, April 25, 1914, Dawson Papers, AAA, reel 64, frame 887.

8. Walter Pach, "The Point of View of the 'Moderns,'" *Century* 87 (April 1914): 851–52.

9. Pach, "The Point of View of the 'Moderns,'" 862, 863.

10. Walter Pach, "Why Matisse?" *Century* 89 (February 1915): 634.

11. Cauman, "Matisse and America," 277.

12. Pach to Quinn, February 3, 1915, Quinn Collection. Pach wrote Mumford in 1923, "In 1914 William C. Brownell asked me to write it for Scribner's (the book house, not the magazine) and have had a couple of other good offers to publish it." Pach to Mumford, July 6, 1923, folder 3764, Mumford Papers. Also quoted in Perlman, *American Artists, Authors, and Collectors,* 205.

13. Quinn to Pach, February 4, 1915, Quinn Collection.

14. Pach to Mumford, July 6, 1923, folder 3764, Mumford Papers.

15. Pach to Quinn, February 2, 1915, Quinn Collection. Also quoted in Perlman, *American Artists, Authors, and Collectors,* 250.

16. John Quinn to Allan Dawson, April 30, 1915, Quinn Collection. Also quoted in Perlman, *American Artists, Authors, and Collectors,* 253–54.

17. Walter Pach, "French Art and War," *New York Times,* March 5, 1916.

18. Antliff, *Anarchist Modernism,* 173.

19. Antliff, *Anarchist Modernism,* 174.

20. Allan Antliff, "Interpellating Modernity: Cubism and 'La Vie Unanime' in America," in *American Modernism Across the Arts: Studies on Themes and Motifs in Literature* (New York: Peter Lang, 2001), 63.

21. Antliff, *Anarchist Modernism,* 176.

22. Antliff, "Interpellating Modernity,"63.

23. Wallace Stevens to Carl Zigrosser, July 10, 1918, quoted in Wallace Stevens, *Letters of Wallace Stevens,* ed. Holly Stevens (New York: Alfred A. Knopf, 1966), 209. Permission to publish courtesy of Peter B. Hanchak.

24. Pach to Quinn, April 26, 1919, Quinn Collection.

25. See "The Dial Magazine: History and Bibliography," http://virtual.clemson.edu/groups/dial/dialhist.htm, 2008.

26. Walter Pach, "The Schamberg Exhibition," *Dial* 66 (May 17, 1919): 506.

27. Ben Wolf, *Morton Livingston Schamberg: A Monograph* (Philadelphia: University of Pennsylvania Press, 1963), 35.

28. For a complete discussion of Pach's ideas on Native American art, see William Jackson Rushing III, "Native American Art and Culture and the New York Avant-Garde, 1910–1950" (Ph.D. diss., University of Texas at Austin, 1989), 154–62.

29. Walter Pach, "The Art of the American Indian," *Dial* 68 (January 1920): 58.

30. Walter Pach, "Notes on the Indian Water-Colours," *Dial* 68 (March 1920): 343.

31. Rushing, "Native American Art and Culture," 156–57.

32. The articles in the *Christian Science Monitor* were unsigned, but Pach was the author.

33. Walter Pach, "The Approach to Modern Art: Ingres and Delacroix as Moderns," *Christian Science Monitor,* January 14, 1920, 14.

34. Pach, "The Approach to Modern Art: And the Enjoyment It Offers," *Christian Science Monitor,* January 26, 1920, 14.

35. Susan Jane Turner, *A History of the Freeman: Literary Landmark of the Early Twenties* (New York: Columbia University Press, 1963).

36. "Art in America: I," *Freeman* 2 (November 10, 1920): 206.

37. "Art in America: II," *Freeman* 2 (November 17, 1920): 233, 232.

38. Walter Pach, "At an Exhibition of Photography," *Freeman* 2 (February 23, 1921): 565–66.

39. Walter Pach, "At the Pennsylvania Academy," *Freeman* 3 (May 18, 1921): 233.

40. Pach first wrote Brooks in 1920 and the two corresponded for the rest of their lives. Walter Pach to Van Wyck Brooks, October 28, 1920, Van Wyck Brooks Papers, Rare Book and Manuscript Library, University of Pennsylvania, Philadelphia (hereinafter Brooks Papers). For Mumford's recollection of his correspondence with Pach, see Mumford to Pach, April 29, 1957, Mumford Papers, courtesy of the Estate of Lewis and Sophia Mumford. Also quoted in Perlman, *American Artists, Authors, and Collectors,* 222.

41. Harold E. Stearns, preface to *Civilization in the United States: An Inquiry by Thirty Americans* (Westport, Conn.: Greenwood Press, 1971), iii.

42. Pach to Mumford, June 9, 1922, folder 3764, Mumford Papers.

43. Walter Pach, "Art," in *Civilization in the United States,* 228, 229, 241.

44. Walter Pach, "The Approach to Modern Art: And the Enjoyment It Offers," *Christian Science Monitor,* January 26, 1920, 14.

45. Walter Pach, "Art: The Contemporary Classics," *Freeman* 3 (July 13, 1921): 424.

46. Herbert, *Seurat and the Making of "La Grande Jatte,"* 15.

47. Herbert, "*La Grande Jatte* and Seurat, 1892–1965," 155.

48. Pach to Quinn, March 22, 1923, Quinn Collection.

49. Suzanne La Follette to Walter Pach, September 10, 1922, Pach Papers, AAA, reel 4217, frame 663.

50. Walter Pach, *The Masters of Modern Art* (New York: B. W. Huebsch, 1924), 3.

51. Pach, *The Masters of Modern Art,* 13.

52. Pach, *The Masters of Modern Art,* 102.

53. Undated *New York Times* clipping, Pach Papers, AAA, reel 4221, frames 88–90.

54. Guy Eglington, quoted in Susan Noyes Platt, *Modernism in the 1920s: Interpretations of Modern Art in New York from Expressionism to Constructivism* (Ann Arbor, Mich.: UMI Research Press, 1985) 40; Robert Allerton Parker, "Review of The Masters of Modern Art, by Walter Pach," *Arts* 7 (January 1925): 51.

55. Platt, *Modernism in the 1920s,* 40.

56. Meier-Graefe praised *The Masters of Modern Art.* He also congratulated Pach on being the first American to attempt, and succeed at, a serious examination of art from Corot to the present, though he pointed out Pach's failure to cite the German contributions. Julius Meier-Graefe to Walter Pach, Pach Papers, AAA, reel 4217, frames 788–90.

57. Mumford to Pach, July 5, 1923, Mumford Papers, courtesy of the Estate of Lewis and Sophia Mumford. Also quoted in Perlman, *American Artists, Authors, and Collectors,* 205.

58. Pach to Mumford, July 6, 1923, folder 3764, Mumford Papers. Also quoted in Perlman, *American Artists, Authors, and Collectors,* 205.

59. Xavier Martínez to Walter Pach, December 3, 1924, AAA, reel 4217, frame 833.

60. Pach to Quinn, November 30, 1920, Quinn Collection.

61. William C. Agee, *Raymond Duchamp-Villon, 1876–1918,* introduction by George Heard Hamilton, notes by William C. Agee (New York: Walker, 1967); Judith Zilczer, "Raymond Duchamp-Villon: Pioneer of Modern Sculpture," *Philadelphia Museum of Art Bulletin* 76 (Fall 1980): 2–24; and "Raymond Duchamp-Villon and the American Avant-Garde," *Archives of American Art Journal* 38 (1998): 14–27.

62. Walter Pach, "Is Cubism Pure Art?—a Debate: Picasso's Achievement," *Forum* 23 (June 1925): 770.

63. Walter Pach, *Modern Art in America* (New York: C. W. Kraushaar Art Galleries, 1928), 7.

64. Pach, *Modern Art in America,* 22.

65. C. J. Bulliet, "Walter Pach Tells How Bad Are Our Bad Artists Today," *Chicago Evening Post,* May 17, 1927.

66. José Clemente Orozco to Jean Charlot, March 10, 1928, quoted in *The Artist in New York: Letters to Jean Charlot and Unpublished Writings, 1925–1929,* foreword and notes by Jean Charlot (Austin: University of Texas Press, 1974), 45. Permission to publish these letters courtesy of Clemente Orozco Valladares.

67. Orozco to Charlot, September 10, 1928, quoted in *The Artist in New York,* 65.

68. Arthur B. Spingarn to Walter Pach, November 1, 1928, Pach Papers, AAA, reel 4218, frame 217.

69. Copy of letter from Orozco to Ruth Raphael, November 14, 1928, Pach Papers, AAA, reel 4218, frames 219–21.

70. Pearl Gross, "Pach Attacks Mediocre Art Shown in U.S.," *Washington Herald,* November 19, 1928.

71. "Pach to Talk," *Cleveland News,* January 6, 1929, Cleveland Museum of Art Archives.

72. Grace V. Kelly, "Pach Also Fires at 'False' Critics: Speaks at Art Museum; Explains and Elaborates on 'Ananias,'" *Cleveland Plain Dealer,* January 12, 1929, Cleveland Museum of Art Archives.

73. Edward Alden Jewell, "Walter Pach Fires a Salvo Against 'Official' Art," review of *Ananias, or the False Artist, New York Times Book Review,* November 25, 1928.

74. Lee Simonson to Walter Pach, December 18, 1928, Pach Papers, AAA, reel 4218, frames 222–23.

75. Lee Simonson, "God and the Esthetic Prig," *Creative Arts,* January 1929, lii.

76. William Howe Downes, "John Ruskin and Walter Pach: Defenders of the Faith," *American Magazine of Art* 20 (June 1929): 458. Emphasis in the original.

77. Walter Pach, *Vincent Van Gogh, 1853–1890: A Study of the Artist and His Work in Relation to His Times* (New York: Artbook Museum, 1936), dust jacket.

78. Pach, "The Approach to Modern Art: And the Enjoyment It Offers," *Christian Science Monitor,* January 26, 1920, 14.

79. Walter Pach, "A Modern Artist," *Freeman* 2 (December 8, 1920): 302.

80. Pach, *Vincent van Gogh,* 10.

81. Edward Alden Jewell, "Mr. Pach's Excellent Study of Van Gogh," *New York Times Book Review,* May 24, 1936, 5.

82. Brooks to Pach, November 9, 1938, Brooks Papers. Also quoted in Perlman, *American Artists, Authors, and Collectors,* 101.

83. Pach to Brooks, November 14, 1938, Brooks Papers.

84. Edward Alden Jewell, "Walter Pach's Reflections on Art," *New York Times Book Review,* December 4, 1938.

85. Oliver Larkin, quoted in Pach to Guggenheimer, November 28, 1938, Guggenheimer Papers.

86. Walter Pach, "Art Must Be Modern," *Atlantic Monthly* 185 (May 1950), 41, 46.

87. Walter to Raymond Pach, March 18, 1946, Pach Papers, DAM.

88. Pach to Sloan, July 11, 1948, Sloan Archives.

89. Pach to Brooks, March 4, 1954, Brooks Papers. Also quoted in Perlman, *American Artists, Authors, and Collectors,* 116.

90. Walter Pach to Jacques Villon, March 1, 1954, Fonds Jacques Villon, Pac. W. 11 8139.271, Correspondence, Bibliothèque Kandinsky, Centre de Documentation et Recherché du Musée National d'Art Moderne—Centre de Création Industrielle, Centre Georges Pompidou, Paris, France, translation courtesy of Susan Berger.

91. Pach to Sachs, October 17, 1954, Sachs File. Also quoted in Perlman, *American Artists, Authors, and Collectors,* 356.

92. Walter Pach to Bernard Berenson, February 3, 1955, the Berenson Archive, the Harvard University Center for Italian Renaissance Studies, Villa I Tatti, courtesy of the President and Fellows of Harvard College. Also quoted in Perlman, *American Artists, Authors, and Collectors,* 91.

93. Platt, *Modernism in the 1920s,* 40.

94. Phillips, "The Art Criticism of Walter Pach," 121.

Chapter 10

1. For Pach's appointment to Berkeley, see *Summer Session Bulletin,* University of California, Berkeley, the Bancroft Library, University of California, Berkeley. I wish to thank William M. Roberts, university archivist, for sending me the materials related to Pach's teaching at Berkeley.

2. Walter Pach, notebooks from his lectures delivered at the University of California, Berkeley, June 24–August 2, 1918, Pach Papers, AAA, reel 4220, frames 278–96, 298–326. Unless noted otherwise, all quotes from Pach's lecture notes and all references to these classes are taken from this source.

3. "Art and Artists Find Spokesman in Walter Pach," *Summer Session* (University of California, Berkeley), July 1, 1918, 1. Courtesy of the Bancroft Library, University of California, Berkeley.

4. "Critic Explains Why Our Bad Art Is Bad," *Summer Session* (University of California, Berkeley), July 25, 1918, 3, courtesy of the Bancroft Library, University of California, Berkeley.

5. "Art and Artists Find Spokesman in Walter Pach," *Summer Session* (University of California, Berkeley), July 1, 1918, last page, courtesy of the Bancroft Library, University of California, Berkeley.

6. Walter Pach to Edward Duff Belkan, December 27, 1923, Carnegie Institute Papers, AAA, reel 32, file 4050.

7. For the summer session at the Louvre, see preliminary announcement for the summer session, 1926, and report of the summer session, 1926, *New York University, Department of Fine Arts, Summer School Art Courses in Paris* (New York: New York University, 1927). I would like to thank Galen J. White, former archival assistant at New York University, for providing me with the materials related to Pach's work for NYU.

8. Pach to Sachs, February 19, 1932, Sachs File. Also quoted in Perlman, *American Artists, Authors, and Collectors,* 343–44.

9. Walter Pach, "Address at the Worcester Opening of the International 1933," *Parnassus* 5 (January 1933): 23.

10. Pach's notes on the Whitney Museum symposium, Pach Papers, AAA, reel 4220, frames 265–70.

11. Typewritten letter by Arthur L. Strasser, September 22, 1937, Guggenheimer Papers.

12. Pach to Guggenheimer, September 26, 1937, Guggenheimer Papers.

13. Pach to Sachs, April 27, 1946, Sachs File.

14. Wallace Stevens to Walter Pach, May 4, 1928, Pach Papers, AAA, reel 4218, frames 192–93. Permission to publish courtesy of Peter B. Hanchak.

15. Walter Pach to Wallace Stevens, May 10, 1928, Wallace Stevens Correspondence, Huntington Art Gallery, San Marino, California. This item is reproduced by permission of the Huntington Library, San Marino, California. Permission also granted by Peter B. Hanchak.

16. Walter to Raymond Pach, November 7, 1946, Pach Papers, DAM.

Chapter 11

1. Nieto, "Mexican Art and Los Angeles, 1920–1940," 123.

2. *Queer Thing, Painting,* 287.

3. Pach to Quinn, May 23, 1922, Quinn Collection. Also quoted in Perlman, *American Artists, Authors, and Collectors,* 311.

4. Pach to Sloan, July 28, 1922, Sloan Archives.

5. Walter Pach to Yvonne Duchamp-Villon, September 30, 1922, Correspondence, Bibliothèque Kandinsky, Centre de Documentation et Recherché du Musée National d'Art Moderne—Centre de Création Industrielle, Centre Georges Pompidou, Paris, France, translation courtesy of Susan Berger.

6. Pach to Quinn, September 20, 1922, Quinn Collection.

7. Pach to Quinn, September 20, 1922, Quinn Collection.

8. Pach to Yvonne Duchamp-Villon, September 30, 1922, Correspondence, Bibliothèque Kandinsky, Centre de Documentation et Recherché du Musée National d'Art Moderne—Centre de Création Industrielle, Centre Georges Pompidou, Paris, France, translation courtesy of Susan Berger.

9. Jean Charlot to Walter Pach, March 31, 1923, Pach Papers, AAA, reel 4217, frames 715–16.

10. Diego Rivera to Walter Pach, July 3, 1923, Pach Papers, AAA, reel 4217, frames 733–34, translation courtesy of Alba Fernández-Keys, © 2009 Banco de México Diego Rivera Frida Kahlo Museums Trust, México, D.F./Artists Rights Society (ARS).

11. "Mexican Independents Accept Local Society's Invitation," *New York Times,* December 17, 1922.

12. For the show of Mexican artists, see Diego Rivera to Walter Pach, December 7, 1922, Pach Papers, AAA, reel 4217, frames 682–85; Nieto, "Mexican Art and Los Angeles, 1920–1940," 124, and Marlor, *The Society of Independent Artists,* 16.

13. "The Independents," *Freeman* 7 (April 18, 1923): 135–37.

14. Rivera to Pach, July 3, 1923, Pach Papers, AAA, reel 4217, frames 733–34, translation courtesy of Alba Fernández-Keys, © 2009 Banco de México Diego Rivera Frida Kahlo Museums Trust, México, D.F./Artists Rights Society (ARS).

15. For Charlot's exhibition, see Walter Pach, "An Exhibition of Art by Mexican School-children and Jean Charlot," *Art Center Bulletin* (April 1926): 244–46. For Rufino Tamayo's shows, see Anna Indych-López, "'None of Those Little Donkeys for Me': Tamayo, Cultural Prestige, and Perceptions of Modern Mexican Art in the United States," in Diana C. du Pont and Rufino Tamayo, *Tamayo: A Modern Icon Reinterpreted* (Madrid: Turner Ediciones, 2007), 344–47, 364, and Ingrid Suckaer, "Chronology," 417. For the other Mexican artists'

exhibition, see Reba White Williams, "The Weyhe Gallery Between the Wars, 1919–1940" (Ph.D. diss., City University of New York, 1996), 123–50.

16. Pach, *Queer Thing, Painting,* 288.

17. Orozco to Charlot, December 21, 1927, quoted in *The Artist in New York,* 27, 28.

18. Orozco to Charlot, March 10, 1928, quoted in *The Artist in New York,* 45.

19. Orozco to Charlot, April 30, 1928, quoted in *The Artist in New York,* 51.

20. For Pach's selection of this print, see Anna Indych, "Made for the USA: Orozco's Horrores de la Revolution," *Anales del Insituto de Investigaciones Esteticas* 23, no. 079 (2001): 164.

21. Walter Pach, "Impresiones sobre el arte actual de México," quoted in Jean Charlot, *The Mexican Mural Renaissance, 1920–1925* (New Haven: Yale University Press, 1967), 222–23.

22. Pach, *Ananias, or the False Artist* (New York: Harper and Brothers, 1928), 205.

23. Walter Pach, "The Greatest American Artists," *Harper's Monthly Magazine* 148 (January 1924): 252.

24. Pach, *Queer Thing, Painting,* 289.

25. Walter Pach to Mrs. Abby Aldrich Rockefeller, May 11, 1933, Rockefeller Family Archives, Record Group 2, Office of the Messrs Rockefeller, Business Interests series, box 94, folder 707, Rockefeller Archive Center, Sleepy Hollow, New York (hereinafter Rockefeller Archives). Also quoted in Perlman, *American Artists, Authors, and Collectors,* 329.

26. See Bertram D. Wolfe, *The Fabulous Life of Diego Rivera* (New York: Stein and Day, 1963), 317–40; Laurance P. Hurlburt, *The Mexican Muralists in the United States* (Albuquerque: University of New Mexico Press, 1989), 170–74; Hayden Herrera, *Frida: A Biography of Frida Kahlo* (New York: Harper Perennial, 2002), 165–66; Irene

Herner de Larrea, Gabriel Larrea, and Rafael Angel Herrerias, *Diego Rivera's Mural at the Rockefeller Center* (Mexico City: Edicupes, 1986).

27. Pach, *Queer Thing, Painting,* 211.

28. Pach to Mrs. Abby Aldrich Rockefeller, May 10, 1933, Rockefeller Archives. Also quoted in Perlman, *American Artists, Authors, and Collectors,* 326–27.

29. Pach to Mrs. Abby Aldrich Rockefeller, May 11, 1933, Rockefeller Archives. Also quoted in Perlman, *American Artists, Authors, and Collectors,* 328.

30. Telegram to John D. Rockefeller Jr., May 11, 1933, Rockefeller Archives. Also quoted in Perlman, *American Artists, Authors, and Collectors,* 329.

31. Pach to Guggenheimer, June 23, 1933, Guggenheimer Papers.

32. Walter Pach, "Rockefeller, Rivera, and Art," *Harper's Magazine* 167 (September 1933): 476.

33. Walter Pach, "The Rivera Mural," letter to the editor, *New York Times,* February 19, 1934, 14.

34. Walter Pach, "Frida Rivera: Gifted Canvas by an Unselfconscious Surrealist," *Art News* 37 (November 1938): 13.

35. Pach to Sloan, August 10, 1942, Sloan Archives. Also quoted in Perlman, *American Artists, Authors, and Collectors,* 378.

36. Pach to Brooks, April 18, 1943, Brooks Papers.

37. Magdalene Pach to Carl Zigrosser, July 1, 1942, Carl Zigrosser Papers, AAA, 4636, frame 514.

38. Pach to Brooks, September 20, 1942, Brooks Papers.

39. Pach to Brooks, September 20, 1942, Brooks Papers. Also quoted in Perlman, *American Artists, Authors, and Collectors,* 111.

40. Pach to Sloan, August 10, 1942, Sloan Archives. Also quoted in Perlman, *American Artists, Authors, and Collectors,* 379.

41. Pach to Brooks, September 20, 1942, Brooks Papers. Also quoted in Perlman, *American Artists, Authors, and Collectors,* 111.

42. Pach to Brooks, April 18, 1943, Brooks Papers.

43. Pach to Brooks, September 20, 1942, Brooks Papers.

44. Walter Pach, "Our Ancestors of the Soil," *Virginia Quarterly Review* 20 (Summer 1944): 413.

45. Walter Pach, "A Newly Found American Painter," *Art in America* 31 (January 1943): 32.

46. Pach, "Our Ancestors of the Soil," 415.

47. Pach to Sachs, February 23, 1943, Sachs File.

48. Pach to Zigrosser, December 9, 1942, Zigrosser Papers.

49. Walter Pach, "Flannagan," *Kenyon Review* 5 (Summer 1943): 384.

50. Pach to Sachs, February 23, 1943, Sachs File.

51. Sachs to Pach, April 8, 1943, Pach Papers, AAA, reel 4219, frames 42–43.

52. Pach to Sloan, July 23, 1943, Sloan Archives.

53. Pach to Sloan, September 8, 1943, Sloan Archives.

54. MacKinley Helm, *Modern Mexican Painters* (New York: Harper and Brothers, 1941), 162.

Chapter 12

1. Pach to Sachs, October 26, 1939, Sachs File. Also quoted in Perlman, *American Artists, Authors, and Collectors,* 347.

2. For the summer session at the Louvre, see preliminary announcement for the summer session, 1927, and report of the summer session, 1926, New York University, *New York University, Department of Fine Arts, Summer School Art Courses in Paris* (New York: New York University, 1927).

3. Pach to Sachs, October 26, 1939, Sachs File. Also quoted in Perlman, *American Artists, Authors, and Collectors,* 347.

4. Walter Pach to Alfred Stieglitz, July 27, 1923, Alfred Stieglitz/Georgia O'Keeffe Archives, Yale Collection of American Literature, Beinecke Rare Book and Manuscript Library (hereinafter Stieglitz Archives). Also quoted in Perlman, *American Artist, Authors, and Collectors,* 392.

5. Pach to Stieglitz, July 27, 1923, Stieglitz Archives. Also quoted in Perlman, *American Artists, Authors, and Collectors,* 392.

6. Carl Zigrosser Papers, AAA, reel 4636, frames 547–49.

7. Henry Miller, *Tropic of Cancer* (New York: Signet Classic, 1995), 62. I would like to thank John Cauman for pointing out this reference to me.

8. Pach to Guggenheimer, July 11, 1937, Guggenheimer Papers.

9. Walter Pach, introduction to Eugène Delacroix, *The Journal of Eugène Delacroix,* trans. Walter Pach (New York: Covici, Friede, 1937), 31.

10. Allen Tucker to Pach, November 1, 1937, AAA, reel 4218, frame 571. Brooks to Pach, November 18, 1937, AAA, reel 4218, frames 573–74. Also quoted in Perlman, *American Artists, Authors, and Collectors,* 100.

11. Frances Winwar, "The Portrait of the Artist: Delacroix's Remarkable Journal Is Rich in Personal Revelation: A Review of *The Journal of Eugène Delacroix,* translation by Walter Pach," *New York Times Book Review,* October 31, 1937, 1.

12. Herbert Read, review of Delacroix, *The Journal of Eugène Delacroix, Burlington Magazine* 72, no. 423 (June 1938): 310.

13. Pach to Mumford, April 16, 1939, folder 3764, Mumford Papers.

14. Walter Pach to Bernard Berenson, February 16, 1940, the Berenson Archive, the Harvard University Center for Italian

Renaissance Studies, Villa I Tatti, courtesy of the President and Fellows of Harvard College. Also quoted in Perlman, *American Artists, Authors, and Collectors,* 78.

15. Brooks to Pach, December 29, 1939, Brooks Papers. Also quoted in Perlman, *American Artists, Authors, and Collectors,* 102.

16. Margery Ryerson, "Ingres and the World of Art," *New York Times Book Review,* January 7, 1940.

17. Walter Pach to Germain Seligmann, November 10, 1939, Germain Seligmann Papers, Archives of American Art, Smithsonian Institution, Washington, D.C., unmicrofilmed. I would like to thank Judy Throm of the archives for pointing these materials out to me.

18. Pach to Brooks, January 10, 1940, Brooks Papers. Also quoted in Perlman, *American Artists, Authors, and Collectors,* 103.

19. Pach to Mrs. Abby Rockefeller, February 28, 1940, Rockefeller Archives. Also quoted in Perlman, *American Artists, Authors, and Collectors,* 332.

20. Pach to Brooks, March 27, 1940, Brooks Papers.

21. Pach to Mrs. Abby Rockefeller, May 6 and 13, 1940, Rockefeller Archives. Also quoted in Perlman, *American Artists, Authors, and Collectors,* 333.

22. Magda Pach to Etta Cone, July 27, 1940, Cone Papers, Archives of American Art, Smithsonian Institution, Washington, D.C., reel 3809, frames 1068–71.

23. Pach to Guggenheimer, August 21, 1940, Guggenheimer Papers.

24. Walter Pach to Bernard Berenson, September 30, 1945, Berenson Archive. Also quoted in Perlman, *American Artists, Authors, and Collectors,* 84.

25. Walter to Raymond Pach, July 7, 1945, Pach Papers, DAM.

26. Walter to Raymond Pach, July 29, 1945, Pach Papers, DAM.

27. Walter to Raymond Pach, July 29, 1945, Pach Papers, DAM.

28. Kurt Wolff to Walter Pach, November 5, 1947, Pach Papers, AAA, reel 4219, frame 160.

29. Walter to Raymond Pach, November 23, 1947, Pach Papers, DAM.

30. Walter to Raymond Pach, July 22, 1945, Pach Papers, DAM.

31. Pach to Villon, June 18, 1958, Fonds Jacques Villon, Pach.W. c 16 8139.276, Bibliothèque Kandinsky, Centre de Documentation et Recherché du Musée National d'Art Moderne—Centre de Création Industrielle, Centre Georges Pompidou, Paris, France. Translation courtesy of Susan Berger.

32. Walter Pach, *The Classical Tradition in Modern Art* (New York: Thomas Yoselhoff, 1959), 56–57.

Chapter 13

1. Pach, quoted in Trapp, *The 1913 Armory Show in Retrospect,* 27.

2. "Art in America: II," *Freeman* 2 (November 17, 1920): 232.

3. For information on the New York subway, see Joseph Cunningham and Leonard de Hart, *A History of the New York City Subway System,* rev. ed. (New York: J. Schmidt, R. Giglio, and K. Lang, 1993), 17, 27, 45.

4. For an early history of Governors Island, see R. Ernest Dupuy, comp., *Governors Island: Its History and Development, 1637–1937* (New York: Governors Island Club, 1937).

5. For the Shot Tower, see Isaac Newton Phelps Stokes, *The Iconography of Manhattan Island, 1498–1909* (New York: Robert H. Dodd, 1918), 3:601.

6. Elizabeth Cary, "The World of Art: Etchings in Variety," *New York Times Book Review and Magazine,* July 18, 1920, 20.

7. Walter to Gotthelf Pach, July 23, 1920, Pach Papers, DAM.

8. Faure to Pach, January 31, 1924, Pach Papers, AAA, reel 4217, frames 758–59.

9. Rivera to Pach, March 13, 1925, Pach Papers, AAA, reel 4218, frame 23. Translation courtesy of Alba Fernández-Keys, © 2009 Banco de México Diego Rivera Frida Kahlo Museums Trust, México, D.F./Artists Rights Society (ARS).

10. Pach to Mumford, February 15, 1925, folder 3764, Mumford Papers. Also quoted in Perlman, *American Artists, Authors, and Collectors,* 208.

11. Henry McBride, "Truth About the Air," *New York Times Magazine,* February 22, 1925, 17.

12. Dreier to Pach, October 4, 1926, Société Anonyme Collection. Also quoted in Perlman, *American Artists, Authors, and Collectors,* 146.

13. Dreier to Pach, January 12, 1927, Société Anonyme Collection.

14. Pach to Dreier, January 13, 1927, Société Anonyme Collection.

15. For further discussion of this show, see Ruth L. Bohan, *The Société Anonyme's Brooklyn Exhibition: Katherine Dreier and Modernism in America* (Ann Arbor, Mich.: UMI Research Press, 1982), and Robert L. Herbert, Eleanor S. Apter, and Elsie K. Kenney, eds., *The Société Anonyme and the Dreier Bequest at Yale University: A Catalogue Raisonné* (New Haven: Yale University Press, 1984).

16. Introduction to Herbert, Apter, and Kenney, *The Société Anonyme and the Dreier Bequest,* 1.

17. Introduction to Herbert, Apter, and Kenney, *The Société Anonyme and the Dreier Bequest,* 4.

18. Edward Alden Jewell, "Grand Central Display: Many Tubes of Bright Paint Used—Walter Pach's Work—a Busy Week at Art Centre," *New York Times,* November 25, 1928, 10.

19. Henry McBride, "Honest Enough, and Tries Hard Enough," *New York Sun,* November 24, 1928.

20. "Exhibitions in New York: Walter Pach, Kraushaar Galleries," *Art News* 27 (November 24, 1928).

21. Pach to Mumford, January 16, 1930, folder 3764, Mumford Papers. Also quoted in Perlman, *American Artists, Authors, and Collectors,* 213.

22. Pach to Guggenheimer, November 1, 1929, Guggenheimer Papers.

23. Pach to Guggenheimer, November 1, 1929, Guggenheimer Papers.

24. The works donated to the Metropolitan Museum of art were *Cyclamen,* 1929; *Portrait of a Girl,* 1930; *Les Invalides,* 1930; and *The Fountain of the Innocents, Paris,* 1930.

25. Burroughs to Pach, October 23, 1930, Pach Papers, AAA, reel 4218, frame 288. Also quoted in Perlman, *American Artists, Authors, and Collectors,* 121.

26. Pach to Guggenheimer, November 21, 1930, Guggenheimer Papers.

27. "Walter Pach: Kraushaar Galleries," *Art News* 29 (March 21, 1931): 14.

28. "Pach, Critic, Revealed as Artist," *New York Times,* March 14, 1931, 25.

29. Pach to Guggenheimer, January 24, 1931, Guggenheimer Papers.

30. Pach to Guggenheimer, May 28, 1931, Guggenheimer Papers.

31. Pach to Etta Cone, October 16, 1931, Cone Papers, AAA, reel 3809, frames 1078–79.

32. Pach to Guggenheimer, March 13, 1932, Guggenheimer Papers.

33. Pach to Guggenheimer, March 13, 1932, Guggenheimer Papers.

34. L. E., "Walter Pach, Knoedler Galleries," *Art News* 33 (May 25, 1935): 9.

35. Walter Pach to Bernard Berenson, August 3, 1936, Berenson Archive. Also quoted in Perlman, *American Artists, Authors, and Collectors,* 73.

36. Pach to Sachs, October 26, 1939, Sachs File. Also quoted in Perlman, *American*

Artists, Authors, and Collectors, 347–48.

37. Walter Pach to Bernard Berenson, August 3, 1936, Berenson Archive. Also quoted in Perlman, *American Artists, Authors, and Collectors,* 73.

38. Pach to Sloan, February 13, 1932, Sloan Archives.

39. Walter Pach, introduction to *Walter Pach: Oils and Water Colors* (New York: Laurel Gallery, 1947), Brooklyn Museum Records: Miscellaneous Exhibition Catalogues, 1809–1945, Archives of American Art, Smithsonian Institution, Washington, D.C., reel BR14, frames 356–57.

40. "Reviews and Previews: Walter Pach," *Art News* 46 (April 1947): 49.

41. Edward Alden Jewell, "Academy by Itself," *New York Times,* March 23, 1947.

42. James Daugherty to Walter Pach, April 22, 1947, Pach Papers, AAA, reel 4219, frame 156. Permission to publish courtesy of the Friends of James Daugherty Foundation.

43. Walter Pach to Bernard Berenson, December 29, 1953, Berenson Archive.

44. Walter Pach to Bernard Berenson, February 3, 1952 (continuation of a letter started January 23, 1952), Berenson Archive.

45. Walter to Raymond Pach, June 20, 1955, Pach Papers, DAM.

Chapter 14

1. Pach to Guggenheimer, November 21, 1950, Guggenheimer Papers.

2. Walter to Raymond Pach, December 4, 1950, Pach Papers, DAM.

3. Walter to Raymond Pach, November 27, 1950, Pach Papers, DAM.

4. Walter to Raymond Pach, December 30, 1950, Pach Papers, DAM.

5. Pach to Brooks, April 7, 1951, Brooks Papers.

6. Walter Pach to Julius Rauzin, April 28, 1951, AAA, reel 2345, frames 943–44.

7. Pach to Guggenheimer, June 4, 1951, Guggenheimer Papers.

8. Pach to Helen and John Sloan, June 2, 1951, Sloan Archives.

9. Walter to Raymond Pach, December 5, 1951, Pach Papers, DAM.

10. Walter to Raymond Pach, January 15 and 29, 1953, Pach Papers, DAM.

11. Walter to Raymond Pach, April 16, 1952, Pach Papers, DAM.

12. Walter to Raymond Pach, October 6, 1954, Pach Papers, DAM.

13. Pach to Villon, November 12, 1957, Fonds Jacques Villon, Pach.W. c 14 8139.247, Bibliothèque Kandinsky, Centre de Documentation et Recherché du Musée National d'Art Moderne—Centre de Création Industrielle, Centre Georges Pompidou, Paris, France. Translation courtesy of Susan Berger.

14. Walter to Raymond Pach, July 26, 1954, Pach Papers, DAM.

15. Walter to Raymond Pach, September 22, 1955, Pach Papers, DAM.

16. Pach to Villon, June 18, 1958, Fonds Jacques Villon, Pach.W. c 16 8139.276, Bibliothèque Kandinsky, Centre de Documentation et Recherché du Musée National d'Art Moderne—Centre de Création Industrielle, Centre Georges Pompidou, Paris, France. Translation courtesy of Susan Berger.

17. Copy of a newspaper notice in a letter from Nikifora Pach to Gabrielle and Jacques Villon, January 24, 1959, Fonds Jacques Villon, Bibliothèque Kandinsky, Centre de Documentation et Recherché du Musée National d'Art Moderne—Centre de Création Industrielle, Centre Georges Pompidou, Paris, France.

18. Walter to Raymond Pach, September 17, 1952, Pach Papers, DAM.

19. Copy of a newspaper notice in a letter from Nikifora Pach to Gabrielle and Jacques Villon, January 24, 1959, Fonds Jacques Villon, Bibliothèque Kandinsky, Centre de

Documentation et Recherché du Musée
National d'Art Moderne—Centre de
Création Industrielle, Centre Georges
Pompidou, Paris, France.

Epilogue

1. Phillips, "The Art Criticism of Walter
Pach"; William C. Agee, "Walter Pach and
Modernism: A Sampler from New York,
Paris, and Mexico City," *Archives of American
Art Journal* 28 (1988): 2–10; Bennard B.
Perlman, "Walter Pach (1883–1958) and
Magda Pach (1884–1950)," in *Exhibition of
the Art of Walter and Magda Pach*
(Youngstown, Ohio: Butler Institute of
American Art, 1988) and introduction to
American Artists, Authors, and Collectors; and
Antliff, *Anarchist Modernism*. Pach is also
briefly mentioned in dozens of books and
articles on artists such as Duchamp, Matisse,
John Sloan, Maurice Prendergast, Rivera,
and Kahlo, to name a few.

Selected Bibliography

Archival Sources and Interviews

Arensberg, Walter Conrad, and Louise. Archives. Twentieth Century Department, Philadelphia Museum of Art, Philadelphia.

Berenson, Bernard. The Bernard Berenson Archives. The Harvard University Center for Italian Renaissance Studies, Villa I Tatti, Florence, Italy.

Brooks, Van Wyck. Papers. Rare Book and Manuscript Library, University of Pennsylvania, Philadelphia.

Carnegie Institute. Papers of the Museum of the Carnegie Institute, Pittsburgh, Archives of American Art, Smithsonian Institution, Washington, D.C. (AAA).

Chase, William Merritt. Papers. AAA.

———. Archives. The Parrish Art Museum, Southampton, New York.

Crotti, Jean. Papers. AAA.

Dawson, Manierre. Papers, 1904–63. AAA.

Dreier, Katherine S. Papers/Société Anonyme Archives. Yale Collection of American Literature. Beinecke Rare Book and Manuscript Library, Yale University, New Haven.

Duchamp-Villon, Raymond. Letters on temporary loan to the Musée des Beaux-Arts de Rouen, courtesy of Marie Pessiot.

———. Correspondence. Bibliothèque Kandinsky, Centre de Documentation et Recherché du Musée National d'Art Moderne—Centre de Création Industrielle, Centre Georges Pompidou, Paris, France.

Gest, Joseph H. Directors' Correspondence. Cincinnati Art Museum Archives, AAA.

Guggenheimer, Ida. Correspondence with Walter Pach and related miscellaneous material, 1929–51. AAA.

Hale, Gardner. Letters to Walter Pach. Courtesy of Myra Bairstow.

Henri, Robert. Papers. Yale Collection of American Literature. Beinecke Rare Book and Manuscript Library, Yale University, New Haven.

Ivins, William. Papers. AAA.

Johns Hopkins University. Peabody Institute. Peabody Gallery of Art. Records, 1860–1972 and undated. AAA.

Kimball, Fiske. Archives and Records. The Philadelphia Museum of Art, Philadelphia.

Klauber, Alice. Collection. San Diego Museum of Art.

———. Papers. Letters, 1907–46. AAA.

Kuhn, Walt. Kuhn family papers and Armory Show Records, 1893–1966. AAA.

La Follette, Suzanne. Interviews. AAA.

Laurel Gallery. Records, 1946–52. AAA.

MacRae, Elmer Livingston. Papers, 1899–1958. AAA.

Matisse, Henri. Archives. Les Héritiers Matisse, Issy-les-Moulineaux, France.

McBride, Henry. Papers. AAA.

Meyer, Agnes Ernst. Meyer Collection. Manuscript Division. Library of Congress, Washington, D.C.

Mumford, Lewis. Papers. Rare Book and Manuscript Library, University of Pennsylvania, Philadelphia.

Museum of Fine Arts, Boston. Directors' Correspondence, 1901–54. AAA.

Pach, Raymond. Interview by the author. Newport News, Va., 26 April 1994.

———. Interview by the author. Newport News, Va., 14 March 2001.

Pach, Walter. Papers and Library, 1883–1980. AAA.

———. "The Politer the Cutt'n'er." Walter and Louise Arensberg Archives. Twentieth Century Department, Philadelphia Museum of Art, Philadelphia.

———. Walter Pach Collection. City University of New York, City College of New York, Archives and Special Collections Division, City College Libraries, New York.

———. Walter Pach Letters and Photographs. Helen Farr Sloan Library and Archives, Delaware Art Museum, Wilmington.

Phillips, Duncan. Correspondence. Archives. The Phillips Collection, Washington, D.C.

Phillips, Sandra S. Research materials on Walter Pach. AAA.

Prendergast, Maurice Brazil, and Charles Prendergast. Selected Papers. AAA.

Quinn, John. John Quinn Papers. Manuscripts and Archives Division, New York Public Library, Astor, Lenox, and Tilden Foundations, New York.

Rauzin, Julius. Papers regarding Walter Pach. AAA.

Rockefeller Family Archives. Record Group 2, Office of the Messrs Rockefeller, Business Interests Series, Box 94, Folder 707, Rockefeller Archive Center, Sleepy Hollow, New York.

Sachs, Paul J. Paul J. Sachs Papers. Harvard University Archives, Harvard Archives HUG 4764.12 [Miscellaneous Correspondence.]

Schoelkopf, Robert. Papers. AAA.

Seligmann, Germain. Papers, AAA.

Sheeler, Charles. Papers. AAA.

Sloan, Helen. Interview by the author. Wilmington, Del., April 1994.

Sloan, John. Archives. Helen Farr Sloan Library and Archives. Delaware Art Museum, Wilmington.

Stein, Gertrude, and Alice B. Toklas Papers. Yale Collection of American Literature. Beinecke Rare Book and Manuscript Library, Yale University, New Haven.

Stevens, Wallace. Correspondence. Huntington Art Gallery, San Marino, Calif.

Stieglitz, Alfred/Georgia O'Keeffe Archive. Yale Collection of American Literature. Beinecke Rare Book and Manuscript Library, Yale University, New Haven.

Villon, Jacques. Correspondence. Bibliothèque Kandinsky, Centre de Documentation et Recherché du Musée National d'Art Moderne—Centre de Création Industrielle, Centre Georges Pompidou, Paris, France.

Zigrosser, Carl. Papers. AAA and Rare Book and Manuscript Library, University of Pennsylvania, Philadelphia.

Writings by Walter Pach

"Abstractionists Appraised." Book review. *New York Herald Tribune,* November 25, 1956.

"Address at the Worcester Opening of the International 1933." *Parnassus* 5 (January 1933): 23–26.

"Amedée de la Patelliere, 1890–1932." *Parnassus* 4 (November 1932): 7–8.

"American Art at the Louvre." *Fine Arts* 20 (May 1933): 18–20, 48, 50.

American Artists, Authors, and Collectors: The Walter Pach Letters, 1906–1958. Edited by

Bennard B. Perlman. Albany: State University of New York Press, 2002.

"America's Ancestral Art." *Virginia Quarterly Review* 19 (Autumn 1943): 635–40.

Ananias, or the False Artist. New York: Harper and Brothers, 1928.

"Anatomizing the Muses." *Freeman* 3 (7 September 1921): 619.

"The Approach to Modern Art: And the Enjoyment It Offers." *Christian Science Monitor,* 26 January 1920, 14.

"The Approach to Modern Art: 'Ideas' Versus 'Truth.'" *Christian Science Monitor,* 19 January 1920, 14.

"The Approach to Modern Art: Ingres and Delacroix as Moderns." *Christian Science Monitor,* 12 January 1920, 14.

"Un aquafortiste américain, M. Herman-A. Webster." *Gazette des Beaux-Arts* 1 (1920): 43–49.

Arnold Friedman Lent by Sixteen Collectors. New York: Marquie Gallery, 1950.

"Art." In *Civilization in the United States.: An Inquiry by Thirty Americans.* New York: Harcourt, Brace, 1922.

"Art: A Half-Century Celebration." *Freeman* 1 (25 August 1920): 568–69.

"Art: A Modern Artist." *Freeman* 2 (8 December 1920): 302–3.

"Art: Art Since the War." *Freeman* 4 (1 March 1922): 589.

"Art: At the Pennsylvania Academy." *Freeman* 3 (18 May 1921): 232–33.

"Art: Brancusi." *Nation* 123 (1 December 1926): 566.

"Art: Modern: Cubism: Its Development." *Freeman* 7 (29 August 1923): 591–93.

"Art: Modern Art: After Impressionism." *Freeman* 7 (25 July 1923): 471–73.

"Art: Modern Art: Cubism: The Early Years." *Freeman* 7 (15 August 1923): 542–44.

"Art: Modern Art: The Modern Period." *Freeman* 7 (4 July 1923): 398–99.

"Art: Modern Art: The Poles of the Modern Movement." *Freeman* 7 (18 July 1923): 448–49.

"Art: Modern Art: The Wild Beasts." *Freeman* 7 (1 August 1923): 495–97.

"Art: Modern Art: To-Day." *Freeman* 7 (5 September 1923): 615–17.

"Art: Modern Art in Perspective." *Nation* 137 (30 August 1933): 249–50.

"Art: Modern Art on Exhibition." *Freeman* 5 (12 April 1922): 112–14.

"Art: Paris in New York." *Freeman* 2 (2 February 1921): 492–94.

"Art: The Century of Grace." *Nation* 141 (25 December 1935): 751–52.

"Art: The Contemporary Classics." *Freeman* 3 (13 July 1921): 423–25.

"Art: The Independents." *Freeman* 2 (9 March 1921): 616–17.

"Art: The Independents." *Freeman* 7 (18 April 1923): 135–37.

"Art: The Living Past." *Freeman* 5 (19 April 1922): 135–37.

"Art: The Modern Period: From the Revolution to Renoir." *Freeman* 7 (11 July 1923): 422–24.

"Art: The Popular Arts of Mexico." *Freeman* 6 (31 January 1923): 496–97.

"Art: We Do More Than Our Part." *Nation* 137 (15 November 1933): 576.

"L'art au Mexique." *L'Amour de l'Art* 7 (1926): 285–94.

"L'art de John Sloan." *L'Art et les Artistes* 18 (October 1913–March 1914): 222–26.

"Art in America: I." *Freeman* 2 (10 November 1920): 206–7.

"Art in America: II." *Freeman* 2 (17 November 1920): 232–33.

"The Artist and the Democratic Way of Life." In *Conference on Science, Philosophy, and Religion.* Edited by Lyman Bryson and Louis Finkelstein. New York: Conference on Science, Philosophy and Religion and Their Relation to the Democratic Way of Life, 1942.

"An Artist's Criticism." *Freeman* 6 (25 October 1922): 165.

The Art Museum in America. New York: Pantheon, 1948.

"Art Must Be Classical." *Virginia Quarterly Review* 27 (Autumn 1951): 568–80.

"Art Must Be Modern." *Atlantic* 185 (May 1950): 44–48.

"The Art of A. S. Baylinson." *American Artist* 16 (March 1952): 24, 28, 55–58.

"The Art of A. S. Baylinson." *Shadowland* 4 (June 1921): 11, 70, 76, 78.

The Art of Odilon Redon. New York: Association of American Painters and Sculptors, 1913.

"The Art of the American Indian." *Dial* 68 (January 1920): 57–65.

"As to Futurists." In *For and Against: Views on the International Exhibition Held in New York and Chicago.* Edited by Frederick James Gregg. New York: Association of American Painters and Sculptors, 1913.

"At the Studio of Claude Monet." *Scribner's Magazine* 43 (June 1908): 765–67.

"La Barricade by Delacroix in America." *Art News* 45 (July 1946): 42–43, 46.

"Cézanne: An Introduction." *Scribner's Magazine* 44 (December 1908): 765–68.

The Classical Tradition in Modern Art. New York: Thomas Yoselhoff, 1959.

"Le classicisme de Barye." *L'Amour de l'Art* 9 (November 1932): 318–20.

"Connoisseurship or Criticism." *Dial* 65 (2 November 1918): 365–66.

"Correspondence: False Art." *Nation* 132 (10 June 1931): 631.

"Correspondance d'Amérique: Une exposition d'art moderne." *La Chronique des Arts et de la Curiosité. Supplement à la Gazette des Beaux-Arts* 28 (16 August 1913): 221–22.

"Correspondence Relating to WPA Art Project." *New York Times,* 4 October 1936.

"The Cubist Room." In *For and Against: Views on the International Exhibition Held in New York and Chicago.* Edited by Frederick James Gregg. New York: Association of American Painters and Sculptors, 1913.

"Delacroix Speaks for Himself." *Art News* 43 (1–14 November 1944): 8–11.

"Delacroix Today." *Magazine of Art* 31 (January 1938): 16–19.

"Descubrimiento de un Pintor Americano." *Cuadernos Americanos* 1 (November–December 1942): 152–63.

"Diego Rivera at Work." *Nation* 137 (6 September 1933): 257–58.

"The Divine Proportion." *Creative Art* 12 (May 1933): 369–71.

"Editor's Letters." *Art News* 55 (September 1956): 6.

"The Eight, Then and Now." *Art News* 42 (1–14 January 1944): 25, 31.

"Elie Faure." *Freeman* 3 (30 March 1921): 58–60.

"Les Etats-Unis." *L'Amour de l'Art* 10 (December 1934): 464–68.

"The Etchings and Lithographs of Odilon Redon." *Print Connoisseur* 1 (October 1920): 45–63.

"The Etchings of John Sloan." *Studio* (14 August 1926): 102–5.

"European and American Art." *American Magazine of Art* 25 (October 1932): 203–6.

"The Evolution of Diego Rivera." *Creative Art* 4 (January 1929): 31–39.

"Ex Libris." *Freeman* 7 (4 April 1923): 95.

"An Exhibition of Art by Mexican Schoolchildren and Jean Charlot." *Art Center Bulletin* (April 1926): 244–46.

First Exhibition of Géricault in America. New York: Marie Sterner Gallery, 1936.

"First Portfolio of American Art." *Art News* 35 (3 October 1936): 11–13, 22.

"French Art Upheld." *New York Times,* 7 December 1941.

"French Art and War." *New York Times,* 5 March 1916.

"Frida Rivera: Gifted Canvas by an Unselfconscious Surrealist." *Art News* 37 (November 1938): 13.

"Gemmeaux of Jean Crotti." *Magazine of Art* 40 (February 1947): 68–69.

"Georges Rouault." *Parnassus* 5 (January 1933): 9–11.

"Georges Seurat." *Arts* 3 (March 1923): 160–74.

Georges Seurat. New York: Duffield, 1923.

"Géricault." *Parnassus* 8 (November 1936): 12–15.

"Géricault in America." *Gazette des Beaux-Arts* 27 (April 1945): 227–40.

"A Grand Provincial." *Freeman* 7 (11 April 1923): 112–14.

"The Greatest American Artists." *Harper's Monthly Magazine* 148 (January 1924): 252–62.

"Hail and Farewell." Introduction to *Memorial Exhibition of the Work of Mary Rogers (1881–1920).* New York: Society of Independent Artists, 1921.

"The Heritage of J. L. David." *Gazette des Beaux-Arts* 45 (February 1955): 103–12.

"Hindsight and Foresight." In *For and Against: Views on the International Exhibition Held in New York and Chicago.* Edited by

Frederick James Gregg. New York: Association of American Painters and Sculptors, 1913.

"Homer Boss." *Shadowland* 5 (December 1921): 11, 70–71, 76.

An Hour of Art. Philadelphia: J. B. Lippincott, 1930.

"Importance of the John Quinn Collection." *Art Center Bulletin* 4 (January 1926): 140–41.

"La Importancia de los Museos." *Letras de Mexico* 4 (15 April 1943): 8–9.

"Impresiones sobre el arte actual de México." *México Moderno,* October 1922.

"The Independents." *Dial* 66 (22 March 1919): 307–8.

"The Indian Tribal Arts." *New York Times,* 22 November 1931.

Ingres. New York: Harper and Brothers, 1939.

"Introducing the Paintings of George Of." *Art News* 55 (October 1956): 36–38, 62–63.

"Is Cubism Pure Art?—A Debate. Picasso's Achievement." *Forum* 23 (June 1925): 769–75.

"Jacques Lipchitz and the Modern Movement." *Magazine of Art* 39 (December 1946): 354–58.

"Jean Le Roy." *Modern School* (October 1918): 296.

"John B. Flannagan." *Cuadernos Americanos* 8 (March–April 1943): 242–50.

"John B. Flannagan, American Sculptor." *Kenyon Review* 5 (Summer 1943): 209–20.

"John Sloan." *Atlantic* 194 (August 1954): 68–72.

"John Sloan." *New Mexico Quarterly Review* 19 (Summer 1949): 177–81.

"John Sloan Today." *Virginia Quarterly Review* (July 1925): 196–204.

"Kitchen with a Hare." *Bulletin of the Art Association of Indianapolis* 40 (October 1953): 31–33.

"Light from the South Seas." *New Republic* 114 (27 May 1946): 769–70.

"'Luscious' Repudiated. Letters to the Editor." *Nation* 172 (20 January 1951): 68.

"M. J. Alden-Weir." *Gazette des Beaux-Arts* (1911): 214–15.

"Manet and Modern American Art." *Craftsman* 17 (February 1910): 483–92.

"Marinot, Artist and Artisan." *Creative Arts* 11 (November 1932): 207–9.

The Masters of Modern Art. New York: B. W. Huebsch, 1924.

"Maurice Prendergast." *Shadowland* 6 (April 1922): 11, 74–75.

"The 'Memoria' of Velasquez." *Scribner's Magazine* 42 (July 1907): 38–52.

"Methods of Criticism." *Freeman* 2 (19 January 1921): 450–51.

"Mexican Art and Culture." *New York Times,* 30 November 1924.

"Miscellany. Review of Jerome Blum's exhibition at the Anderson Galleries." *Freeman* 5 (5 April 1922): 87.

"Modern Art Expounded in Terms of Evolution." Review of *Entwicklungsgeschichte der modernen Kunst,* by Julius Meier-Graefe. *New York Times Book Review,* 27 December 1925.

Modern Art in America. New York: C. W. Kraushaar Art Galleries, 1928.

"Modern Art Today." *Harper's Weekly* 62 (19 April 1916): 470–71.

"A Modernist Visits Greece." *Archaeology* 6 (Autumn 1953): 137–41.

"The Morgan Collection." *Outlook* 100 (10 February 1912): 345–46.

"Le mouvement artistique a l'étranger. Etats-Unis." *L'Art et les Artistes* 86 (May 1912): 92.

"Le mouvement artistique a l'étranger. Etats-Unis." *L'Art et les Artistes* 90 (September 1912): 281–82.

"Mr. Pach Replies to Mr. Field." *Brooklyn Daily Eagle,* 14 March 1920.

"Museums Can Be Living Things." In *Laurels Print Portfolio.* New York: Laurel Gallery, 1947.

"New Found Values in Ancient America." *Parnassus* 7 (December 1935): 7–10.

"A 'New' Portrait by Ingres." *Art Quarterly* 15 (Spring 1952): 2–8.

"New York as an Art Centre." *Harper's Weekly* 54 (26 February 1910): 12.

"Newly Discovered Ingres, 'The Lovers.'" *Art in America* 30 (October 1942): 206–10.

"A Newly Found American Painter: Hermenigildo Bustos." *Art in America* 31 (January 1943): 32–43.

"Notes on the Indian Water-Colours." *Dial* 68 (March 1920): 343–45.

"Notes on Museums. Apropos of a Recent Publication." *Gazette des Beaux-Arts* 24 (July 1943): 59–62.

"Notes sur le classicisme de Delacroix." *L'Amour de l'Art* 6 (June 1930): 241–53.

"The Old and the New in Art Forgery." *New York Times Magazine,* 4 September 1927.

"On Albert P. Ryder." *Scribner's Magazine* 49 (January 1911): 125–28.

"On Cézanne's Water Colors." *Christian Science Monitor,* 23 February 1920, 14.

"On Owning Pictures." *Fine Arts* 20 (August 1933): 27–29, 46–47.

"One Sculptor's Progress: New York, Paris, London." Review of *Epstein: An Autobiography. New York Herald Tribune,* 7 August 1955.

Origins of Modern Art. Foreword by Walter Pach. Chicago: Arts Club of Chicago, 1940.

"Our Ancestors of the Soil." *Virginia Quarterly Review* 20 (Summer 1944): 413–26.

"Outlook for Modern Art." *Parnassus* 8 (April 1936): 5–8, 43.

"A Painter of Dramas Who Made the Unreal World Seem Real." *Current Opinion* 61 (November 1916): 340–41.

"Painting. A Modern Art Exhibition." *Freeman* 1 (23 June 1920): 354–55.

Paintings, Watercolors, and Sculptures Selected from the John Quinn Collection. New York: Art Center, 1926.

"The Past Lives On: Part I." *American Artist* 12 (October 1948): 28–31, 64–66.

"The Past Lives On: Part II." *American Artist* 12 (November 1948): 40–43, 64.

"Pierre Auguste Renoir." *Scribner's Magazine* 51 (May 1912): 606–12.

"The Point of View of the 'Moderns.'" *Century* 87 (April 1914): 851–52 and 861–64.

"Probing the Mind and Heart of Van Gogh." Review of *Passionate Pilgrim: The Life of Vincent Van Gogh,* by Lawrence and Elizabeth Hanson. *New York Herald Tribune,* 20 November 1955.

Queer Thing, Painting: Forty Years in the World of Art. New York: Harper and Brothers, 1938.

"Quelques notes sur les peintres américains." *Gazette des Beaux-Arts* 2 (1909): 324–35.

"The Raphael from Russia." *Virginia Quarterly Review* 12 (January 1936): 43–55.

"Raymond Duchamp-Villon." *Formes* 15 (May 1931): 84–85.

Raymond Duchamp-Villon, Sculpteur, 1876–1918. Paris: Presses de l'Imprimerie Crozatier, 1924.

"A Recollection of Arthur B. Davies." In *Arthur B. Davies: A Centennial Exhibition.* Utica, N.Y.: Munson-Williams-Proctor Institute, 1962.

"Relaciones entre la cultura notreamericana y la obra de Diego Rivera." In *50 años de su labór artistica.* Mexico: Museo Nacional de Artes Plastica, 1951.

"Renoir, Rubens and the Thurneyssen Family." *Art Quarterly* 21 (Autumn 1958): 278–82.

"The Rivera Mural." Letter to the editor. *New York Times,* 19 February 1934.

Review of *Jacques Villon: His Graphic Art,* edited by William S. Lieberman. *The Saturday Review* (7 November 1953): 50–51.

Review of *Seeing and Knowing,* by Bernard Berenson. *Catholic World* 178 (March 1954): 479.

Review of *Seeing and Knowing,* by Bernard Berenson. *New Yorker* 30 (27 February 1954): 102–3.

Review of *Seeing and Knowing* and *Caravaggio,* by Bernard Berenson. *Atlantic* 193 (March 1954): 87.

Review of *The ABC's of Art,* by Leo Stein. *Architectural Record* (1928).

"Rockefeller, Rivera, and Art." *Harper's Magazine* 167 (September 1933): 476–83.

"The Role of Modern Art." *Virginia Quarterly Review* 21 (Summer 1945): 399–412.

"The Schamberg Exhibition." *Dial* 66 (17 May 1919): 505–6.

A Sculptor's Architecture. New York: Association of American Painters and Sculptors, 1913.

The 75th Anniversary Exhibition of Painting and Sculpture by 75 Artists Associated with the Art Students League of New York. New York: Metropolitan Museum of Art, 1951.

"The Shilling Fund." *New Republic* 114 (4 February 1946): 159.

"The Significance of Redon." *Dial* 66 (22 February 1919): 191–93.

"Some Reflections on Modern Art Suggested by the Career of Arthur Burdett Frost, Jr." *Scribner's Magazine* 63 (May 1918): 637–39.

"Some Women Artists of Today." *Charm* (October 1924): 37+.

"A Splendid Courbet for Smith College." *New York Times,* 10 March 1929.

"The Stake of the Arts in the Democratic Way of Life: A Postscript." In *Perspectives on a Troubled Decade: Science, Philosophy, and Religion, 1939–1949.* New York: Conference on Science, Philosophy and Religion in Their Relation to the Democratic Way of Life, 1950.

"Submerged Artists." *Atlantic* 199 (January 1957): 68–72.

"The Talent of the Brush." *Dial* 65 (28 December 1918): 613.

"The Temple of the Muses." *Freeman* 4 (9 November 1921): 212–13.

"Les tendances modernes aux Etats-Unis." *L'Amour de l'Art* 1 (January 1922): 29–30.

Thomas Eakins Exhibition. New York: Kleeman Galleries, 1937.

"Thus Is Cubism Cultivated." *Art News* 48 (May 1949): 23–25, 52–53.

"Tradition." *American Magazine of Art* 27 (December 1934): 641–47.

"Two Exhibitions, I: French Art Before the Dawn." *New Republic* 104 (10 February 1941): 181.

Two Masterpieces of Renaissance Painting from the Collection of Carl W. Hamilton. New York: Anderson Gallery, 1929.

"Universality in Art." *Modern School* (February 1918): 46–55.

"Unknown Aspects of Mexican Painting." *Gazette des Beaux-Arts* 24 (October 1943): 209–20.

"Vincent Van Gogh." *International Studio* 74 (November 1920): 72–76.

Vincent van Gogh, 1853–1890: A Study of the Artist and His Work in Relation to His Times. New York: Artbook Museum, 1936.

"War Still a Game for the French." *New York Times,* 17 February 1918.

"The Weyhe Book and Print Shop." *Publishers' Weekly* 115 (16 March 1929): 1396–98.

"What Passes for Art." *Harper's Magazine* 155 (June 1927): 89–97.

"Why Matisse?" *Century Magazine* 89 (February 1915): 633–36.

"William Glackens." *Shadowland* 7 (October 1922): 11, 74.

"Winslow Homer." *Gazette des Beaux-Arts* 16 (November 1912): 73–79.

"With Hair and Hammer." Review of *History of Art, 1921–1930,* by Elie Faure. *Saturday Review* (4 July 1953).

"The Wood-Carver, Charles E. Prendergast." *Shadowland* 8 (May 1923): 11, 72.

Years of Art: The Story of the Art Students League. Introduction by Walter Pach. New York: Robert McBride, 1940.

Other Published Sources, Theses, and Dissertations

Abrams, Ann Uhry. "Catalyst for a Change: American Art and Revolution, 1906–1915." Ph.D. diss., Emory University, 1975.

Agee, William C. "Walter Pach and Modernism: A Sampler from New York, Paris, and Mexico City." *Archives of American Art Journal* 28 (1988): 2–10.

Alexander, John W. "Art and the Average Man: An Interview with Walter Pach." *Outlook* (1912): 197–203.

Antliff, Allan. *Anarchist Modernism: Art, Politics, and the First American Avant-Garde.* Chicago: University of Chicago Press, 2001.

Archipenko, Alexander. In *1913 Armory Show 50th Anniversary Exhibition, 1913–1963.* New York: Henry Street Settlement and Munson-Williams-Proctor Institute, 1963.

A. S. Baylinson: A Memorial Exhibition. Foreword by Walter Pach. New York: Art Students League, 1951.

Association of American Painters and Sculptors. *The Armory Show: International Exhibition of Modern Art, 1913.* 1913. Reprint. New York: Arno, 1972.

Avrich, Paul. *The Modern School Movement: Anarchism and Education in the United States.* Princeton: Princeton University Press, 1980.

Barr, Alfred, Jr. *Matisse: His Art and His Public.* New York: Museum of Modern Art, 1951.

Bell, Clive. *Art.* 1914. Reprint. New York: Frederick A. Stokes Company, 1949.

Berger, Klaus. *Japonisme in Western Painting from Whistler to Matisse.* Translated by David Britt. Cambridge: Cambridge University Press, 1992.

Bolger, Doreen. "Hamilton Easter Field and the Rise of Modern Art in America." Master's thesis, University of Delaware, 1973.

Boyle-Turner, Caroline. *Paul Sérusier.* Ann Arbor, Mich.: UMI Research Press, 1983.

Brinton, Christian. "Current Art, Native and Foreign." *The International Studio* 49 (May 1913): 51–58.

———. "Evolution Not Revolution in Art." *The International Studio* 49 (April 1913): xxvii–xxxv.

Brooks, Van Wyck. *Days of the Phoenix: The Nineteen-Twenties I Remember.* New York: E. P. Dutton, 1937.

———. *From the Shadow of the Mountain: My Post-Meridian Years.* New York: E. P. Dutton.

———. *John Sloan: A Painter's Life.* New York: E. P. Dutton, 1955.

———. "John Sloan and the Armory Show." *Arts Digest* 29 (1 February 1955): 6–8, 35.

———. *The Van Wyck Brooks–Lewis Mumford Letters: The Record of a Literary Friendship, 1921–1963.* Edited by Robert E. Spiller. New York: E. P. Dutton, 1970.

Brown, Milton W. *The Story of the Armory Show.* New York: Abbeville Press, 1963.

———. *The Story of the Armory Show.* Rev. ed. New York: Abbeville Press and Joseph H. Hirshhorn Foundation, 1988.

Bryant, Keith L., Jr. *William Merritt Chase: A Genteel Bohemian.* Columbia: University of Missouri Press, 1991.

Buffet-Picabia, Gabrielle. "Introduction à l'art moderne aux Etats-Unis." *XX siècle* 40 (June 1973): 63–68.

Cabanne, Pierre. *André Derain.* Paris: Editions Aimery Somogy, 1990.

———. *The Brothers Duchamp: Jacques Villon, Raymond Duchamp-Villon, Marcel Duchamp.* Boston: New York Graphic Society, 1976.

Calo, Mary Ann. *Bernard Berenson and the Twentieth Century.* Philadelphia: Temple University Press, 1994.

Camfield, William A. *Marcel Duchamp Fountain.* Houston: Houston Fine Art Press, 1989.

Cancel, Luis R, Jacinto Quirate, Marimar Benitez, Nelly Perazzo, Lowery S. Sims, Eva Cockcroft, Feliz Angle, and Carla Stellweg. *The Latin American Spirit: Art and Artists in the United States, 1920–1970.* New York: Bronx Museum of the Arts in association with Harry N. Abrams, 1988.

Cauman, John. "Henri Matisse's Letters to Walter Pach." *Archives of American Art Journal* 31 (1991): 2–14.

———. "Matisse and America, 1905–1933." Ph.D. diss., City University of New York, 2000.

Cézanne. New York: Montross Gallery, January 1916. Unpaginated.

Charlot, Jean. *The Mexican Mural Renaissance, 1920–1925.* New Haven: Yale University Press, 1967.

Chase, William Merritt. "Import of Art by William M. Chase: An Interview with Walter Pach." *Outlook* 95 (25 June 1910): 441–45.

Chave, Anna C. *Constantin Brancusi: Shifting the Bases of Art.* New Haven: Yale University Press, 1993.

Chipp, Herschel B., comp. *Theories of Modern Art: A Source Book by Artists and Critics.* Berkeley and Los Angeles: University of California Press, 1968.

Churchill, Alfred Vance. "Is Cubism Pure Art?—a Debate: Picasso's 'Failure.'" *Forum* 23 (June 1925): 776–83.

Cohen-Solal, Annie. *Painting American: The Rise of American Artists, Paris 1867–New York 1948.* Translated from the French with Laurie Hurwitz-Attias. New York: Alfred A. Knopf, 2001.

Courtois, Martine, and Jean-Paul Morel. *Élie Faure: Biographie.* Paris: Librairie Séguier, 1989.

Coyle, Laura. "Amadeo and America." In *At the Edge: A Portuguese Futurist, Amadeo de Souza Cardoso.* Lisbon: Textype Artes Graficas, Gabibete das Relações Internacionais, 1999.

Crunden, Robert M. *American Salons: Encounters with European Modernism, 1885–1917.* New York: Oxford University Press, 1993.

Daix, Pierre. "Portraiture in Picasso's Primitivism and Cubism." In *Picasso and Portraiture: Representation and Transformation.* Edited by William Rubin. New York: Museum of Modern Art, 1996.

Davidson, Jo. *Between Sittings: An Informal Biography.* New York: Dial Press, 1951.

Delacroix, Eugène. *The Journal of Eugène Delacroix.* Translated by Walter Pach. New York: Covici, Friede, 1937.

———. "On Art Criticism." Translated by Walter Pach. Gallery Notes: *The Buffalo Fine Arts Academy* 12 (1947): 3–9.

Downes, William Howe. "John Ruskin and Walter Pach, Defenders of Faith." *Magazine of Art* 20 (1929): 455–59.

Dreier, Katherine S. *Western Art and the New Era: An Introduction to Modern Art.* New York: Brentano's, 1923.

Du Bois, Guy Pène. *Artists Say the Silliest Things.* New York: American Artists Group, Duell, Sloan and Pearce, 1940.

Duchamp, Marcel. *Affectionately, Marcel: The Selected Correspondence of Marcel Duchamp.* Edited by Francis M. Naumann and Hector Obalk. Ghent: Ludion Press, 2000.

Duchamp-Villon, Raymond. *Memorial Exhibition of the Works of Raymond Duchamp-Villon.* Introduction by Walter Pach. New York: Brummer Gallery, 1929.

Dunlop, Ian. *The Shock of the New: Seven Historic Exhibitions of Modern Art.* London: Weidenfeld and Nicolson, 1972.

Eddy, Arthur Jerome. *The Arthur Jerome Eddy Collection of Modern Painting and Sculpture.* Chicago: Art Institute of Chicago, 1931.

———. *Cubists and Post-Impressionism.* Chicago: A. C. McClurg, 1914.

Egan, Eloise. *Paintings by Eloise Egan.* Foreword by Walter Pach. Boston: Grace Horne Galleries, 1940.

Eldredge, Charles. "The Arrival of European Modernism." *Art in America* 61 (July–August 1973): 35–41.

Exhibition of Modern Art. New York: Bourgeois Gallery, 1916.

Faure, Élie. *Cézanne.* Translated by Walter Pach. New York: Association of American Painters and Sculptors, 1913.

———. *History of Art.* Translated by Walter Pach. 5 vols. New York: Harper and Brothers, 1921–1930.

———. *Paul Gauguin.* Translated by Walter Pach. New York: Association of American Painters and Sculptors, 1913.

———. *The Spirit of Forms.* Translated by Walter Pach. New York: Harper and Brothers, 1930.

Federal Writers Project. *New York: A Guide to the Empire State.* New York: Oxford University Press, 1940.

Field, Hamilton Easter. "An Answer to Walter Pach." *Brooklyn Daily Eagle,* 21 March 1920.

———. "The Opening of the Independent Show." *Brooklyn Daily Eagle,* 14 March 1920.

Filreis, Alan. *Wallace Stevens and the Actual World.* Princeton: Princeton University Press, 1991.

Frèches-Thory, Claire, and Ursula Perucchi-Petri. *Nabis: 1888–1900.* Munich: Prestel-Verlag, 1993.

Freeman, Judi. *The Fauve Landscape.* New York: Abbeville Press, 1990.

Fry, Roger. *The Last Lectures by Roger Fry.* New York: Macmillan and Cambridge: At the University Press, 1939.

———. *Vision and Design.* New York: Brentano's, 1921.

Goetz, Thomas H. *Taine and the Fine Arts.* Madrid: Playor, 1973.

Gogh, Vincent van. *Letters to an Artist: From Vincent van Gogh to Anton Ridder van Rippard, 1881–1885.* Introduction by Walter Pach. New York: Viking Press, 1936.

Goodman, Helen Evelyn. "Robert Henri: The Teacher." Ph.D. diss., New York University, 1975.

Goodrich, Lloyd. *Pioneers of Modern Art in America.* New York: Whitney Museum of American Art, 1946.

Gregg, Frederick James. "A Remarkable Art Show." *Harper's Weekly* 52 (15 February 1913): 13, 20.

Hamill, Peter. *Diego Rivera.* New York: Harry N. Abrams, 1999.

Haskell, Barbara. *Joseph Stella.* New York: Whitney Museum of American Art, 1994.

Helm, MacKinley. *Modern Mexican Painters.* New York: Harper and Brothers, 1941.

Henri, Robert. *The Art Spirit.* 1923. Reprint. New York: Harper and Row, 1984.

Herbert, Robert L., with essays by Neil Harris and contributions by Douglas W. Druick, Gloria Groom, Frank Zuccari and Allison Langley, Inge Fiedler, and Roy S. Berns. *Seurat and the Making of "La Grande Jatte."* Chicago: Art Institute of Chicago in association with University of Chicago Press, 2004.

Hey, Kenneth R. "Manierre Dawson: A Fix on the Phantoms of the Imagination." *Archives of American Art Journal* 14 (1974): 7–12.

Homer, William Innes. *Alfred Stieglitz and the American Avant-Garde.* Boston: New York Graphic Society, 1977.

———, ed. *Avant-Garde Painting and Sculpture in America, 1910–1925.* Wilmington: Delaware Art Museum, 1975.

Homer, William Innes, and Lloyd Goodrich. *Albert Pinkham Ryder: Painter of Dreams.* New York: Harry N. Abrams, 1989.

———. *Robert Henri and His Circle.* Ithaca: Cornell University Press, 1969.

Hulten, Pontus, Natalia Dumitresco, and Alexandre Istrati. *Brancusi.* New York: Harry N. Abrams, 1987.

Hurlburt, Laurance P. *The Mexican Muralists in the United States.* Albuquerque: University of New Mexico Press, 1989.

Hyland, Douglas K. S. "Agnes Ernst Meyer: Patron of American Modernism." *American Art Journal* 12 (Winter 1980): 64–81.

Jewell, Edward Alden. "Grand Central Display." *New York Times,* 25 November 1928.

———. "New Pach Fresco on Public View." *New York Times,* 21 May 1935.

———. "Pach, Critic, Revealed as Artist." *New York Times,* 14 March 1931.

———. "Walter Pach Fires a Salvo Against 'Official' Art." *New York Times Book Review,* 25 November 1928.

Karlstrom, Karl, ed. *On the Edge of America: California Modernist Art, 1900–1950.* Berkeley and Los Angeles: University of California Press, 1996.

Kuhn, Walt. *The Story of the Armory Show.* New York: [Printed privately], 1938.

Kyle, Jill A. "Cézanne and American Painting, 1900 to 1920." Ph.D. diss., University of Texas at Austin, 1995.

La Follette, Suzanne. *Art In America.* New York: Harper and Brothers, 1929.

Larrea, Irene Herner de, Gabriel Larrea, and Rafael Angel Herrerias. *Diego Rivera's Mural at the Rockefeller Center.* Mexico City: National Autonomous University of Mexico and EDICUPES, S.A. de C.V., 1987.

Larrea, Juan. *Guernica, Pablo Picasso.* Translated by Alexander H. Krappe and edited by Walter Pach. New York: C. Valentin, 1947.

Laurvik, J. Nilsen. *Is It Art? Post-Impressionism, Futurism, Cubism.* New York: International Press, 1913.

Leonard, John W., ed. *Who's Who in New York City and State.* New York: L. R. Hamersly, 1907.

Lukach, Joan M. "Severini's 1917 Exhibition at Stieglitz's '291.'" *Burlington Magazine* 113 (April 1971): 196–207.

MacLeod, Glenn. *Wallace Stevens and Modern Art: From the Armory Show to Abstract Expressionism.* New Haven: Yale University Press, 1993.

Marlor, Clark S. *The Society of Independent Artists: The Exhibition Records, 1917–1944.* Park Ridge, N.J.: Noyes Press, 1984.

Mather, Frank Jewett, Jr. "The Armory Exhibition: II." *Nation* 96 (13 March 1913): 267–68.

———. "Authority in Art Criticism." *Scribner's Magazine* 48 (December 1910): 766–68.

———. "Old and New." *Nation* 96 (6 March 1913): 240–43.

———. "The Society of Independent Artists." *Nation* 104 (10 May 1917): 574–75.

Matisse, Henri. *A Gallery of Women: A Portfolio of Sketches by Henri Matisse.* Introduction by Walter Pach. New York: Beechhurst Press, 1955.

McBride, Henry. *The Flow of Art: Essays and Criticisms of Henry McBride.* Introduction by Daniel Catton Rich. New York: Atheneum, 1975.

McCarthy, Laurette E. "Modernists on Tour: A New Look at an Historic Show." *Archives of American Art Journal* 37, nos. 3–4 (1997): 2–16.

———. "The 'Truths' About the Armory Show: Walter Pach's Side of the Story." *Archives of American Art Journal* 44, nos. 3–4 (2004): 2–13.

———. "Walter Pach: Artist, Critic, Historian, and Agent of Modernism." Ph.D. diss., University of Delaware, 1996.

Mecklenburg, Virginia McCord. "American Aesthetic Theory, 1908–1917: Issues in Conservative and Avant-Garde Thought." Ph.D. diss., University of Maryland, College Park, 1983.

Mellow, James R. *A Charmed Circle: Gertrude Stein and Company.* Boston: Houghton Mifflin, 1974.

Meyer, Agnes Ernst. *Journey Through Chaos.* New York: Harcourt, Brace, 1944.

———. *Out of These Roots: The Biography of an American Woman.* Boston: Little, Brown, 1953.

Moffett, Kenworth. *Julius Meier-Graefe as Art Critic.* Munich: Prestel-Verlag, 1973.

Monod-Fontaine, Isabelle. *Daniel-Henry Kahnweiler: Marchand, éditeur, écrivain.* Paris: Centre Georges Pompidou, 1984.

Morgan, H. Wayne. *Keepers of Culture: The Art-Thought of Kenyon Cox, Royal Cortissoz, and Frank Jewett Mather, Jr.* Kent: Kent State University Press, 1989.

Mumford, Lewis. "Beauty and the Picturesque." *Freeman* 3 (13 July 1921): 419–20.

———. *The Brown Decades: A Study of the Arts in America, 1865–1895.* New York: Harcourt, Brace, 1931. Reprint. New York: Dover, 1971.

———. *My Works and Days: A Personal Approach.* New York: Harcourt Brace Jovanovich, 1979.

———. "Painting. A Very Royal Academy." *Freeman* 1 (16 June 1920): 327–28.

———. *Sketches from Life: The Autobiography of Lewis Mumford; The Early Years.* New York: Dial Press, 1982.

Myers, Bernard S. *Mexican Painting in Our Time.* New York: Oxford University Press, 1956.

Myers, Jerome. *Artist in Manhattan.* New York: American Artists Group, 1940.

Nathanson, Carol A. "The American Reaction to London's First Grafton Show." *Archives of American Art Journal* 25 (1985): 3–10.

Nathanson, Carol Arnold. "The American Response, in 1900–1913, to the French Modern Art Movements After Impressionism." Ph.D. diss., Johns Hopkins University, 1973.

Naumann, Francis M. "Amicalement, Marcel: Fourteen Letters from Marcel Duchamp to Walter Pach." *Archives of American Art Journal* 29 (1989): 36–50.

———. "The Big Show: The First Exhibition of the Society of Independent Artists." *Artforum* 17 (February 1979): 34–39.

———. "The Critical Response." *Artforum* 17 (April 1979): 49–53.

———. "Frederick C. Torrey and Duchamp's *Nude Descending a Staircase.*" In *West Coast Duchamp,* edited by Bonnie Clearwater. Miami Beach: Grassfield Press, 1991.

———. *New York Dada, 1915–23.* New York: Harry N. Abrams, 1994.

———. "Walter Conrad Arensberg: Poet, Patron, and Participant in the New York Avant-Garde, 1915–20." *Philadelphia Museum of Art Bulletin* 76 (1980): 2–32.

———. ed., *Affectionately, Marcel: The Selected Correspondence of Marcel Duchamp.* Ghent: Ludion Press, 2000.

Neil, J. Meredith. "The Impact of the Armory Show." *South Atlantic Quarterly* 79 (Autumn 1980): 375–85.

Nieto, Maragarita. "Mexican Art and Los Angeles, 1920–1940." In *On the Edge of America: California Modernist Artists, 1900–1950.* Berkeley and Los Angeles: University of California Press, 1996.

New York World's Fair: Catalogue of European and American Paintings, 1500–1900. Introduction by Walter Pach. New York: Art Aid Corporation, 1940.

Parker, Robert Allerton. "Review of *The Masters of Modern Art,* by Walter Pach." *Arts* 7 (January 1925): 51–52.

Perlman, Bennard B. "Walter Pach (1883–1958) and Magda Pach (1884–1950)." In *Exhibition of the Art of Walter and Magda Pach.* Youngstown, Ohio: Butler Institute of American Art, 1988.

Persin, Patrick Gilles. *Daniel-Henry Kahnweiler: L'aventure d'un grand marchand.* Paris: Solange Thierry Editeur, 1990.

Petruck, Peninah. *American Art Criticism, 1910–1939.* New York: Garland, 1981.

Phillips, Sandra. "The Art Criticism of Walter Pach." *Art Bulletin* 65 (March 1983): 106–22.

Pisano, Ronald G. *A Leading Spirit in American Art: William Merritt Chase, 1849–1916.* Seattle: Henry Gallery Association, 1983.

———. *The Students of William Merritt Chase.* Huntington, N.Y.: Heckscher Museum and the Parrish Art Museum, 1973.

———. *William Merritt Chase in the Company of Friends.* Southampton, N.Y.: Parrish Art Museum, 1979.

Platt, Susan Noyes. "Formalism and American Art Criticism in the 1920s." *Journal of Theory and Criticism of the Arts* 2 (1986): 69–84.

———. *Modernism in the 1920s: Interpretations of Modern Art in New York from Expressionism to Constructivism.* Ann Arbor, Mich.: UMI Research Press, 1985.

———. "Responses to Modern Art in New York in the 1920s." Ph.D. diss., University of Texas at Austin, 1981.

———. "Sheldon Cheney: Crusader for Modernism." *Archives of American Art Journal* 25 (1985): 11–17.

Prendergast, Maurice. *Maurice Prendergast Memorial Exhibition.* Introduction by Walter Pach. New York: Whitney Museum of American Art, 1934.

Quinn, John. *The Letters of John Quinn.* Edited by Peter Kavanagh. New York: P. Kavanagh Hand-Press, 1960.

Ratcliff, Carter. "Art Criticism: Other Minds, Other Eyes, Part III (1863–73)." *Art International* 18 (20 May 1974): 52–57.

———. "Art Criticism: Other Minds, Other Eyes, Part IV." *Art International* 18 (20 September 1974): 49–54.

———. "Art Criticism: Other Minds, Other Eyes, Part V." *Art International* 18 (15 December 1974): 53–57.

Redon, Odilon. *Lettres d'Odilon Redon.* Paris et Bruxelles: Librairie Nationale d'Art et d'Histoire, 1923.

———. *Odilon Redon.* Introduction by Walter Pach. Chicago: Albert Roulliers Art Galleries, 1919.

———. *Odilon Redon.* Introduction by Walter Pach. New York: Ehrich Galleries, 1919.

Reid, Benjamin Laurance. *The Man from New York: John Quinn and His Friends.* New York: Oxford University Press, 1968.

Renoir, Pierre Auguste. *Pierre Auguste Renoir.* Introduction by Walter Pach. New York: H. N. Abrams, 1950.

Rewald, John. *Cézanne and America: Dealers, Collectors, Artists, and Critics, 1891–1921.* Princeton: Princeton University Press, 1989.

Richardson, Joan. *Wallace Stevens: The Early Years.* New York: Beech Tree Books, William Morrow, 1986.

Risatti, Howard Anthony. "American Critical Reaction to European Modernism, 1908–1917." Ph.D. diss., University of Illinois at Urbana-Champaign, 1978.

Rushing, William Jackson, III. "Native American Art and Culture and the New York Avant-Garde, 1910–1950." Ph.D. diss., University of Texas at Austin, 1989.

Russell, John. *Matisse: Father and Son.* New York: Harry N. Abrams, 1999.

Saarinen, Aline. *The Proud Possessors: The Lives, Times, and Tastes of Some Adventurous American Art Collectors.* New York: Random House, 1958.

Seurat, Georges. *Exhibition of Paintings and Drawings by Georges Seurat.* Foreword by Walter Pach. New York: Brummer Galleries, 1924.

Sheon, Aaron. "1913: Forgotten Cubist Exhibitions in America." *Arts Magazine* 57 (March 1983): 93–107.

———. "1913: Pittsburgh in the Cubist Avant-Garde." *Carnegie Magazine* 56 (July–August 1982): 12–17, 38–39.

Simon, Linda. "Alice B. Toklas." In *American Writers in Paris, 1920–1939.* Vol. 4, *Dictionary of Literary Biography,* edited by Karen Lane Rood. Detroit: A Bruccoli Clark Book, Gale Research Company, Book Tower, 1980.

———. *The Biography of Alice B. Toklas.* Lincoln: University of Nebraska Press, 1991.

———. *Gertrude Stein Remembered.* Lincoln: University of Nebraska Press, 1994.

Sloan, John. *John Sloan's New York Scene.* Edited by Helen Farr Sloan and Bruce St. John. New York: Harper and Row, 1965.

Special Exhibition: Paintings, Drawings, Etching, Lithographs, and Sculpture by Henry Matisse. New York: Montross Gallery, 1915. Unpaginated.

Spurling, Hilary. *Matisse the Master: A Life of Henri Matisse: The Conquest of Colour, 1909–1954.* New York: Alfred A. Knopf, 2005.

———. *The Unknown Matisse: A Life of Henri Matisse: The Early Years, 1869–1908.* London: Hamish Hamilton, 1998.

Stavitsky, Gail. *Gertrude Stein: The American Connection.* New York: Sid Deutsch Gallery, 1990.

———. "John Weichsel and the People's Art Guild." *Archives of American Art Journal* 31 (1991): 12–19.

Steegmuller, Francis. *Stories and True Stories.* Boston: Little, Brown, 1973.

Stein, Gertrude. *The Autobiography of Alice B. Toklas.* New York: Random House, 1933.

———. *The Flowers of Friendship: Letters Written to Gertrude Stein.* Edited by Donald Gallup. New York: Knopf, 1953.

———. *Two: Gertrude Stein and Her Brother and Other Early Portraits.* 1951. Reprint. Freeport, N.Y.: Books for Libraries Press, 1984.

Sterne, Maurice. *Shadow and Light: The Life, Friends, and Opinions of Maurice Sterne.* New York: Harcourt, Brace and World, 1965.

Stevens, Wallace. *Letters of Wallace Stevens.* Edited by Holly Stevens. New York: Alfred A. Knopf, 1966.

Stewart, Patrick L. "The European Art Invasion: American Art and the Arensberg Circle, 1914–1918." *Arts Magazine* 51 (May 1977): 108–12.

Strand, Paul. "Aesthetic Criterion." *Freeman* 2 (12 January 1921): 426–27.

———. "The Independents in Theory and Practice." *Freeman* 3 (6 April 1921): 90.

———. "The Subjective Method." *Freeman* 2 (2 February 1921): 498.

Tomkins, Calvin. *Duchamp: A Biography.* New York: Henry Holt, 1996.

Trapp, Frank Anderson, ed. *The 1913 Armory Show in Retrospect.* Amherst: Amherst College, 1958.

Trow's New York City Directory. New York: Trow Directory, Printing, and Bookbinding, 1883–1958.

Troyen, Carol. *Charles Sheeler, Paintings and Drawings.* Boston: Little, Brown, 1987.

Turner, Susan. *A History of the Freeman: Literary Landmark of the Early Twenties.* New York: Columbia University Press, 1963.

Villon, Jacques. *Jacques Villon.* Edited by Daniel Robbins. Cambridge, Mass.: Fogg Art Museum, Harvard University, 1976.

———. *Villon.* Foreword by Walter Pach. New York: Brummer Gallery, 1928.

Walker, Lester Carl. "Art in Average America: The Cultural Pattern of Des Moines, Iowa." Ph.D. diss., Ohio State University, 1951.

Wattenmaker, Richard J. *Maurice Prendergast*. Washington, D.C.: National Museum of American Art in association with the Smithsonian Institution, 1994.

———. *Puvis de Chavannes and the Modern Tradition*. Rev. ed. Toronto, Ontario, Canada: Art Gallery of Ontario, 1975.

Wertheim, Arthur Frank. *The New York Little Renaissance: Iconoclasm, Modernism, and Nationalism in American Culture, 1908–1917*. New York: New York University Press, 1976.

Wildenstein, Alec. *Odilon Redon: Catalogue raisonné de l'oeuvre peint et dessine*. Vol. 1. Paris: Wildenstein Institute, 1992.

Williams, Reba White. "The Weyhe Gallery Between the Wars, 1919–1940." Ph.D. diss., City University of New York, 1996.

Wolf, Ben. *Morton Livingston Schamberg: A Monograph*. Philadelphia: University of Pennsylvania Press, 1963.

Wolfe, Bertram David. *The Fabulous Life of Diego Rivera*. New York: Stein and Day, 1963.

Wood, Beatrice. "I Shock Myself: Excerpts from the Autobiography of Beatrice Wood." *Arts Magazine* 51 (May 1977): 134–39.

Wright, Brooks. *The Artist and the Unicorn: The Lives of Arthur B. Davies*. New City, N.Y.: Historical Society of Rockland County, 1978.

Wright, Willard Huntington. "An Abundance of Modern Art." *Forum* 55 (March 1916): 318–34.

———. "The Aesthetic Struggle in America." *The Forum* 55 (February 1916): 201–20.

———. "Art. The Future of Painting. I: The Confusing of Two Distinct Arts." *Freeman* 6 (22 November 1922): 255–57.

———. "Art. The Future of Painting. II: The Art of Colour." *Freeman* 6 (29 November 1922): 278–80.

———. "Art. The Future of Painting. III: A New Art-Medium." *Freeman* 6 (6 December 1922): 303–4.

———. "The Forum Exhibition." *Forum* 55 (April 1916): 457–71.

———. *Modern Painting: Its Tendency and Meaning*. New York: John Lan, 1915.

Yount, Sylvia. *To Be Modern: American Encounters with Cézanne and Company*. Philadelphia: Museum of American Art at the Pennsylvania Academy of the Fine Arts. Distributed by the University of Pennsylvania Press, 1996.

Zayas, Marius de. *How, When, and Why Modern Art Came to America*. Edited by Francis Naumann. Cambridge: MIT Press, 1996.

———. "How, When, and Why Modern Art Came to New York." *Arts Magazine* 54 (April 1980): 96–126.

Zigrosser, Carl. "My Catalogue." *Art in America* 51 (February 1963): 45.

———. *My Own Shall Come to Me; A Personal Memoir and Picture Chronicle*. Haarlem, The Netherlands: J. Enschede en Zonen, 1971.

———. *A World of Art and Museums*. Philadelphia: Art Alliance, 1975.

Zilczer, Judith. "The Aesthetic Struggle in America, 1913–1918: Art and Theory in the Stieglitz Circle." Ph.D. diss., University of Delaware, 1975.

———. "Alfred Stieglitz and John Quinn: Allies in the American Avant-Garde." *American Art Journal* 17 (Summer 1985): 18–33.

———. "The Armory Show and the American Avant-Garde: A Reevaluation." *Arts Magazine* 53 (September 1978): 126–30.

———. "The Dispersal of the John Quinn Collection." *Archives of American Art Journal* 19 (1979): 15–20.

———. "John Quinn and Modern Art Collectors in America, 1913–1924." *American Art Journal* 14 (Winter 1982): 56–71.

———. *"The Noble Buyer": John Quinn, Patron of the Avant-Garde*. Washington, D.C.: Hirshhorn Museum and Sculpture Garden, Smithsonian Institution Press, 1978.

———. "Raymond Duchamp-Villon: Pioneer of Modern Sculpture." *Philadelphia Museum of Art Bulletin* 76 (Fall 1980): 2–24.

———. "Raymond Duchamp-Villon and the American Avant-Garde." *Archives of American Art Journal* 38 (1998): 14–27.

———. "The World's New Art Center: Modern Art Exhibitions in New York City, 1913–1918." *Archives of American Art Journal* 14 (1974): 2–7.

Index